# BIBLICAL HERMENEUTICS

# BIBLICAL HERMENEUTICS

Gerhard Maier

Translated from the German edition,
*Biblische Hermeneutik*
by Robert W. Yarbrough

CROSSWAY BOOKS • WHEATON, ILLINOIS
A DIVISION OF GOOD NEWS PUBLISHERS

*Biblical Hermeneutics*

First English edition. Copyright © 1994 by Gerhard Maier

Published by Crossway Books
        a division of Good News Publishers
        1300 Crescent Street
        Wheaton, Illinois 60187

Edited by Tom Raabe and Leonard G. Goss

Cover design: Bob Fuller Creative

Art Direction: Mark Schramm

First printing, 1994

Printed in the United States of America

Text: 11.2/15 Times Roman x 26

Bible quotations not marked NIV, NASB, RSV, etc. are translations of the author's own renderings of the Greek and Hebrew texts.

**Library of Congress Cataloging-in-Publication Data**
Maier, Gerhard, 1937-
    [Biblische Hermeneutik. English]
    Biblical hermeneutics / Gerhard Maier : translated by Robert W.
Yarbrough. — 1st English ed.
        p.    cm.
    Translation of: Biblische Hermeneutik.
    Includes bibliographical references and indexes.
    1. Bible—Hermeneutics.  I. Title.
BS476.M213   1994        220.6'01—dc20                93-42342
ISBN 0-89107-767-7

| 02 | 01 | 00 | 99 | 98 | 97 | 96 | 95 | 94 |
|----|----|----|----|----|----|----|----|----|
| 15 | 14 | 13 | 12 | 11 | 10 | 9 | 8 | 7 | 6 | 5 | 4 | 3 | 2 | 1 |

# TABLE OF

# Contents

# Translator's Preface

The completion of this project is due to timely help from a number of people. Jürgen and Franziska Schwarz of Wilhelmsdorf, Germany, made valuable suggestions on early chapters and furnished translations of a number of Latin and French quotations. Eckhard Schnabel, Bergneustadt, Germany, solved a vexing riddle concerning J. T. Beck's dialect. More locally, Vicki Barrs put her considerable command of French at my disposal at a strategic juncture. V. Philips Long likewise gave generously of his time on sabbatical to read the entire manuscript in both the original and translation. Dan Doriani helped enlarge my hermeneutical understanding, and therefore translational capacity, with his own literary and historiographical observations about some of Maier's proposals.

Tim Phillips, Wheaton College Graduate School, cheerfully decoded numerous Latin quotations that were inaccessible to me. I am grateful for his competent readiness to tackle someone else's problems on short notice. My former teacher, J. Julius Scott, Jr., also of Wheaton, first introduced me to the formal study of hermeneutics over a decade ago; he deserves a word of thanks for piquing an interest that has never waned since. Helmut Ziefle of the Wheaton College foreign language department lent generous assistance with an enigmatic Luther quote.

Lane Dennis of Crossway Books and Jan Dennis, now with Thomas Nelson, had the vision to arrange for an Anglophone edition of

Maier's study. Crossway Books is to be commended for their continuing dedication to the publication of quality scholarly and literary works.

Covenant Theological Seminary provided necessary computer and other logistical support. I am grateful to the trustees as well as to President Paul Kooistra and Dean Bryan Chapell for their encouragement. Students at Covenant Seminary kindly showed interest in the content of this book as its hold on my thinking surfaced in courses that may or may not have had anything to do with hermeneutics.

Professor Maier has been magnanimous and patient in correspondence over many months. I am deeply grateful to have had this opportunity to benefit from interaction with his insights and scholarship.

Finally, my wife and two sons were encouragingly solicitous about the state of both translation and translator as work progressed. To them I dedicate my small effort in this aspect of Professor Maier's ministry by way of thanks.

# Foreword to English-language Edition

**B**iblical Hermeneutics grew out of long-term involvement in the modern theological-hermeneutical discussion.

I had my first formative experience in the encounter with critical theological hermeneutics when I switched to theological studies after completing training in the field of law. At that time practically everyone in German theology was speaking of the "significance" of this or that biblical account. At the same time the "facticity" of those accounts was widely denied. As a lawyer I had learned that the facts must be ascertained before their significance can be assessed. In German Protestant theology the procedure was precisely the reverse. But is such spiritualizing legitimate? Can the historicity of the Christian message be placed in question and its authority and significance still upheld?

A second far-reaching experience was the transition from pastoral work to academic theological instruction. As a pastor, in entirely normal circumstances with neither charismatic nor other unusual factors at work, I had preached and prayed, shared people's awakening to faith, observed the effectiveness of God's Word, and learned increasingly to the trust that Word. The "critical" vantage point of theology in the sixties and seventies, however, stood diametrically opposed to this burgeoning trust. Now, which basic posture was correct? Trust or doubt? Confidence or skepticism?

Striking connections and confirmations of the biblical reports became evident in that moment when I honestly and openly wrestled with the possibility that the biblical Word—even with respect to historical events—could be true. This was not the world of legends, of contrivances, of falsifications. Rather I detected here "the scent of truth," as Wolfgang Schadewaldt once put it. I therefore opted for a basic posture of trust, of remaining open to the possibility that the biblical reports are reliable. All my subsequent work followed from this basic posture.

I would like to pose this question to those who prefer a different position: How can we remain Christians when we call biblical revelation in doubt? How is God's voice supposed to remain perceptible when we subject everything to the violent constraints of explanation based on the purely immanent?

It may be that the great upswing of historical interest that the Enlightenment brought with it is beginning to ebb. In this situation there remains a twofold task. First, against long-standing and still virulent tendencies of modernity we must speak confidently of the history of God's dealings with mankind. Second, at the same time we must take to heart that the Bible can mediate encounter with God at many levels—not only at the historical. A communicative hermeneutic, a hermeneutic of encounter, seems essential at the present time. Yet this encounter with God will flourish only where the Bible is permitted to be no less than what God intends: namely, the Word of God.

I express my deeply felt thanks to Dr. Robert Yarbrough, Covenant Theological Seminary, St. Louis, for shouldering the load of translating, thereby giving English-speaking readers access to this book and the discussion in which it is rooted.

Tübingen
20 April 1993
Gerhard Maier

# CHAPTER ONE

# Defining the Hermeneutical Task

"Hermeneutics": what do we mean by that word? What is the basic aim of "hermeneutics"? These are the primary questions that must be answered at the outset of this book.

Over the course of history hermeneutics has been defined in countless different ways. In ancient Greek *hermeneuein* means to impart or convey. This can denote a "simple" oral translation. Even in such a "simple" act, however, there are two components constantly involved: #1) the correct conception, and #2) the correct representation of that which needs to be conveyed.[1] This already suggests the two basic possible meanings of "hermeneutics." While the second component, understood as a skillful interpretation, has tended to dominate the discussion in the English-speaking world,[2] German thought has observed an increasing focus on the act of understanding itself. Clearly the first component has been dominant in German-speaking circles. We are therefore confronted at the outset with a decision. Because of our ties with the history of theology in its continental European form, we concern ourselves below primarily with component #1) above: the correct conception. To borrow from F. Lücke, we will be concerned with a "science of the first principles of a theory of exegesis, along with the act of exegesis itself."[3]

Plato was presumably the first to strike out in this direction. In any case he uses the formula *he hermeneutike techne* (literally "the art of interpreting") to denote "the art of correctly apprehending something."[4] This characterization of hermeneutics as an "art" then persists through the centuries. Dilthey's definition of hermeneutics eventually became famous: "the theory of the art of understanding textually fixed living utterances," or again, "the theory of the art of the interpretation of textual monuments."[5] As one can see, Dilthey concentrates on written texts. Christian exegetes tend to proceed in an even more restricted fashion than the philosophers. Thus Mussner explains that hermeneutics is the "theory of the understanding of a text."[6] Schleiermacher, however, whose heir Dilthey understood himself to be,[7] spoke of the "art" of "correctly understanding the speech of another, primarily in its written form."[8]

If hermeneutics came to be restricted to texts, a further development is no less interesting. Since the eighteenth century the concept of "scientific" has insinuated itself more and more into definitions of hermeneutics. Semler (1725–91) praised his teacher Baumgarten for producing "the first German scientific outline of hermeneutics."[9] Bultmann, who placed himself in the Schleiermacher-Dilthey heritage,[10] defined hermeneutics as "the art of scientific understanding."[11]

Since, however, science itself is based on presuppositions and presents the outcome rather than the presupposition of understanding, we are operating here in an unfruitful circle. Harnack could still speak of the "pure knowledge of the object" as the goal to be striven for.[12]

In the meantime, both Protestant and Catholic thinkers have come to concur that interpretation and understanding can "never" take place "without presuppositions."[13] Basically, therefore, nothing is gained by the designation "scientific."

Such various authors as Lücke, Heinrici, and Torm make use of the concept of "theory" as part of their definitions. Heinrici formulates it this way: hermeneutics is "the theory of the interpretation of that which has been handed down."[14] The danger this entails is best seen in Lücke; he defines biblical hermeneutics as "the true theory of the concept and practice of exegesis."[15] Its content is "the study of the laws and rules according to which the sense of an utterance or writing should be interpreted."[16] Here, however, hermeneutics runs the risk of becoming a sterile application of rules, and the interpreter is tempted as a skilled theoretician to want to understand everything.

To what extent is it even possible, however, to understand someone else? The history of hermeneutics yields somewhat astonishing answers to this question. Both Schleiermacher and Dilthey were convinced that the interpreter might well be able to understand an utterance better than its own author. "The task," says Schleiermacher, "is to be expressed as follows: to understand an utterance at first as well as, and then better than, its author."[17] Dilthey reiterates: "The ultimate aim of the hermeneutical process is to understand the author better than he understood himself."[18]

How is that possible? Dilthey explains that this follows from "the doctrine of unconscious creation."[19] Behind the person of the author stands a greater "It" which speaks and acts through him. One senses behind this conception the outlook of German idealism and the belief in a world spirit.

Here two central questions arise, both important for defining hermeneutics. The first question runs: what is it, really, that we are trying to understand? Should hermeneutics "lead to the understanding of the human personality" of the author? Torm, who advocates this view, states very clearly that if this is the case, then an "inexplicable remainder" still persists. Here he cites Plato's Gorgias: *oudeis heteros heterou tauto ennoei* ("No one thinks just the same way as anybody else").[20] Or is our task rather to comprehend and set forth the concrete life utterance (text, etc.), i.e., to practice an *ars interpretandi* (interpretative art) as suggested by Dannhauer, among others?[21] Or must we enter the world on the other side of the text, as e.g. Ricoeur suggests? He has reduced his concern to the statement: "Not what is said, but about what it is said" is the object of hermeneutics.[22] The text opens up to us a "text world." The key matter is "the sort of world intended beyond the text as its reference."[23] It is clear that such a conception is attractive for those theologians who follow Karl Barth in distinguishing between revelation itself and the Bible as a mere "witness of God's revelation."[24]

If, however, the focal point of interpretation lies on the other side of the text, then a second question arises: how is an overweening subjectivity in the understanding process to be controlled? As with our first two questions, we are in no position here to furnish a comprehensive answer. It suffices at this preliminary stage to see the problem. In recent decades a battle has raged over this subjectivity. Here we must come back to Ricoeur once more; his ultimate aim is indeed an altered self-understanding in a process of participation and distanciation with respect to the world of the text.[25] Thus hermeneutics becomes a contribution to the interpreter's personal self. But if I am #1) dependent on an appropriate understanding of that which lies on the other side of the text, and #2) caught up into an exchange with this "text world" that continually alters me, then subjective factors end up playing a decisive role. How can one ever arrive, then, at that "universal validity in interpretation" with which Dilthey wrestled?[26]

Interestingly enough, it is most of all nontheologians who have been at pains to secure objectivity in the process of understanding. Betti is a good example. He interacts aggressively with existentialist interpreters, especially Bultmann and Gadamer, reproaching them for losing objectivity. Their hermeneutic, charges Betti, is "determined by its content" from the outset; it no longer permits any "hermeneutical autonomy of the object."[27] Although they strove for a hermeneutic of "consent to the subject matter" of the text (a favorite theme of Gadamer), their understanding changed into a "monologue."[28] For his part, Betti is convinced of the possibility of objective knowledge. He wants to attain this through linking "subordination" (objective element) with "recreating that which becomes one's own possession" (subjective element).[29] Surprisingly, just like Bultmann or Dilthey, his starting point is "the great Schleiermacher."[30] No less than Betti, who was a historian, the philosopher Spranger commits himself to the objectivity of the understanding process. A striking similarity is thereby exposed between Spranger and Betti. That is, they both presuppose an "objective spirit" and the "common humanity" that permits such a common understanding.[31] Spranger's appeal to Hegel and Plato[32] makes it clear that we are dealing here as well with the heritage of German idealism. And just as Betti dissociates himself from existentialist interpretation, Spranger dissociates himself from Kierkegaard.[33] He seeks rather to build on the universal human "consciousness of truth."[34] Precisely this makes the essential objectivity possible. At this point Spranger refers to Ranke: "I wished, so to speak, to obliterate myself. . . ."[35]

As the struggle for objectivity of understanding teaches us, it matters a great deal whether or not in the other person "the same human spirit" speaks "to us."[36] The biblical interpreter, however, falls into a predicament here. For the Bible, which it is his task to interpret, makes a claim directly contrary to the thesis that "the same human spirit" speaks "to us." It is rather the case that here, in the Bible, God wants to talk with us! For that reason Oepke formulated the "central problem of biblical hermeneutics" in this way: "How can the human word of a time long since vanished be understood as God's word to the present?"[37] Can this "central problem" be solved by excluding the word of God in the Bible, strictly limiting interpretation to "the human speech, the human testimony about God, not God himself"?[38] That would be an attractive possibility. In that way we would come to an understanding of the human author, to an enrichment of our own possibilities of understanding, and more besides. As we will see, however, this solution is ruled out, since it stands in direct contradiction to the self-understanding of the biblical witnesses. We appear to have arrived, then, at a dead end.

A first way out of this dead end opens up if we consciously restrict ourselves to the understanding of the Bible as we seek the definition and task of hermeneutics. Here we are not denying that hermeneutics as such is at home in numerous scientific areas, e.g. jurisprudence, philology, philosophy, aesthetics, and psychology.[39] But understanding and interpretation of the Bible have to do with the unique case: they encounter a message that has taken written form, and the message appears with a unique demand. For it claims that here, and here alone, God speaks reliably.[40] At this point we concur even with Ricoeur: "It is a unique case because all its partial forms of discourse are referred to that name which is . . . the name of the unnameable."[41] We begin to build the case, therefore, for a special biblical hermeneutic which we will later ground more fully. On the basis of our reflections thus far we can now assert this much: our task consists in understanding the Bible of the Old and New Testaments commensurate with their own claim. A biblical hermeneutic serves this task in that it establishes the leading lines that correspond to this claim and form the foundation of interpretation.[42]

# CHAPTER TWO

# A Special Biblical Hermeneutic?

Should there be a special "biblical hermeneutic" (*hermeneutica sacra*)? For centuries this question has provoked controversy. Some answer in the affirmative, while others are adamantly opposed. These contrasting opinions are not easily relegated to different theological camps. The thesis, for example, that all German Pietists affirm a *hermeneutica sacra* is simply false. A special biblical hermeneutic is rejected by theologians of quite various stripes, among them Baur, Harnack, Hofmann, Lutz, and Schleiermacher.[1]

## REASONS FOR A SPECIAL BIBLICAL HERMENEUTIC

1. In favor of a special biblical hermeneutic is, first, the observation that the Bible—if what it says is true even to a small degree—is the most unusual and unique object there is. It is incomparable. There is nothing else like it in all of world literature. No other work can compare with the prophetic array of sixty-six books hailing from various centuries, all furnishing a pregiven framework pointing to the one God and the one Messiah. The Koran is either imitation or future speculation. In the

Bible, however, the fulfillment of prophecy is reported at the same time. In this Bible the unique and incomparable claim is raised that *only here* God speaks in written form.[2] In this respect the Bible is less tolerant than the Koran.

Should this Bible be handled like any other book? Should it "be studied according to the very same methods" as the other "religions"?[3] This would amount to the hermeneutical surrender of its singularity. In Girgensohn's formulation: "The foremost law of all scientific thought is unconditional respect for reality in its givenness in all its forms of manifestation."[4] When a unique reality confronts us, then such unconditional respect requires that we approach it in a unique fashion. This is exactly what Droysen called for when he wrote, "All empirical research regulates itself according to the facts to which it devotes itself."[5] Accordingly, "every method" is "determined by its object."[6]

We would be giving up this basic principle of all cognition if we studied the Bible just like any other book. Torm is correct, then, when he writes that "the content of the New Testament . . . [is] so unusual that a special handling of New Testament hermeneutics proves to be fruitful, also in view of the content; for . . . the more specialized the crafting of a hermeneutic, the more productive it will be."[7] Later we will demonstrate to what extent a specialized biblical hermeneutic is more fruitful than a general one.

2. In favor of a special biblical hermeneutic is, second, the observation that the biblical writers seek consciously to recede into the background. They point away from themselves to *God as the author* of their message. They spare no effort in putting God before the reader. God, however, is the Entirely Other (Eccl 5:2). It is not feasible to want to retain accustomed categories of understanding and thinking when dealing with this God.

This principle finds application in a number of directions. We can no longer, e.g., take as a starting point that that which is uttered in alien individuality "is also contained in the comprehending [= interpreting] living entity."[8] God is not "alien individuality" in the normal sense of those words; he is our creator and sustainer. Nor is it permissible to equate in principle the one who speaks (God) with the one who hears (man).

We can, then, also no longer trust our own reason. Spranger had declared it as "in the nature of the case impossible to erect a science on the basis of the consciousness of sin instead of on the basis of the consciousness of truth." He concluded with this dogmatic assertion: "We believe that today we cannot lead a life of high intellectual and ethical integrity apart from the pervasive illumination of science and the purging fire of its purifying flames."[9] In light of the Bible, however, man is a sinner, and his reason and science are radically affected by this. It is rather God whose "purging fire" purifies man—if he harks to God's activating voice (Isa 6:5ff.). We cannot evade the fact that centuries of interaction with the Bible lead again and again to the conclusion that reason is "in no sense the source from which the knowledge of saving truths flow to man."[10] Luther was right, therefore, in rejecting humanism and faith in reason.[11]

The Bible likewise transforms the usual modern concept of history. In the Bible's view all history unfolds under God's planning and direction. He created the "arena of history," creation itself. He created the movement of history, time. He made man to be an entity inhabiting history. History is always that which proceeds from God. Still today the Bible proclaims "an activity of God with us that extends his effective influence into this history."[12] That means the end of a purely immanent conception of history. At the same time it means the end of purely mechanical-causal explanation.[13] It is noteworthy that even historians distance themselves from purely mechanical-causal explanation. Droysen, e.g., in 1843 outlined a "theology of history" and saw the highest task of historical science in theodicy.[14]

If purely mechanical-causal explanation is not viable, the dominant positivistic and rationalistic concept of science is unusable for a hermeneutic that is applied to the Bible. "Modern science," says Gadamer, "follows . . . the principle of Cartesian doubt, accepting nothing as certain that admits of any doubt whatsoever."[15] True, lively protest is presently underway against Cartesianism.[16] But the accustomed, shallow Cartesian intellectual starting point is still commonly found in theology.[17] Systematic doubt is, however, the most inappropriate procedure imaginable for dealing with the Bible. Girgensohn once cited three principles of modern science: #1) "the autonomy of human reason," #2) "the principle of immanent explanation," and #3) "the bias in favor of a mechanistic-causal explanation of reality."[18] He himself sees the biblical proclamation as standing "in direct contradiction to the fundamental tendencies of scientific procedure."[19] Mark carefully: today these tendencies are under examination and at times siege.[20] But to the extent that they continue to be influential, we must reject them as unusable. Theology is science sui generis, because it deals with the living biblical God.[21] The struggle to establish such independence characterizes e.g. Lücke's grand scheme, in which he sought to escape "merely human science" and demanded a "biblical hermeneutic."[22]

3. In favor of a special biblical hermeneutic is, third, the observation that the Bible sets up a singular, unmistakable *relation between God and the interpreter*. Later we will develop the view that an interpretation without the Holy Spirit cannot be a correct interpretation. For now we simply state that the Bible intends a transformation of the interpreter and his existence.

This intended transformation of the interpreter includes, however, the interpreter's obedience. Procksch characterizes this obedience as an act of submission. He sees the battle between God and man taking place in the very act of biblical interpretation. Understanding does not emerge from this battle until submission occurs.[23] In addition to submission, Procksch also speaks of "faith in Christ."[24] Oepke argues along the same lines. He holds that "the special quality of the biblical text lies precisely in that it demands a decision from the hearer."[25]

Decision, faith, obedience, transformation in view of our salvation—these are all goals that transcend a general hermeneutic and once again suggest a special biblical hermeneutic. In this sense Ricoeur is correct to state: "The event is our master."[26]

4. In favor of a special biblical hermeneutic is, fourth, the insoluble difficulties into which the interpreter unavoidably falls.

True, every hermeneutic has ongoing problems, tensions, and unsatisfactory features. In addition to this, however, the attempt to understand the Bible possesses the character of a risk whose successful outcome is attended by unavoidable difficulties.

"Every interpreter presupposes something prior to taking up the task," wrote Gustaf Wingren years ago in his essay "The Question of Methods in Theology."[27] Actually, we have seen that a "presupposition-less" exegesis presents "a phantom, a self-deception."[28] Yet it is precisely our presuppositions that the Bible wants to place in question, correct, and to some extent obliterate. One of the difficulties cited above is this: I as a human can never work without presuppositions and must at the same time constantly realize that my presuppositions are shaped by sin.

A further difficulty consists in the encounter between incomparable persons. Ultimately the Bible is, indeed, a medium of encounter rather than a collection of neutral information. In this exchange one of the encountered parties, man, does not know who he is. "We do not know what man is," runs one of C. G. Jung's insightful observations.[29] Much less does man know who God is. "God is in heaven / and you are on earth" (Eccl 5:2 NIV). "No one has ever seen God" (Jn 1:18 NIV). How can encounter take place under such conditions? Bultmann was convinced that we can, with the help of philosophy, know who man is— indeed, "man can very probably know who God is, i.e. in asking the God-question."[30] This is surely a totally erroneous assessment.

Where, then, does the "point of connection" lie in that encounter? With this question we take aim at an additional difficulty. To the extent that we are dealing with understanding, human thought is challenged. On the one hand, man's reason is depraved, according to ecclesiastical and biblical teaching. On the other hand, reason must possess at least the gift of hearing. For this reason, dogmatic theologians of past centuries are ambivalent in their assessments of reason. As "the intellectual capacity for apprehension" it is to be regarded positively.[31] There is no question, however, of it being a building block for a harmonious relationship with God. These viewpoints collide head-on. So here, too, there remains a fundamental insoluble difficulty.

During the Deist controversy in England, the question was posed sharply how historical events, which happened once and can never be repeated, could possibly be the vehicle of a universally valid revelation.[32] This question later generated debate in Germany through Lessing's formulation regarding "accidental truths of history" and "necessary truths of reason."[33] The relationship, however, between revelation and history, between the historically particular and the universally valid, also ranks among the difficulties that no biblical interpreter can fully overcome. In itself the "revelation of the unconditioned [i.e., God] in historically conditioned form"[34] would seem to require a separation between revelation and its manifestation. We will see, however, that this solution is not a viable way out. Thus, study of the Bible encounters yet another unavoidable difficulty at this point.

The observations (1–4) we have just made compel us to affirm a special "biblical hermeneutic." It should be noted yet again that we are not abandoning the discussion of hermeneutics as it is carried on in jurisprudential hermeneutics, philosophical hermeneutics, and in other areas. On the contrary, we will discover numerous overlaps and similarities. We would be closing our eyes to reality, however, if we were to deny the exceptional character of the divine revelation found in the Bible by seeking to subordinate understanding of the biblical message to some subfield of "normal" hermeneutics as generally applied.

## OBJECTIONS TO A SPECIAL BIBLICAL HERMENEUTIC

Two objections require sifting at this point. The first was brought forward by Harnack, among others, and asserts "that one constantly distances himself farther and farther from the pure knowledge of the object"[35] when one seeks to apply a *hermeneutica sacra*. Harnack's objection was sharpened, in part, by the insistence that a *hermeneutica sacra* was historically untenable. In response to Harnack, we hardly need to rehearse the fact here that there simply is no "pure knowledge of the object"—and there never has been. Furthermore, a *hermeneutica sacra* is at least as tenable and fruitful, historically speaking, as a *hermeneutica profana* (secular hermeneutic). It must be especially emphasized here, however, that the "object," the Bible itself, demands a special hermeneutic. The person who, for the sake of a universal hermeneutic, obliterates the claim to once-for-all-ness and uniqueness found in the biblical revelation distances himself much further from the so-called object than the advocate of a special hermeneutic.

A second objection bears greater weight. Are we not arbitrarily carving up reality as a unified entity, the solitary order ordained by the Creator, when we place a biblical hermeneutic alongside the customary hermeneutic used elsewhere, special knowledge alongside universal? Or to put it more sharply: are we not then guilty of pious disobedience?[36] Answer: creation has long been torn by the Fall (see Ge 3). A rift has entered the scene. The thesis that one ought to apprehend the world using a unified knowledge dismisses the effects of the Fall at a crucial juncture. For the communication of the Creator with his creation has been disturbed at its most important point: the relationship with persons. Precisely for this reason the Creator appears as a stranger to fallen man. "He came to that which was his own, but his own did not receive him" (Jn 1:11 NIV). The revelation comes from the One with whom we once had fellowship; it seeks to restore us to that fellowship. But that is why it seems alien in the present world. "Who has believed our message / and to whom has the arm of the LORD been revealed?" (Isa 53:1 NIV). A new, special understanding is necessary to overcome the alienation of a world to whom God has become a stranger.

With the name "biblical hermeneutic" we take up a designation that has been used by Baumgarten, Dilthey, Gadamer, Heinrici, Hofmann, Keil, Lücke, Moldaenke (regarding Flacius), Mussner, and

Oepke.[37] According to Dobschütz the concept of "hermeneutics" "appears to be an invention of the pseudo-classicism of the 17th century." He observes it first in Joh. Conr. Dannhauer in Strassburg (1654).[38]

## RESULT

Despite a few misgivings, it seems to us that the name "biblical hermeneutics" is still the most appropriate and usable name available.

# CHAPTER THREE

# The Starting Point of Hermeneutics

## THE FUNDAMENTAL ALTERNATIVE

We would contradict our previous deliberations if we located the starting point of hermeneutics in the listening person. The most significant hermeneutical decision is probably whether we take revelation itself or man as our starting point.

## MAN AS STARTING POINT

At least since René Descartes' *Discours de la méthode* (1637), "the thinking self has moved to the center of the universe," as Scholder stated it.[1] The thinking self is the Archimedean point from which all else is judged. Outside of the thinking self, however, nothing is certain. Tradition that is passed along must be tested. Two corollaries follow: #1) as a matter of principle a "break with tradition" and all its conventional claims to authority,[2] and #2) "the principle of universal doubt,"[3] with which truth can first be discovered. Even if Descartes finally remained convinced that God exists, it was still human reason that proved his existence.[4] The Cartesian turn in thought is more decisive than the Copernican. For from Descartes on, the idea of "truth" was bound primarily to reason and no longer to revelation. The consequence became clear first among natural scientists. They experienced God's revelation not only in the Holy Scriptures but also in nature. Galileo held that one could not be deceived by natural processes, but might be deceived by Holy Scripture. For that reason the Scripture must be interpreted on the basis of the findings of natural science.[5] The principle established itself: "Non tam autoritate quae nihil valet apud eos qui ratione duci volunt, quam necessariis argumentis" ("Not on the basis of authority, then, which is worthless for those wishing to give reason its due, but rather through the necessary arguments").[6] Out of the certainty of reason grew the "pathos of truth."[7] Kepler and La Peyrères reverse the principle: "At magis mihi veritas" ("Truth is what means more to me").[8] How great a shift this represents from, e.g., the older humanism of that era is seen by recalling that Erasmus (1466?–1536) still described theology as the mother of all sciences.[9]

From this time on a demanding battle for the reconciliation of both—reason and revelation—sets in for those unwilling to give up the Holy Scripture. Here authors are guided by a number of concerns, including a desire to exclude the notion of twofold truth (i.e., reason and revelation) in favor of the unity of knowledge.[10] Isaac de la Peyrères championed the slogan "Per hanc rursus positionem conciliatur fides cum recta ratione" ("Through this approach, the faith is again reconciled with correct reason").[11] This could be achieved in the manner of Spinoza by making God and nature into one.[12] Much more recently Schelling still advocated this approach: "deus est res cunctas" ("God is all things").[13] Or one could proceed from the unity that Scripture and nature, reason and revelation, find in the one God who created them both. So runs the formulation of Balthasar Bekker: "Et deus tam rationis quam revelationis autor" ("God is the creator of both reason and revelation").[14] We can pass over the related battle waged in England centering most of all on the "Reasonableness of Christianity"[15] as well as on the problem of miracles.[16] In any case the result was that German theology fell under strong English influence.[17] Wolff guaranteed "reason the right to have a decisive equal voice in matters of faith."[18] He sought "to join reason and revelation together, for without this combination they will contradict each other."[19] Unless the two are equally yoked, they will be pulling in opposite directions.

Increasingly, the major emphasis is placed on reason. Gottsched could say: "I abide, then, by that which is most certain, which is what the pure light of reason teaches about God and my actions."[20]

The outcome here is threefold: #1) Germany witnesses the demise of any *hermeneutica sacra*.[21] There is indeed no more independent realm for it. #2) Truths of reason are placed above factual truths. In his study of monads Leibniz states, "The truths of reason are necessary and their opposite impossible, factual truths are contingent and their opposite possible."[22] Instead of truths of reason and factual truths one can also speak of "eternal truths" and "temporal, contingent truths."[23] As a result the contingence of biblical revelation receives a telling blow. The Neologists then emptied the idea of revelation of its historical content to a great degree.[24] #3) Man becomes the measure of all things by virtue of his reason. He is basically good. The doctrine of original sin is rejected. It is no accident that "in the age of the Neologists the most hated man" was Augustine.[25]

Clearly this line of thinking in its historical development does not permit revelation to serve as the starting point. It must rather constantly return to man. This theological tendency is strengthened by similar tendencies that had long since established themselves among historians and philosophers. Already in 1566 the historian Jean Bodin declares himself independent from the Bible's account of history. He decides to serve "the progress of mankind."[26] Three hundred years later the historian Droysen refers to Descartes and speaks of "cogito ergo sum" as "the most certain fact we possess."[27] We remember the stress that the philosopher Spranger placed on the human consciousness of truth.[28] We also recall that historians and philosophers repeatedly insisted that we can only understand the artifacts of the past from person to person, by means of an interpersonal congeniality with the earlier authors. To cite Droysen one more time: "We are illumined only by the trace that man has left behind, by that which the human spirit and hand has formed, impressed, and touched."[29]

It is also clear that a theological hermeneutic rooted in this tradition, and supported by the conviction that the Bible is a book like any other, had to seek its starting point in man. It did this in a twofold manner. First, it made its point of departure contemporary man in his quest for understanding. Second, it assumed that it was *man* with which the Bible offered an encounter. Modern "existential" interpretation expresses this most sharply. Bultmann's primary concern was the "question concerning the understanding of human existence that comes to expression in the Scripture."[30] His student Fuchs formulated it even more radically: "the question about God . . . means . . . indeed that we are asking about human existence itself." For Fuchs there is no other theological and scientific interpretation apart from the "existential."[31] Of course, Bultmann and his followers were prepared "to let themselves be questioned by the text" and "to hear its claims."[32] But this was thoroughly confined to the level of human understanding of being. It is interesting that Bultmann, referring explicitly to Dilthey, Schleiermacher, and Herder, emphasizes the "relatedness" between the biblical author and the modern interpreter.[33] At the same time he sees himself bound by the "law of veracity, which commands that nothing be seen as true which contradicts the truths that are the factual presupposition of my . . . worldview."[34] That is very much in line with the thought of Isaac de la Peyrères and the Neologists. Gadamer, a cofounder of the "New Hermeneutic,"[35] basically holds the same position, even though he seeks links with Hegel rather than Schleiermacher.[36] "To understand means first of all to understand each other," according to Gadamer. "Understanding is first of all consent."[37] "Consent" thus becomes a key idea of a hermeneutic that seeks its starting point in man. "Consent," "to understand in relation to others," can only take place where in principle equal entities engage in exchange and relationship with each other. The consequence is a relativizing of truths. Carson, who rejects the idea of "consent," speaks of a "sea of historical relativity."[38]

Ricoeur has lodged a protest against both Cartesianism and existentialism.[39] There is no autonomy of human consciousness. For every consciousness is determined by some given. The given, the event, becomes our "destiny." Immanence is thereby ruptured. For an event that is determinative cannot be purely immanent. Human consciousness, then, must be seen as an entity determined and derived from outside itself.[40] Yet this dependency is not heteronomy, because it does not consist in force and subjection but rather in an openness of the self as events make their "nonviolent appeal," as Ricoeur puts it.[41] But for Ricoeur "the most formidable obstacle to the idea of revelation" is making consciousness the starting point.[42] He opts rather for revelation. His goal is a "hermeneutic of revelation."[43]

## REVELATION AS STARTING POINT

We have cited Ricoeur in order to indicate how unsatisfactory it is to take the human person as the starting point of hermeneutics. Such a starting point contradicts the intent expressed in biblical revelation. Indeed, it contradicts the idea of revelation itself.

Is there some other approach? If we look back over church history, we observe that Reformation thinkers embraced a quite different starting point from the ones that became dominant in the seventeenth, eighteenth, or nineteenth centuries. The statement "Holy Scripture is its own interpreter"[44] would be senseless if it were not assumed that Scripture possessed priority over the human interpreter. Revelation forms the interpreter's consciousness, thinking, and willing: he does not understand revelation on the basis of his consciousness, thinking, and willing. Revelation makes itself understandable to the interpreter. Luther's basic position was pondered from all sides in a voluminous study by Flacius, who is rightly regarded as the father of Protestant hermeneutics.[45] Flacius is an enemy of the thesis "that the [divine] word is to be measured by the object, rather than the object by the [divine] word."[46] This concern was for the most part furthered in Protestant Scholasticism. E.g., for Quenstedt the "certa et infallibilis scripturae interpretatio" ("sure and infallible interpretation of Scripture") comes only from Scripture.[47] In the same manner scientific Pietism holds that truth can be recognized only from Scripture itself.[48] This revelatory starting point is still clearly visible in the middle of the nineteenth century in Philippi's *Kirchlicher Glaubenslehre*. Interacting with Schleiermacher, Philippi emphasizes that at issue is not the Christian mental condition and the like but rather the unfolding of the content of revelation.[49]

If we have rightly defined our task, namely, to understand the Bible in accordance with its own basic claim, and if we have rightly observed that the Bible is the most unique "object," then our guiding principle must be to proceed consistently from the revelation that encounters us in the form of the Bible. The starting point must strictly and consistently be revelation itself. Let us attempt to clarify this point.

The Bible brings new dimensions to our experience. The person God calls is one "whose eye sees clearly," who "hears the words of God," "who sees a vision from the Almighty" (Nu 24:3f., 15 NIV). He cleanses persons who hear his message and bear it among other hearers (Isa 6:1ff.). He places his words in their mouths so they may speak his words in his name (Jer 1:9). He speaks "face to face" with chosen individuals (Nu 12:8). He gives "revelation," disclosure, apocalypse in seeing and hearing (Rev 1:1). He explains what is hidden (Da 2:22, 24). He proves he is God—and he alone!—by describing what will take place before it comes to pass (Isa 44:7; cf. 41:22ff.; 43:9).

Even the person to whom this all appears impossible must lay aside all standards of prior experience in order to hear. The worst thing that can befall the hearer is this: to restrict, for reasons of principle, the right of that which encounters him as revelation to speak. When this occurs, he will invariably fail to hear. In place of encounter there will surely be opposition.

None of the three standards established by Troeltsch as his "historical method" meets this fundamental demand of hearing. These standards are analogy, (immanent) causality, and correlation.[50] Their deficiency cannot be overcome by adding an additional "principle."[51] To the credit of historians it should be noted that they have never wielded the "principle of analogy" with such strictness.

It can be said that the demand of revelation has a correlate in the personal openness on the human side. This opening of oneself is a process involving the whole of one's being. It includes thinking and willing and is thus the opposite of ecstasy and meditative self-contemplation. The Formula of Concord (1577) expressed this in very simple language by stating that people should not stop up their ears.[52] It is noteworthy that this statement is embedded right in an overwhelmingly predestinarian context. In man's personal openness God lays claim to his created capacity to think. It was that very listening faculty of reason, that capacity for intellectual perception to be put to its proper use, which old Protestant orthodoxy regarded as given and essential despite the human condition due to the Fall.[53] In opening oneself all prior experience and knowledge remain present. To that extent a discerning and in that sense "critical" (better: diacritical, or discriminating) hearing is thoroughly possible. This personal openness ultimately means the willingness to turn loose of former certainties on the very broadest scale.

Personal openness and a revelatory starting point would be seriously impaired if we felt that our ability to hear depended on some philosophy or other. In retrospect, every confidence that theology placed in philosophy proved unfounded. Eighteenth-century English and German theology languished in the chains of English Deism to a large degree.[54] Strauss sought the key first in Hegel's philosophy before going over to Feuerbach in 1839.[55] Baur attached himself first to Schleiermacher, then to Hegel, and confessed: "Without philosophy history remains eternally dead and silent to me."[56] Lohmeyer was dependent on Hönigswald,

Schlatter on Baader.[57] Bultmann entrusted himself to Heidegger,[58] although the Tübingen philosopher Walter Schulz later called Heidegger's *Being and Time* "a 'godless' book."[59]

All these and other considerations do not exactly encourage us to cling to philosophical preunderstandings or to take them as our guideposts in listening to revelation.[60] As already stated, conscious and unconscious philosophical influences will always accompany our hearing. But they are present in order to be divested of their leading role.

Starting with revelation prevents us, furthermore, from thinking in terms of an already established doctrine of evolution. Long before Troeltsch, e.g., Harnack assumed "the evolutionary development" of biblical revelation. For him the Old Testament was permeated with "all stages" of religion, "from naive barbaric folk ritual to the religion of the Psalmists."[61] Wellhausen went on to develop and present these "stages of religion"[62] exegetically. But Dilthey as well, probably dependent on Hegel, spoke of the "development of religion." Religion has "its law in the essence of the [human] spirit, determined as it is by history."[63] Here revelation is pressed into the schema of an immanent causality. Philosophically based evolutionary viewpoints restrict the interpreter's hearing and determine in advance the contents of revelation. In extreme cases Christianity then appears as "a syncretistic religion,"[64] in which the concept of revelation is either entirely dissolved or transmuted into the mystical.[65]

Starting with revelation is, however, also to be insisted on in contrast to every form of experiential theology. It is precisely conservative theologians that have often readily pointed to inner certainty and the like. Martin Kähler is an especially impressive example. He grounds the Bible's authority using the "experience" of the Christian that the "words of Scripture retain the capacity to generate and preserve the church, as well as furnish the standard for judgment, purification, and renewal."[66] Here a distinction must be made. Without question experience *can* provide an argument in the area of hermeneutics. This argument will, however, always suffer from a twofold weakness. First, the experiences of various persons diverge from one another. Second, experience as such offers no possibility to distinguish true and false doctrine from each other. Most important, however, Scripture opens entirely new human experiences to us. In interpreting Scripture, therefore, the leading principle must be determined by a theology based on revelation rather than a theology based on experience.

If the revelatory starting point be taken seriously, then interpreting and understanding Scripture can basically only take place inductively. That is, knowledge and standards are gleaned from continually fresh listening to Scripture. It is perhaps here that the deepest difference lies between a Pietist and a fundamentalist hermeneutic. Representing the latter view, J. I. Packer can say, e.g., "No Christian will question that God speaks truth and truth only"—"then Scripture as such must be infallible and inerrant, because it is God's utterance."[67] That is a rationalistic and deductive conception. Because #1) in the Bible God speaks, and #2) God cannot speak what is not true ("untruths cannot be God's word"),[68] then all that the Bible says is true and reliable. C. F. Henry follows a similar line in his monumental work. For him it is "logically deducible" that the Bible is without error precisely because it presents the inspired word of God.[69] Here he is able to refer to John Wesley.[70] One should not, however, simply label this outlook as "fundamentalistic."[71] We observe a similar approach among orthodox Lutherans, e.g., Philippi, who writes: "It can be derived a priori [!] from the concept of divine revelation itself that divine revelation must have preserved itself with perfect integrity."[72] In addition, theologians who may be fairly designated fundamentalists also wish to stress the need for inductive work.[73] Three reasons speak against a deductive approach. First is the danger of rationalism which readily appears. It suffices to recall Descartes' proof of God's existence. Descartes assumed "that God as absolutely perfect being cannot desire to deceive," and that "to the being of God as perfection . . . necessarily" belongs "existence."[74] Such concepts are not all too far removed from statements made by scholarly fundamentalism. Second is the danger of placing dogmatic principles over biblical exegesis.[75] Third is the knowledge that man can know nothing certain in matters of faith unless revelation discloses it to him.

We thus remain dependent on an inductive procedure that lets itself be led step by step in listening to revelation, gaining all its knowledge from the Scripture.

If in interpreting Scripture we decline to entrust ourselves either to philosophy or to traditional dogmatics, then we must repudiate even more firmly every claim that other sciences domineeringly assert against theology. That applies first of all to the science of history. Lücke has already stressed that one must "keep . . . theology safe from the thoroughgoing sole sovereignty of historical knowledge."[76] It is true that theology, as talk about God and with God and as task of the church, has numerous points of contact with historical science. Yet at the same time it possesses a healthy independence. This applies no less to natural science. Fascher observes that the humanities and especially theology up to the First World War stood "under the covert dictates of natural science's ways of thinking and formulating concepts."[77] To read Bultmann's essay "The New Testament and Mythology" is to see that these dictates exerted a measure of influence into the time of World War II and beyond. It was precisely natural scientists who helped free theology from these dictates.[78] Questions concerning ethics and religion are moreover now much in the forefront in the natural sciences. So it hardly befits theology to give in to the "spell" of these or those scientific hypotheses.[79]

We state once more: biblical hermeneutics starts with the enscripturated revelation and subordinates all other demands to this listening to the Scripture.

But is such a hermeneutic, rooted in revelational-theological considerations, rightly deemed a "science"?

# CHAPTER FOUR

# Theological Hermeneutics as Science

## THE INDEPENDENCE OF THEOLOGICAL SCIENCE

It is disputed whether theology, and along with it hermeneutics, can comprise a "science." L. Wittgenstein and the Vienna circle deny it. For them, only statements of (human) logic and mathematics and the empirical sciences have meaning.[1] Theological statements thus become "sense-less" in the strictest sense.

Such a viewpoint is untenable. It would in fact mean that broad reaches of human existence, e.g., in philosophy and religion, would become "sense-less" and remain removed from ordered mental reflection. It would end in irreparable damage to our comprehension of reality. In addition, it contradicts the history of the West, in which theology was "the mother of all sciences" (Erasmus),[2] not an intruder having no rights.

Granted: if one insists that in modern science "the critical, thinking person" is "the measure of all things,"[3] then theology appears as a stranger in the circle of other sciences. For it maintains that it finds the measure of all things in God. In its very essence, then, theology is non-rationalistic and nonpositivistic.[4] Yet this observation by no means removes its right to call itself a science. It can point out that to this present hour no unanimously recognized concept of science has been found.[5] In this situation we must content ourselves with a formal concept of science. "Science" may be defined as follows: methodologically ordered reflection, making use of all available means, which can be executed and tested under the same conditions by others.

In this sense theology along with its hermeneutic bear the character of a science. Yet, because it deals with God and his revelation, it remains a science sui generis. This finding corresponds to what we have already shown above in chapter 2 regarding a special hermeneutic. And precisely because it involves a science sui generis and *suae rationis*, no one can demand of theology that it "emulate" every "major variation in all the sciences."[6] That would be to give up its own distinctive legitimacy and ultimately its scientific character as well.

Incidentally, in the early twentieth century, liberal theology fought for that distinctive legitimacy in exemplary fashion. At that time a battle was underway regarding whether theology faculties in the universities "had a right to exist . . . only as a faculty of general religious studies."[7] Scholars like G. Krüger or H. Weinel viewed the presence of an independent "New Testament" science, or any analogous theological discipline, as a "chief hindrance" in the way of "the research of early Christianity" and of "healthy theological-scientific teaching activity."[8] They demanded that traditional theology be subsumed under a comprehensive history-of-religions approach. In response, A. Harnack in his university presidential address of August 1903 referred to the uniqueness of Christianity: it is *"the* religion, because Jesus Christ" is *"the* master."[9] Perhaps the Prussian king whom Harnack called "our king and lord"[10] contributed to the preservation of independent theology faculties—an objectively justified decision.

## RELATIONSHIP TO OTHER SCIENCES

Let us now attempt to bring a bit more clarity to the relation between theology and the other sciences.

1. Theology also works with methodological rigor. That is, it takes pains to demonstrate how it arrives at its results and how they may be thoroughly tested. It employs expert knowledge, makes use of appropriate resources, and attempts to spot subjectivity so as to overcome its harmful effects.[11]

2. Like other sciences it serves the interests of truth. Yet as soon as one asks what "truth" is, disputes rage within theology as well as between theology and other sciences. For Spranger, e.g., all science takes its cue from the (Platonic) "idea of truth" and must be measured by that standard.[12] The Catholic J. Blank sees himself obligated "to the ethos of scientific truth," which he interprets as renunciation of dogmatic authority regarding truth.[13] The Protestant Bultmann adheres to the (Enlightenment-based) "principle of truthfulness, which requires us to accept nothing as true which contradicts truths that form the factual presupposition of my understanding of the world."[14] For others Christ embodies the truth. Nevertheless, despite all differences one can cautiously state that most sciences and scientists feel they are obligated to a truth that stands in contrast to deception and error.

3. In addition, it is essential to recognize that theology is ready to revise its methods and ways of posing questions.[15] Such self-criticism links it with the rest of the sciences.[16] It is disputed, however, to what extent such self-criticism is justified. Should it extend to "self-criticism of its foundations"? The philosopher Spranger affirms this.[17] The Catholic Blank comes to a similar result when he says, "Whoever comes to the Bible with firm, unshakable convictions and is not willing radically to risk and expose to scrutiny the entirety of his inherited theological understanding in order to listen more precisely, to learn, and to give something new a hearing—that person may be suited for much, but he is totally unsuited for exegesis."[18] Since, however, divine revelation is

the foundation of theology, and since theology can gain its knowledge of God only from that source, a revision or even rejection of this foundation is not an option. In this restriction we see once more the sui generis character of theological science.

4. Yet precisely at the point of this nonnegotiable given, the discussion flares up anew. How can theology, e.g., still be called a science when it refuses to engage in criticism of the content of revelation? Here it should first be recalled that nonnegotiable givens also play determinative roles in other sciences. A legal scholar is, e.g., bound by existing laws and precedents. Yet he can arrive at radically new conceptions in the area of philosophy of law. But even there he will infer the law ultimately from the given, e.g., from morality or history or political goals. In the same way the historian is bound by actual extant data of history. Doing away with this givenness would place him in the category of a storyteller or dreamer. Still more to the point, P. Ricoeur maintains that life and reflection generally depend on givens ("external testimonies").[19] In that sense theology is scientifically legitimate in starting with the inalterability of its foundation in the form of revelation.

5. But what about preunderstanding? Doesn't theology require faith? And doesn't this entangle it in unscientific ties? The battle over this question is ancient. Once more, the dispute rages not only between theologians and proponents of other sciences but also within theology. On the one hand liberal theologians emphasize that theological research presupposes a "complete freedom."[20] William Wrede laid out this demand even more clearly in his essay "Über Aufgabe und Methode der sogenannten Neutestamentlichen Theologie" ("On the Task and Method of So-called 'New Testament Theology'") (1897). "A pure, disinterested quest for knowledge" should "lead" the theological interpreter. He must "be adept at holding himself entirely aloof from" his own "outlook, be capable of suspending it, so to speak."[21] It is clear that in this view personal faith is unwelcome. Still in 1958 (a half century after Wrede), Rylaarsdam demanded a "presuppositionless" exegesis.[22]

Since then, however, it has been widely recognized that there is no presuppositionless exegesis or biblical research. Harnack furnishes an instructive example. He spoke of "the pure knowledge of the object" and insisted on the "freedom" of theological research.[23] At the same time he described how "a new concept of science has established itself since the 18th century" and "gained ascendency in the universities."[24] As Harnack's words reveal, this was a conception of science that pushed into the universities by storm, bringing with it certain substantial implications. Blank referred to a few of these when he reflected on the reception of Protestant biblical criticism in Catholic research. Modern methods have also "ushered modernity's autonomous historical-critical reason into theological thought." This is not a matter of "taking over a neutral tool" but rather "an entire complex of additional new problems, behind which lies a comprehensive, novel understanding of truth."[25] Even the "sound reason" (*sana ratio*) of the Socinians was, in fact, decisively informed by their convictions.[26] In the same manner theology in the age of Neology and rationalism worked "with philological-historical means" and presuppositions that dictated results.[27]

The insight that there is no presuppositionless understanding is also widely acknowledged outside the confines of theology. "Every hermeneutic"—whether in the realm of law, philology, philosophy, psychology, or some other realm—"will be grounded in certain metaphysical convictions."[28] Among philosophers many have spoken of the presuppositions that are innate to science, including Theodor Litt, Erich Rothacker, Max Scheler, and Eduard Spranger. "All knowledge is nourished, finally, by a . . . world-view."[29] Spranger wrote: "Even in the act of pure observational understanding there is always a silent measuring against some ideal."[30] H. G. Gadamer went so far as to speak against the "methodological ideal of the objectivity of science."[31] Even if this bears the scent of subjectivity, one must agree with Gadamer that every form of tradition grows out of preunderstanding.[32]

So then, theology loses nothing by admitting that "as a science" it is "continually borne along and informed by faith."[33] For now it must remain open as to when faith steps in and what the consequences will be. For the moment all that matters is that faith be affirmed and recognized as a presupposition and aid in understanding Scripture.[34] Whoever wishes to infer the "unscientific character" of theology from this must submit to Oepke's question: "since when is color blindness necessary for the history of painting, or tone deafness for the science of music?"[35]

6. Still, faith belongs to the level of immanence. Doesn't the idea of science leave off where talk of God begins? Everything changes at the point where "the question of God is included in the scope of the discussion."[36] From this many theologians have drawn the conclusion that they must use "atheistic methods," so to speak.[37] Against this speak three considerations: #1) No one would deny philosophy its status as a science because it speaks of God. Thus Hegel sought a "reconciliation of faith and knowledge." Even more striking, he wanted "now once more to place God absolutely at the forefront, on the pinnacle of philosophy as the sole ground of everything, as the only principium essendi and cognoscendi [principle of existence and of knowing]."[38] #2) The historian is also permitted to consider God without ceasing to pursue the science of history. Thus Droysen acknowledges in persons a "most personal realm" "in which they commune with themselves and God alone."[39] True, he adds: "Into this holy sanctuary the eye of research gains no entrance."[40] It suffices, however, that a place must be reserved for this sanctuary if one seriously pursues the historian's craft. #3) It is still the case that "theology . . . [is] the mother of all the sciences."[41]

Talk of God does not, therefore, cause theology to forfeit its right to describe itself as "science."

## RESULT

To restate: the idea of science must be formally determined. Assuming this, theology along with its hermeneutic is a science. It is, nevertheless, a science sui generis, distinguished from all others by its dependence on revelation and its relation to faith.

# CHAPTER FIVE

# The Interpreter

Precisely the independence of theology sharpens the question of the interpreter. Who can understand the Bible in accordance with its own claim? Which presuppositions are appropriate?

## INTERPRETATION WITHOUT PRESUPPOSITIONS?

In the history of interpretation it has not always been self-evident that understanding presupposes a positive relationship to that which, or the one who, is to be understood. Thus Jean Alphonse Turretin (1671–1737) in his methodological treatise "De Sacrae Scripturae methodo tractatus bipartitus" assumed this standpoint: "An empty head . . ., a veritable tabula rasa . . . must be brought to the Scripture."[1] He thereby consciously set himself apart from the Pietist hermeneutic of the day and inaugurated a long chain of demands aimed at securing exegesis that was presuppositionless.[2] Recently J. Barr has been at the forefront in championing the thesis that critical distance aids a better, more objective apprehension.[3] The interpreter's faith or lack of faith, therefore, makes no difference: "the presence or absence of personal religious commitment cannot function as a test of the validity of methods or results."[4] Meanwhile, however, the acceptance of presuppositionlessness has proved to be "self-deception" (see previous chapter).[5] It remains only to inquire "which presuppositions are justified."[6] The question is, "which assumptions are legitimate?"[7]

As Dilthey put it, the "degrees" of understanding are "conditioned by interest." "If interest is restricted, so is understanding."[8] Spranger argues in similar fashion: "All understanding in the area of the humanities is tied to the intellectual breadth (capacity) and maturity (fullness of spirit) of the researcher's personality."[9] From this can be inferred the hermeneutical axiom that understanding increases and deepens to the extent that the seeker engages with openness what he wishes to understand.

## CONGENIALITY?

It is therefore only consistent if "capacity for religious empathy"[10] or a "religious sensitivity"[11] was demanded in theology. The term *congeniality* is often used, however, to express the requisite nearness.[12]

In specific cases, this congeniality was conceived in quite various fashions. It was thought of in terms of the capacity of creative, imitative imagination,[13] imitative sensitivity,[14] "intuition" as "soul [merges into] soul,"[15] a similar form of "experience of spirit,"[16] "inner relatedness of choice,"[17] inner "agreement" with the biblical authors,[18] or simply "affinity" and "sympathy" with them.[19] This congeniality could, however, also be separated from the authors and regarded as a positive "relationship of the interpreter's life to the matter being communicated" as expressed in the words of the text.[20] In any case there had to be a similar quantity present on both sides: "Just as an abstemious person would hardly be an apt interpreter for the songs of an Anakreon or Sappho," a nonreligious person would be ill-suited to interpret the Bible.[21] Still, those who were united in calling for congeniality were also clear that an unbridgeable gap still remains. This gap involves the uniqueness of the individual. Both Dilthey and Torm state, "Individuum est ineffabile."[22] All understanding "remains only relative."[23]

The principle of congeniality's necessity is largely correct and worthy of recognition. It is to be affirmed so long as it is not based on the genius or "brilliance of the interpreter."[24] It should rather be based on the same (Holy) Spirit who created the Scripture and takes hold of the interpreter. Yet precisely out of regard for the Holy Spirit, it would be more appropriate to speak of a "co-spirituality" than a "con-geniality."

First, however, it must be asked whether such a "kinship of spirit" between the interpreter and written revelation is sufficient. It is all too easy to equate *spiritus* (spirit) with intellect and "kinship of spirit" with intellectual capacity.[25] An additional element, then, must enter the picture to enable adequate understanding. J. G. Hamann perceptively recognized this; he stated, "interpreters have had plenty of arguments but absolutely no, or very little, *affectus* (emotion) and *mores* (moral sense)."[26] Amazingly, nontheologians have, with special emphasis, demanded love. "Certainly one person understands the other, but only peripherally. It is quite another thing when a friend trusts a friend, so that in love one person captures the image of another's true self."[27] This statement by Droysen is underscored by Treitschke: we understand only that which we love. "This applies to the highest degree in understanding religious tradition."[28] If revelation (as we will show more clearly below) has to do most of all with an I-Thou relationship, then faith and love are all the more necessary to initiate an adequate understanding of the Bible.

## HOLY SPIRIT AND SPIRITUAL REBIRTH?

Before we follow this trail any farther, we need to ponder the word *spirit* in the heading above. In the previous section we stated that it is the Holy Spirit who binds together God's revelation and the interpreter. Is, then, the reception of this Spirit the necessary presupposition for understanding revelation and interpreting it for others? Is Philippi's inference correct: "only the person who has the Holy Spirit has spiritual relatedness to the content of the Bible"?[29] Philippi went on to speak, consistently enough, of the "folly of presuppositionlessness" committed by those who want to understand and interpret without the Holy Spirit.[30]

With this we touch on the hotly debated "theology of the spiritually reborn" (*theologia regenitorum*). Some insist on it doggedly, while others repudiate it as unworkable and obsolete.[31] In the scope of church history an imposing range of voices call for it. Paul definitely viewed a true understanding of the Holy Scriptures as possible only through the Holy Spirit (cf. 1Co 2:13f.; 2Co 3:14ff.; 4:3ff.).[32] Origen shared this view that only persons renewed by the Spirit, "qui dignos se et capaces ad recipiendam capientiam praepararent" ("who thereby render themselves worthy and receptive for the appropriation of Scripture"),[33] grasp the full content of the Bible. Both Luther and Calvin[34] emphasized that every interpreter is dependent on the Holy Spirit. Quite typical of Luther is the passage quoted by Karl Holl from Luther's lectures on the Psalms: "nam nullus alium in scripturis spiritualibus intelligit, nisi eundem spiritum sapiat et habeat" ("for none understands the spiritual Scriptures unless he tastes and possesses the same Spirit").[35] The Protestant Scholastics likewise advocated a *theologia regenitorum*. Here they were at pains to make a distinction. Hollaz taught that a grammatical-lexical understanding is thoroughly possible for the person who is not spiritually reborn.[36] But full understanding presupposes divine illumination. The *Institutiones Theologiae dogmaticae* (1723) by Joh. Franz Buddeus is indebted to both Protestant Scholasticism and Pietism. It lays special stress on the *theologia regenitorum*. Only spiritual regeneration, with the faith and practical obedience it brings, equips one for theology.[37] Not until the incursion of the Enlightenment does Mosheim (d. 1755) give up the *theologia regenitorum*. Mosheim explains that it affects only the communication and persuasive force of knowledge, not knowledge itself.[38] In pietistic hermeneutics, then, it was most of all the interpreter who was at the center of deliberations. From Francke to Bengel there is agreement regarding the principle "that reason must subordinate itself to faith."[39] There is also agreement in the goal of "becoming more spiritual through the reading of Scripture."[40] Francke, referring to the academic instruction he gave, states, "No theology lecture is held that does not aim for the heart and that does not attempt to pierce the soul of every listener."[41] Prayer is as important as thoroughness in theological study.[42] For biblical exposition, consequently, the individuality of the author is important. Thereby the psychological element pushes into hermeneutics. This is readily visible in Francke's *Praelectiones hermeneuticae* (1717).[43] Finally, the major work on hermeneutics in Pietism was the *Institutiones hermeneuticae sacrae* (1724) by Johann Jakob Rambach (1693–1735). He elevated illumination by the Holy Spirit, love for Jesus, and love for God's Word to decisive presuppositions of scriptural exegesis.[44]

The Enlightenment in no way signaled the end of *theologia regenitorum*. It is interesting that Schleiermacher's student Friedrich Lücke consciously began with J. Franz Buddeus and Johann Jakob Rambach.[45] For Lücke the Holy Spirit was indispensable to the interpreter. We need "the pious and persistent prayer to the Angel Interpreter," and we need "faith in league with science."[46] In some sections Lücke reads like an introit to the later "pneumatic exegesis" (see below). Lücke laments that interpreters have become "even mockers of that which is sacred."[47] We must have "apostolic love and evangelical faith"[48] to arrive at an understanding of the Holy Scripture. J. Samuel Lutz and Friedrich Adolf Philippi cling to *theologia regenitorum* in the mid-nineteenth century.[49] Martin Kähler then passed on to his students, among them H. E. Weber, the sure conviction that "the theological enterprise calls for the believing apprehension of revelation."[50] Or in Weber's formulation, faith forms the "key of understanding."[51] R. Seeberg and—in recent times—F. Beisser are examples of advocates of a *theologia regenitorum* in the twentieth century.[52] It is virtually self-evident that such a *theologia* is promoted by scientific fundamentalism to this present day.[53] It also holds an important place among representatives of the so-called pneumatic exegesis such as Karl Girgensohn, Otto Procksch, or Hellmuth Frey, whose thought relies on Johann Tobias Beck.[54] The papal Bible commission renewed the normative status of *theologia regenitorum* in its "Instructio de historica Evangeliorum veritate" of April 21, 1964.[55]

In view of all these precedents from church history it is impossi-

ble to declare a *theologia regenitorum* to be unworkable or outmoded.[56]
There should rather be substantive discussion at this point regarding its
justification.

## THE ANSWER OF REVELATION

It would be thinkable—and perhaps not entirely false—to make man the
starting point at least in view of a *theologia regenitorum*. But here, too,
we must think rigorously from the basis of revelation. What presuppositions are laid down by revelation itself to enable us to arrive at understanding? The answer is found along two lines:

1. A knowledge of Scripture and serious study of it are also possible without the Holy Spirit. That is evident from Jesus' discussions with
the Bible scholars, the scribes, of his time (cf. Mt 23:2f.; Jn 5:39) as well
as from Jewish religious instruction (cf. 2Ti 3:14f.) and many other
sources (e.g., Ac 17:11).

2. A sufficient understanding is, however, possible only for the person who has become Jesus' disciple (cf. Mt 13:11ff., 52) and is led by
the Holy Spirit (cf. Jn 6:45; 16:13; 1Co 2:13f.; 2Co 3:14ff.). From the
point of view of the New Testament, knowledge is an outcome of faith
(Jn 6:69; Ac 2:38).

Both #1) and #2) above are affirmed at the time of the
Reformation. Luther emphasized "the general understandability of the
Bible"[57] and ascribed some cognitive competence to "the natural light
of reason."[58] Calvin held "that some knowledge of God resides indelibly
in the human heart"[59] and "that in spite of everything sensitivity for the
divine cannot be extinguished."[60] He also held, however, that without the
Holy Spirit and faith we have nothing more than "only a very approximate impression of the divine essence"; there is "nowhere a pure and
reliable religion . . . where the only basis is natural reason."[61]
Melanchthon seems to have in mind a sequence of stages when he writes
that every good theologian must be "primum grammaticus, deinde
dialectus, denique testis" ("first grammarian, then dialectician, finally

witness").[62] We recall, moreover, the view of Hollaz, who conceded that even the unregenerate have grammatical-lexical knowledge, but then continued: the "summus et infallibilis interpres" ("highest and infallible interpreter") is the Holy Spirit.[63]

We repeat: revelation itself presupposes the Holy Spirit and faith for a sufficient and appropriate understanding on the part of the interpreter. To that extent there can be no doubt that a biblical hermeneutic includes a *theologia regenitorum.*

Yet that does not mean that *every* reading and *every* understanding is dependent on faith. Revelation rather also offers itself to the reading and understanding of that person who does not yet have faith. We may refer here to the attractive principle laid down by Hollaz that man is converted and renewed in the act of reading.[64] It is thus impermissible to demand spiritual rebirth for all Bible study. It rather remains up to the sovereign work of God's Spirit when and how he will lead the person he addresses to renewal and rebirth. A consequence of #1) and #2) earlier in this section is that according to Scripture there may be circumstances and certain areas in which the unregenerate make discoveries that elude the regenerate. E.g., a linguistically gifted Moslem can shed light on linguistically difficult Old Testament passages. A further consequence is, e.g., that a person in prison can find his way to faith through Bible reading. On the other hand, believing and Spirit-led interpreters are not impervious to error, as both revelation (Ac 11:2ff.; 15:1ff.) and church history prove.

## FAITH AS AID TO UNDERSTANDING

This much, however, can be said: according to all the above, the faith of the interpreter is a welcome, helpful, and indeed ultimately indispensable presupposition of understanding.

  1. It would be thoroughly unnatural, as Lutz observed, "to deny the Christian faith in the process of interpreting the Bible."[65]

  2. We are not in a position to divest ourselves of our encounter with

Christ and our prior Christian background in order to hand them over, so to speak, to critical research for safekeeping. Such a move would also be entirely unscientific.[66] To be scientific rather means to examine critically one's own prejudgments and predecisions and to render them fruitful.

3. It would also not be desirable to detach faith and love for God's Word from the person doing biblical research. Faith does not, after all, stand in opposition to an objective, i.e., appropriate, understanding. R. Bring has shown this to be an insight of Martin Luther.[67] Even for philosophers, "one's own certainty and desire for open-eyed objectivity need not exclude each other."[68] How much less ought we to separate faith and interpretation from each other when revelation itself binds them together!

We must now call attention to the consequences of separating believing encounter with revelation, on the one hand, from understanding it in the course of research, on the other. One of two things takes place. One either avoids the risk of pursuing both lines as far as they extend, or one ends up forcibly dislocating the wholeness of one's own personality. E. Barnikol relates the confession of the Tübingen Old Testament scholar G. F. Oehler (1847): "With my heart a foe of destructive criticism, with my mind ensnared by it, I swim here between two waters, charging myself with unbelief on the one hand and lack of integrity on the other."[69] In 1882, J. Wellhausen quit the theology faculty in Greifswald and instead took up a post as professor of Semitic languages in Halle—all because he could not unite the two sides. He argued, "I became a theologian because scientific investigation of the Bible interested me. Only gradually did it dawn on me that a professor of theology has the practical task of preparing students for service in the Lutheran church, and that I did not fulfill this practical task. Rather, despite all my discretion, I made my listeners unfit for their office."[70] Dibelius accepted a dualism between faith and thought but conceded, "The dualism between the two modes of approach, that of believing and that of knowing, can lead to the point of *forcible dislocation within the whole of one's personal life.* "[71] Presumably many thought, and still think, like E. von Dobschütz, who held that "only science and not edification" belong "in the academy."[72] Even among the proponents of "pneumatic exegesis," who sought a synthesis between "the critical sharpness of contemporary science" and the "strength and depth of biblicists,"[73] the end result was a "form of double-talk."[74]

Such dislocation between thinking and believing, the researching and the practicing self, is hermeneutically the most infelicitous position thinkable. Already at the anthropological level it impairs congeniality. It makes contradiction a normal form of living, which is then consciously or unconsciously imposed on the object. And this all takes place in opposition to the devotion that revelation demands.

In contrast, the renewed person endowed with the Spirit of revelation itself, who opens himself in commitment of his entire person to this revelation, who enters this encounter in trust and love—this person turns out to be better suited as an interpreter.

## THE DIFFERENCE BETWEEN THE REGENERATE AND THE UNREGENERATE INTERPRETER

The question often arises, What distinguishes the regenerate from the unregenerate interpreter? Calvin placed high value on the certainty that the Holy Spirit gives to the interpreter. He considers it "established that only persons inwardly taught by the Holy Spirit take their stand clearly and securely on the Bible."[75] Calvin seeks the difference, then, not primarily in the results but rather in the interpreter himself. Buddeus moves in a similar direction. The unregenerate lack two things: #1) agreement with that which transcends human reason, and #2) the vitality of the word of Scripture.[76] Yet how foolish it would be to want to lead others to salvation and at the same time forget one's own soul. In addition, Buddeus continues, the theologian must be familiar with the *oratio-meditatio-tentatio* (prayer-reflection-struggle) sequence.[77] The unregenerate person is thus capable of relaying tradition to others only in an insufficient fashion. And he is further disadvantaged with respect to content, because he finds acceptance of the supernatural difficult. Like other advocates of a *theologia regenitorum*, J. C. K. von Hofmann also distinguishes between an outward knowledge, which he called the "grammatical-historical," from an inward.[78] The inward is available only to the regenerate.

To be more specific and explicit, however, involves obvious problems. In this connection Hofmann says no more than that only the regenerate can equip the church for the right use of the Holy Scripture.[79] Without the Holy Spirit, says M. Kähler, "the full effectiveness of God's word" would be lacking. It could "therefore not be known and acknowledged as God's word at all."[80] The aspect of the Bible, therefore, that makes it God's Word falls out of consideration. When Kähler speaks of "acknowledgement" through the interpreter, this most surely involves the personal relationship of the exegete to revelation. Girgensohn too places strong emphasis on this personal relationship. The "application of the word of Scripture to oneself" is essential.[81] Then one arrives at "the actual core"[82] of the Holy Scripture, a core which the purely "scientific" theology therefore does not reach. Yet, what is "the actual core"? In recent times Torm has ventured an answer to the question, What can a believing exegete do any better? He cites three advantages: #1) "tenacious energy" for research, #2) the capability for "directing" the right "questions to the text," and #3) better knowledge of the "fine nuances."[83] Of these at least #1) and #3) belong to the so-called outward knowledge of the Scripture. Nothing extra is visible here in terms of content.

If these and other[84] attempts are soberly assessed, it must be said that it so far "has been impossible" to formulate in a really precise way "the difference between illuminated understanding of Scripture and unilluminated exegesis."[85]

It follows that we must replace the anthropocentric question with the pneumatic. The question is thus no longer: how does this or that interpreter differ from others seen from the human perspective? Nor is it: in what respect does he achieve better exegesis? The question is now rather: what does the Holy Spirit, who encounters us in revelation, want to effect with the interpreter? In what follows we proceed from this question.

## THE WORK OF THE SPIRIT ON THE INTERPRETER

The Bible is far more than a treasure trove of doctrinal truths. To view it as a catalog of God's utterances would be to mistake its character. It is primarily a communication of God—communication in the literal sense: God himself communes with us. He wants us to experience communion with him. To that extent the Bible is termed "revelation" with good reason. It is, so to speak, an encounter related in the clear form of words. Or to put it another way: it is transmission of the discussion between God and man—communicative mediation.

This mediation would be utterly misunderstood were it seen as revelation "only insofar as it affects me." The Bible knows no truth that is truth only insofar as it presents "truth for me." Existential categories, therefore, have never sufficed to apprehend it.[86]

If we consistently recognize this character of communication, of revelation, then "conversation" becomes the overarching concept that describes all biblical research. Understanding takes place within that framework of question and answer, address and decision, sometimes even contradiction. The I-Thou relationship becomes decisive in what the Bible says.[87] In the wake of this encounter the interpreter makes decisions that he previously never made. His world of experience is changed. This is the point at which Ricoeur's concept of "understanding oneself in the presence of the text" actually possesses a certain nearness to revelation.[88] What Ricoeur terms "expos[ing] oneself to receive from it [i.e., the world of the text] a larger self" indeed takes place.[89] One should not, however, overlook the difference that lies in the fact that revelation does not merely present an absolutized world of the text; it is also transmission, the mediation of divine speech.

In making encounter our starting point,[90] i.e., the encounter related in the clear form of words in scriptural revelation, we are at the same time taking up a concern of Spener and Bengel. Both could describe the Bible as a letter from God.[91] As Spener puts it, it is "the divine letter of grace, in which the heavenly father announces to us his will to give us blessedness." Bengel states similarly, "This is a letter that my God caused to be written to me, according to which I should orient myself and according to which my God will guide me. . . . Every person must handle it as if it had to do only with him or her."[92]

If we find ourselves in an I-Thou relationship, then it is evident that our understanding cannot make use only of "categories of objects." A purely "object"-ive study of Scripture would once more misconstrue revelation.

It has already been intimated that the encounter mediated by the Bible seeks to elicit decisions. Oepke has rightly underscored this element: "the distinctiveness of the biblical text lies in its demand for a decision from the hearer."[93] "Hearer"—that is, first and foremost the exegete. There are, then, no "neutral" exegetes.[94] And there is also no "neutral" zone of research that lies isolated from the decision process. As G. N. Stanton remarks, not even so-called textual criticism is possible without hermeneutical presuppositions.[95]

Yet the concept of "decision" is too narrow to encompass what we are discussing here. What the Holy Spirit seeks to effect in the interpreter is far more comprehensive: transformation, renewal. In 2 Corinthians 4:6, Paul compares his new existence, especially his new-found and burgeoning understanding, with the divine act of creation. Before Paul could preach and exegete, the old Saul had to become the new Paul. The Holy Spirit seized him, indwelt him, transformed him, and illuminated him. According to Scripture, the same should happen to every interpreter (cf. Jn 3:1ff.; 14:16ff.; 16:13ff.; Ac 13:2; Ro 12:4ff.; 1Co 2:10ff.; 12:28ff.; 1Pe 1:12). An interpreter who sets himself against this transformation by, e.g., claiming some sort of "neutrality" falls into existential contradiction of the revelation that he wishes to interpret and understand. This contradiction is far more dangerous and profound than can be described by simply pointing to its deficiencies at individual points where they crop up. It would be a trivialization of the contradiction to ask naively: "*What* is inaccessible to me when I close myself to the encounter that revelation seeks to convey?" Not a *what* becomes inaccessible but a *who*: God withdraws himself precisely in that revelation that should disclose him, and the interpreter withdraws himself as one who is addressed. Yet only as one touched by revelation's claim on him can he arrive at understanding.

The Holy Spirit teaches the interpreter to conceive of the understanding process as a part of Christian discipleship. The interpreter transformed by the Spirit asks with the first disciples, "Lord, where else can we go? You have the words of eternal life" (Jn 6:68). At work here is a personal knowing reminiscent of what the Hebrew *yada'* (to know) conveys: entering a relationship, experiencing through practice, confirming through involvement.[96]

The "starting point" of our exegetical work is, therefore, emphatically not "scientific skepticism."[97] For skepticism is rooted, after all, in Cartesian thinking, for which from the outset all that lies outside the thinking self is to be doubted. This relates most closely to the notion of autonomous reason as this made its victorious march during the Enlightenment.

The starting point is rather obedience, the obedience of the person whose communion with God is one of fervor ("Be fervent in the Spirit," Ro 12:11) through God's own working. This communion manifests itself in hearing, compliance, and service. We are thus not speaking of blind obedience but obedience illuminated by the Spirit. This is certainly similar to what Ricoeur termed "a nonviolent appeal."[98] But Ricoeur misses an essential feature of revelation when he conceives it as directed to "our imagination" rather than "our obedience."[99] This loses sight of the close proximity of obedience and knowledge. Indeed, Jesus made knowledge dependent on obedience when he said, "If anyone wants to do his will, he will know whether this teaching is from God or whether I speak from my own initiative" (Jn 7:17). Without the practice of discipleship, therefore, no Christian hermeneutic can be constructed. These connections have often been noted in the literature. As soon as God's voice "becomes recognizable," says Girgensohn, "every possibility of human superordination over his word ceases. As soon as God's voice sounds, man can do but one thing: hear and obey unconditionally."[100] Elsewhere he defines the "key to the Holy Scripture" as the "bending of one's own person to the will of God."[101] From an entirely different theological position, Elert stated that God's revelation subjects the interpreter along with his prejudgments to divine judgment: "The Scripture is understood rightly as God's word only if the exegete is willing to hand himself over to the Lord who speaks here, i.e., willing to receive God's verdict regarding him from that which he wants to understand."[102] Accepting this judgment means giving up the value judgments and prejudices that arise from autonomous reason. For the renewed person such willingness to be corrected is a thoroughgoing possibility.[103]

It cannot be denied: in that the Holy Spirit leads the interpreter into the obedience of knowledgeable and practicing discipleship, he specifies to him at the same time the authority to which he is subject. This authority is the eternal Lord. And this eternal Lord encounters him by "the one word of God, which we must hear and to which we must give trust and obedience in life and in death."[104]

Claiming that the interpreter stands under an authority outside his own self meets the gravest objections today. It sounds patronizing. It carries the bad associations of Protestant Scholasticism. Why should the person who has found "the way out of his self-imposed intellectual immaturity" (Kant) surrender again to the sorry state of being subject to external authority? If revelation takes on the quality of an authority, is it not inevitable that the authority of e.g., the Koran or the *Book of Mormon* will be unshakably binding for persons of other cultural and religious backgrounds? Christian revelation answers: there has been no arrival at some intellectual adulthood by modern man. There has simply been an exchange of authorities. If once it was the Holy Scriptures, later it became successive contemporary dogmas of autonomy. "Light," "wisdom," "knowledge," "truth," "freedom"—all these are present where God is the Lord (Pss 36:10; 119:18, 105, 130, 142, 154; Pr 1:7; 4:18; Jn 8:12, 32, 36; 9:39ff.; 14:6). Where, however, God's lordship is nullified, the *stoicheia tou kosmou* (basic principles of unregenerate humanity) with their dogmas are in control. These are enslaving (*dogmatizesthe:* Col 2:20) dogmas. Against this background it becomes intelligible why e.g., Buddeus and Bengel energetically battled the rationalism of their time. They saw its consequence as bondage, not liberty. They preferred the *praeiudicum auctoritas alienae* (presupposition of an alien—i.e., divine—authority) to the *praeiudicum auctoritatis propriae* (presupposition of one's own—i.e., human and "reason"-based— authority), because they were convinced that truth and freedom lay only in the former. The latter, in Buddeus' view, becomes a *praeiudicum praecipitantiae* (a presupposition of unrestraint).[105] Two and a half centuries later, we have opportunity to test their thesis. The test results are positive. We have become authorities unto ourselves without, generally speaking, arriving at a better understanding of the Scripture. A revision, therefore, of the way "alien" authority is viewed is a pressing priority.[106] But is it really an "alien" authority? Is it not rather the authority of him who in Jesus Christ has become closer to us than a brother, who knows man better than he knows himself because he created him, who loves him more than all his self-love is capable of (1Sa 16:7; Ps 139; Jn 2:25)? A true distinction, however, between the various authorities that lay claim to us in the form of Bible or Koran or some other source is only possible through the experiment of discipleship (Jn 7:17). So we see once more that our understanding is embedded in the experience of discipleship.

Discipleship, obedience, renewal, encounter, trust, love in the Holy Spirit—these have all by now become clear to us as essential aspects of understanding revelation. Starting from revelation, we asked the Spirit-centered question: What does the Holy Spirit seek to effect in the interpreter? It is now time to consider that our understanding comprises a process—even and precisely if we speak of the Holy Spirit, as is appropriate given revelation. Process: that refers to the Spirit-led understanding that takes place in increments. Sometimes this may involve circuitous, even erroneous routes. Nowhere is it promised that our understanding is infallible (cf. 1Co 13:9). Yet, a *basic disposition of trust* in the enscripturated revelation will accompany the interpreter at every step, as long as he works as a Christian interpreter in a comprehensive sense. This basic disposition of trust expresses itself in the *preliminary extension of trust* that the interpreter grants to the Bible. This extension of trust forms an indissoluble element of the faith that arises through encounter with Christ. It renews itself continually as it feeds on the vindication of the biblical message in the entire life of the interpreter who has been transformed by the Spirit. Decisive, irrefutable facts are required to imperil the trustworthiness of the Scriptures in this or that passage. That means that the burden of proof lies on the one who wishes to dispute a scriptural utterance. "In the absence of contrary evidence belief is reasonable."[107] On the other hand, we admittedly cannot provide irrefutable proof of the trustworthiness of Scripture. Revelation preserves its validity in a realm that transcends our proofs. The Holy Spirit who speaks in revelation remains independent of human ingenuity. Perhaps it could be put like this: the Christian interpreter's experience resists the hostile claims of criticism, but it is not the supporting pillar of biblical revelation.[108]

The Holy Spirit leads the interpreter into the fellowship of believers (Ps 119:63; Ac 2:42; 4:32; Ro 12:4ff.; 1Co 12:4ff.; Eph 4:3ff.). The presuppositions we have listed in this chapter are not, therefore, exclusively his. They are shared by all believers. For this reason these presuppositions cannot be dismissed as something "subjective" or arbitrary. They are rather transsubjective.[109] Hofmann expressed it in these words: the interpreter must necessarily bring with him a "prejudice," namely, that "which is based on the faith that he holds in common with Christendom."[110]

On purely temporal grounds it makes sense that the interpreter who has been renewed by the Spirit approaches the Scripture "as a member of the church . . . whose faith he shares."[111] That is, his understanding of revelation is influenced by a tradition upon whose existence he had no influence and whose effect in history [*Wirkungsgeschichte*] must be carefully pondered.[112] A perennial difference exists between Catholic and Protestant exegetes with respect to this tradition. For Catholics church tradition possesses "the function of a norm for interpretation."[113] "Every Catholic priest and teacher of the Holy Scripture obligates himself in his interpretation to obey the *sensus* established by the Mother Church in her tradition."[114] The "Instructio de historica Evangeliorum veritate" of the papal commission on the Bible of April 21, 1964, refers the interpreter "to the help of God and the light of the Church."[115] Indeed, he should work under care of the Church (*ductu Ecclesiae*), fall in line like others with the "admonitions of the Popes (hortamentis Summorum Pontificum obsecundentes)," and in his publications make it a matter of conscience "never to diverge in the slightest from the clear teaching and tradition of the Church (numquam a communi doctrina ac traditione Ecclesiae vel minimum discedere)."[116] Actual practice may look otherwise, developments may be running in another direction. But until further notice this fundamental tie to the tradition recognized by the church's teaching office remains in place. We are, then, dealing with an authoritative exegesis in which the decisive aspect is furnished by the ecclesiastical fellowship of faith.

It is well known that on the Protestant side there exists neither a comparable tie to tradition (in spite of the confessions!) nor a comparable ecclesiastical teaching office. Precisely for this reason the attempt must be made to give a pneumatological account of what belonging to the fellowship of faith means for the interpreter's understanding of Scripture. First, it is to be assumed that "the interpretation of the Holy Scripture . . . [is] a task of the entire church"[117](cf. Eph 3:18f.; 4:13f.; 5:10, 17; Ac 17:11). It is therefore not to be handed over to a "guild" of biblical specialists. Second, then, the various gifts should serve to further unity (cf. Ro 12:4ff.; 1Co 12:7ff.; Eph 4:12ff.). For the interpreter of Scripture this means that he is dependent on exchange with and fraternal correction of other believers. Third, however, the interpreter is an "advocate for the contemporary Christian community."[118] He does not represent merely himself but also the body of Christ, to which he belongs. Moreover, he stands "in the service of the Gospel proclamation."[119] Like all theology, interpretation of Scripture is not *l'art pour l'art* (art for art's sake) but rather responsible activity within the parameters of the fellowship of Jesus Christ. Francke therefore defined theological science as a "means of the furtherance of the kingdom of God under the leadership of the Holy Spirit."[120] This expresses the apologetic and missiological dimension of scriptural interpretation (cf. 1Pe 3:15; Col 3:17). This way of looking at the theological task was widespread, however, far beyond the pietistic, orthodox, and fundamentalist tradition, as E. von Dobschütz's admonition shows: "Every scientific exegete should nurture the awareness that the goal of his work is practical application."[121] There has also been protest, nevertheless, in liberal circles against linking scientific exegesis with church and practical application.[122] If one bears in mind the idea of incorporation into the body of Christ, then F. Lücke's remark makes sense: "all the theological disciplines" are "thoroughly . . . subordinate" to the church "by rights" and "must be obedient to" it.[123] In any case it is not workable, looking at the matter from a pneumatico-centric point of view, to *set* theological science as teacher, monitor, or the like *over against* the church. It is rather to be *integrated into* the church. The body's understanding is deeper, broader, and better than that of any individual member.

## NECESSARY CAUTION

Every hermeneutical chapter has its dangers. If to this point we have stressed the effect of the Holy Spirit on the interpreter, it is appropriate here to warn against exaggerated emphasis on pneumatology. Such exaggeration can threaten a proper understanding of revelation and shows disdain for methodological rigor.[124] We will deal with this more fully below. For the moment we merely assert that the Spirit of the Scripture discloses himself through "due painstaking research," as Bengel put it.[125] Or in biblical terms: in the fully devoted *akriboō* (accurate understanding) that is actualized in the Bible itself (cf. 1Co 3:11f.; Pss 1:2; 119:59, 66; Da 9:2; Lk 1:3; Eph 5:15, to name only a few passages).

# CHAPTER SIX

# Ways of Understanding Revelation

## RESTRICTION TO HISTORICAL UNDERSTANDING

Interpretation is presently restricted through an almost exclusive fixation with historical understanding. What can be illuminated historically is regarded as understood. This view becomes still further restricted when the origin of a living utterance is confused with its hermeneutical decoding. Many share H. Gunkel's "cardinal conviction" that "we are not in a position to understand a person, a time, an idea, in isolation from their pre-history. Only when we know the history out of which they emerge can we speak of actual, vital understanding."[1]

A number of reasons have contributed to the rise of this restricted view. An external reason might be that after 1875 or so almost no comprehensive presentations of hermeneutics were produced in Protestant circles.[2] It is no wonder that historical-critical research and hermeneutical reflection came to resemble look-alike twins. Another reason lies in concentration on the intention of the human author, pioneered by Herder and Schleiermacher and energetically opposed today by

Ricoeur.[3] A fine example here is the textbook on hermeneutics by Karl August Gottlieb Keil (1810), in which we read: "To understand the sense of a statement or writing means nothing other than to think just the same thing when encountering the statement or writing that the speaker or author thought when he wrote it, or that he wanted his hearers or readers to think." Keil called this "with justification a historical" explanation.[4] A third reason presumably lies in the rejection of the multiple sense of Scripture, which grew in the course of the nineteenth century—in resistance to Schleiermacher![5] The same K. A. G. Keil mentioned above permitted there to be only one sole sense of any Scripture, reasoning that "no rational author" would give his words "more than one sense," not even in the New Testament.[6] Dilthey went so far as to call allegory an "utterly useless artifice."[7] Writers like H. Olshausen, whose 1824 essay "Ein Wort über tieferen Schriftsinn [A Word Regarding Scripture's Deeper Meaning]" proposed a renewal of allegorical interpretation, are exceptions.[8] A fourth reason is glimpsed in the tight relation that was posited between "scientific character" and "intellectual understanding."[9] That turned out to mean that historical-scientific exegesis was the exclusive means of assuring an adequate understanding of the biblical texts. Thus U. Wilckens arrived at this conclusion: "The only scientifically responsible interpretation of the Bible is an investigation of the biblical texts that" operates "according to methodologically consistent application of historical reason."[10]

## OPPOSING TENDENCIES

If some were convinced that only historical-scientific research could arrive at an appropriate understanding of the Bible, others took a different view, raising objections from two sides.

One side took note of the so-called laity. It must be admitted, even in view of the sharpest points of disagreement between critical science and "church belief," that "those who are unable to read are nevertheless also among the blessed."[11] This was to assume, however, that an adequate grasp of the biblical message was also accessible to those bereft of "historical" understanding. This in turn forced recognition of the fact that, generally speaking, access to the Scripture could not be seen as "dependent on scientific research." Otherwise a "papacy of experts" would be founded, a situation worse than undue exercise of interpretive authority by the papacy itself.[12] Occasionally the viewpoint was even expressed that on the whole the laity is "by no means inferior or disadvantaged in comparison to the theologians."[13] The importance of lay-level scriptural interpretation was underscored by the fact that substantial impetus in the lives of theologians has come about through laypersons. For example, the blind Peter Köhn in Lübeck became a highly influential spiritual advisor for A. H. Francke.[14]

This positive assessment of lay input met energetic opposition, however. "One must acquire a very high level of intellectual prowess before the intellectual world takes note of what one has to say."[15] This quote from Spranger is indicative of the attitude of a number of theologians. While "church belief" was glibly characterized as "artless," "simplistic," and so forth, a "competent,"[16] intellectual-congenial interpretation was seen to be at work precisely where the concern was for "scientific" interaction with the text. Today this kind of high regard for "scientific exegesis" may be found, e.g., especially in the work of Barr: "For critical scholarship the standard and criterion for judging the validity of exegesis lies no longer in church doctrine, but in research."[17] Mussner countered this and similar claims with the objection that they amount to a "private gnosticism."[18]

Apart from questions raised regarding lay understanding, the monopoly of the historical understanding of the Bible was disputed by a second line of thought. This was the much-discussed area of the multidimensionality of scriptural interpretation. If one wished, e.g., to give a positive assessment of Luther, then one must also acknowledge that historical-critical procedure is not necessary to understand the Bible aright. Researchers like R. Bring accordingly called attention to dimensions of the Bible "that a purely historical observation would not have been able to discover."[19] Oepke emphasized in discussion with Windisch that "historical exegesis" is not the only exegesis that is scientific.[20] Even without confessional considerations exegetes came to the conclusion that historical understanding should not be granted absolute status: "it would be false," says Westermann, "for us to presume to have found [i.e., in historical understanding] the exclusively correct, absolute, and eternally valid method of explaining the Bible."[21] In his study of hermeneutics Torm attempts to reflect also on "other forms of understanding."[22] Most of all it is Catholic theologians who champion the view that alongside of historical research there are "rightly also other ways to the truth of the Scripture."[23]

Regarding the Catholic position, it unambiguously involves a connection with the doctrine of the multiple meaning of Scripture.[24] Does that also apply to Protestants? We will have to consider this connection below.

## A LOOK AT THE HISTORY OF EXEGESIS

The most emphatic rejection of the exclusive dominance of historical understanding comes from the history of scriptural exegesis itself. A summary glimpse of the history of interpretation will suffice to illustrate this point.

Early Christian exegesis of the Bible arose in a milieu where attributing multiple meaning to Scripture was totally acceptable. Jewish interpreters of the first century were convinced that the Holy Scriptures contained more than what the *sensus literalis* offered. Longenecker distinguishes between four forms of Jewish interpretation: literalist, midrashic, pesher, and allegorical.[25] Yet it was "literalistic" exegesis that furnished the starting point—also for Philo and at Qumran.[26] All of these forms of interpretation were used by Jesus and the authors of the New Testament.[27] Longenecker thinks that for Jesus the pesher method was the most characteristic. Pesher viewed Old Testament prophecy as having "a veiled eschatological meaning."[28] Scholars commonly attribute allegorical and typological interpretation to Paul.[29]

In the second and third centuries A.D. a multidimensional approach to interpretation continued. Thus Justin interpreted the Old Testament both historically and Christocentrically.[30] The role of allegory was disputed. Marcion rejected it—proof that even the pure *sensus literalis* cannot prevent heresy.[31] In view of the allegorical excesses of the Gnostics, interpreters like Irenaeus saw themselves forced to insist on the clarity of scriptural expressions and to stem the allegorical tide.[32] Alexandrian interpretation, on the other hand, systematically developed allegorical approaches, first through Clement and then most notably through Origen.[33] For Origen, it is true, all of Scripture's statements possessed a spiritual meaning, but not all possessed a literal meaning. He developed a doctrine of threefold meaning: somatic (historical), psychological (moral), and pneumatic (mystical).[34] Nevertheless, the Egyptian bishop Nepos protested against Alexandrian allegorizing in the name of biblical realism.[35]

In the fourth and fifth centuries one finds alternating positions. The Antiochene school and Jerome are at least reserved toward allegory. According to Grant, the Antiochenes insisted on the "historical reality of the biblical revelation."[36] He speaks of a "literal-historical method" in Antioch.[37] Still, Jerome clung to Scripture's typological meaning. The "intellegentia spiritualis" is necessary and results in a plus—not a minus!—over against the "carneus sensus."[38] Augustine, who was helped to conversion by allegorical explanation of the Scriptures, wrote *De doctrina christiania* (A.D. 397), a work that became the hermeneutical standard for the era after him. He based his views on the *Liber Regularum*, which he regarded as the "premier manual of biblical hermeneutics," written by Ticonius (A.D. 382?). Ticonius focused on the illumination of Old Testament prophecy. Accordingly he sought to interact responsibly with allegorical interpretation.[39] Augustine seeks to grasp as much of the Scripture as possible under the rubric of our salvation. He is convinced of the legitimacy of a "multiplex *sensus liter-*

*alis* of Scripture."[40] This conviction was closely related to a similar view that the biblical writers themselves had intended Scripture to have a multiple sense.[41]

This adage is commonly quoted as a summary of the Middle Ages: "Littera gesta docet, quid credas allegoria, moralis quid agas, quo tendas (quid speres) anagogia" ("The letter teaches the events; the allegorical [sense of Scripture] teaches what you should believe; the moral [sense of Scripture] teaches what you should do; the eschatological [sense of Scripture] teaches what you should strive for, place your hope in").[42] Next to this fourfold meaning of the Holy Scripture—historical, dogmatic, ethical, eschatological[43]—other forms of interpretation make their appearance. Allegory was variously assessed.[44] The multiple meaning of Scripture, however, remained generally recognized. Its hermeneutical advantage lay in the fact that the text "was worked through thoroughly."[45]

It is well known that Luther concentrated on the *sensus literalis*: "whoever interprets according to the literal sense finds in [Scripture] strength, doctrine, and skill."[46] Yet Luther's approach was differentiated. For not only the "simple sense of Scripture's words" but also "the experience of the heart" possesses authority.[47] One is reminded of Luther's remark two days before his death: "Scripturas sacras sciat se nemo gustasse satis, nisi centum annis cum Prophetis Ecclesias gubernarit" ("No one should suppose that he has fed sufficiently on the Holy Scriptures if he has not led the church for a hundred years with the prophets").[48] Because #1) Scripture presents words having a clear, "simple" sense[49] and #2) the practical experience of faith is decisive, laypersons can also interpret the Bible adequately. "Therefore every Christian is able to extract truth from the Bible. He is not tied to human authorities that mandate certain interpretations."[50] Sometimes laypersons are superior interpreters.[51] By no means did Luther categorically reject allegory. There are times when allegorical interpretation is necessary, as e.g., when the text's context or the intention of the author demands it.[52]

In general it can be asked whether the rise to dominance of the *sen-*

*sus literalis* is only the fruit of the Reformation, or whether it is not also due to the Renaissance.[53]

On the so-called left wing of the Reformation among the Anabaptists and spiritualists are the most varied hermeneutical outlooks. The Anabaptists generally held to the strict sense of the words of the Scripture.[54] The spiritualists, in contrast, turn away from the surface meaning of the words. Decisive for Hans Bünderlin is the inner word. The outer word is only the midwife and witness.[55] For Christian Entfelder all depends on the Spirit who gives the living word. Without the living word the Scripture remains a dead letter and subject to all manner of error.[56]

Matthias Flacius, the "greatest theoretician of old Protestant hermeneutics,"[57] rejected the multiple meaning of Scripture.[58] He observed, however, that the genre of allegory is found in Scripture itself. For such cases he prescribes allegorical interpretation.[59] This confirms that even where revelation is the starting point, interpretation can be broader than only "literal" or "historical."[60]

Protestant Scholasticism's interpretation of Scripture insists on the preeminence of the literal sense. As the memory of Flacius recedes, however, there was the tendency to recognize a "spiritual sense" alongside the literal. Hollaz, e.g., endorses a "mystical sense" which he further subdivides into allegorical, typical, and parabolical senses. But the literal sense remains the basis and primary framework.[61]

In the era following Protestant Scholasticism the streams of interpretation divide. Federal theology and Pietism show renewed concern for Scripture's multiple sense.[62] Coccejus, following his teacher Amesius, proceeds from the assumption of a twofold meaning in Scripture: the grammatical sense and the spiritual sense. That makes possible a typological interpretation of the Scripture.[63] Bengel likewise looks for a spiritual meaning in Scripture.[64] In 1771 Christian Friedrich Schmid of Leipzig, influenced by Bengel, describes "two stages" of the art of interpretation. Meaning emerges first from a preliminary, philological stage and then from a deeper, spiritual stage.[65]

On the other hand, where the Enlightenment holds sway, both typological and allegorical interpretation fall on hard times.[66] As early as Spinoza the demand for a purely historical interpretation comes to the fore.[67] Increasingly, the historical-critical method is regarded as the only legitimate exegetical approach. Grant states that "many critics came to regard criticism as identical with exegesis."[68] This outlook furnished the chief line of analysis for the nineteenth and early twentieth centuries.[69]

Not until the rise of so-called pneumatic exegesis does the question of Scripture's multiple meaning become urgent once more. The first stirrings are found in one of the movement's forerunners, J. L. Samuel Lutz (1849).[70] A fundamental new beginning was then carried out by Karl Girgensohn in the 1920s. In his treatise on the inspiration of Holy Scripture (second edition, 1926) he asks, among other things, "Does the present hour perhaps dictate that we seek a renewal of the doctrine of Scripture's twofold meaning? Could it perhaps be that here lies nothing short of a liberating solution to the great difficulties that modern theology is enmeshed in due to overemphasis on the historical mode of analysis?"[71] In the same connection we read: "Is it not calamitous that we still cling to the doctrine of Scripture's simple meaning and ignore the motives that have again and again led to acceptance of Scripture's multiple meaning in the history of interpretation?"[72] Girgensohn and those who follow him seek the solution in a two-stage exegesis.[73] The first stage is called historical, historical-psychological, literal, or critical. The second stage of interpretation is the pneumatic, normative-pneumatic, or superhistorical.[74] Within this framework allegorical interpretation is hermeneutically assessed and endorsed.[75] We will consider this two-stage doctrine separately at a later point. For the moment we simply point out that the multiple meaning of Scripture finds renewed recognition here in pneumatic exegesis.[76]

In the interest of completeness it should be mentioned again that Roman Catholicism has expressly endorsed the *sensus spiritualis* in the sense spoken of by Pius XII ("Non omnis sane spiritualis sensus a sacra

Scriptura excluditur" ["Not every spiritual sense is excluded from Holy Scripture on the basis of reason"]).[77]

What is the result of this survey of the history of exegesis? Times and schools that exclusively or almost exclusively venerate a single-meaning approach to Scripture are the exception. Restriction to the historical understanding is limited to certain trends since the Enlightenment. It has been normal for both Jewish and Christian interpreters to work with a multiple-meaning approach.

## REVELATION AS STARTING POINT

By now we need to return to the basic principle established earlier of making revelation the starting point. What help does revelation give us toward an understanding of itself? In putting the question this way we orient ourselves "to discern the claim of revelatory occurrence enshrined in Scripture itself."[78]

According to biblical revelation, understanding takes place at three levels: dynamic, ethical, and cognitive.

Dynamic understanding occurs where revelation addresses the person directly and transforms him. The addressee grasps that he must change his ways, or has the opportunity to make major changes in himself. When the tax collector at the tollbooth heard Jesus' summons "Follow me," he understood that he must cease the kind of activity that had characterized him to that point and take up a new course in life (Mt 9:9). Therefore "he rose and followed him" (RSV). When a powerful evangelist calls for decision and the hearer is inwardly smitten, he will along with others or perhaps alone make a conscious commitment of his life to Jesus Christ. When my morning devotional guide says, "Do not worry about tomorrow" (Mt 6:34 NIV), I can commit my cares to the Lord in prayer. In all these cases a helpful preunderstanding is present. But the point is not so much the cognitive or other enlargement of that preunderstanding. Rather, God's revelation uses this preunderstanding as an instrument to call forth transformation. Understanding and response form a unified event. Understanding takes place dynamically, or, to put it another way, through transformation.

Ethical understanding takes place where a person already lives in a positive relationship to revelation and now desires its long-term application to his practical life. Here understanding takes place because a person wants to obey. And that person wants to understand in order to be able to obey. An illustration of this is seen in the question posed to Jesus by the rich young ruler (Mt 19:16): "What good thing should I do in order to acquire eternal life?"

Cognitive understanding takes place where a person wants to comprehend revelation rightly in order to clarify it in terms of form and content prior to making inferences from it or passing it along to others. Cognitive understanding is preparation or transition. This is exemplified, e.g., in the question directed to Jesus, "Which is the greatest command in the Law?" (Mt 22:36; cf. Mk 12:28–34).

Below we will reflect with more precision on these various ways of understanding revelation.

## DYNAMIC UNDERSTANDING

As we have seen, dynamic understanding takes place where revelation meets the person directly, transforming and profoundly altering him. Through contact with the Word the person is not who he was before. A dynamic transformation has taken place. The Word "cut[s] to the heart" (Ac 2:37 KJV).

It must be graphically underscored that this has nothing to do with emotionalism or ecstatic excess.[79] Revelation meets a person in the heart, and thus also in the intellect. It does not meet him somewhere beyond the person as a central whole. Nor does the dynamic transformation mentioned above remove the responsibility of response, of decision. Dynamic understanding takes place just as well in a situation where the person is compliant as where the person drags his heels. In any case the coordinating center of his life has been profoundly touched. Even if he is recalcitrant, he is not merely the same person that he was before. When the rich young ruler—in contrast to the tax collector in Matthew 9:9—declined to accept the call to discipleship (Mt 19:22), his life was nevertheless altered from that which it had previously been: "He went away sad" (NIV). Those who at Pentecost were "cut to the heart" (Ac 2:37) were also affected in their intellect, in their understanding. They had to give a responsible, conscious answer. "There is no repentance in a state of ecstatic excess."[80]

What does this say about our understanding? First, where and when the dynamic word of revelation penetrates our lives is beyond our control. That means that we can, to be sure, reflect on it hermeneutically, but we cannot furnish hermeneutical systematization of it.

Second, we have to recognize that the occurrences that are often most important take place where particularly hermeneutical systematization, and thus also strict methodological description, lie beyond our ken. The boundary of scientific hermeneutics is to be set down clearly here. It must clearly acknowledge this: what makes the creature into a believer, what makes the "old person" a reborn person, is basically inaccessible to it. There is no hermeneutical penetration to the essence of conversion. This is, then, an early indicator that hermeneutics must restrict itself to a considerable extent to the cognitive sphere.

What role, then, does human understanding play in dynamic encounter with the revelatory word? First, we note that revelation as it really took place in the Bible used normal human languages (Hebrew, Aramaic, Greek). The Spirit did not choose a unique language. Revelation does not go forth in glossalalia; at most it is occasionally responded to in that way. To this extent philological understanding on the part of people is presupposed and possible. We do not know to what extent man's fall into sin changed human speech. This much is, however, clear from revelation: human speech that was actually uttered could serve as an adequate medium of communication of divine revelation even after the Fall. And precisely for this reason, philological understanding has its place even in a fallen world (cf. chaps. 5 and 13). So then, the revelatory word goes out to concrete human creatures who are gifted in keeping with the will of the Creator (Pss 8:6ff.; 139:13ff.), chosen in the state they are and in places and times that God determines (cf. Da 2:21ff.; Gal 4:4). Included in all this is the prior preunderstanding of the one who receives revelation. Now God reveals himself precisely in the midst of this human condition. The concrete creatureliness, the concrete historical place, the concrete time, the concrete preunderstanding become instruments with whose help God makes himself accessible and understandable.[81] This all still applies when in this dynamic encounter changes are carried out at the same time. By opening himself up—which is possible due to the way he was created as well as his prior history—man permits God to carry out the necessary changes. If he closes and hardens himself, then his seeing eyes have not seen and his hearing ears not heard (cf. Isa 6:9ff.; Mt 13:13ff.). The Epitome of the Formula of Concord brings the heart of the matter to expression: "the hearing of God's word" is necessary, and it is God's will "that one hear his word and not cover his ears" (II, Affirmativa, 3). In this dynamic encounter with the revelatory word, then, the close tie between understanding and obeying is especially impressive. If the person opens himself, if he complies with what has been revealed, then he obeys, and only after that has truly understood. Understanding issues forth in new understanding. It becomes a process, and thus becomes whole.

From the above it follows that on the level of dynamic understanding there is no difference in principle between "theologians" and "laypersons." That is, in many cases so-called laypersons possess better and deeper understanding than so-called theologians. That can be seen most of all in testimonial, missionary, evangelistic, and confessional preaching, which evince a marked affinity for the dynamic dimension of revelation.

## ETHICAL UNDERSTANDING

Ethical understanding is characterized by its focus on the application of what has been understood rather than primarily on the enlargement of understanding. Typical is the searching question, "What must I/we do in order to . . . ?" (cf. Mt 19:16; Ac 2:37; 16:30). Here revelation is no longer impetus to new life but an outline for new life. Obedience is already basically established. What is sought is its concrete expression.

Clearly, the intellectual interest here is different in principle from the interest typifying, say, historical research. Perhaps rabbinic doctrinal discussion is most closely related to ethical understanding.

In chapter 5 we attempted to reflect on the effect of the Holy Spirit on the interpreter. The question arises whether the effect of the Holy Spirit as described in revelation does not evince a particular nearness to that act of understanding that is determined by deliberate obedience. This question must be answered negatively for this reason: the Holy Spirit's effect encompasses all areas, the dynamic, the ethical, and the cognitive. Another reason for a negative answer is because the ethical understanding, or the intended obedience, is not automatically identical with faith.

It is rather the case that the process of understanding in the ethical sphere is more variegated, and in some cases more complicated, than in dynamic understanding. For ethical understanding is characterized far less by that directness that binds together Word and response, God's revelation and transformation of the person, in dynamic understanding. Clearly, in ethical understanding research and reflection occupy a more prominent place.

As a result, ethical understanding makes greater use of cognitive forms that we will become familiar with below. Indeed, it can subordinate itself to cognitive modes of understanding to achieve its goal. It is also more noticeably open to hermeneutical reflection and regulation than dynamic understanding is. Consequently, this is a point where "theologians" and "laypersons" begin an increasing divergence from each other. A marked shift in the direction of "theology" takes place. Yet the formation of a special science is not yet so far advanced as in cognitive understanding. Those possessing ethical understanding typically serve as the doctrinal instructors for the church.

One factor demands particular attention here. To the extent that human reflection exerts influence, the danger of subjectivism grows. It is thus entirely natural that teachers with distinctive views arise and begin to form schools of thought, and that battles over true and false doctrine continually ensue.

To offset the danger of subjectivism, integration of the person within the fellowship of believers must be emphasized. This took place already in the New Testament. For in 1 Corinthians 14:29 the testing of what was preached was made obligatory. The early Christian worship service was the place where the fellowship made its appearance as the body of Christ. In the setting of the fellowship of believers, doctrinally sound proclamation was laid down and purified.

## COGNITIVE UNDERSTANDING

If dynamic understanding tends toward transformation through revelation, and ethical understanding toward the application of revelation, then cognitive understanding stresses the knowledge of revelation (i.e., Scripture). Its focus is on the enlargement of previous understanding.

Here the course leading to application is longer, as a rule, than in ethical understanding. The danger thus also increases that knowledge itself will be viewed as a sufficient goal in and of itself. That is, in a sense, the gnostic heresy that has plagued the church from the beginning.

An additional danger lies in the direction of increasing abstraction. The distance from the directness that characterizes dynamic encounter grows beyond even that found in ethical understanding. In extreme cases the "relevance of understanding" is lost sight of.[82] Practical ministry and Christian experience may then be entirely negated. At times exegesis then loses itself in hypotheses and threatens to become an idle game.

The danger of subjectivism remains a continuing threat. It is counterbalanced, however, by the verifiability of results that the science of exegesis demands.

It is in the realm of cognitive understanding that the problem of the so-called laity becomes acute. For here, in the cognitive sphere, processes of understanding lend themselves most readily to methodological regulation. Indeed, this is where scientific theology practically demands a reflected hermeneutic with related methods. These postulates—appropriate in themselves—facilitate the scientific enterprise. But they tend to exclude the laity.

To counteract this, it must be insisted that cognitive understanding is only the preparation, albeit a necessary one, for the witness of Christian believers. Whatever is attained cognitively is worthless if it hinders or prevents this witness. In that sense one could say that theological science furnishes the bridge from revelation to the ministry of Christian believers. This way of looking at the matter excludes two common errors: #1) hostility toward science, and #2) gullible acceptance of all of science's claims.

What makes cognitive understanding essential? By way of summary, the following four considerations may be mentioned: #1) for appropriately comprehensive praise of God; #2) for doctrine; #3) for the missiological spread of the faith, which should not be allowed to take place only under emotion-driven auspices; and #4) for apologetics (1Pe 3:15).

We observe that cognitive understanding can be achieved through various pathways. Starting from revelation, we attempt in what follows to describe individual possibilities under the rubric of cognitive understanding. It is surprising to find that currently only a few concrete distinctions are being made, although many authors defend or even demand recognition of a pluralistic approach to possible ways of understanding. Frederik Torm, one of the few who bucks the trend by making concrete distinctions, cited the following "principles of interpretation" in 1930: "dogmatic" interpretation, "allegorical" interpretation, "typological" interpretation, and the "analogy of Scripture."[83] In 1979 Ralph Martin described five approaches to or perspectives on the New Testament: #1) the "dogmatic approach," #2) the "impressionistic approach," #3) the "grammatical-historical method," #4) "the meaning for the twentieth century," and #5) the "salvation history" approach. Only #3) and #5) appeared to Martin to hold much promise.[84]

Below we discuss in turn the historical, dogmatic, typological, allegorical, and prophetic understandings of Scripture. Each of these amounts to a subset of cognitive understanding.

## HISTORICAL UNDERSTANDING

In historical understanding, the Bible is understood using the vantage point that history furnishes. It is based first on the assumption that God acted in keeping with the claims of revelation. Indeed, it views God as constitutive for our concept of history: his action is what creates that which we call "history" in the first place. Without God there would be no existence and no occurrence. It is based second on the assumption that the Bible is itself a document arising out of this action and is thus also a document of history. For God acts in steps. His revelation is progressive. That is seen, e.g., in the sequence of covenants he establishes. Historical understanding is based third on the assumption that the enscripturated revelation itself goes back to history in its origins and what it relates.

Let us clarify these three considerations underlying historical understanding as each is offered to us in revelation itself.

"God . . . calls things that are not as if they were" (Ro 4:17). All that exists, except God himself, arose through God's creative word. "Without him," and that includes his creative word, "nothing was made that has been made" (Jn 1:3 NIV). All that exists is enabled to exist and to have a history because God wills it. And it goes no further or longer than he permits. An "atheistic" concept of history is, looked at from the standpoint of revelation, a contradiction in itself. Yet creation does not simply follow some rigidly predetermined course. The sovereign God rather exerts influence on what occurs where and when he wishes. He himself generates fresh history out of fresh acts. His word and deeds direct and alter even the space-time world that arose after the Fall. There is only a difference in degree between "salvation history" and "secular history." Both are God's creations (cf. Isa 45:5–7), just as are the times in which persons live their lives (cf. Rev 10:6 with Da 2:21; 12:7). Within this framework God extends his call to man (cf. Ge 12:1ff.), places him under his promise (cf. Ge 12:2f.; 15:5; etc.), and fulfills his word to him (cf. Jos 21:45; 24:2ff.). God establishes his people, protects them, instructs them, and brings them to the goal toward which his promise was directed (cf. Heb 3:7–4:13). None of this, however, takes place in a side alley of the cosmos or in an enraptured state of altered consciousness: it is rather carried out before the eyes of the nations (Ex 12:29ff.; Est 7–9). Revelation in the form of the Bible exposes this activity of God. It contains fact and interpretation simultaneously. Revelation offers us a historical dimension of the Bible so that it can be read with profit and understood more readily.

Revelation in its biblical form has itself come into existence, moreover, in the course of history. Prior to Moses there were the traditions of the patriarchs. The Mosaic Pentateuch does not yet know of the proclamation of the prophets. Over the span of a millennium and a half the Old Testament grew to its present extent. Not every word fits perfectly into every later time. Similarly, the New Testament required a half century to reach its present dimensions, a compilation of various individual revelations. We speak here of "progressive revelation." Its growth to enscripturated form, the Bible, presents research with a fruitful opportunity. If we accompany it along the course of its growth, it will grant us valuable insights into the work of God.

Finally, revelation in its biblical form wishes to direct our attention to the history for which we have God to thank. Long ago Moses was called on to remind Israel, which had just emerged in Egypt, of the "God of your fathers" (Ex 3:15). The generation of the Exodus was supposed to pass on to its children the memory of the events that took place in those years. Historical understanding of the Bible is made unavoidably necessary simply for the sake of children's questions as well as their instruction (Ex 12:26f.). No wonder that historiography as it arose in the

Middle Ages and then in modern history owes its origins to the Bible! With Israel's confession of Deuteronomy 26:5ff., the history-based confession in general was born. Every Israelite was instructed in history and in the grateful recollection of God's deeds (cf. also Pss 78, 106). No religion shows such a close tie between faith and history as the religion of the Bible. Close consideration of history becomes an admonition and thus a part of the Bible's proclamation (Jos 24:2ff.). The prophets refer back to the history of Israel ( cf. Hos 2:16ff.; 8:13; 9:3ff.; Am 9:7ff.; Mal 3:22). Indeed, the entire New Testament is unthinkable without its view of the history described in the Old Testament. For this reason, historical understanding of the Bible is necessary and worthwhile.

## DOGMATIC UNDERSTANDING

The dogmatic understanding of Scripture uses the doctrinal teaching that it has gained from the Bible to arrive at a comprehensive understanding of the Bible.

While the legitimacy of historical research is hardly disputed today, dogmatic understanding of the Bible is hotly debated. Protestant assessment of a dogmatic approach to scriptural interpretation was burdened from the beginning with the precedent in Catholicism, in which church tradition and thereby also church dogma assumed normative status. Thus Montaigne, e.g., charged Luther with subjecting the Scriptures to the interpretation of men. One ought rather, insisted Montaigne, tread "the way of dependence on the Church established by the Church."[85] What Montaigne wanted is clear: the transsubjective, dogmatically supported interpretation of the church ought to hinder Protestant subjectivism. Montaigne's reflections become understandable when one considers the profound shaking of faith's certainty and the conflicting conclusions to which critical Protestant research led. In the eyes of philosophers the situation looked like this: "The Protestant principle of individual liberty of conscience, which indeed first made possible unfettered science and its 'autonomy,' leads to the troubling result that no finally certain standard of universal validity seems to reign in this personal realm of conscience. The outcome is the anarchy of values. . . ."[86] Looked at in this way, one cannot simply push aside the demand that the Bible be interpreted in keeping with the church's confession ("the analogy of faith").

This demand appeared in various forms. An extreme position was taken here by Ferdinand Delbrück, who in 1826 wanted to elevate the rule of faith rather than the Scripture to the highest norm.[87] J. L. Lutz (1849) proceeded from the assumption that the church was there before Scripture was; therefore the demand for scriptural interpretation that supports church teaching is justified. Scripture must be interpreted according to the analogy of faith.[88] For Hans Emil Weber historical research performed only a "preliminary function," albeit a "foundational" one. The dogmatician, not the exegete, makes the decisions in interpreting Scripture.[89] Yet the dogmatician to the present hour suffers from the real "contradiction" between the exegetical and dogmatic disciplines of theology.[90]

It should also be noted that the demand for a dogmatic understanding of the Scripture is not restricted to parties within the church. The same demand arises where Marxist literary theory is applied to the Bible.[91]

How much justification should be accorded to a dogmatic understanding of Scripture from the basis of a theology that is based on revelation? For the decisive factor is not a demand derived from experience but rather the way of understanding that revelation itself affords. Every proclamation should take place "in keeping with the analogy of faith," as Romans 12:6 puts it. In this context "faith" is the relationship with God that comes about by the new covenant as specified by Jesus and the Holy Scriptures of Israel. Romans 12:6 does not, then, refer to an ecclesiastical confession. It likely speaks rather of the content of the faith that the new covenant community possesses. According to 1 Corinthians 14:29, the congregation's proclamation is undergirded by the discerning judgment of the believers who are present. In this and similar statements in the New Testament two things become clear. #1) Scriptural interpretation, even when it is called "prophecy," creates no new revelatory source to be placed alongside the revelation divinely given to Jesus and his apostles. #2) Scriptural interpretation is not a purely individual act but depends on the agreement and mutual responsibility of the congregation.

To apply this to our question regarding a dogmatic understanding of Scripture: such an understanding is a legitimate way of cognitive understanding so long as "dogmatic" refers to the content of the faith of Christian communities in all times.

The concept "dogmatic" may not, therefore, be interpreted as a certain theological school of thought. It may also not be understood as a grid of understanding that is placed on a higher level than Scripture and into which Scripture is made to fit. Every impression that "dogmatic" amounts to a "confessional" interpretive schema must be avoided. In the same way the impression must be avoided that dogmas, traditions, or church confessions comprise a second, equally authoritative source of knowledge alongside the Scriptures.

Positively, a "dogmatic" understanding of revelation validates the point of view of biblical doctrine. It preserves interpretation from bogging down in atomistic exegesis or individual, fragmented points of view.[92] Moreover, it obligates the interpreter to take note of other interpretations that have arisen in Christian circles, whether in the hoary past or the fluid present. The more that these interpretations have determined the church's way, the less they should be overlooked. For this reason the confessions, especially those of early Christianity, play a prominent role. Here it is obvious by what was said above that every ecclesiastical confession and Christian tradition is subordinated to Scripture, not placed over it. No council, no confession has the power to alter a clear statement of Scripture. A third positive effect of dogmatic understanding lies in the help and spadework that it accomplishes for later interpretations. Understanding of revelation is not furthered by a propensity for "talking about and listening to the latest ideas" (Ac 17:21). What matters is rather the fruitful preservation of continuity with the apostolic doctrine in all times (cf. Ac 2:4; Php 3:1). The dogmatic understanding of Scripture brings with it a protective, almost "conservative" element into interpretation. This is, however, a necessary conservatism that establishes the Christian community in understanding.

One more item should be noted: it would be a misunderstanding to regard "dogmatic" understanding as an exclusive concern of the theological discipline of "dogmatics." The participation here of both exegesis and dogmatics is called for, along with all other activities in the Christian community that impinge on the interpretation of Scripture.

## TYPOLOGICAL UNDERSTANDING

Typological understanding of Scripture makes use of the doctrine latent in the history God has brought to pass. It does so in order to understand the Bible more comprehensively. It presupposes that there are important points of analogy between what took place long ago and what takes place today. These comparable features of disparate times bridge the centuries. They are enduring. At the same time they repeat themselves in certain respects. They are, in a word, "typical." Typological understanding also presupposes that God brought about the recording of what took place long ago in order to furnish later generations with information that transcends mere reminiscence. That is, he wished to point the way for subsequent generations. This quite oversteps the normal bounds of historical research. It also indicates that such a typological understanding can only succeed if the Scripture possesses a "spiritual" sense along with its literal meaning.

Now the expression "spiritual sense" is not entirely appropriate. Strictly speaking, historical understanding itself has a "spiritual" sense. For historical understanding is no less than an activity of the Christian community under the leading of the Spirit for the purpose of edifying the community. We speak, therefore, of a distinct "spiritual" sense only because this concept has become a fixture in church history and can hardly be dispensed with at this late date.

A second preliminary observation: typological understanding has a long history in the church. We saw that it is encountered everywhere that interpretation does not consciously restrict itself to a *sensus literalis*. What we describe as "typological" was often called the "sensus moralis" or "allegoria" in medieval times.

The decisive question, however, is: to what extent does revelation itself offer such a typological understanding? Without question it *does* offer one. The New Testament describes the generation of Israel that wandered in the desert as virtually our *typoi* (types, examples; 1Co 10:6). What took place at that time occurred with us in view "so that we would not desire evil as they did" (1Co 10:6). Looking back at that occurrence, 1 Corinthians 10:11 summarizes, "These things happened to them as examples [*typikōs*] and were written down as warnings for us, on whom the fulfillment of the ages has come." The concept *typos* and the phenomenon of typological interpretation are already present in the Scriptures.[93] Exegesis must grapple continually with the question of what the Scriptures mean by "typological" understanding.[94] In modern times, however, this has been dealt with primarily as a *historical* question: how did typological understanding function back then? The more pressing question now, however, is the legitimacy and boundaries of a *contemporary* typological understanding.

Decisive here is the knowledge that God's actions stand in a salvation-historical connection. What takes place today was already proclaimed by God (Isa 41:22f.; 43:8f.; 44:7). What took place earlier was already preparatory for today. God's actions are teleological in nature. In God's word and act lies an intention that already allows for what is to come. What comes to pass is a key, therefore, to the meaning of the past. Here the era of the new covenant takes on great importance, first because it is the time of fulfillment, and second because God had it in mind from the beginning of his redemptive acts (Eph 1:3ff.; 1Pe 1:12). From that standpoint we gain access to the statement that God's dealings with the Israelites in the desert contained an announcement to the community of Jesus Christ, both in word and in deed. This helps us understand the statement that the Pentateuch was "written down . . . for us" (1Co 10:11 NIV). Typological interpretation, which sees the Old Testament from a New Testament viewpoint, is not merely a bygone phenomenon to be explained historically. It is also a possibility and task that gives those alive today access to revelation.

A question then arises, however, regarding the boundaries of the typological understanding of Scripture. How far should it be taken? Can it be constantly and everywhere applied? Is there not a danger, seen again and again in church history, that uncontrolled exegesis will result? Is there not even the danger of arriving at an additional source of revelation, one that adds to the clear statements of Scripture?

First of all, this much is certain: an essential feature of typology is that it presupposes a historical event of another time in all its concreteness and distinctiveness. Typological understanding, then, always adds to and augments historical understanding. Yet it never replaces it. In this necessary link with historical understanding lies the first safeguard against uncontrolled exegesis.

Second, we observe in Scripture itself that typological understanding never creates new revelatory data. It only underscores, illustrates, and amplifies what has already been stated clearly. In other words: typological understanding enriches but does not replace a previous understanding of revelation. It is checked by philological-grammatical understanding.

Third, New Testament typology is possible only because of the new covenant community's basis in the Christ event. First Corinthians 10, with its relating of the Exodus "rock" to Christ (1Co 10:4), shows this quite clearly. Jesus Christ is thus the norm of a legitimate typological explanation of Scripture. Typological interpretation is Christological in its focus.

Proceeding from the above three assumptions, a typological interpretation of the entire Old Testament is possible in principle.[95] The same may be said for the historical reports found in the New Testament. It should, nevertheless, be asked in each individual case whether a given text does not preclude a typological interpretation, and whether a typological meaning can be attributed to a passage without contradicting the passage's own expressed intent.

## ALLEGORICAL UNDERSTANDING

Allegorical understanding of Scripture uses the surface meaning of words merely as a starting point for unmasking the statement that lies behind it. This does not mean that the surface meaning is irrelevant. Indeed, it essentially determines the allegorical understanding insofar as it furnishes the concrete basis for that understanding and thereby at the same time its boundaries. Yet for typological interpretation the surface meaning itself is emphatically not what the text "actually" asserts. The "actual" meaning, the intended statement itself, lies beyond the words. In a sense the interpreter becomes "apocalyptic" in his outlook, a hermeneutician who leads the way in uncovering that which would not have emerged without his activity and thus would have remained unnoticed and ineffective.

It is no accident that it is precisely apocalyptic literature that shows great interest in allegorical understanding. Unlocking and deciphering hidden meaning is the whole point here. Another outlook that made much use of allegory was gnosticism. We have already seen that a bitter controversy raged over the legitimacy of allegorical interpretation of Scripture in Egypt during the third century A.D. The dispute was decided, finally, in favor of the allegorists. Ticonius and Augustine attempted to steer allegory along somewhat ordered paths. In the Middle Ages allegorical interpretation came to mean, in the words of the previously mentioned saying, "what you should believe." Without question the allegorical understanding of Scripture, like the typological, has a long history in the church.

In contrast to typology, allegorical interpretation can be fully independent from history. Indeed, the converse can also be affirmed: where interest in actual history recedes, interest in allegory as a rule increases. This is remarkably confirmed by the theology of the Enlightenment. On the one hand it sought to do away with typology and allegory in favor of exclusive attention to philological-historical understanding. On the other hand it sought to understand Scripture as instruction for true morality and for that reason lost interest in the historical books of the Bible. In this connection Aner wrote of a "prevalence of moral concern" and a "transformation of Christianity into ethics."[96] It was precisely those Old Testament books which dealt with history that Semler rejected as unnecessary.[97] So a very high degree of allegorization of the biblical message took place due to constant attention to highly valued virtues.

If we examine revelation itself for the light it sheds here, we see that the term *allegoroumena* appears only in Galatians 4:24. That may serve as a warning to us. On the other hand, the New Testament does not exclude the possibility of allegorical understanding. This possibility enlarges as soon as one moves from the term proper to the thing it signifies. Then it is most of all the parables of Jesus that play an important role. The Gospels report that Jesus gave allegorical interpretations to some parables (cf. Mt 13:18ff., 36ff.). True, researchers like Joachim Jeremias have declared such interpretation on Jesus' part as unhistorical. Jeremias saw in allegory the work of the early church.[98] This view, however, is untenable. For Jesus' procedure corresponds almost precisely to that which Longenecker has found in use among Jewish scribes of the first century. Longenecker points here to both "midrashic interpretation" and "allegorical interpretation."[99] David Flusser rightly concludes from his investigation of Jesus' parables that it is highly probable, from a historical point of view, that Jesus' interpretations sometimes made use of allegory.[100] Along with Jesus' parables, the allegorical tendency of Revelation deserves mention. There, too, one finds the characteristic interpretive formula "that is . . ." (cf. Rev 1:20; 4:5; 5:6; etc. with Mt 13:18ff., 36ff.). The whole realm of images, visions, similes, metaphors, and other figures of speech found in the Bible cries out for allegorical interpretation. Indeed, such interpretation can be applied even to names. Along with the example of Galatians 4:24f., one thinks also of the notable instance found in Hebrews 7:2f.

Yet, to what extent do the parameters and potential of allegorical understanding suffice for modern interpretation? The question is even more pressing for allegorical than for typological understanding, since the tie to history is much looser in the former than in the latter.

As already stated, because allegory does not necessarily presuppose a historical event, and because this makes correction by way of historical understanding difficult, allegorical interpretation must proceed with even more caution than typological. The extent of agreement between the scope of a given concrete text and an allegorical interpretation of it must be subjected to the greatest and most careful scrutiny. Here we detect a fine boundary, easily violated but necessary to protect with great zeal: we do not make use of allegorical interpretation because we wish to imitate the biblical authors. Rather, we use allegory because, and insofar as, it is opened to us by the authors and by the revelation they have enscripturated. We strive, not for imitation (*imitatio*), but for obedience (*oboedientia*). For this reason the ingenuity of a Spirit-led biblical author is not an unconditional standard for application to ourselves. We do well to exercise far more reserve than they did.

Just as for typology, two presuppositions apply to allegorical understanding of Scripture as well: #1) It cannot create new revelatory content. The clear words of Scripture, or of the understanding of Scripture that philological-grammatical analysis yields, provide a general restriction.[101] #2) Jesus Christ remains the norm of a legitimate understanding. I.e., an allegorical interpretation can only be sustained in a close inner relation to the actual Christ event.

## PROPHETIC UNDERSTANDING

Prophetic understanding of Scripture uses the eschatological content of revelation to understand revelation more fully. It takes the progressive character of revelation seriously. Just as typology presupposes a salvation-historical *connection* in revelation, the prophetic understanding presupposes a salvation-historical *movement* in revelation. And just as allegorical understanding builds on the premise that God can use words as signs pointing to a still-to-be-discovered meaning, prophetic understanding assumes that God can give words of guidance into an as-yet-unrealized future.

What distinguishes prophetic understanding from typological and allegorical? Typology and allegory emphasize the presently given scriptural expression (typology), or the meaning that the expression yields (allegory). Prophetic understanding attempts to understand what will happen in and emerge from the future as God sees it. Obviously, prophetic understanding is closely related to the other ways of understanding revelation. It may very well be the case that one and the same biblical text will be interpreted the same way typologically (or allegorically) and prophetically. Yet for two reasons it is advisable to accord prophetic interpretation a place of its own. First, the Bible's eschatological dimension is of special importance. Second, the prophetic understanding has played an independent role in the history of interpretation.

In the context of ancient Judaism, the prophetic understanding is similar to the pesher method observable in apocalyptic prophecy[102] and in some of the Qumran material.[103] In the Middle Ages the *anagogia* (higher sense) was said to indicate *quid speres* (what hope should be placed in). Many Christian interpreters stressed the essential prophetic understanding most of all when it came to interpreting Revelation.[104]

Within biblical revelation two forms of prophetic meaning are discernible. We may call them the presentistic and futuristic forms. The presentistic form consists in this contemporary characterization: "This is that." Thus Jesus says in the synagogue, "Today this scripture is fulfilled in your hearing" (Lk 4:21 NIV). He refers to Isaiah 61:1f. Jesus and his hearers are agreed that historically speaking Jesus' text deals with "the prophet Isaiah" (Lk 4:17). They are also not discussing which typological or allegorical meaning can be derived from the Isaiah passage. Of fundamental interest is the prophetic understanding, similar to

Jewish pesher, that is announced here. Jesus states that he is the one of whom Isaiah spoke in his very different place and time. That is the presentistic or contemporary form of prophetic interpretation.

We also encounter a second form, the futuristic. Again we can discover it in the Jesus tradition, this time as he discusses Psalm 110:1 (Mt 22:41ff.). There David spoke "in the Spirit" (NASB). So far Jesus and his discussion partners are in agreement. "In the Spirit" likely means under prophetic illumination. The matter at issue in Jesus' time, then, is the prophetic understanding of what David described. Who is it that David calls "my Lord" in Psalm 110:1? Jesus' indirect answer runs: it must be more than the son of David; otherwise the father would not, against social convention, have named the son "my Lord." Jesus' concern is with this "more," which is in point of fact the Son of God. Yet it is the Son of God whose enemies are a footstool for his feet. And that is not the present Son who came in earthly weakness but rather the future Son, the Son of God who will return in divine might.

Prophetic understanding uncovers the identity of the person named in Psalm 110:1. But that person is one yet to come. Therefore we speak here of a future form of prophetic meaning.

In what way can prophetic understanding take place today? Although "prophetic" interpretation is far more often used in practical settings than it might seem, the answer to this question is by no means easy to supply. And for this reason: it is precisely in the realm of prophetic interpretation that truth and falsehood mingle in highest measure, without there at first sight being criteria for discovering what is true.

The first rule must be to distinguish between the presentistic and futuristic forms, just as we do in looking at revelation itself, some of which clearly applies to its own time and some of which has more extended or universal application.

The second rule must be that in contemporary prophetic interpretation ("This is that") the utmost reserve is to be exercised. That is, the justification of the interpretation must ultimately remain open. For we do not possess that infallibility of interpretation that the New Testament has in relation to the Old. A constantly recurring error in the history of interpretation is to want to make contemporary prophetic statements without trusting in God's decision. In this respect Bengel is exemplary. He reckoned with "major failure" in his "system" and called for testing of his interpretations.[105] Since Bengel's time we have learned especially from how the book of Revelation has been handled not to favor facile identifications of what Revelation says with world historical developments, but rather to pay attention first to the "essential structure" that comes to expression in the prophecy contained in Revelation.[106]

A third rule is that prophetic understanding of Scripture also does not lead to new revelation that transcends Scripture's own clear and sufficient words. The futuristic form of prophetic understanding is especially exposed to this danger. A contemporary interpretation can go wrong without in any way affecting the revelation of Scripture that lies in clear view. It actualizes only the word that seems to apply to the present situation. Futuristic interpretation, however, concretizes and unfolds what will allegedly take place in the future. Because the implicit claim here is that the meaning of God's word is being "discovered," that for the first time its content is being clarified, the boundary leading to a claim of new revelation is quickly crossed. For this reason, futuristic interpretation must be securely bound to the content of Scripture as a whole as this is opened up through other means of understanding.

A fourth rule involves respect for the order that 1 Corinthians 14 establishes for Christian worship. The interpreter bears responsibility for the prophetic understanding he proffers, not the Holy Spirit as if he were directly present. "The spirits of the prophets are subject to the prophets" (1Co 14:32 KJV). That means that the interpreter cannot simply equate his words with the Holy Spirit's, as if the latter had irresistibly implanted this or that statement. He must rather take personal responsibility for his claims, representing his interpretation in the context of the entire community, allowing it to be corrected as need be (cf. 1Co 14:29). For that reason an understanding that comes to us as "prophetic" can also never be binding. It can only be confirmed through revelation, thereby being commended to revelation-bound faith (cf. Dt 13:2ff.; 18:20ff.).

Nevertheless, we cannot dispense with prophetic understanding of Scripture. Both in preaching and in biblical instruction it occasionally must occupy our attention. It is necessary in the midst of the struggle that the Christian community faces in every age, and most of all under end-time conditions. If we relegate it to the no-man's-land of unreflected practice, or leave it to be exercised only by groups we consider to be heretical, then the risk that inheres in this method of understanding will become uncontrollable and outweigh its benefits.

## RECIPROCAL RELATIONSHIP OF THE VARIOUS WAYS OF UNDERSTANDING

At the close of this chapter the question arises: what is the relationship of the various means of understanding to each other?

We have discussed a few of the ways they relate. But only a few: a presentation of the ways of understanding can never be complete, if for no other reason than because new ways are constantly being pondered, and often tried out, in the course of the church's history.

Let us cling to the conviction that historical, dogmatic, typological, allegorical, and prophetic understanding all without exception offer *cognitive* possibilities for understanding. That is also to say that they require supplementation, i.e., must be augmented with the help of *dynamic* and *ethical* understanding.

Overall it may be said that no individual possibility of understanding may be absolutized. Rather, all are only concrete expressions of discipleship. We recall the apt words of Hans Schlaffer: "a disciple of Christ—that's who a Christian is."[107] To be Christ's disciple means to lead a renewed existence in faith. Understanding at various levels belongs to this renewed existence. If these dimensions of discipleship are detached from each other, the individual parts grow abstract, mere *l'art pour l'art*, and die.

But it is not only one's personal existence in faith that demands a unity and comprehensiveness of understanding. The integrity of the faith at the community level is also at stake. All the possibilities of understanding described above are, indeed, activities within one and the same community. Their goal is its building up in the best sense. As the individual members of the community make up the whole body, the various ways of understanding are functions of the one body. That is why we must reject a division between "theology for the church" and "theology for the university." A university theology that at the same time has no desire to be theology for the church is in the strict sense no longer theology at all. And a church theology that has no desire to articulate its convictions in the university sphere is in the strict sense no longer a theology that will serve the church.

The end that must be striven for, then, is a sound development and tight consolidation of all the possible means of understanding that revelation opens up to us.[108]

# CHAPTER SEVEN

# The Inspiration of Scripture

## A DEAD ISSUE?

When it came time for Karl Girgensohn to publish his essay "The Inspiration of Holy Scripture," he wrote: "When the topic of inspiration is broached, people appear to treat it as a dead issue."[1]

When did inspiration come to be regarded as "a dead issue"? Certainly since the time of W. Hermann's and J. Kaftan's protest against a renewal of the doctrine of inspiration. They argued that "the notion of an inspired Scripture actually [would complicate] the knowledge of revelation as well as obedience to it." Gennrich called this a "radical break" with the traditional doctrine of inspiration.[2] But for the majority of theologians on the Continent, the doctrine of inspiration had become a "dead issue" much earlier, as early in fact as the end of the Enlightenment. O. Merk and G. Hornig concur in their judgment: "At no point in dogmatics" did "the historical-critical theology of the 18th century Enlightenment break so radically with orthodox traditions as in the area of the doctrine of inspiration."[3]

We can readily trace the progress of the collapse of the doctrine of Scripture and, as a result, the doctrine of inspiration.

Jean Alphonse Turretin of Geneva (1671–1737) dissociated himself from the notion of Scripture being "God-breathed" (θεόπνευστοσ; cf. 2Ti 3:16).[4] Johann Salomo Semler completely gave up the doctrine of inspiration.[5] Gotthold Ephraim Lessing had anticipated Semler in denying the inspiration of Scripture.[6] Soon the only tenable views maintained inspiration of Scripture's content, or of the person, as opposed to verbal inspiration; Schleiermacher exemplifies belief in personal inspiration.[7] Friedrich Wilhelm Jerusalem (1709–89) reads Moses with the same eyes as he reads Homer, Virgil, or Plato.[8] Rationalism turned against every conception of inspiration that infringed on human autonomy (an example here would be Wegscheider).[9] Even relatively conservative theologians like Tholuck or Rothe come out against verbal inspiration.[10]

A. Tholuck spoke of the "necessity of a freer conception of inspiration." This suggested itself as a necessity for him because Scripture was inerrant only "in the essentials."[11] R. Rothe distinguished between revelation and Scripture. Only the former was inspired; in the latter he saw mistakes and errors.[12] Fr. H. R. Frank argued in similar fashion.[13] When changes in the traditional doctrine of inspiration were criticized in the Baltic churches, Theodosius Harnack replied, "We don't believe in a book but in Jesus Christ.[14] . . . The preached word is the actual means of grace; the written word serves only [!] as plumbline and norm."[15] O. Zöckler saw no room for verbal inspiration in the state church: "The ultimate consequence of a full doctrine of verbal inspiration would be a free church system"; no theologians would be forthcoming "from the teaching institutions of the state church" who held such a view.[16] The Herrnhuter seminary in Gnadenfeld was expressively permitted to adopt modern-critical views according to a ruling of the Herrnhuter synod of 1897; the unity of "faith in the inmost heart" would be sufficient.[17] Theologians like Köhler (Erlangen), Öttli, or Sellin strove for a "positive criticism," forsaking the traditional doctrine of inspiration, because they were convinced that ("negative") criticism could only be refuted by ("positive") criticism.[18] For court preacher Stöcker in Berlin the doctrine of verbal inspiration was "a grave error."[19]

This was the situation in Germany in 1900. We have canvassed the views of conservative theologians because they furnish the best evidence for what developed. As far as liberal theology is concerned, William Wrede could state concisely and colorfully in 1897: "Science has recognized the old doctrine of inspiration to be untenable."[20] His main argument runs: "inspired" and "historical" are irreconcilable opposites.[21] It speaks for the honesty of the liberal standpoint when Wrede rejected all "one-quarter and three-quarter doctrines of inspiration" as unsatisfactory compromises.[22]

The dissolution of the doctrine of inspiration in Germany triggered great theological battles in America at the turn of the century. The outcome there was also similar. An example is the so-called Chicago school headed up by W. R. Harper.[23]

From the turn of the century to today, two characteristics dominate. First, for the majority of Continental and perhaps also many Anglo-Saxon theologians, there is no longer any battle over inspiration. Second, the doctrine of inspiration seems to be irretrievably lost. The same view is shared by many Catholic voices.[24] It will suffice to cite a few—primarily "conservative"—examples. Heinrich Frick, who inclined to the pneumatic exegesis of the 1920s, opined in 1927: "Whoever takes part in theological learning even to the slightest extent can no longer argue for a naive trust in the verbal infallibility of the Bible."[25] That is, the stance toward biblical inspiration is decided by "theological learning." Whoever possesses it no longer maintains "a naive trust" in the Bible. W. Elert placed the following heading over a paragraph in his book on the Christian faith: "Inadequacy of the doctrine of inspiration." He called the Christian and Protestant Scholastic "dictation theory" a "heresy."[26] W. Joest in 1966 went even further. He explained the historical-critical solution to the doctrine of inspiration as simply "a correction made by God himself to our theological notions."[27] Thus the

conviction of Scripture's inspiration, widely accepted for many centuries, is given up as ungodly and heretical. In its wake the modern critic
becomes God's spokesman. Erich Dinkler, a Bultmannian following in
the steps of Bultmann's teacher Wrede, argued in 1950 that the earlier
doctrine of inspiration must give way in the light of historical-critical
research: "there can be no talk of inspiration."[28] "Historical" and
"inspired" are mutually exclusive. Popular presentations infer from all
this "that the Bible as a witness to its divine origin collapsed under the
cross-examination to which historical-critical research subjected it."[29]
Somewhat more cautiously Finlayson (1959) speaks of a "displacement
of the authority of Scripture by that of human experience and enlightenment."[30]

This background must be kept in mind when seeking to outline a
doctrine of inspiration today. But there is another dimension to consider.
For broad segments of the church have not gone along with the developments sketched above regarding conceptions of inspiration. In the
German-speaking context this is true above all for believers at the local
level. Gennrich's monograph (1898) expressly described how university
theology continually referred to the injuries it had inflicted on the traditional approach to the question of inspiration; "the division between
theology and the faith of common believers" became "greater and
greater."[31] As recently as 1981, assembled members of the influential
Gnadauer Federation[32] approved this formulation: "We believe and confess that the entire Bible is God's word, produced and permeated by the
Holy Spirit and therefore unconditionally true and trustworthy."[33] True,
technical terms are avoided in their statement. But the tendency to hold
fast to the inspiration of the "entire Bible" is clear. Individual Protestant
theologians like L. Gaussen or F. A. Philippi fought for verbal inspiration even during the nineteenth century.[34] Even where verbal inspiration
was rejected, there is some acknowledgment that the orthodox evangelical doctrine of inspiration was a legitimate continuation of what the
Reformers believed.[35] On the evangelical side, scholarly fundamentalism has continued to defend the verbal inspiration of Scripture right up

to the present hour: among others one thinks of Geisler, Henry, Mickelsen, Packer, Ramm, and Warfield. Finally, it should be noted that official Catholic doctrine continues to affirm both the inerrancy of Scripture and its inspiration. The papal encyclical on the timely furtherance of biblical studies of September 30, 1943, begins with the words: "Divino afflante Spiritu, illos Sacri Sciptores exararunt libros" ("Prompted by the Holy Spirit, holy authors wrote those books").[36] Here we encounter concepts like "verbum divinitus inspiratum" (divinely inspired word), "divina inspiratio" (divine inspiration), "exceptum errore" (without error), and "ab omni errore immunis" (immune from all error).[37] Somewhat more reserved, then, is the instruction of the papal Bible commission of April 21, 1964, which appears to move in the direction of personal inspiration.[38] Yet one reads again and again that inspiration "preserved" the writers of the Gospels "from all error" (ob omni errore praeservabat).[39]

If, in addition to the above, one considers the careful attempts, also from the evangelical side, to make renewed connections with the biblical statements about inspiration,[40] then it is hardly possible to declare the doctrine of inspiration a "dead issue."[41]

It could not possibly be a "dead issue" anyway, however, because it is based on statements that are revealed,[42] that are not to be obliterated, and that place before every generation the task of a renewed and biblical doctrine of inspiration.

It is now time for us carefully to test the arguments that were pondered in the centuries-long disputes over the inspiration of the Bible. Even and especially here, however, we observe the starting point established earlier: we proceed from revelation itself.

## THE ANSWER OF REVELATION

Strangely enough, the question whether the writings of the old covenant are inspired is easier to answer than the question concerning the inspiration of the New Testament.

Second Timothy 3:16 declares, "All Scripture is θεόπνευστοσ."[43] The translation "All Scripture is given by God" is superior to the more restrictive translation "All Scripture that is given by God. . . ."[44] "Scripture" here denotes what we call the Old Testament. It has the quality of a "Holy Writing." As a result, Paul can use the term "Holy Writings" (Ro 1:2). They are "holy," however, in the sense that here "the words of God" lie before us (Ro 3:2).

Our first result is this: in the NT the entire "Old Testament" as it existed at that time—its precise compass is not our concern at this point—is viewed as "given by God." This result is also widely acknowledged among exegetes.

The question arises, however, whether this "given by God" or "inspired" receives a more precise definition. With this question in mind we turn first to another locus classicus,[45] 2 Peter 1:21. There we read: "men spoke from God as they were carried along by the Holy Spirit" (NIV). The content of this statement can be summarized in three steps. #1) "Men spoke"; that is, representatives of "normal" persons at a particular place and time, not "instruments," "writing implements," or the like; and they used a "normal" human language, not glossalalia, ecstatic sounds, or some similar means. #2) None of them, curiously enough, spoke from the standpoint of men, but "from God"; that is, sent from him, empowered, proceeding from his vantage point and bringing across a message from him that is no less than a "divine" message. #3) The one who brought about this peculiar state of affairs is the "Holy Spirit." He "carried" them, that is "compelled," "moved," "led," "directed," "steered." These basic determinations form the core of any doctrine of inspiration that can be called biblical.

Thus far we have left the written form of the "Old Testament" out of consideration. The Old Testament, however, contains unambiguous statements that must be weighed. The testament of Moses seeks to exclude every alteration of his teaching: "Do not add to what I command you and do not subtract from it . . ." (Dt 4:2 NIV; cf. 12:32; Pr 30:6). From Revelation 22:18f. the inference can be drawn that such unalterability was accorded precisely to Scripture's written form[46] in New Testament times at the latest. This is confirmed through Jesus' statement in John 10:35: "The Scripture cannot be broken."[47] It is precisely the written Torah that Joshua is told to heed carefully (Jos 1:8). Psalm 119 (vv. 6, 18, etc.) likewise presupposes the written form. The prophets are also supposed to support the permanence and lasting quality of their message through writing (Isa 8:16; Jer 36; Da 12:4). On the other hand, the prophets proceed from the conviction that Torah is extant in written form (Hos 8:12; Mic 6:8; Mal 4:4), and they themselves refer back to written materials of earlier prophets (Da 9:2). Here we should also mention numerous passages that presuppose a revelation in written form and address the adherence to or rejection of these passages in the history of Israel—e.g., Joshua 8:31ff.; 1 Samuel 10:25; 1 Kings 2:3; 2 Kings 14:6; 18:4ff.; 23:2, 21; 1 Chronicles 16:40; 28:11, 19; 2 Chronicles 17:3ff.[48] All in all, revelation in written form regards itself as #1) unalterable and #2) absolute. The deepest reason for this is that God himself is the ultimate origin of these utterances.[49] Therefore God himself is essentially the writer (Ex 24:12; 31:18; 32:15f.). Therefore we encounter the formula "the scripture says," which is interchangeable with the formula "God says; cf. Mt 22:31f.; 1Co 15:3f.; Gal 3:8."[50]

This knowledge serves to lead to the further knowledge that it is the Holy Spirit who created that writing of revelation.[51] Moses is regarded as bearing the Spirit (Nu 11:17, 25; Dt 18:15ff.), as are the prophets.[52] David, too, knows that "the Spirit of the LORD spoke through me" (2Sa 23:2 NIV). The NT recognizes this about David, who as *pars pro toto* (part for the whole) represents the entire book of Psalms (Lk 24:44; Mt 22:43; Ac 1:16; Heb 1:7; 3:7), just as it recognizes the prophets (Mt 1:22; Lk 24:44; Ac 28:25; 1Pe 1:11; 2Pe 1:21; Heb 10:15) and the Torah (Heb 9:8; 2Ti 3:16).

This goes along, once more, with the fact that the human authors of the so-called Old Testament recede into the background. It is "the Lord who spoke through the prophets" (Mt 1:22; cf. other Old Testament citations in Matthew). It is "Scripture" that "says" something (Gal 3:8).

It is "the Scriptures" that proclaim something (1Co 15:3f.). And it is also the "Scripture" itself and not only a chosen proclaimer that is filled with and formed by the Spirit (2Ti 3:16).

It remains to be noted that in the presentation above we are in agreement with Jewish interpreters known to us from the first century A.D. As Longenecker says, they were all convinced of the "divine inspiration of the Scriptures" and that the Scriptures were "the very words of God" (cf. Ro 3:2).[53]

But what about the New Testament? The question is difficult to answer because for Christians there is no authoritative Koran to confirm definitively the authority of the New Testament. Rather, God's revelation reached its final conclusion in the time of Jesus (Heb 1:1f.). Furthermore, the New Testament contains no binding list or definition of its own dimensions.

In this situation the only option is to proceed inductively in keeping with the procedure we have established above. That is, we must hear the claims of the individual writings of the New Testament, and only then press on to an assessment of the New Testament in its entirety.

With the book of Revelation there can be little question. By the statement in 22:18f. it places itself on the same level of binding normativity as the Mosaic Torah (Dt 4:2). It sees itself from the outset, then, as "Holy Scripture." The opening chapters serve only to support this claim (cf. Rev 1:1, 10f.; 2:1, 12, etc.).[54]

Moreover, 2 Peter 3:15f. shows that already in New Testament times there was a Pauline corpus, the extent of which we can admittedly no longer be certain. As to the character of this collection of Pauline writings ("all his letters," 2Pe 3:16), we can infer the following from Peter's statement: #1) Paul's letters consist of a number of letters. #2) Paul composed these letters under the direction of God-given wisdom ("the wisdom that God gave him," v. 15 NIV). #3) These Pauline utterances are cited as if they were Holy Scripture (cf. v. 15, "just as . . . Paul also wrote" [NIV] and e.g., Ro 3:4, "As it is written . . ."). #4) The Pauline writings are placed on the same level as "the other Scriptures" (v. 16).

It can be said, then, that a collection of Pauline letters was viewed as Holy Scripture as early as the time of the writing of Peter's second epistle.

When one scrutinizes Paul's letters with this in mind, one encounters Paul's claim to be writing under the leadership of the Holy Spirit (1Co 7:40; 14:37; 2Co 3:5ff.; 4:13). Paul expressly described his oral proclamation "not as the word of men, but as it actually is, the word of God" (1Th 2:13 NIV). He is "taught by the Holy Spirit" (1Co 12:13; cf. Gal 1:8, 11). That which he preaches was "revealed by the Spirit" (1Co 2:10).[55] The internal witness of Paul's letters agrees, then, with the external testimony of 2 Peter. That gives us the right to regard the Pauline letters in the New Testament as "Holy Scripture," in keeping with the New Testament's own statements.

At first glance the situation appears less clear in the case of the Gospels. For example, the Lucan prologue (Lk 1:1–4) can be regarded as a historical outline.[56] Luke alludes to his role as author but says nothing about the Spirit.

More careful study, however, modifies this first impression. Let us start with the gospel of John. It contains a key phrase that describes the eyewitness and author of the report (cf. Jn 21:24 and 19:35) as someone whose "testimony is true" (Jn 21:24). *True* is a term that encompasses various dimensions: #1) subjectively "true" = convincing; #2) objectively "true" = reliable, true to the facts; #3) in agreement with God's will, just as God's Word and his incarnation in Jesus are "truth" (cf. Jn 14:6; 17:17). In this way the entire gospel is legitimated as standing in agreement with God. To this corresponds Jesus' repeated prophecy that his disciples, one of whom is the author of the fourth gospel, will be led by the Spirit (Jn 14:26; 16:13). Finally, it is striking that the opening of John's gospel, in part right down to the very wording, runs parallel to Genesis 1. This can really only be interpreted as an implicit claim that John's gospel stands on the same level of legitimacy and authority as the Holy Scriptures of Israel.[57]

If we return now to Luke's two treatises (Luke-Acts), a few key emphases of the Lucan prologue grab our attention. So far there is no unanimity over the precise meaning of *kathexes* (in order; Lk 1:3).[58] But there is broad consensus that for Luke "assured reliability" (*asphaleia;* Lk 1:4) is a central concern.[59] Du Plessis defines *asphaleia* as "certainty or reliability" whose aim is "the historically verified and theologically reflected truth."[60] This understanding of *asphaleia* is supported from two sides. First is the accompanying word *akribōs* (precisely, carefully; Lk 1:3). Second is a word that appears in Luke 1:1, *diēgēsin* (narrative, account). Parallels in Josephus (*Jewish War* I, 1ff.) indicate that the word refers to a well-attested and solidly grounded report.[61] If Luke thereby emphasizes the "truth" of the report in the sense of its "reliability" (cf. Jn 21:24)—explicitly stated with mention of eyewitnesses and tradition in Luke 1:2—then a second element comes to light when he alludes to the "servants of the word" (Lk 1:2). When Luke bases his writing on these persons, he consciously highlights a subset among the eyewitnesses in order to introduce a new criterion. What is the nature of this criterion? "Eyewitnesses" and "servants of the word" are first of all apostles, according to Acts 6:2–4. More precisely, this refers to the Twelve. And it is precisely to these that Jesus' promise in Luke 10:16f. applies: "The one who hears you, hears me." They are the ones who received the Spirit in keeping with Jesus' promise (Lk 24:48ff.; Ac 2). When Luke, therefore, refers to the "servants of the word" in the prologue of his two treatises, he is basing his writing on those who bore the Spirit. When he at the same time emphasizes "reliability," he is not only laying claim to historical veracity; he is also implying that he serves as an extension, so to speak, of the Spirit-led apostles and founders of the earliest church. If all this does not amount to a *direct* claim to be producing "Holy Scripture," it comes very close. Luke's writings leave it up to the Spirit-led judgment of the early Christian community (cf. Ac 2), one might say, whether to regard those writings as Holy Scripture.

With respect to Matthew's gospel, the carefully crafted beginning section, containing literal resemblance to Genesis 5:1, likewise shows an intention to continue the Holy Scriptures of Israel. Matthew 1:17

emphasizes this continuity with its claim that the (sevenfold: compare Rev 1:4; 3:1; 4:5; 5:6 with Zec 4:2, 10) Spirit of God has determined the history of Israel and of the nations up to the time of Christ. This story of God's work must, in keeping with the history of the old covenant, be chronicled. From Christ come Spirit-filled "prophets and wise men and teachers" (Mt 23:34 NIV; cf. 3:11; 28:19) who can do this. Indirectly, therefore, Matthew also lays claim to be writing Holy Scripture.

For Mark there is as little as nothing to be said. Perhaps it would be otherwise if we still possessed the original ending to that gospel.

In discussing the inspiration of the Gospels, however, there remains one important argument that we have not yet taken into account. I refer to the manner in which other parts of the New Testament treat the material found in the Gospels. How does the handling of Gospel tradition (which predates the New Testament epistles) show those epistles' special regard for that tradition? First, 1 Corinthians 7:10ff. suggests that a collection of Jesus' sayings existed which Paul placed on the same level of authority as the Holy Scripture of Israel. The Pauline epistle that is likely the oldest confirms this (1 Th 4:15ff.). If one sifts through Peter's first letter in search of the Jesus traditions it contains,[62] similar observations can be made. Without question, 1 Timothy 5:18 quotes a saying of Jesus (Lk 10:7; Mt 10:10) as "Scripture" and places it on the same level with the Torah (Dt 25:4). We can even go a step farther: John's gospel handles Jesus' words in just the same way as Old Testament statements that must be fulfilled (cf. Jn 18:9, 32). All these observations combine to support the conclusion that the words of the eschatological, Spirit-filled Messiah possess the same worth as the "Holy Scriptures" of the old covenant. That has considerable significance for a proper conception of the inspiration of the Gospels.

Let us expand our search to include the Johannine Epistles. The author of 1 John introduces himself as an eyewitness and empowered herald (1Jn 1:1–4). The central formula of 3 John, "you know that our testimony is true" (3Jn 12 NIV) is highly reminiscent of John 21:24. The author of all three epistles, who is obviously one and the same person, speaks with the certainty that he is anointed with the Holy Spirit (1Jn 2:20; 4:1ff.; 5:6). The Johannine Epistles are, therefore, likewise inspired according to their own self-testimony.

To summarize the results of the preceding: by far most of the writings of the New Testament are inspired based on the statements they make about themselves (Revelation, Paul's letters, John's letters, Jesus' words). In other cases indirect claims justify the inference that the writings are inspired (the gospels of Matthew, Mark, and Luke; Acts). Only a few letters say nothing along these lines (Petrine letters, James, Jude, Hebrews). With the exception of Hebrews, however, even these may be viewed as the writings of eyewitnesses and authorized (i.e., Spirit-led) teachers of the earliest Christian fellowships.[63]

When the church later acknowledged the inspiration of all New Testament writings on the basis of the testimonium spiritus sancti internum (internal testimony of the Holy Spirit), it was taking its stand on firm historical ground. Moreover, its claim was in harmony with the claims of revelation itself.

The question can, then, by no means be *whether* the writings of the New Testament are inspired, according to revelation (i.e., Scripture) itself. The question can rather only be what we *mean* when we describe them as "inspired."

In what follows we will attempt to lay out the basic pattern that the Bible gives us.

## THE RANGE OF REVELATION

We proceed here with two comments in mind. One comes from Alan M. Stibbs (and not only from him) and asserts that in investigating revelation we have to guard ourselves against overly detailed questions.[64] That is doubtless a necessary reminder! The other remark is by Albert C. Sundberg: "that the Bible is inspired . . . is a universal Christian doctrine."[65] The second statement is no less important than the first.

## 1. PERSONAL INSPIRATION

The prevailing critical tendency is to treat inspiration, if it recognizes it at all, as personal inspiration. That is, by inspiration it understands—to use W. Schmidt's formulation—"the subjective transmission of revelation to the holy writer" or "God's breathing of himself into the inmost reaches of the person."[66] Richard Rothe stated it even more briefly when he spoke of the "inspiration of the writers," not of the Scripture.[67] Today one occasionally hears of the "empowering" of the biblical authors "for witness."[68] This conception of personal inspiration has won ground since Schleiermacher.[69]

The advantage of such a solution is obvious and was already described by Schleiermacher himself. If inspiration does not extend to revelation as expressed in Scripture but only to the writer who was active in producing it, then "all individual features can be handled as purely human."[70] Then criticism possesses free reign over the word of revelation. E.g., Schleiermacher could thereby deny the inspiration of the Old Testament.[71] Rothe came to the conclusion that "there can be no talk of an infallibility and absolute inerrancy of the Scripture."[72] Similar statements can be found in H. E. Weber.[73] W. Abraham draws parallels to a human teacher who "inspires" his pupils and suggests that, since along with the teacher there are other influences, the pupils will obviously make mistakes.[74]

In critiquing this view its partial truth should be acknowledged. There can, in fact, be no doubt that biblical statements on inspiration emphasize that the writers are Spirit-filled.[75] Nor can it be doubted that the early church, Protestant Scholasticism,[76] Catholic doctrine, and both pietistic and fundamentalist writers teach personal inspiration—though that is not the full extent of what they teach. To take a few examples: according to Justin God "moves" (*kinein*) the writers; the Spirit breathes on them (*empnein*).[77] For Origen the Holy Scriptures were "written down as the result of what the Holy Spirit breathed out (*ex epipnoias*)."[78] Flacius emphasizes the inspiration of the authors in speaking of their "empowerment."[79] Johann Tobias Beck came up with a similar formulation: "In the Scripture holy men of God speak and write due to the impetus and input of the Holy Spirit. They are taught by him internally and led into the truth."[80] The "Instructio" of the 1964 papal Bible commission speaks of the "spirits" of the authors which were "led and guided" as the authors "composed" their works.[81]

However—and here we turn to criticism of another side of the matter—this doctrine of personal inspiration remained, until the Enlightenment, linked with the doctrine of verbal inspiration. For Protestant Scholasticism Preus concludes that verbal inspiration was explicated *first*, and after that personal inspiration. The point at issue, then, is not *whether* personal inspiration is a tenable view. For this is really a settled question. The disputed point is rather whether personal inspiration is the *only* sense in which inspiration affects the Bible's writings.

Additional critical consideration is in order regarding the modern shaping of the doctrine of personal inspiration, which represents a theological setback in the face of the Enlightenment's triumphal march. Gennrich describes the matter thus: "Finally it was enough to say nothing beyond the bare fact that the writers were illumined; or to be content with affirming the writer's piety (which as proclaimers of divine truth was certainly suitable for them anyway). The divine element of inspiration came to be viewed as simply that which reason already recognized as true and good." At that rate a special doctrine of inspiration became quite unnecessary.[82] Here we glimpse the danger that a truly biblical doctrine of inspiration must avoid by all means: loss of assurance regarding the God-givenness of the content of the Bible.

This danger is clearly exemplified in Shailer Mathews, a leading theologian of the Chicago school. He believed "in the inspiration of men, not words." As a result the Bible appeared to him as "a trustworthy record of the human experience of God."[83] This conclusion is nearly paradoxical, if also understandable: the human is deemed reliable, while the divine falls prey to doubt. The humanly subjective triumphs over the divinely objective. As we saw earlier, this form of theory runs counter to what revelation intends to be.

Precisely at this point we must return once more to Paul Ricoeur. For Ricoeur the "manifestation of the absolute" is found in the biblical testimony. Without such manifestation, our interpretation would "forever be only an interpretation of an interpretation."[84] We require "the objective dimension of revelation."[85] From there Ricoeur succeeds in locating the locus of revelation: it lies "between the secret and the revealed."[86] Here, now, we glimpse the crux of the matter. The purpose of inspiration is to vouchsafe the reliability of statements that come from God (2Pe 2:21) and to assure that they endure for the future (cf. Isa 40:8; Mt 5:18; 24:35). An inspiration that extends only to the concrete person and not to the message permits the message to sink into oblivion. The "absolute" would then have disappeared.

## 2. INSPIRATION OF IDEAS

Like the notion of purely personal inspiration, the view that just the ideas (not the actual words) of Scripture are inspired represents a dogmatic retreat in the face of the Enlightenment's forward march. According to Gennrich, "people now began to distinguish between words and ideas and to ascribe divine prompting only to the latter. And they went even farther: they restricted inspiration to the religious content of the Bible, excluding other material, which they deemed to be purely human."[87] This restriction to certain kinds of statements offered the same advantage as the doctrine that inspiration was purely personal in nature—namely, it made room for criticism of the Bible's content (Sachkritik). It also offered an additional advantage of permitting a basic endorsement of Scripture's inspiration to continue. Inspiration of the Bible's ideas is a view partially in evidence in late Protestant Scholasticism. Calixt would be an example here, for whom it would have dishonored the Holy Spirit to reveal that which was nonessential ("leviculae").[88] Similar ideas are present yet earlier among Catholic authors such as Franz Suarex.[89] With Musaeus we then encounter the more sharply defined concept that the "contents" of Scripture are inspired.[90] Ernesti (1707–81) evinces for the first time the formulation that became typical for subsequent thought. His work combines criticism of content (Sachkritik) with the idea of divine inspiration. But in that case we are dealing here with nothing other than a view that Scripture's contents (not its words) are inspired.[91]

It is tempting to try to trace how this view branched out. We would see, among other things, that personal inspiration and idea inspiration are compatible and can crop up alongside each other. But what is important here is to work out the considerable inner tension inherent in the view that inspiration involves primarily only the Bible's ideas. This tension almost inevitably results in a view of *partial* inspiration. Ernst Bloch saw the tendency to sunder unities as a primordial human phenomenon: "Man's darkness and confusion find a correlate in his disunification."[92] It appears that man tends to project this indwelling disunification onto that which ought to put it to flight—revelation. Let us clarify this phenomenon by looking at an example. Both Schleiermacher and Rothe distinguish between (inspired) revelation and (noninspired) Scripture. For Rothe this resulted in the task of separating out "that which is appropriate to revelation" in the Bible. Only this is inspired and has unconditional authority.[93] Both basically arrive at the result that only certain parts of the Bible, which it is theology's job to determine, are inspired. For Marheinecke inspiration grants protection only "from errors in the substantial truths of the Christian faith."[94] Tholuck speaks in similar terms: only "in that which is essential" is the Bible without error and inspired.[95] Nor does J. S. Lutz think that all in the Bible is divinely given. Only soteriological material is "God's word," not "historical data, depictions of customs and morals, comments on insignificant persons." The "historical calls for critical investigation."[96] The dogmatic implications of an approach to inspiration centering on ideas (as opposed to words, the actual text in its fullness) becomes especially clear in the work of W. F. Gess (1819–91). Passages like Judges

19 or Nehemiah 7:68f. "relate totally to our fleshly world" and are not inspired. Uninspired biblical writings are Jude, James, Hebrews, Ecclesiastes, Esther, and Chronicles. The Synoptic Gospels, Judges, and Samuel are only partially inspired.[97]

Criticism of this view must again stress that element of truth it contains. In fact, the Christian church has long taught that the ideas found in the Bible are inspired. God determined the contents of the writings, as e.g., Augustine states.[98]

Until the Enlightenment,[99] however, this teaching was embedded in the overarching doctrine that Scripture's very words are inspired. To remove inspiration from its embeddedness in the larger framework had to mean that 2 Timothy 3:16 could no longer be upheld.[100] The inescapable conclusion is this: a doctrine that adds nothing more substantial to personal inspiration than idea inspiration is no longer compatible with biblical revelation. It rather marks out the borders, before exegetical work ever begins, of what may count as revelation and what may not.

Idea inspiration, just like personal inspiration, results in uncertainty about the divinely worked content of the Bible, or, as Ricoeur would say, about the "objective dimension of revelation." For "where is the boundary between essential and non-essential?"[101] Such questions will confront us again when we take up the subject of canon. But they already carry decisive weight with respect to inspiration. Finally, a view of inspiration that extends merely to the ideas is no more satisfactory than one that applies only to the person.[102]

Let us bring the point in question back to this formulation: it is not a matter of whether one should *also* affirm that inspiration extends to ideas. The question is rather whether inspiration should extend *only* to ideas.

## 3. VERBAL INSPIRATION

The doctrine of verbal inspiration is the third classical conception. It predates the view that inspiration extends merely to ideas.

In order to grasp its traditional weight let us turn once more to a historical overview.

Jesus' interpretation of Scripture is not undisputed. Yet Matthew 5:17f. in conjunction with John 10:35 shows that Jesus understood Holy Scripture, as it existed in his day, as authoritative, inspired, and able to bring about its own fulfillment, right down to the finest details (the very smallest letter!).[103] Clearly Paul's position is an affirmation of verbal inspiration. "No one can believe more adamantly in the Scripture than he."[104] At the end of the first century, the inspiration of Holy Scripture in its entirety is affirmed in Clement's first epistle.[105] Justin (mid-second century A.D.) is "the first orthodox theologian who possessed something akin to a 'doctrine of Holy Scripture,'" according to Campenhausen (p. 106). The inspiration of the whole of Scripture was a set starting point for him.[106] The same can be said with respect to Irenaeus and Tertullian.[107] Campenhausen (p. 365) expressly describes Origen as "an advocate of verbal inspiration." He makes "the Bible a subject of dogmatics."[108] As a result he sees the Bible as "totally perfect," without contradiction, "written down under the influence of the Holy Spirit"; his preferred designation of the Bible is "divine writings" (*theiai graphai*).[109] For all these writers, Scripture's freedom of contradiction, infallibility, perfection, unity, and truth are important. Augustine, too, taught the doctrine of verbal inspiration.[110] Most of all he emphasized Holy Scripture's infallibility and absence of contradiction ("nihil in eis omnino errasse, nihil fallaciter posuisse" ["in them there is absolutely no error; nothing presents a deception"]).[111] Divine inspiration determined, e.g., the content and the order of the Gospels in the New Testament.[112] Even failures in the apostles' memory were caused by the Holy Spirit in order to instruct us.[113] Augustine prized the idea that the gospel served as the present Lord ("quasi praesentem dominum") and the "mouth of Christ" ("Os Christi").[114] Thus were laid the essential basic lines of a doctrine of inspiration that endured right down to the Reformation. The medieval Scholastics viewed God as the sole ultimate originator of the Scripture. The human authors receded into the background. They were called secretaries, writing instruments, scribes, and so on. The absolute inerrancy of the Bible was roundly affirmed.[115] According to Gabriel Biel (d. 1495) the Bible "arose through dictation and inspiration by the Holy Spirit."[116] Kropatscheck summarized the doctrine of Scripture of the Middle Ages in this way: "Scripture is without error, perfect, sufficient, clear" (p. 434). Presumably a doctrine of "sola scriptura" could not have arisen without this "common Catholic" conception.[117]

Luther's stance toward verbal inspiration remains disputed. Outstanding researchers occupy various positions. While R. Bring holds the view that Luther developed no doctrine of verbal inspiration,[118] O. Scheel arrived at the conclusion that "Luther appears even to have presupposed the doctrine of verbal inspiration."[119] Presumably Scheel is correct that Luther's approach to Scripture contains contradictions.[120] Calvin's view is clearer. For him the writers of the New Testament are "authorized scribes of the Holy Spirit" (Inst IV, 8, 9). The entire Bible is dictated by the Holy Spirit.[121] In Flacius we encounter formulations that remind us of Augustine: "Scripturam esse divinitus . . . inspiratam" ("Scripture is inspired through divine prompting") and "Spiritus s. et Pater ipse per os Prophetarum et Apostolorum locutus est concripsitque sacram Scripturam" ("The Holy Spirit and the Father himself spoke, and the Holy Spirit wrote, through the mouth of the prophets and apostles").[122] Here the inspiration of all of Scripture, with God as the ultimate author and actual speaker, comes to clear expression. It is well known that Protestant Scholasticism thought through verbal inspiration in detail. It is *Scripture* that is inspired, it is the *entire* Scripture.[123] Inspiration also applies to related things like "res historicae, chronologicae, genealogicae, astrologicae, physicae et politicae" ("matters of history, chronology, genealogy, astronomy, physics, and politics"). True, these are not essential to salvation, but they aid in understanding the overall setting.[124] Hollaz furnishes a classical formulation of the doctrine of verbal inspiration: "Omnia et singula verba, quae in s. codice leguntur, a spiritu s. prophetis et apostolis inspirata et in calamum dictata sunt" ("Every individual word that is read in Holy Scripture was given from the Holy Spirit to the prophets and apostles and dictated into their pens").[125] God is the ultimate author of Scripture (causa principalis); the human authors serve only as his instruments (causa instrumentalis).[126] Inspiration encompasses both the suggestio rerum (inspiration of the content) and also the suggestio verborum (inspiration of the words). Obviously it also encompasses the commission to write.[127] Thus we again encounter the combination of all three conceptions of inspiration: personal inspiration, idea inspiration, word inspiration.

It remained for "modern knowledge of the world and insight into the historically conditioned nature of the biblical testimony," as this knowledge and insight gained dominance in the course of the Enlightenment, to shake and suppress verbal inspiration more and more.[128] Yet scholarly Pietism and fundamentalism, along with official Roman Catholic dogmatic teaching, have held to verbal inspiration right down to the present time.[129]

## 4. CRITICISM OF VERBAL INSPIRATION

Following the above historical survey, our task is to lay out the many-sided critique that has been leveled at the doctrine of verbal inspiration in the history of modern theology. Criticisms emerge at various levels.

A 1972 publication edited by Heinrich Ott and others (*Antwort des Glaubens*) calls the "theory of literal inspiration" "fundamentalistic" in view of historical facts.[130] The theory is to be rejected in light of three considerations: #1) "historical consciousness," #2) "intellectual honesty," and #3) "the fact of the incarnation."[131]

Consideration #2) resembles more the verdict of a moral judge than the sober observation of a theologian. It would bar from the discussion, on the grounds of alleged dishonesty, all advocates of verbal inspiration who have lived since the Enlightenment. Consideration #3) overlooks that in the course of history a parallel was actually drawn between the "doctrine of the divine-human nature of the Bible" and

Christology in order to support the inspiration of the Bible.[132] Taking the form of word and taking the form of flesh (incarnation) seemed to furnish mutually supporting, comparable events. For this reason it is preferable not to adduce the fact of the Incarnation as evidence against verbal inspiration. Indeed, otherwise the implication of the Divine Son's sinlessness would be the errorlessness of God's Word. On the other hand, consideration #1) above does possess some weight. On the whole, however, the doctrine of verbal inspiration cannot be so quickly dismissed as it is in *Antwort des Glaubens*.

But what is the substance of the criticism? One of the objections runs thus: the doctrine of verbal inspiration is logical and abstract and thereby incapable of grasping "the actual composition of Scripture."[133] In point of fact the doctrine as such possesses a somewhat scholastic feel and misleads in the direction of deductive thinking. If the *doctrine*, however, suffers from abstraction, that is not yet necessarily an indictment against *Scripture* itself.

A second objection asserts that Scripture contains mistakes.[134] This objection implies that the Holy Spirit would be incapable of inspiring errors to be written. But is this implication true? Is it really unthinkable that the Holy Spirit, for one reason or another, might let this or that miscue stand—or even make use of it (see Augustine!)? Hofmann, e.g., had the provocative insight that the Scripture is a unity and inspired, while at the same time he emphasized that in a few places it erred.[135]

A third objection suggests that the Scripture makes no claim "to be the product of the Holy Spirit's direct dictation" in each and every passage.[136] As a matter of fact, this is correct. If verbal inspiration depends on the idea of dictation, it must at least be modified.

A fourth objection charges that the doctrine of verbal inspiration transforms that living book called the Bible into a "law book"[137] "whose individual paragraphs are to be binding for all alike without any differentiation of their internal value."[138] Our historical survey indicates, however, that this assertion is untenable. Long ago Flacius made note of the "difference as well as convergence of law and gospel."[139] Protestant Scholastic dogmatics distinguished constantly between what was essential to salvation in Scripture and what was not. It used the expression "unimportant" ("leviculae"), e.g., for 2 Timothy 4:13.[140] The differences of style and character of the human authors were recognized.[141] Above all Bengel emphasized levels of inspiration[142] and so forth. It is not true, therefore, that to defend verbal inspiration is to be a "legalistic biblicist and hair-splitter."[143]

A fifth objection runs that the various readings and other phenomena that stem from text-critical researches no longer permit a doctrine of verbal inspiration.[144] As soon as verbal inspiration is related to the original manuscripts, however, this objection loses force.

A sixth objection sees historical research and verbal inspiration as fundamentally antithetical. E.g., Abraham states that we cannot "maintain their [evangelicals'] position about [verbal] inspiration and at the same time take history seriously." This applies all the more, he continues, in view of the relation between inspiration and historical-critical work: "We must either abandon critical historical study and honestly admit this or we must abandon the theology of inerrancy."[145] Why? Because of the established dictum: "Historical research handles the Bible like any other human book."[146] And because precisely in the course of executing this approach "many of its assertions" have turned out to be "incorrect."[147] Yet if verbal inspiration really did exclude historical understanding of the Bible, it would find itself in contradiction with revelation itself (cf. chap. 6 above).

A seventh objection proceeds from the assertion that we as believers are not dependent on verbal inspiration. It is not the Scripture that is the foundation of faith in Jesus Christ but the opposite: faith in Christ confers "a special reputation" on Scripture.[148] That argument is at least as old as Schleiermacher.[149] But which Jesus is it, then, that we are dealing with? Our faith is, after all, not mythical. It is historically bound and to that extent also transmitted through the content of the Bible.

An eighth objection occasionally encountered is that a return to verbal inspiration would mean "a complete break with [contemporary] science."[150] Abraham demands that our doctrine of inspiration be "contemporary,[151] coherent, and credible."[152] Isn't it rather true, however, that it is more important for the doctrine to correspond to its object? And is science static? Is it not rather undergoing constant revision?

The ninth objection claims that Scripture contains contradictions.[153] If this objection can be sustained, then a doctrine of inspiration is no longer possible.

Positively, the advantages of the doctrine of inspiration should now be assessed. The doctrine possesses #1) a logical and consistent comprehensiveness. It is #2) in a position to hear what all of Scripture has to say. It has no need, then, to attempt the Sisyphean task of separating between the "husk" and the "kernel," between "eternal truth" and "contingent appearance"[154] in Scripture. It can #3) successfully press the claims of the "absolute" dimension of revelation and imparts certainty to us regarding the God-given content of the Scripture. It is the view that #4) comports most readily with Scripture itself (2Ti 3:16).

A revelational theology cannot give up these advantages. Above all it cannot dispense with being in agreement with Scripture. It will maintain close connection, therefore, with verbal inspiration. At the same time it will desire to respond adequately to justified criticism.

Without going into details to be covered below, let us state this preliminary conclusion: it is *Scripture* that is inspired.[155] Mere personal inspiration or idea inspiration cannot satisfy. Yet in Christian tradition both personal and idea inspiration are included in the notion of inspired Scripture. Corresponding to this inspiration, an inspiration of the interpreter is also present (see chap. 5 above). Nevertheless, inspiration of the interpreter lies on a different level, as we will clarify below. We may add here that this conception of inspired *Scripture* is in essential agreement with Jewish understanding at the time of the apostles.

What we have just said deals with the inspiration of Scripture in its *entirety*. We speak therefore of the *entire inspiration* of Scripture.

## 5. ENTIRE INSPIRATION

It will now be our task to unfold what we mean in speaking of entire inspiration.

Once more we take revelation itself as our starting point. The concept of "entire inspiration" is directly from the Bible. It is rooted in 2 Timothy 3:16: "All Scripture is given by God" (Revised Elberfelder Bible). Instead of "all Scripture" some prefer to translate "every Scripture passage"[156] or "every Bible passage."[157] With Holtz, Jeremias, Schlatter, Schrenk, Stuhlmacher, and others we understand 2 Timothy 3:16 in the extensive, not limited, sense.[158] It speaks, therefore, of the entire Holy Scripture as it existed at that time, transmitted through Israel. Schlatter comments that Paul "did not speak of certain or of a few passages, but of all that stands written in the Bible, in asserting that Scripture brings us a divine gift."[159] The extensive translation of the verse is also supported by early church history.[160]

Applying an overtly biblical term like *entire inspiration* is preferable to resorting to some other conceptual formation. For neither personal nor idea inspiration can base itself directly on biblical terms.

In addition, *entire inspiration* offers the advantage of furnishing a terminological bridge to conceptions stemming from the background of historical theology, where one encounters such phrases as "plenary inspiration"[161] or "pleine inspiration."[162]

The third advantage is that we can thereby take up influential traditions out of our own theological background. Preus has made clear that in Lutheran orthodoxy the *entirety* of Scripture was regarded as inspired.[163] The prophetic/salvation-historical theology could likewise emphasize that we must begin with the inspiration of "Scripture as a unified whole."[164] This was but a furtherance of what J. A. Bengel had left as a legacy for future generations: to hear and heed the whole of Scripture.[165] Pietism attempted to stay on this same track. Accordingly the Gnadauer Federation stated in a resolution published in 1981: "We believe and confess that the entire Bible is God's word, effected and permeated by the Holy Spirit."[166]

Fourth, the term *entire inspiration* offers hope of dismantling misunderstandings and blunders associated with the traditional doctrine of "verbal inspiration."

There is one aspect of the hotly disputed doctrine of verbal inspiration that we share, however: God's Spirit brought forth and permeates absolutely no less or other than the *entire* Scripture. Any notion of partial inspiration remains excluded.

We have thereby already decided how we will answer the old controversial question: "Is" the Bible God's word, or does it only "contain" God's word? At least since Thomas Hobbes' *Leviathan* (1651) the notion has spread that the Bible and God's word are two different things.[167] In volume one of his treatise on the canon, Johann Salomo Semler coined the classical formulation, "Holy Scripture is quite entirely to be distinguished from word of God."[168] In Karl August Keil's hermeneutic (1810), e.g., there is a definite distinction made between "that which is appropriate to all times and persons" and "that which was expressed only for former times and needs."[169] Among conservative theologians "God's word" was most preferably located in a soteriological sphere. Martin Kähler's procedure is instructive here. He too proceeds from the premise that "God's word and the Bible are not to be automatically equated."[170] It is therefore a theological task to determine the "essential content," "midpoint," and "major focus" of Scripture.[171] "One must therefore experience the word of God from the Bible."[172] For Kähler it is "faith in justification" that forms the Bible's midpoint.[173] H. E. Weber,[174] among others, has followed him in this, although the definitions and delimitations vary regarding what God's word is. Thus F. Traub, e.g., begins with the "fact of Christ": "All in the Scripture that 'Christum treibet,' i.e., either is a direct expression of the fact of Christ or stands in necessary inner connection with that fact, is word of God."[175] For Traub this excludes, e.g., "the reports about the empty grave"; they are therefore not "word of God."[176] A further possibility of distilling the word of God from the Bible involves discerning whether a certain statement becomes word of God *for me*. Traub mentions this possibility as well: "Only a certain content, one that legitimates itself as divine in heart and conscience, can arouse in me the impression that God is addressing me through it."[177] In this way the subjectivity of the hearer becomes the decisive criterion for the word of God. In any case, however, this amounts to the distinction already alluded to between "shell and kernel," essential and nonessential.[178]

On the other hand there can be no doubt that Luther,[179] the confessional documents, and Protestant Scholasticism,[180] along with Bengel[181] and scientific Pietism including salvation-historical theology of the nineteenth century[182] stood firm in holding that Scripture *is* God's Word.

We have no choice but one. Only the assertion that the Bible as a whole "*is*" God's gift and revelation is able to do justice to Scripture itself.

That leads us into interaction with the doctrine of the three-stage word of God: #1) God's actual revelation, #2) the witness to this revelation (the testified word), and #3) the preached word.

Karl Barth (1886–1968) gave this doctrine classic expression in modern times. It is good, wrote Barth in his *Church Dogmatics*, "to take note of the special significance of the fact that we must call the Bible precisely a witness of God's revelation. Therein, undoubtedly, lies a restriction: we thus distinguish the Bible as such from revelation. A witness is, indeed, not simply identical with that which is witnessed to by and in him."[183] The Bible is, therefore, "not itself revelation."[184] To the extent that the Bible is "merely" "a human word," it must be "historically" investigated and understood.[185] To put it in other words: revelation passes into the Bible only fragmentedly. Elsewhere Barth says that we must distinguish "between the flow of words, on the one hand, and that which lies 'back behind' them and seeks to become visible."[186] That which lies "back behind" is the actual revelation. Bible and proclamation, however, are only derivative phenomena. This is obviously an attractive modern garb for the older dictum: The Bible "contains" God's word.

Beyond those we might call "Barthians" in a narrow sense,[187] Barth's doctrine of the three forms of God's word is mirrored in Bultmann and his students,[188] in modern Lutherans,[189] and by those theologians who wish to relate their work positively to Barth and Bultmann.[190]

The line in which Barth stands can, as already indicated, be traced back farther. First mention goes to Barth's teacher Adolf Harnack, who could say: "Religion always lies behind its material manifestation."[191] Related to Harnack's view is Gunkel's statement: "Cutting loose from the letter teaches one to grasp the Spirit who gives life."[192] Still earlier W. Schmidt (1869) emphasized the testimonial quality of the Bible: "God's revelation is not transmitted to us in and of itself; it is rather transmitted to us in the garb in which it formerly clothed human hearts that had already experienced it."[193] Once more we recall Thomas Hobbes' *Leviathan*, for which the Bible was not revelation but "the record of that revelation."[194] For all these authors the "actual" or "genuine" lay behind the Bible. This "actual" is no longer accessible in pure form. We must content ourselves with the world of "appearance," to which the Bible also belongs, with all its errors and imperfections. Girgensohn's view is much the same; for him revelation stands "behind" the Bible.[195] Similarly, Schrenk sees the Bible as the bearer of revelation.[196] Clearly, an affinity exists here in continental thought with German idealism and the Platonism that attends it. This has been rightly criticized by Esking and Traub, among others.[197] Traub goes so far as to say that in Karl Barth's work "the Bible in its full scope is surrendered to literary and historical criticism."[198]

It has now become clear why we cannot befriend the doctrine of the three forms of the word of God. It devastates Scripture's God-givenness (2Ti 3:16) at the decisive juncture, namely, precisely where Scripture should take form as the ultimately intended word of the Holy Spirit. It breaks the bond with the biblical word that has gone out in concrete and contingent form, in that it ultimately binds us to a nonconcrete, timeless "back behind." It also contradicts the position of both Luther and other Reformers, for whom the biblical word was the actual will of God.[199]

In contrast, with the concept of entire inspiration we wish to emphasize that what God's Spirit has brought into being is precisely *this concrete*, biblical revelation. *This* word—precisely in its concreteness and contingency—is what God had to say to us. God's own revelation states that he did not intend to direct any other word to us (Heb 1:1f.). It is *this* word, not some "back behind" or "actual." Such is the humble form that Scripture takes.

One aspect that we have not yet treated remains to be emphasized. This aspect concerns the word *entire*. In contradistinction to verbal inspiration, the concept of "entire inspiration" directs attention to the overarching, interrelated whole. Verbal inspiration is constantly open to the charge that various textual readings have been transmitted, or that the biblical text contains gaps here and there.[200] Can the term *verbal* be used if the actual *verbum* (word) is uncertain or missing? Still, one must consider that the doctrine of verbal inspiration is not unconditionally committed to removing individual words in atomistic fashion from their context.[201] The doctrine is also aware of the problems of text transmission and therefore concentrates on the original autographs.[202] The concept of entire inspiration, however, avoids from the start the misunderstanding that it amounts to an atomistic viewpoint, proof-texting, or the like. Instead, it reminds us that inspiration involves the connection of promise and fulfillment, of word and response, of origin and goal of God's ways. In this comprehensive connection little importance can attach to individual words of the tradition that may be uncertain. The understanding of the whole cannot thereby be imperiled.[203]

Entire inspiration relates therefore to the original text.

## THE RELATION BETWEEN WORD OF GOD
## AND WORD OF MAN

Once entire inspiration is accepted, the question immediately arises: What is the relation between God's word and the words of men? If the entire Scripture is inspired, what is the role of the human authors in the rise of the Bible? Is the Bible "a book that fell down from heaven" (to use a famous cliché whose actual use has never been documented, as far as I know)?

Once more the task will be to lay out the basic contours of revelation itself. "Men spoke from God as they were carried along by the Holy Spirit," says the New Testament (2Pe 1:21 NIV).

In his *Gnomon* Bengel emphasized the passivity of the persons involved and the activity of God: "Non ferebant, sed ferebantur. Passive, non active se habuerunt. Quod fertur, non sua vi, non suo labore movet et promovet" ("They do not set themselves in motion but are set in motion. They act passively, not actively. What is set in motion is not of its own initiative and comes neither by its own strength nor from its own effort"). Thus he could also praise the beauty of the divine speech: "Deus, non ut homo, sed ut Deus verba facit, se ipso digna" ("God does not make words like a human does but like God, words that are worthy of him himself").[204] That is entirely in line with traditional Christian theology, which through the centuries regarded God as the ultimate source of enscripturated revelation. The view was that here God himself speaks. Matthew and other New Testament authors made this clear through the citation formulas they used. Thus it was "the Lord who spoke through the prophets" (Mt 1:22; 2:15; cf. Lk 1:70). Justin,[205] Tertullian,[206] and Origen agree that "the sacred books" do not present "writings of men"; they were "rather written down according to the will of the Father."[207] Augustine, like Bengel, traces even the use of individual words back to the will of the Holy Spirit.[208] This line of thinking persists through Thomas Aquinas,[209] Luther,[210] and Flacius, thus extending well into Protestant Scholasticism. Flacius can occasionally say that God "wrote through the hands" of human authors ("per eorundem manus conscripsit").[211] Bengel's words are not essentially different: "Paracletus per apostolos est locutus" ("The Spirit speaks through the apostles").[212] The fathers of Pietism did not hesitate to liken the Bible to a "letter from God."[213] Through Pietism and Johann Tobias Beck the same line extends into present times.[214] In 1967 Hermann Sasse could write that it is a "dogma of the entire church" that the Holy Scriptures "have God as their author."[215] James Barr's view that Scripture is a "product of the church"[216] is a conception that could never have been accepted as Christian during four-fifths of the whole of church history.

Even in the Scripture people "speak from God"; if the authors of the biblical writings were really "moved by the Holy Spirit," then we in fact must regard God as the ultimate author of Scripture. Through the messengers we hear him. It is his word.

Occasionally the question has arisen whether "moved by the Holy Spirit" means a form of special inspiration, or whether it rather denotes the general gift of the Spirit conferred on all believers. Speaking for the latter option is, e.g., Albert C. Sundberg.[217] Certainly one will not be able to speak of two "forms" of the Spirit. Still, the commissioning and empowering to author a revelatory writing bears a special character. Therefore, one must speak of a special, distinctive leading of the Spirit, though a different sense than that envisioned by Sundberg and others.[218] The goal of the Spirit's work here was to confer a distinctive, normative dignity to the Sacred Scriptures, while no such normative force attached to the oral and other proclamation.[219] This is the way the matter was seen in earlier dogmatics, as well.[220]

But what is the nature of human participation in the biblical writings? If God's activity is emphasized, the danger easily arises of regarding persons as mere media.

Surprisingly, however, we discover that the church as a whole has held itself quite aloof from a conception of ecstatic inspiration. The occasionally leveled charge[221] that the church's doctrine of verbal inspiration depends on Philo's concept of inspiration and is therefore also ecstatic in nature lacks historical foundation. True, Chmiel has established Philo's influence in Justin,[222] but he judged that Justin by no means viewed the writers of the Bible as passive transmitters. Rather, these writers were involved in an "action consciente et propre" ("action at once cooperative and individual").[223] Campenhausen stresses the difference between Origen and Philo: Origen taught neither a disengagement of human consciousness nor an ecstasy of the human authors.[224] Augustine's reflections are instructive here; in spite of his doctrine of verbal inspiration, he does not hold to a view of mechanical inspiration.[225] Kropatscheck's studied conclusion is that the early church rejected ecstasy as a major explanatory factor of inspiration.[226] Typical of the attitude of old Protestant Scholasticism is Quenstedt, who defended the full consciousness of the writers against any notions of trance, ecstasy, or enthusiasm.[227]

Moreover, according to recent research Philo himself did not advocate an ecstatic doctrine of inspiration.[228] There is, therefore, no longer any ground to work with an alleged "Philonic" concept of ecstatic inspiration.

If one seeks elsewhere for a Jewish parallel to the early Christian doctrine of inspiration, then it is more likely to be found in Josephus[229] or the rabbis than in Philo.[230]

Christian tradition does not tend, therefore, to an elimination of the personality of the human authors. It does, however, lay emphasis on God's speaking, and for that reason it often misapprehends the human factor. Yet it is significant that we are dealing with emphasis and not with an either-or judgment. So terms are employed like *pens*, *styli* (since Gregory the Great; otherwise also in Luther),[231] *scribes*, *secretaries*, *notaries*, *actuaries*, and the like, through the course of the many centuries of church history. As recently as 1943, Pius XII in "Divino afflante spiritu" likened the "sacred writers" to an "organon seu instrumentum" ("musical instruments or tool").[232] It is clear that the accent was shifted to the opposite extreme at the beginning of the Enlightenment.[233] Early on Richard Simon in his *Histoire critique du texte du Nouveau Testament* (1689) emphasized the active participation of men in the rise of Holy Scripture.[234] From a mediating position Childs describes the present situation in these words: "few theologians in this postcritical era would wish to deny that the active human participation . . . is an absolutely necessary feature for correctly understanding the text."[235]

A doctrine of inspiration that does justice to revelation must attempt to arrive at an emphasis that comports with Scripture itself. Earlier we pointed to the "men spoke from God" dimension (2Pe 1:21); we must now also unpack what it means that "men spoke." True, being filled with the Holy Spirit alters those so affected.[236] It renders them competent to hear, obey, and receive. Yet to a great degree it leaves intact their creative constitution and their unmistakable personal identity. "The human distinctiveness of the person affected by inspiration is not destroyed."[237] The inspired authors retain their consciousness, their personal capacities and intellectual strengths, their memory, their free will—as even Augustine insisted long ago.[238] They also maintain their characteristic literary style.[239] They select the material they use, at least in part (cf. Jn 20:30f.; 21:24f.).[240] They occupy a concrete historical locale and write with certain recipients and opponents in mind. That is the powerful kernel of truth in Bengel's statement that there are various "degrees of *theopneustie*."[241] Nevertheless, the view that there are "levels" of the Spirit is unacceptable. One may, however, assume that various writers were charged with differing mandates such that, e.g., the various Gospels evince varying degrees of accuracy and precision. Bengel was likewise justified in speaking of an apostolic "liberty" of word choice.[242] The erring human memory comprises an area for a judgment call involving the interrelationship of free human activity and the Spirit's activity. Both Augustine and Bengel were exercised by this question. The solution at which both[243] arrived in fundamental agreement may be regarded as exemplary: #1) there are such "errors of memory"; #2) the supernatural power of the Scripture, or the superintendence of the Spirit, renders these errors to the advantage of the readers.[244] God makes, therefore, even the errors of the messengers his servants—a view, to be sure, that crowds the edge of what we can affirm on the basis of revelation. All in all it would be good, then, to speak no more of "styli" or "instruments" when referring to the biblical writers. They are rather messengers.

This idea of messengers proves its value once more when we pose the question: How much insight did they have into the message that they conveyed? Revelation itself answers: their insight was limited. Both the content and the fulfillment of their message remained partially hidden to their eyes (1Pe 1:10f.; Mt 13:17).[245] Just getting the message to the messenger was sometimes attended by great difficulties, as accounts of divine calls and angel visitations indicate. The disciples had problems understanding Jesus' words and passing them along in the appropriate manner (cf. Mt 13:9ff., 36ff.; 16:5ff.; Jn 2:22; 12:16; 16:12, 25ff.; 21:23). The essential characteristic, then, of the biblical messengers is their fidelity, not their understanding.

Because comprehensive understanding on the part of the messengers was not a factor, even persons who did not belong to God's people could become God's messengers (e.g., Balaam).[246] On the other hand, revelation made use of purely human speech, because it wished to show thereby what man is. J. T. Beck called this a "mirror of the truth."[247] This is evidently where some statements of Ecclesiastes belong (e.g., 3:19; 9:2). One must therefore constantly inquire who is speaking in a given passage. Finally, it is not necessary that every individual writer has known that his work was destined to become part of Holy Scripture. The Holy Spirit could allow him to become a messenger taking part in revelation's enscripturation even without such foreknowledge.

What we have just tried to describe as the human participation in the biblical writings may finally be summarized in the idea of the "messenger." His two characteristic features are commitment and limitation. The second of these, limitation, precludes the writer's becoming a coauthor. Coauthorship would mean synergism. Synergism, however, would annul not only entire inspiration but also the givenness—what Ricoeur refers to as the "absoluteness"—of biblical revelation.[248] God must, then, remain in place as the ultimate author. At the same time the qualitative difference between the divine ultimate author and the human messengers must remain in place as well.

In concluding this section there remains the task of presenting more specifically *the intermingledness* of the sender and those sent, of the ultimate author and the messengers, of the speaker and the mediators of what was spoken *at the level of the word.*

An approach suggested by Karl Girgensohn may serve in orienting our discussion here. He sees two forces at work in enscripturated revelation: #1) a human "factor," and #2) a divine (pneumatic) "factor."[249] Infallibility belongs to the divine factor. The human factor, on the other hand, is responsible for errors and individual discrepancies.[250] Girgensohn believes he can separate the two factors from each other. E.g., there are "passages to which it would be grotesque to apply the idea of inspiration," such as in 2 Timothy 4:13 or 1 Timothy 5:23.[251]

J. I. Packer suggests a different approach. More recently I. H. Marshall has followed a similar line.[252] They describe the relation between the God who acts and the persons who write as "concursio." This means that the divine and human relate to each other complementarily.[253] Scripture can be explained at the level of human activity, but it can also be explained at the level of divine working. Indeed, both levels are at work at the same time and in an interpenetrating way.

Packer's and Marshall's model is well suited to make sense of the intertwinedness of divine word and human word. The unity of revelation remains intact. Girgensohn's approach, in contrast, threatens to bisect Scripture into two "Bibles," a divine and a human. His model, therefore, will not do justice to the coexistence and intertwinedness of divine and human word. Entire inspiration is excluded by Girgensohn's approach. The Packer-Marshall approach, however, which we may term concursive, possesses the advantage of being compatible with ancient Christian doctrine. To take Augustine as an example once more: for the Bible was "both entirely . . . God's work and also entirely . . . the work of man." Augustine thereby forewent "the determination of what is to be charged to the account of one and what to the account of the other."[254] Matthias Flacius' example is likewise instructive. He spoke of an "ultimate identification of human and divine word" and of the connection between "docens" (teaching) and "discens" (learning).[255]

This points the way ahead for us. Revelation, formed through the

Holy Spirit, given written form by people, meets us as something unified and entire. It offers us no key with which to chop it into two levels or strata. It seeks to be heard as a whole and in its interconnectedness—in spite of its obvious differentiation between such varied individual speakers as God, other supernatural created beings, or man. As Scripture took form, word of God and word of man became fundamentally and indissolubly intertwined:[256] God wanted to speak in just this manner through human agency (2Pe 1:21). Just as Jesus Christ is truly God and truly man, yet is not divisible into two persons, but remains thus the Son of God, so Scripture is simultaneously God's word and man's word, yet not divisible into two "words." It remains, finally and ultimately, God's word.

## THE RELATION BETWEEN INSPIRATION AND HISTORY

In previous sections we have already touched on the relation between inspiration and history. How does the divine Spirit who brings inspiration about enter the world of humanity—a realm bound to space and time? Conversely, how does historical research as modern man pursues it relate with the inspired quality of enscripturated revelation?

It has become customary to regard historical investigation of the Bible as militating against inspiration.[257] As if man by his power could tear God's work from its hinges! Behind this understanding, however, stands the conviction that history comprises an immanent causal nexus into which God can hardly be integrated. As is well known, E. Troeltsch (1865–1923) elevated this idea to a redoubtable principle of interpretation. Yet today it should be noted that causality has lost its former fame as an omnicompetent explanatory factor. C. G. Jung could even state that causality is "a statistical truth and not an axiom."[258]

Our starting point is, however, somewhat different. Within the horizon of revelation we understand history as that which God works or makes possible.[259] God is constitutive for our concept of history, one derived from revelation. For us, therefore, there can be no opposition in principle between historical investigation of the Bible and inspiration of the Bible.

Indeed, we regard inspiration itself as a historical phenomenon. Historical phenomenon means: God establishes communication with certain persons in certain places at certain times so that they become active as he intends. Or should the statement that "men spoke . . . as they were moved by the Holy Spirit" (2Pe 1:21) be understood as something "unhistorical"?

We unfold this starting point as we now consider the variegated nature of the steps of inspiration. For we are dealing with diversity and variegation, as the *polutropōs* (in various ways) of Hebrews 1:1 decisively indicates: "God spoke . . . at many times and in various ways."

In a few eras of the history of interpretation, it was emphasized that the Bible was dictated. The dictation theory reigned e.g., for Augustine[260] and in old Protestant Scholasticism, indeed up to the time of Mosheim (1694–1755). Concepts and turns of phrase like "divinitus esse dictum" ("What is given from God has been dictated"— Augustine), "omnia dictata sunt" ("all is dictated"—Hollaz), "verbatim dictata" ("literally dictated"—Hutter), and "auctorem et dictatorem illius esse Deum" ("God is the ultimate source, the one who dictated, of every [Scripture]"—Schröder), are characteristic here.[261] Yet the desire shows itself repeatedly to avoid a mechanical doctrine of inspiration.[262] Thus for Flacius there was plenty of room for recognizing that Mark had read Matthew, Luke had read Mark and Matthew, and John all three Synoptic Gospels.[263] We observe this same striving to establish distance from a mechanical doctrine of inspiration in modern scholarly fundamentalism.[264] This warns us against polemical oversimplification.

In reacting to Protestant Scholasticism's dictation theory, some went so far as to declare the theory as "heresy."[265] This, too, is a path we decline to follow.

We must rather conduct a careful test. Such a test will show that by no means all of the Bible is dictated. There are, however, individual sections that prove to be products of divine dictation. This applies, e.g., to the Sinaitic Covenant Law in the narrower sense (Ex 34:27f.), the Song of Moses (Dt 31:14ff.), the letters to the seven churches in Revelation, or to Isaiah 8:1.

Dictation is to be distinguished from the command to write. Such a command indicates that something is to be written but avoids dictation that is written down word for word. Commands to write include, e.g., God's instruction to Moses after the battle with the Amalekites (Ex 17:14 NIV): "Write this on a scroll as something to be remembered. . . ." Also, Jeremiah 36 and Revelation go back to commands to write (Jer 36:1f., 27f.; Rev 1:11). Under the command to write, freedom of word choice is preserved.

Precisely these last-named examples, however, show right at the outset how complicated the matter of inspiration is. If John is to write what he sees, then this command implicates the hearing, seeing, and writing down using his own choice of words. This all extends itself over a considerable period of time. Not until completion of the entire book is the goal of the command in Revelation 1:11 attained (cf. Rev 22:18f.). If inspiration is not to be arbitrarily limited to special "paralogical" (irrational) factors or the like, then it must be in effect at least till the goal in writing has been reached. At the same time we observe that the act of writing things down presupposes at least a reflected, conscious effort on the part of John.

Still more variegated is the process lying behind Jeremiah 36. The prophet hears the word of the Lord (v. 1). It calls on him to prepare writing material, to write down his recollections of the words God previously spoke to him (v. 2: "from the time I began speaking to you in the reign of Josiah till now," NIV). The prophet springs into action, calling on his scribe Baruch and dictating to him. Later he discovers that the words Baruch records are destroyed (vv. 4, 23). At renewed divine behest a second document is prepared in a manner similar to the first. But there is a difference: "And many similar words were added to" the original words (v. 32). The document is, therefore, considerably expanded (cf. vv. 27-32). Not until completion of this collection of words could the Lord speak to posterity by the mouth of his prophet (cf. Lk 1:70; Heb 1:1f.; 2Pe 1:21). For later generations, for whose sake the document is designed (cf. 1Co 10:11), the completed collection under Jeremiah's name is as a whole God's word (cf. Da 9:2). Here they are addressed "from God" (2Pe 1:21!). To restrict inspiration to certain segments of the entire process would be, once more, arbitrary. Inspiration rather extends to the whole sequence right up to the final phase of a canonized writing. The comprehensive inclusiveness of this process as a whole also aptly illustrates the concept of "entire inspiration" that we have already touched on.

Apart from the command to write, there is the additional consideration that *God confirms the completed book of an author*. Isaiah and Daniel, e.g., are to hand down their writings to disciples, and to later generations, in secure fashion (Isa 8:16; Da 12:4). Here Daniel 12:4 is of special interest. For "the words of the scroll" spoken of there must be seen as applying to the whole of the book of Daniel as it existed at that time. In composing his treatise, Daniel presumably made use of the archives of the Neo-Babylonian and Persian empires.[266] In addition there were his own writings (7:1). Daniel 12:4 may possibly incorporate an Assyrian loanword that must be translated: "preserve the words and seal the book until the time of the end!" In any case it is to provide instruction and insight for later generations. Once more the concept of inspiration must be conceived of in broad terms. In the case of Daniel it encompasses the preservation of his own writings, the preservation of national archives, the discerning use of both in a reflected literary work, and the subsequent rise of the book of Daniel in its entirety. Not until the book's completion has inspiration attained its goal.

A restriction to a moment of enlightenment would be, therefore, purely arbitrary. To conclude otherwise would be to confuse *illuminatio* (illumination) and *inspiratio* (inspiration).[267] The use of the book of Daniel by Jesus and the apostles (Mt 24:15) shows that they regarded the entire book as inspired.

Let us now turn to the Luke's two volumes. His prologue (Lk

1:1–4) presents the most comprehensive account given by any biblical author regarding what lies behind his work. We have already devoted considerable attention to Luke (cf. section 2 above: "The Answer of Revelation"). Let us now determine what Luke has to teach us regarding the relation of inspiration and history. Luke emphasizes both #1) the historical reliability of what he reports and #2) the fact that his sources are the apostolic bearers of the Spirit ("servants of the word," Lk 1:2). That is, in his own way he binds historical investigation with divine inspiration. When the early church, invoking the idea of apostolicity, recognized the work of Luke, the student of Paul the apostle, as inspired Scripture, the die was cast under the leading of the Holy Spirit, so to speak, for seeing just this coalescence of historical investigation and divine inspiration as part of God's own intention. In Luke's case inspiration encompasses numerous stages and individual incidents and matters: the rise of sources (e.g., the "we" sections of Acts); the gathering of data, the comparison and assessment of these data (cf. *akribōs*, "carefully," "accurately," in Lk 1:3); the incorporation of sources; the editing of the work in its entirety; and so forth. We see, therefore, that sources and documents that were already complete and available to Luke are contained within the entirety of the revelatory phenomenon—even, of course, if the human creators of the sources were oblivious to how their work would later be put to use.

We select the next example to make clear that inspiration is to be distinguished from normativity. As little as inspiration is to be confused with illumination, just so little is inspiration to be confused with obligation. In 1 Corinthians 7 we find the case of Paul citing a saying of Jesus (v. 10). This dominical saying is both inspired (Jesus bears the Spirit!) as well as normative. Two verses later Paul issues orders in his own name ("I, not the Lord"; v. 12). As the context shows, this apostolic command is likewise inspired (cf. 1Co 7:40!) as well as normative. A few verses earlier, however, the apostle makes a "concession," which he sharply distinguishes from a "command" (v. 6; 2Co 8:8; Phm 8f.). Even this "concession" is inspired (1Co 7:40). By its very nature, however, it cannot be normative. Here, therefore, inspiration is seen to involve a certain latitude. We are dealing with biblical-inspired pastoral care which as such is not intended for use as a universal decree. A similar conclusion is in order regarding the "judgment" (*gnōmē*) that Paul expresses in verses 25 and 40 (cf. vv. 28, 36, 38).

The list of examples could be extended. This suffices, however, to show that inspiration entails a historical process in its entirety, the course of which is superintended by God in such a way that, in the end, there arises the word that is revelatory of God.

The "how" of this divine superintendence of history remains hidden from us. It is ultimately identical to the mystery of divine revelation itself. Dogmaticians of earlier times were well advised to forgo trying to explain the "how" of the "suggestio verborum."[268]

Nevertheless, it contradicts the character of the entire inspired process to detach individual elements from it or to attempt to qualify such elements as "human." Much can be classified as "unimportant" when judged from man's point of view. The tendency has shown itself repeatedly to deny this "unimportant" material any inspired status. This has been attempted, e.g., with respect to cosmological, historical, geographical, or chronological data that some regard as nonessential for salvation.[269] Such detachment or qualification, however, is damaging on two counts. First, it is an assault on the character of a history whose very self-presentation involves an entire nexus. Second, it is an assault on the character of inspiration, which makes use of the entire nexus and in fact itself comprises a historical process. Presumably it was not scurrility but insight into these matters that moved post-Reformation dogmaticians, in their disputes with Jesuits of their day, to extend dictation by the Holy Spirit even to that which the human writers knew prior to writing.[270] In any case they argued—quite rightly, in objective terms—using the context established by biblical statements, a context that is not to be torn to pieces and whose even apparently "unimportant" features offer aids to understanding.[271] They rightly repulsed a move toward inappropriate atomistic consideration and upheld that aspect of inspiration that involves its unified entirety.

Finally, we must still take up a special case that belongs on the one hand to the issue of inspiration and history, and on the other to the issue of God's word and man's word. The matter before us is form criticism. To put it more precisely, we must deal with the problem of human-collective activity in the rise of biblical revelation. Can a collective production be inspired? Can it serve as a messenger of God? When form-critical investigation of the Bible arose, somewhat critical judgments were made about the human authors. Wrede called the writers of the New Testament "quite subordinate entities."[272] For Wrede, the individual conceptions are generally less important than the "general type."[273] In addition to this, many form critics tended to explain the biblical writings in purely immanent fashion and to deny the significant involvement of a personal God. The "Instructio" of the papal Bible commission (1964) called for caution in the use of form criticism due to such philosophical, anti-individualistic, and antisupernatural tendencies.[274] Since then there have been a few significant changes. Unchanged, however, remain #1) close association with research into the transmission of folklore,[275] and #2) the "axiom" that the Synoptic Gospels are part of a larger body of folk or popular literature.[276]

It appears now that this very "axiom" needs reworking. Riesenfeld, Gerhardsson, Schürmann, Ellis, and Riesner see Jesus as the point of origination of the Gospel tradition. Rather than an "untamed stream,"[277] we are dealing with reflected and carefully protected tradition. The proverbial[278] "ditch" between Jesus and the Gospels is, therefore, beginning to close.[279] This is supported from the tendency to date the Gospels earlier.[280] Researchers like H. Schürmann, S. H. Travis, R. Riesner, or E. E. Ellis go a step farther. They take it as a serious possibility that certain traditions were already committed to writing before Jesus' crucifixion.[281] It becomes increasingly clear that "folk literature" or "folk tradition" is an ill-suited analogy for understanding the "sacred" tradition enshrined in the Gospels.[282] As far as the New Testament is concerned, therefore, the idea of a "creative collectivism" has lost its attractiveness. That does not mean, however, that we have no need to subject these matters to fundamental scrutiny.

There is need here as well to make careful distinctions. Where revelation itself justifies it, the idea of collective authorship presents no difficulties. E.g., the chronicles and archives that are used in the Bible (Daniel, Ezra, Esther, and others) go back to multiple authors or groups of authors. Then their work, too, is included in the entirety of the revelatory occurrence. The same goes for other sources used by biblical authors, such as travel diaries (Ac 16:11ff.). We cannot even exclude the possibility that Luke made use of group recollections, judging from Luke 1:3. The idea of collective activity as such cannot, therefore, simply be dismissed summarily for the entire span of Scripture's formation. Revelation does lay down, however, three clear guidelines: #1) The idea may not serve to nullify clear statements of Scripture that refer to a certain author, nor may it transfer responsibility for such a writing to a merely presumed collective entity. One may not, e.g., refer authorship of John's gospel or Paul's letters to a collective entity (cf. Jn 21:24; Ro 1:1; 1Ti 1:1; etc.). #2) The idea may not serve to turn biblical writings or parts of them into more or less "accidental" products of literary history and thereby call in question the inspired final form of the texts. The danger of such leveling comes to the fore, e.g., in W. Marxsen's remarks about synoptic exegesis, in which he opines that each stage of textual formation—which, in addition, must remain hypothetical—can be exegeted.[283] #3) The idea may not serve to present the messengers, to whom God entrusted the production of the texts' final form, as merely immanent-historical redactors or the like. From the purely immanent standpoint, W. Wrede may be right when he depicts the biblical writers as "quite subordinate entities."[284] Revelation, however, demands that these writers be regarded at the same time in their relation to the ultimate source of revelation—and that means as inspired authors (cf. Mt 23:34; Jn 20:21; Eph 2:20). It goes without saying that this also applies to cases in which the author remains unknown to us, as e.g., the book of Hebrews, or a few historical and wisdom books of the Old Testament.

## ERRORS OF SCRIPTURE?

Any sketch of a doctrine of inspiration must take up the question of possible errors in Scripture. The predominant conviction today is that Scripture has errors and that they are at least a grave liability for this doctrine.

The question of errors in Scripture did not first arise with the Enlightenment. It was posed first within the church itself. This is illustrated by comments in the so-called Muratorian Canon that seek to explain the origins of the various Gospels: "Though various ideas are taught in each of the Gospels, it makes no difference to the faith of believers, since in all of them all things are declared by one sovereign Spirit. . . ."[285] Study of the Bible itself, therefore, reveals a variety of expression that necessarily gives rise to the question of whether what one source says might bear correcting by another. Questions regarding errors were posed from the outside, too. The Gnostic Ptolemy (second century A.D.) observed contradictions between the Sermon on the Mount and the Pentateuch.[286] The pagan philosopher and writer Porphyry (d. ca. A.D. 304) sought to prove the book of Daniel guilty of historical inaccuracies.[287]

What response to these questions do we find in Christian tradition? Before the end of the first century we find Clement of Rome writing that "nothing incorrect or perverse is written" in the Holy Scriptures (1Cl 45:1ff.).[288] Justin (d. ca. A.D. 165) emphasized that Scripture is true and free of contradictions.[289] In dialogue with Trypho the Jew he states: "I am simply convinced that no scripture passage can contradict another one. I would rather admit that I do not understand what is being said."[290] Irenaeus infers Scripture's perfection from its inspiration.[291] Both Tertullian and Origen advocate the perfection, freedom from contradiction, and infallibility of the entire Bible.[292] Augustine devotes a separate work (*De consensu evangelistarum*) to the question of biblical contra-dictions. He comes to the result that "every form of error" is to be ruled out with regard to the Gospel accounts (2.12, 29).[293] He writes similarly in Epist. 82, 3, 24: "ut conscriptores earum nihil in eis omnino errasse, nihil fallaciter posuisse non dubitem" ("I have no doubt that the authors of those [Gospels] err in absolutely nothing they wrote, that they mis-represent nothing"). Augustine, therefore, mirrors the views found in early ecclesiastical writers and interpreters: Holy Scripture is without contradiction and error. It is historically true. The methodological ques-tion arises already at this point: did the early-church interpreters read the Bible less intensively or grasp it less adequately than modern criticism? Or why is it that they arrived at such results?

Luther, on the one hand, reckoned with "errors" in Scripture.[294] On the other hand, he could say: "Scripture is God's word, not the word of man, which lies; not an iota is there for nothing" (WA V, 184).[295] Also here Flacius thought in more unified fashion. Inspiration did not render the biblical authors sinless, but it rendered their doctrine inerrant.[296] Interestingly, however, in Flacius' view, only the apostles—not the dis-ciples of the apostles—are free of error in this manner, because only they are called by God.[297] Protestant Scholasticism, which F. Lau grants here a "great dogmatic achievement,"[298] expended much energy on fur-nishing a basis for the inerrancy of the Bible.[299] A. Calov (1612–86) for-mulated the correct doctrine as follows: "Nullus error, vel in leviculis, nullus memoriae lapsus nedum mendacium ullum locum habere potent in universa Scriptura S" ("No error, even in entirely insignificant mat-ters; no error of memory nor miniscule lie, can have a place in the entirety of Holy Scripture").[300] Yet the Devil or wicked people whose speech is recorded in Scripture are naturally not inerrant.[301] Scripture contains no contradictions.[302] It must be recalled that Calov fought against Socinians and Catholics who held open the possibility of lapses in memory or even additional errors in Scripture. In view of the battle lines drawn at the time, Calov argued that if the Scripture errs at even one point, then the entire Scripture becomes unreliable.[303]

A certain tension is present in Bengel (1687–1752). On the one hand he sees the Evangelists as "without mistake or error."[304] On the other, he concedes, even apostles are subject to "mistakes of memory." He therefore agreed with the possibility of a lapse of memory. Yet the efficacy of the Scripture so overshadows these human mistakes that they do not jeopardize our assurance.[305]

Nowhere did the Enlightenment break so radically with Christian tradition as in the question of errors in the Bible. Jacques Le Brun stated that in the Enlightenment "secular knowledge and scientific methods" became "judges of the truth claims of the books of the Bible."[306] The orator Richard Simon (1637–1712), who shared many views with the Jesuits,[307] wrote the trailblazing *Histoire critique du Vieux Testament* (1687), which asserted that the Bible contains errors. In the foreword of his treatise he freely explained that he wished to deal a death blow to the Protestant Scripture principle.[308] He believed that the textual alterations he observed in biblical manuscripts "totally destroy the principle of Protestants and Socinians, who look solely to just these manuscripts."[309] In Reventlow's judgment[310] this is "the origin of a systematically pursued biblical criticism based on the spirit of the Enlightenment." It should not be forgotten that Simon could submit the Bible to such criticism because he presumed to have a superior vantage point in the tradition of the Catholic Church. Johann Salomo Semler (1725–91) republished Simon's *Histoire critique du Vieux Testament* and built his own work upon it.[311] The rationalism of the Enlightenment sidelined the conception of the inerrancy of the Bible in a comprehensive manner.[312] Some of what was claimed along this line, to be sure, strikes one as curious—e.g., John Craig of England calculated the end of the Bible's believability as the year A.D. 3144, because all that is in this world must pass away.[313]

The effects of this radical turn can be clarified best by following the development of salvation-historical, biblicistic, or otherwise "positive" theology. Here, as we saw in "The Range of Revelation" and "The Relation Between Word of God and Word of Man" above, inspiration was limited more and more to certain parts of the Bible. It was believed that the noninspired parts could certainly contain errors and mistakes. Thus, e.g., von Hofmann declared, "The Bible is something better than a book without errors."[314] He not only endorsed secondary interpolations in the text; he also identified contradictions in it (e.g., 1Co 10:8 with Nu 25:9; Ac 7:4 with Ex 11:32). He also accepted the presence of mistakes in the areas of cosmology, anthropology, psychology, and historiography.[315] An Erlangen contemporary, the dogmatician Fr. H. R. Frank (1827–94) held the view that the Bible was only infallible with respect to truths that are essential for salvation. No more can be said from the standpoint of theological science: "I do not wish to take responsibility for teaching a Christian that saving faith involves faith in the absolute inerrancy of Holy Scripture. . . ."[316] The view is also present that the divine provision for us is simply an errant Bible.[317] Even G. Schrenk argued in this direction when he wrote that "God himself" never intended verbal inspiration;[318] "repetitions, contradictions, gaps, and seams" in the biblical text are undeniable signs of the errancy of the Bible.[319]

This state of affairs meets various responses in our time. The range of solutions stretches from, say, B. S. Childs, who regards the Bible as the context sui generis through which the Holy Spirit worked,[320] to R. W. Jenson, who advises us to give up all theories of inspiration, inerrancy, and the like.[321]

This critical survey of history, which we can here only sketch, drives us to the question: Why did Christian tradition for about 1,700 years invest so much erudition in the task of upholding the view that the Bible is without error, if it is now just as clear that this errorlessness is nonexistent? Further, what is the truth?

The latter question becomes still sharper when one notes that segments of contemporary Christendom are very staunch advocates of an error-free Bible. They seek support in the complete reliability of the Word of God in the sense expressed in this bit of verse by Carl Bernhard Garve:

*My merciful Lord himself has spoken;*
*Should I twist the promise proffered?*
*N'er forsake me what he's offered:*
*His word's my never-failing token.*[322]

Charles Haddon Spurgeon, speaking at a pastor's conference in 1891 that was later dubbed his "spiritual will and last testament,"[323] called "the complete, verbal inspiration of Holy Scripture" a "fact, not a hypothesis." For him this involved the infallibility of the Bible: "If this book is not infallible, then where are we to find infallibility?"[324] To detractors he put the question, "Are these critics of the Scripture infallible?" "Is that which goes by the title 'science' infallible?"[325] Recent position statements of the Catholic Church still speak "of the complete inerrancy of the Holy Scripture."[326] It is well known that the "inerrancy" of Scripture maintains its long-standing status as a hermeneutical presupposition of scholarly fundamentalism.[327]

Once more we decline to issue a deductive answer to the questions raised. It is not permissible to argue: Because the Bible is God's word, and because God does not lie, the Bible is without error. We must rather base our answer on what revelation itself states.

Revelation ascribes primarily four attributes to the word of God. First, it is trustworthy. God's word "is right and true; he is faithful in all he does" (Ps 33:4 NIV). We can depend on it because what God says is "certain" (2Pe 1:19). Second, it is efficacious; God's word becomes accomplished deed. From the first page of the Bible the pattern is established: "He spoke, and it came to be; he commanded, and it stood firm" (Ps 33:9 NIV). Jesus emphasized this aspect when he indicated that "everything" in the law will be "accomplished" (Mt 5:18). Third, it uncovers God's will and thereby the way of salvation. It is redemptive instruction (*torah*). Accordingly, one can say with the psalmist that God's word "is a lamp to my feet and a light for my path" (Ps 119:105 NIV; cf. Pr 6:23; 2Pe 1:19). In it the divine wisdom manifests itself (Sirach 1:5, 24). Fourth, it is binding. As God's word it puts man under obligation. Obedience to it brings life, disobedience death (Dt 28:1ff.; 30:15ff.). Jesus states that also during the time of the new covenant, "the Scripture cannot be broken [annulled]" (Jn 10:35; cf. Mt 5:17f.).

We observe, therefore, that concepts like "inerrancy" or "infallibility" are not used in the Bible. Still less does it reflect on "errors" or the like. We need, therefore, first of all to subject our conceptual arsenal to critical scrutiny. It will prove advisable to use concepts that are as close to what revelation itself expresses—and that means what the Bible says—as possible. An example of such a concept: perfect trustworthiness.

It was just this perfect trustworthiness of Scripture that was lived and implemented in apostolic times. In his investigation of Paul's use of Scripture, Campenhausen arrived at the judgment, "No one can be more of a believer in Scripture than he was."[328] Why? Scripture "was for him the unerring, infallibly revealed 'word of God.'" Scripture is "absolutely true" in "all that it says."[329]

With this conception Paul stands in the mainstream of Judaism of his time. In *Contra Apionem* I, 38–41, Josephus submits that the Holy Scriptures of Israel are in themselves without contradiction, possessing full trustworthiness.[330] According to Longenecker, all Jewish interpreters of the first century held that the words of the Bible present "in fact the very words of God."[331]

If we take revelation's own cue and begin with the perfect trustworthiness of the written word of God, then we note that one aspect of this trustworthiness involves concern with and motion toward the way of salvation (see above). That is to say that the Bible has an overriding purpose that informs all it says. Inspiration in its historical entirety—in our terminology, entire inspiration—serves the purpose of our redemption. That forces us to the question: What is the purpose, then, of this or that individual scriptural statement? This insight is important for our understanding of revelation, as authorities representing many viewpoints have underscored.[332] Thus, e.g., one can infer from the context of Matthew 14:1–12 that Matthew 14:9 does not intend to instruct us about the legal definition of the position held by Herod Antipas. He is there called "king." Yet in Matthew 14:1 he is quite correctly referred to as "tetrarch." It is possible to describe the usage of "king" in verse 9 as "technically and objectively imprecise."[333] Perhaps Herod Antipas, corresponding to custom from the days of his father Herod the Great, was still styled "King" by the people. Be that as it may, it would be inappropriate to measure 14:9 with a juristic-technical yardstick, because to do so would be to miss the point of the purpose of the statement in its whole context. To cite another example: what Peter says in Matthew 16:22 is not divine but human (16:23). He speaks like a tool of Satan (cf. again 16:23). It would not occur to anyone to say: because Peter was wrong, the Bible contains mistakes. It is rather the visible purpose of Matthew 16:21ff. to lay bare the lack of understanding of Jesus' disciples at that time and to show how Jesus was tried by his companions. Early-church interpreters were already aware that where the Bible gives the words of evil persons, or even of the Devil himself, it cannot be assumed that what is said is free of error. Why? Because such an assumption would run counter to the clear purpose of the corresponding report. We see, then, that God's inspiring Spirit wished for statements of wicked persons to be taken up in the Bible, yet that such statements are not free of error or mistake. To put it quite sharply: such statements are inspired (= consciously taken up into written revelation), but not errorless.

It may appear hazardous to appeal to the goal-oriented nature of the Bible. Isn't it left, then, to every person's caprice to determine what the purpose of a statement is? Because of the importance of this question, we will devote an entire section to it below. For now let just this be said: if revelation itself and its recognizable purpose be observed, then the alleged or presumedly established errors in Scripture dwindle considerably.

The question of errors in Scripture must, however, be set forth from yet another fundamental point of view. We observe that errors are often debated only in the historical realm. The "historical," however, is only a subcategory of the cognitive understanding of revelation (see chap. 6,

"Cognitive Understanding"). Conversely, the question of errors does not even arise under the dynamic understanding of Scripture (see chap. 6, "Dynamic Understanding"), and the question is at most only remotely significant under the ethical understanding (see chap. 6, "Ethical Understanding"). The transforming and renewing power of the word proves itself without doubt and error in the ongoing history of the Christian community. The ethical understanding, as we underscored already (chap. 6, "Revelation as Starting Point"), occurs where a person lives in a positive relation to revelation and desires its application to his practical life. Even if he wavers as to which biblical command he ought to apply in a given case, or which he should apply first, he still presupposes that the biblical statements are correct. It turns out, then, that the "errors" in Scripture play a role only for the cognitive understanding.

Strangely, this fact has to my knowledge been largely overlooked in the literature on this subject. The logical consequences have not been drawn. Writers act as if it is a question of errors "of the Bible."[334] In reality we are dealing simply with errors for cognitive understanding, or errors that are pressed by cognitive understanding of revelation. Or to put it more sharply: the problems involve our *cognitio* (cognition), not our *oboedientia* (obedience) or our *conversio* (conversion).

What is the outcome? First, the Bible is without error in the areas of dynamic and ethical understanding.[335] Second, it is likewise without error in the area of cognitive understanding once we grasp the Bible in light of its divinely ordained purpose. These two affirmations are not claims to be able to explain all that is in the Bible. They are also not claims that there are no tensions or insoluble questions for our understanding, or that we ought to approach such questions blindly or dishonestly. These affirmations rather make allowance for the fact that in spite of the Holy Spirit's aid we can err in understanding. Difficulties remain. Ongoing debate must be joined regarding the true purposes of Scripture. These affirmations seek, in sum, to assert that we must proceed from the basis of what revelation itself expresses, and that revelation furnishes us with a twofold mandate at this point:

1. The enscripturated word of God is perfectly trustworthy and without error in the sense of its divinely intended purpose, or we might say, looked at from God's point of view.

2. The human interpreter must let revelation say what revelation itself wishes to express. He may not subordinate it to his own demands and wring from it (historical or other) data that it never intended to provide. The demand of the interpreter becomes arrogance when it places itself at the same level as revelation. To recall Luther's memorable formulation: "the apostles and prophets occupy the place of authority, while we listen at their feet. We hear what they have to say. We do not say what they have to hear."[336]

# CHAPTER EIGHT

# The Canon

## THE HISTORY OF THE CANON

What are the writings that make up inspired Scripture? In reply to this question the church sets forth the "canon," i.e., the normative list of biblical books.[1]

In order to arrive at an answer for ourselves it is necessary to be reminded of some events in history.

As Leiman has shown, the Torah (books of Moses) and Prophets of the Old Testament were accepted as normative by "ca. 500–450" B.C.[2]

The precise time of completion and acceptance of the third division of the Old Testament, the *ketubim* ("Writings"), is disputed. In critical circles it was long accepted that this step was not taken until about A.D. 100. Reference was made to the so-called Council of Jamnia, said to have taken place about A.D. 90.[3] Now we know that there was probably some kind of academy in Jamnia at the time in question, but there was no such "synod" or "council" as earlier believed. Furthermore, there were no binding decisions made there concerning the extent of the (Old Testament) canon.[4]

The sources point in another direction. Josephus writes at the end of the first century A.D.: "We do not have ten thousand books, all of them contradicting and battling against each other, but only twenty-two. . . ."[5] This claim is not to be explained (away) facilely as "school tradition"[6] or regarded as simply incorrect.[7] If we take Josephus at his word here, he clearly intends to present the conception of Judaism as a whole at that time.[8] The twenty-two books of which he speaks are probably: five books of Moses; thirteen prophetic books (Joshua, Judges-Ruth, Samuel, Kings, Isaiah, Jeremiah-Lamentations, Ezekiel, Minor Prophets, Job, Daniel, Ezra-Nehemiah, Chronicles, Esther); four additional books (Psalms, Proverbs, Ecclesiastes, Song of Solomon).[9]

The New Testament never cites those parts of the Greek Old Testament (LXX) that extend beyond the Hebrew canon.[10] This fact can only support Josephus's claim.

It appears that the New Testament writers took as their basis the same Old Testament canon as Josephus and other Jews[11] of the New Testament era (cf. Mt 23:35; Lk 24:44).[12] When 4 Ezra 14:44–46 gives the number of Old Testament books as twenty-four, it is likely that Ruth and Lamentations are being reckoned as independent books. In this case 4 Ezra 14:44ff. testifies to a canon having the same proportions as Josephus's.[13] On the other hand, the prologue to Sirach reveals that already at that time a third division of the biblical books existed alongside the Law and Prophets.[14] The book of Sirach itself found no acceptance within the Hebrew canon. It arose about 175 B.C.[15] In sum, Leiman is surely correct in dating the recognition of the "Writings," and thereby the recognition of the entire Hebrew canon, in the first half of the second century B.C. at the latest.[16]

The New Testament canon as we know it today stood established in the second half of the fourth century A.D. Two events were decisive: Athanasius' thirty-ninth festal Easter missive for the Eastern church (A.D. 367), the Roman synod under Damasus for the Western church (A.D. 382). Subsequent synodal decrees merely enacted and confirmed these events. However: the process of canonization was already underway in New Testament times.[17] The book of Revelation views itself as a canonical writing from the outset.[18] Pedersen correctly views Colossians

4:16 and 2 Peter 3:15f. as early evidence of the canonization process.[19] The last-named passage indicates that already at the time of 2 Peter a Pauline corpus existed, the extent of which was known among the churches. Canon formation can be traced in the writings of the apostolic fathers.[20] The basic contours of the New Testament canon were complete at around A.D. 200. According to Zahn it included the four Gospels, thirteen Pauline letters, Acts, the book of Revelation, 1 Peter, 1 John, and perhaps 2 and 3 John and Jude.[21] Yet this protocanon had open boundaries. I.e., the status of individual writings remained disputed because of dogmatic or other considerations, of which today we have only partial knowledge.[22] Surprisingly, these open boundaries did not seem to be a great source of unrest in the early church.[23] In any case, the determinations of canon already mentioned above (A.D. 367 and 382) are, as to its character, an acknowledgment of what already prevailed in the church. They were not new definitions of what the canon comprised. Aland's verdict is apt: "The church as such, itself a product of divine authorship, did not create the canon; it acknowledged the canon that had been created."[24]

The difference between the Catholic and the Jewish canon in the area of the Old Testament forms a special problem. As is well known, on April 8, 1546, the Catholic Church at the Council of Trent acknowledged as canonical the books of Tobit, Judith, 1 and 2 Maccabees, Wisdom of Solomon, Sirach, and Baruch. The books are absent from the Hebrew Bible. The Catholic Bible also contains additions to Esther and Daniel that considerably exceed the text of those books in the Hebrew version. These additions are explicable given the acceptance of the Greek Bible (Septuagint) by the early church.[25] But this acceptance was never formalized until Trent. Cajetan, Luther's Catholic discussion partner and opponent, still regarded the Old Testament Apocrypha with reserve, feeling it could not be used to decide doctrinal questions.[26] The Reformation churches wavered back and forth concerning the scope of inspired Scripture. They doubted least their overall position relative to the Old Testament. They went back to the Hebrew canon and excluded the expansions of the LXX as "apocryphal," by which they meant not divinely inspired. In addition, Eusebius's influence moved Luther to separate Hebrews, James, Jude, and Revelation from the regular canon of the New Testament in the so-called September Bible of 1522. Luther himself based this separation, first, on church-historical grounds: these books had "been seen quite differently long ago."[27] Second, as to their content, Luther claimed that they did not measure up to the standard of "preaching and promoting Christ."[28] After 1530 Luther revoked the separation of these books. Yet Lutheran orthodoxy accorded them secondary rank, as they had been characterized as "antilegomena" (disputed) in antiquity. Johann Gerhard called them deuterocanonical or "canonicos Novi Test. libros secundi ordinis."[29] Chemnitz regarded as deuterocanonical books the following: Hebrews, 2 Peter, 2 and 3 John, James, Jude, and Revelation.[30] As late as the mid-nineteenth century Philippi called these same books "deuterocanonical writings" and "norma normata (having secondary authority in comparison with known canonical writings)."[31] The uncertainty of the Lutheran tradition also shows up in the absence of lists of biblical writings in the various confessional statements, which settled for definitions that left a certain amount of latitude. Thus, e.g., the Confessio Virtembergica of 1522 stated: "We call Holy Scripture those canonical books of the Old and New Testaments whose validity in the church was never in doubt."[32]

Among Reformed churches the situation was a bit different. Calvin clung to the New Testament canon in its modern form.[33] Reformed bodies produced lists of the canonical books, e.g., in the Confessio Gallicana of 1559 (art. 2), in the Confessio Belgica of 1561 (art. 5), and in the Westminster Confession of 1647 (chaps. 1, 2).[34]

The Enlightenment shook the concept of canon more and more. Theologians shifted their argument away from Protestant Scholasticism's stress on usage in church history. Instead they centered on the content of the writings. This is seen already in Hugo Grotius' annotations to the New Testament (1650).[35] In J. S. Semler's investigations into the history of the canon (1771–75) the issue emerged sharply.[36]

Strangely, the consequences, which would necessarily have led to the dissolution of the canon, were not drawn. True, there are occasionally judgments with formal similarity to Luther's approach. An example is Schleiermacher's rejection of the book of Revelation: "I cannot hold that the Apocalypse is canonical, because it contains too little religious material."[37] On the other hand, the old distinction between proto- and deuterocanonical persists right down to Nitzsch-Stephan's dogmatics textbook (1912; see p. 291). Critical researchers could declare that Jude, James, 2 Peter, Ephesians, and the Pastoral Epistles are no better than the extrabiblical apostolic fathers.[38] And yet a consensus arose that the canon decisions of the early church were all in all not so hopelessly mistaken, and that it was not desirable to alter the transmitted, factually given canon.[39] To put it another way: there remained a pragmatic canon.[40] This has to a large degree shaped discourse on the problem right down to the present in Protestantism.

Can we, however, be content with a pragmatic basis?

## THE FOUNDING OF THE CANON

We are constrained, then, to take up the question just raised regarding the proper basis for the canon. Not until that is settled can we deliberate on the original question, the extent of the canon.

The attempt has been made to base canonicity "on the witness and inner assurance of the Holy Spirit." This is how the Confessio Gallicana of 1559 put it (part 4).[41] Behind this confession stands Calvin. In his *Institutes* he built "on the inner conviction of the Holy Spirit."[42] This "inner witness of the Holy Spirit" (*Testimonium Sancti Spiritus internum*) should not be overhastily dismissed as "subjective." For in it the spiritual experience of the church in the most various times and places comes to light. It is accordingly a transsubjective element. And yet the inner testimony of the Spirit is an occurrence that takes place precisely in the realm of the church, and therefore it is disputed just as other spiritual experiences are.[43]

Another attempt to establish a basis for canonicity has turned to the idea of inspiration: canonical means that which is inspired. This was the path taken, e.g., in Lutheran dogmatics of the seventeenth century.[44] The Westminster Confession (1647) argues similarly: books that are "not . . . of divine inspiration" are "no part of the canon of the Scripture" (chaps. 1, 3). Certainly the inspired Scripture is congruent with the canonical books insofar as—as we have already noted—the entirety of the Scripture we have before us is inspired. It remains an open question at the outset, however, whether there are not also inspired writings that did not make it into the canon. If the epistle to the Laodiceans, e.g., which Colossians 4:16 mentions, were discovered, we would surely have to regard it as inspired. But would we also have to make room for it in the canon? In any case there is the possibility that the concepts "canonical" and "inspired" are not congruent.[45] But that means that further explanation must be furnished to clarify what canonicity comprises.

A third means used to try to give a basis for canonicity involves the core content of the Scriptures. An example here is found in Luther's statements in the September Testament of 1522. The "acid test" of canonicity is the question whether the books in question "promote Christ or not." Luther separated canonicity from the authors of the writings, stating in pointed terms: "What does not teach Christ is not apostolic, even if St. Peter or St. Paul teaches it. Again, what does teach Christ is apostolic, even if Judas, Ananias, Pilate and Herod say it."[46] If the principle is applied consistently, then #1) the meaning of "what promotes Christ" must be defined, and #2) sufficient criteria must be established to determine which contents of the Bible correspond to this definition. But this would be throwing open the door to a quite subjective appraisal.

On the other hand, one can throw out criteria based on content—which ultimately rest on subjective decisions!—and relate canonicity to certain persons. The status of apostolicity has been used in this way. As is well known, the early church accepted as canonical that which was generally viewed as having come from an apostle or the disciple of an apostle.[47] To the extent that Reformation churches harked back to the early church,[48] apostolicity remained also for them a determinative consideration. Yet there are Scriptures whose apostolicity is disputed, e.g., Hebrews.[49]

There have been other attempts to give objective foundation to canonicity. An example would be the essay by H. Ridderbos, who seeks to ground canon in the reality of salvation history.[50]

## REVELATION AS STARTING POINT

In this book so far we have consistently made revelation itself our point of departure. That appears to be impossible in this case. For we possess no "Koran," no overarching and higher-level source of authority, that would define the New Testament for us. Are we then caught in circular reasoning when we seek a basis for the canon which makes it possible to *delimit enscripturated revelation*—and then attempt to argue based on the revelation that has not yet been delimited?

We should not give up a revelatory starting point here prematurely. It might indeed turn out that the books that we find, in fact, already present in the Bible contain references, guidelines, or promises for delimiting revelation. If so, then it is primarily revelation that offers possibilities for determining the extent of the canon. In this sense we see ourselves "actually referred back to Scripture itself for answering the question of what is canonical."[51]

Now, there can be no doubt that revelation understands itself as a *fundamentally closed entity*. When Joshua is commanded to proceed according to the Law "in all things," and is at the same time warned "to turn neither to the right nor the left" of what the Law says (Jos 1:7f.), then it is clear that the Torah is complete and unalterable (cf. also Dt 4:2; Mal 3:22). It is just as clear that for the New Testament writers, the Holy Scriptures of the Old Testament were a closed entity that could not be expanded or reduced at will (cf. Mt 5:17ff.; 22:40; Lk 24:44f.; Jn 5:39; 10:35; 2Ti 3:16). In 2 Peter 3:15f. Paul's epistles are likewise spoken of as an entity that is in principle complete. In 2 Thessalonians 2:2 Paul himself spoke out against the danger of letters circulating falsely under his name. Jesus' words, too, have a definite scope, according to 1 Corinthians 7:10ff.[52] Finally, Hebrews 1:1f. states that God's revelation culminates definitively in the time of Jesus. What these and other observations amount to is this: biblical revelation arrives in its final form in the time of Jesus. It informs us that the history of revelation has now arrived at its goal. Its completion is found in the Messiah. That is, it clearly informs the church that further revelations are not to be expected, though that which was given earlier should remain in force. Basically then, the church is charged with the task of determining and accepting a canon.

Along with the knowledge that biblical revelation is to be viewed as a closed entity, there is a second consideration. *In the New Testament that will becomes visible which vouchsafes the doctrine of the apostles and thereby also the doctrine of Jesus for all future times.*[53] "They remained in the apostles' doctrine" (Ac 2:42)—that line from Luke's account of apostolic times is practically a motto of church history. John takes pains to protect the message of the apostles against divergences and heresies (cf. Jn 21:23; 1Jn 2:18ff.; 4:1ff.; 2Jn 9; Rev 22:18f.). Paul pronounces a curse on those who preach a gospel different from the one he proclaimed and passed along (Gal 1:18; 2:2; 1Co 15:1ff., 11). Here the apostles could rest on the promise of Jesus that the Spirit would "lead them into all truth" (Jn 16:13). To be a teacher, i.e., to pass along the true teaching, was a distinctive *charisma* (gift) from the Holy Spirit (Ro 12:7; 1Co 12:28; Eph 4:11). In short: the New Testament intends to uphold the doctrine of Jesus and the Spirit-led apostles as the norm for all times. This too suggests a canon whose very purpose is to delimit what belongs to this doctrine.

Further, we already noted that inspiration comprises an entire occurrence that extends to the point of enscripturation. What confronts mankind, however, in the form of Scripture is not speech bereft of context or interconnection. *The various parts of revelation stand in a tem-*

*poral and material connection*—most of all when their relationship is direct. One such direct connection, e.g., is when a scripture is the fulfillment of a promise that was contained in an earlier scripture. It is one and the same Spirit who leads the human authors (2Pe 1:21). From this the question necessarily arises: which writings are to be counted as belonging to the interconnected whole of God's inspired revelation? The answer, again, can basically only be given through speaking in terms of a canon.

We conclude that revelation itself pushes inexorably in the direction of a canon. The church did nothing wrong but rather fulfilled one of the tasks that revelation set before it when it determined the canon of Holy Scripture. The only thing that revelation itself left open was: what is the ultimate compass that this canon should have?

## DELIMITING THE CANON

How could a definitive delimitation of the canon ever have been arrived at? The decision process entailed both "subjective" and "objective" elements. Revelation, and with it the divine originator of it, intended for there to be a canon. Canonization formed, we might say, the final stage of inspiration. This is, so to speak, the more "objective" side of the occurrence. The inner witness of the Spirit then moved the church to recognition of the canonicity of the writings in question. This is, so to speak, the more "subjective" side of the occurrence.

It remains important that the church "did not create the canon; it recognized the canon that had been created," as K. Aland puts it.[54] "To that extent the decision to canonize is not so much a decision but rather simply an act of declaration."[55] In the church's decision-making process, therefore, the conviction is expressed that revelation encounters us in this ensemble of writings. The canon is not a product of the church[56] but a product of the same divine Spirit who brought forth the various individual writings.

On the human, "subjective" side it is most of all the "apostolic" heritage of the New Testament writings (apostolicity) that plays a leading role. Here apostolicity is tantamount to inspiration. If apostolicity is restricted to a strictly historical understanding, i.e., those who belonged to the circle of the Twelve and Paul including their disciples, then difficulties may arise. We have seen this, e.g., in the case of the book of Hebrews. If apostolicity, however, is broadened to connote the special sending and inspiration that God conferred on the biblical authors, then the argument from apostolicity maintains its biblical justification. It can adduce the fact that Jesus wished to be identified with his disciples: "He who listens to you listens to me" (Lk 10:16 NIV).

On the other hand, application of alleged "material criteria" (e.g., "what promotes Christ") in the canon question is a dead-end street. This would presuppose that one already knows what revelation is. It ends in the subjectivism of very different criteria. And it leads necessarily to a "canon within the canon," about which we will speak further below.

Let us attempt once more to glimpse the entire event of the canonization of the biblical books. It presents itself to us as a process flowing forth from God, driven forward by revelation, and finally brought to completion under the leading of the Spirit. In that it is bound to revelation itself, the process is prevented from being handed over to the subjectivity of the persons involved. The foundational and overarching reality is the "divine superintendence," of which Flacius spoke long ago.[57] Without this providence of God the rise of the canon is inexplicable.[58]

## QUESTIONING THE CANON

Today the canon is called into question from two sides.

First, some attempt to expand the Protestant canon. Starting with the concept of an interconnected history of tradition, e.g., H. Gese wishes to make the unity of the Old and New Testaments visible once more using the Apocrypha that lies historically between them. He expressly states that "the reformation church did not promote a unified view of biblical tradition by culling the Apocrypha out of the corpus of inspired Scripture."[59] We should, therefore, follow the Catholic Church in recognizing the Old Testament Apocrypha as canonical books. A. C. Sundberg argues along similar lines.[60]

What should we say to this? It must first be admitted that this proposal brings us into something of a difficult position. We are not able to speak, as K. Barth did, of the "church" which in this case "determined," "discovered," or "heard" something.[61] For the testimony of the church is split into Roman Catholic and Protestant versions. The question may be raised, however, whether God's revelation in the more limited Protestant canon has not spawned spiritual rebirth, founded church bodies, and made people certain of their salvation. If the answer is yes—and it must be, judged from centuries-long, transsubjective experience—then there is no reason for enlarging the Protestant canon. The unity of both testaments can be recognized and presented even without the "history of tradition" as proposed by Gese and Sundberg. On the other hand, expanding the canon through the Apocrypha à la the Roman Catholic Church does not necessarily have to be undone. It would, however, be advisable for all Christians to grasp the conception that the apocryphal books are to be read only under the standard of the other, unquestionably canonical books (norma normata). To reiterate: the "inner" boundary of the canon is fixed. It consists in the minimal canon of the Reformed churches. This canon does not admit of further reduction. The "outer" boundary, on the other hand, is not fixed. That is, until further developments the question remains open to what extent use may be made of the Apocrypha. What is debatable, then, is only the question of expansion, not of reduction.

A second assault on the canon comes from those who wish to call its validity into question without altering its external form. This occurs through a so-called canon within the canon.

The concept "canon within the canon" occurs first in Schleiermacher.[62] The undertaking that he describes is typical of Enlightenment thinking. True, the attempt has been made to discover a "canon in the canon" already with Luther.[63] Lönning rightly points out, however, that this is reading a later controversy into Luther's work.[64] Luther's *canon-critical* judgments are limited to those writings that appeared questionable to him on *canon-historical* grounds. For the other writings, however, he seeks principles of interpretation that comprehend the entirety of Scripture and do not limit this entirety to certain "strata" or the like. The same can be said for Flacius. For him Paul was "the unrivalled hero and scholar of Scripture," especially in Romans and Galatians.[65] He openly commits himself, therefore, to a Pauline interpretation of Scripture. Yet Flacius remains committed to the unity of the canon.[66] What unites Luther and Flacius is this: #1) Like all other interpreters they operate with a de facto "canon within the canon." #2) But this "canon within the canon" serves to open up the whole unified canon. #3) The de facto canon is, therefore, an interpretive and not delimiting principle![67]

The situation alters fundamentally with the rise of the Enlightenment and the historical-critical method. Now Scripture is combed for the binding-eternal universal that will free us from the temporal and particular. The binding-eternal, however, is the "canon within the canon." The forms of determining it are various. Hofmann, e.g., distanced himself from the attempt to use doctrinal principles as a means of differentiation. He spoke instead of a "state of affairs" in Scripture that would furnish an internal plumb line. He describes it as "the relationship between God and mankind mediated by Jesus."[68] Hofmann does not succeed, however, in furnishing clear grounds by which to determine what belongs to this "saving truth" and what does not.[69] Instead of the sort of dogmatic definition that Hofmann used, one could try historical definitions. One such possibility would be, e.g., to separate what is "authentic" from what is "inauthentic." Where, however, would there be any secure ground here? As S. Pedersen stated, we must assume "that from the first stage of the tradition there was the possibility that either objective errors crept in or that the bearers of the tradition . . . gave" a different "form" to what they passed along.[70] Or are there "material criteria" of an interdisciplinary nature that make possible a distinction between "essential and non-essential, central and peripheral, important and unimportant . . ."?[71] If so, which criteria? Blank says, "There is no getting past the difference between time-conditioned expressions and the abidingly valid." One must postulate a "hierarchy of truths."[72] We find ourselves, then, in a peculiar situation that on the one hand demands a "canon within the canon," yet on the other hand offers no help with the question of how to arrive at one. Instead of an illuminating procedure that produces convincing insights based on revelation, we meet rather subjective judgments such as: "In this matter I see the pauline-reformation proclamation of justification as the truly central interpretation of the word of God."[73] How little is to be gained from such theories is shown in the examples of H. Küng and P. Lengsfeld.[74] Or in the present setting ought one simply give up any concrete working-out of a "canon within the canon" and regard the task rather as an essential process, a program of continual truth seeking? I. Lönning appears to move in this direction when he says the matter should "not be settled once for all by a theological formula," though there is a "theological necessity" for such a program.[75] F. Hesse strikes out once more in another direction. For him the canon in the canon exists first in the New Testament: "The New Testament is norma normans. . . . The Old Testament . . . norma normata."[76] But then he makes the qualification: "Of course one can basically describe the New Testament too only as norma normata. For the actual and final norm, the norma normans in the strictest sense, is the Gospel of Jesus Christ." The New Testament, he continues, is after all not unified.[77] Yet this confronts us once more with a question: what is, then, this "Gospel of Jesus Christ" in concrete terms? In the end F. Hesse too fails to lead us out of the dilemma of difficulties.

In view of the two-hundred-year search for a "canon within the canon" that will convince everyone on all sides, we are today in a position to strike a balance. We see that the search was in vain. The contributing factors have been rehearsed repeatedly elsewhere.[78] Let us cite them now once more in brief.

From the standpoint of tradition-historical continuity, a "canon within the canon" defies the basic principle of such a tradition history. "It is ridiculous, tradition-historically speaking," says H. Gese, "to labor at identifying a so-called 'canon within the canon'—a concept that totally contradicts the essence of the idea of a canon. Apart from the fact that to make such a choice is to indulge theological prejudice, it also misunderstands the Bible's historical character as it comes in view through the history of revelation, the progressive unfolding of truth. The tradition-historical approach to arriving at a 'canon within the canon' approach absolutizes traditions that seek to be understood only in the most minute relations and dependencies to other traditions."[79] The same could be said from a salvation-historical standpoint.[80] Again the "canon within the canon" idea is subject to the charge of arbitrariness. It has, indeed, not succeeded at achieving a general consensus. All the proposals that have been made betray the subjective preference of the scholars who made them.[81] Further, we observe that the end effect is an attenuation of the biblical contents. Only what belongs to a given selected "canon within the canon" may be listened to and pondered without reservation.[82] To this should be added that having a "canon within the canon" mutilates the continuity of Christian history. For the early church knew of no such thing,[83] and the modern church does not accept it.[84] We can only conclude that revelation itself contains absolutely no indications that would permit us a "canon within the canon."

The undertaking of arriving at a "canon within the canon" must, therefore, be abandoned.

## THE CANONICAL CONNECTION OF INTERPRETATION

If the canon is consistent with revelation, then the interpretation we engage in must be connected to this canon.

This connection has a twofold consequence. First, it forbids us to treat texts outside the canon as if they stood on the same level as texts within. We have seen in the case of the Old Testament Apocrypha that such a procedure causes problems. In any case it is impossible to dissolve the Old Testament, New Testament, or both together into a general history of religions (Religionsgeschichte).[85]

Connection to the canon, then, means that the final form of the text is normative. What revelation intends to convey is precisely what, in fact, it does say in this inspired final form. The focus for understanding revelation is not a more or less hypothetically reconstructed earlier tradition or an "Ur-Markus" (a theoretical earlier form of Mark's gospel which some claim existed) or the like. While there may be plausible and historically interesting arguments for such documents, they are documents that God has seen fit to reject. They are not ordained to mediate a redemptive encounter with God to us in this *preliminary* form. They are not that around which the church gathers. To that extent it is not "inappropriate," not "unscientific," but rather quite appropriate if the church wishes to have little to do with them.[86]

We find concern for such a "canonical" interpretation advocated emphatically in recent times by Brevard S. Childs and others under the rubric of "canonical shape."[87] For Childs this means that we understand the Old Testament as "canonical scripture," which in turn means most of all that we place biblical expressions within the context that the canon furnishes. It also means that we understand the canon in its entirety in light of its embeddedness within the fellowship of faith.[88] Even if Childs' conceptions are not always balanced, this is still certainly a step in the right direction.[89]

# CHAPTER NINE

# The Authority of Scripture

## THE QUESTION OF THE BASIS FOR SCRIPTURAL AUTHORITY

There are *very different ways of furnishing a basis* for the authority of Scripture. According to W. Schadewaldt, Scripture has "the scent of truth" about it.[1] Others point to the human necessity of possessing a "bedrock of truth." "Thinking persons seek a secure foundation for faith."[2]

Yet can the thinking person of modern times come to grips with an authority that lies outside himself? K. Scholder has established that since Descartes' *Discours de la méthode* . . . (1637), "the thinking 'I' has moved to the center of the universe." As a consequence, reason has "nothing on which to base itself except for itself alone."[3] This confidence in human reason has, however, sustained such hefty blows in recent decades that it can no longer bear the load it once did. The same can be said of reason viewed as only relatively, as opposed to absolutely, binding. C. G. Jung makes this clear:

> In a pensive mode the intellect may arrive at the con-
> clusion that there is no truth. When, however, a per-
> son loses his money, it is lost, and that is as true as
> an absolute truth, and no intellectual pensiveness
> can mollify that person. There is such a thing as a
> convincing truth, but we have lost sight of it. And it
> is most of all to our frivolous intellect that we owe
> thanks for this.[4]

Presupposing, however, that we are inclined to accord to the Bible
the status of "convincing truth" and to that extent authority, then this
conviction can quite readily be combined with other authorities. We are
faced, therefore, with the subsequent question of whether the Bible is
the only, absolutely final authority in matters of Christian doctrine. The
Enlightenment tradition replies in the negative. It consciously abolished
the view that Holy Scripture is unique.[5] From that point on it matters little whether one continues to claim some degree of authority or privilege
for Scripture.[6] The only decisive consideration is what and how many
authorities make claims that rival the Bible's own in depth and scope.

This leads once more to the question of how one establishes the
authority of Scripture. Because this question relates quite closely, however, to views of the number and relationship of Christian norms, we first
consider these views and the various normative authorities they suggest.

## NORMATIVE AUTHORITIES ALONG WITH SCRIPTURE

1. To the present hour, Roman Catholicism supplements Scripture
by means of the church's teaching office. True, highest authority is
claimed for Scripture. But in that the interpretation of Scripture is a
function of the teaching office, a de facto authority of high effectiveness
and importance is erected next to the Bible. One of the most essential
statements of Vatican II runs: "All that pertains to the form by which
Scripture is explained is subject ultimately to the judgment of the

Church (Ecclesiae iudicio ultime subsunt), whose God-given commission and ministry it is to preserve and interpret the word of God."[7]

There is no need to belabor the point here that the Reformation church, obligated to the principle of *sola scriptura*, rejected such a teaching office. This does not affect recognition that understanding and interpreting Scripture are actually tasks of the community of believers. For now we also leave open the question—which we will take up later—of the extent to which Scripture's authority ought to be derived from the church.

2. Rejection of the Roman Catholic teaching office, however, sharpens the question whether comparable parabiblical authorities were not created by Protestants. One thinks of Martin Kähler's famous expression "papacy of scholars," a reference to what develops when the Bible's authority is spurned.[8]

"The radical Enlightenment's criticism of revelation" reached its first high point with Baruch Spinoza.[9] His *Tractatus theologico-politicus* (1670) criticized the prejudice that "reason must subordinate itself to the reason-transcending revelation that is laid down in Scripture."[10] Once the freedom and superiority of human reason is established in this fashion, however, "the criticism of revelation truly" becomes the "presupposition of scientific investigation of the Bible."[11] This is what G. Ebeling has called the "proclamation of reason as h.[ermeneutical] norm."[12] In other words: the Catholic teaching office has been replaced over time in Protestant circles by reason and a reification of what is "scientific"—the exact nature of which is disputed. This has taken various individual forms. For Harnack and Gunkel, e.g., history acquires the character of a norm alongside of Scripture.[13] In extreme cases historical interest has caused the "abiding normative sense of Scripture for all times" to be overlooked[14] or the normativity of Scripture to be entirely rejected.[15] "Scientific thought" is a similar authority that can confer relevance to the present on biblical expressions—or deny them this relevance. Thus W. R. Harper, the head of the Chicago school at the beginning of the twentieth century, felt himself obligated to two authorities: #1) Scripture, and #2) "scientific investigation."[16] Occasionally the concept of "scientific thought" is expanded or modified by appeal to the "modern consciousness,"[17] "consciousness of truth,"[18] "historical reason,"[19] or the like. These establish the frame of reference within which biblical statements are made to fit. U. Wilckens illustrates this approach in the following formulation: "A scientifically responsible interpretation of the Bible can be claimed only for that investigation of the biblical texts which [works] under methodologically consistent application of historical reason."[20] It is evident that this "modern consciousness" occasionally combines with moral categories. Two examples along this line are Shailer Mathews and Rudolf Bultmann. Mathews accords "equal respect" to both the "sanctity" of the Bible and "intellectual integrity."[21] Such an interpretation, therefore, is again responsible to two authorities. Bultmann places no less emphasis on the moral components of this responsibility. He sees himself bound to a "command of veracity which mandates that I hold nothing to be true that stands in contradiction to truths that are the factual presupposition of my . . . understanding of the world."[22] Veracity and modern understanding of the world are here ethical and intellectual presuppositions that combine to form a second authority alongside the Scripture. This authority is acknowledged even in very moderate forms of critical theology. An example would be H. E. Weber, who states that interpretation of Scripture occurs "when there is informed application of the assured results of historical-critical investigation of the Bible."[23]

3. We said earlier that even in more recent Protestant theology a second authority alongside of Scripture has emerged. We now need to mention a second and contrary development related to this.

Not all talk of reason amounts to the establishing of a second authority alongside of Scripture. E.g., Wiclif and Luther appealed to "scriptura vel ratio" ("Scripture or reason") in the conviction that both are ultimately identical.[24] As the Reformation progressed Luther clearly placed Scripture over reason. Its authority is unique and incomparable; it is the final norm: "The first principles of Christians, then, should be nothing other than the divine words."[25] Like Bengel later on, Luther favored the Bible in the dispute between secular historians and Scripture.[26] For Francke's or Bengel's scholarly Pietism there is absolutely no question that Holy Scripture comprises the highest, sole, and unconditionally valid authority.[27] Pietism still champions this view today.[28] Even moderately critical biblicists like H. E. Weber battled against the "modern world-view" becoming normative alongside of Scripture.[29] Karl Barth went so far as to call for "subjection to the Bible."[30]

One cannot say that the debate over Scripture's authority, or the norms that inform the interpreter, has arrived at its destination or is over. The question remains open. On the one side are those who maintain that we cannot undo post-Enlightenment developments: we must rather subject ourselves to historical criticism.[31] On the other side are those who see things in flux and tend to affirm the uniqueness of biblical authority. To this latter group belongs, e.g., E. H. Amberg, who states—his purview limited, it is true, to the time prior to World War I—that "the problem of the authority of Scripture has given dogmatics no rest."[32] With respect to this problem dogmatics has yet to find rest right down to the present.

We will now consider a few possible ways of furnishing a basis for the authority of Scripture.

## POSSIBLE BASES FOR THE AUTHORITY OF SCRIPTURE

1. Certain *attributes of Scripture* have often been adduced as grounds for its authority. This was already the case with Josephus as he defended the Jews' sacred writings over against those of other peoples. He appealed, e.g., to the absence of contradiction and the gift of prophecy in the Old Testament.[33]

A further example would be Melanchthon's *testimonia*. Miracles, the antiquity of Scripture, its superiority to pagan teaching, the inner witness of the Spirit, the martyrs, the preservation of the church, and the punishing of the enemies of the Gospel establish the authority of Scripture.[34] Still more comprehensive is the catalog of arguments in M. Flacius. He sees all the following as speaking in favor of the authority of Scripture: the divine author, the apostles and prophets, miracles and attesting signs, antiquity, simplicity, freedom from contradictions, reasonableness, confirmation through history (e.g., the triumph of the Reformation), fulfillment of promises, the grim end met by infidels and apostates, and the inner witness of the Spirit.[35] Protestant Scholasticism follows this line in using similar criteria.[36]

These arguments should not be facilely rejected. Some of them, e.g., the connection of promise and fulfillment, cannot be attested in any similar manner in all of world literature, whether judged from the standpoint of quantity, or quality, or both. Still, others are less certain, among them age, miracles, lack of contradiction, and so on, and even prophecy. In principle these can also be found elsewhere, even among false prophets. Consequently, they may be prized as significant indicators, but not built upon as sure foundations.

2. Some appeal to the *"powerful redemptive effect"* of Scripture.[37] Here the focus is on how Scripture leads to faith, gives assurance of salvation, and in general empowers the community whose trust is in Jesus Christ. This argument is meaningful to the extent that it sheds light on the *factual* authority of Scripture in its practical manifestation. But again it must be said: effects can be interpreted in various ways. The justification for Scripture's authority cannot be decided in this fashion.

3. From the opposite direction come those who appeal to the *church as the origin of Scripture*. Lutz argues for this view along two lines. On the one hand he maintains that Scripture must be explained by Scripture "because it is God's word." On the other hand he states that "the Scripture did not form the church; rather the latter existed prior to Scripture."[38] Lutz's second statement is put even more sharply by Reinhold Seeberg, who poses the question: "Who would ever think of reading this book [i.e., the Bible] devotionally if its authority had not been transmitted to him by the Christian community?"[39] From here it is

only a short step to the Catholic conception that all dealings with the Bible whatsoever are governed by the Spirit-led teaching office of the church.[40] In that case it is, in fact, the fellowship of believers that guarantees the Bible's authority. That is, the Bible's authority becomes derivative, even if not intentionally.

This view that appeals to the church as the basis for Scripture's authority exists in a slightly different form among those who derive the Bible from the productivity of faith. James Barr argues in this direction; typically, he voices praise of the Catholic conception.[41]

4. The attempt has been made repeatedly to employ *Christian experience* as a basis for the authority of Scripture. This undertaking can be traced at various levels and in different schools of thought. According to D. F. Strauss, e.g., it is a Protestant principle "not to permit oneself to believe anything in advance, but rather to believe only that which one experiences personally within."[42] Formulated positively: what one experiences personally within is trustworthy and receives normative validity. K. Girgensohn in his outline of dogmatics places "Christian experience" next to Holy Scripture and church confession as a source of dogmatics.[43] We find similar moves among existential interpreters. Thus Trillhaas states that the Protestant faith rests "on contemporary encounter with the word." To this encounter "belongs on the one hand the dynamic individual whom the word confronts, and [on the other] the dynamic 'particular' word, the 'text' which touches us, as it is released from all connections except for the solely important one: the contemporaneity in time with me myself."[44] The mystery of this "dynamic" decides, therefore, what becomes binding word for me. With respect to what this dynamic leaves no room for, or where it is simply inadequate, there can be no talk of either bewilderment or scriptural authority. The outcome of all this is that the person must become the foundation of the authority of Scripture.[45] Now it is true that experience is valuable—as a *witness* to the authority of Scripture. But it is no less true that it is grandly unsuited to serve as this authority's *foundation*.

5. Can Scripture's *material content* (*Sachgehalt*) serve as the

ground for its authority? W. Elert has argued for this.[46] In his view "only the material content of Scripture" can "make it authoritative for us" (p. 170). He believes that in this move he emulates Luther. In fact, a number of Luther scholars say that Luther, in contrast to biblicism, understood the authority of Scripture in "material" and not "formal" terms.[47] What does this mean? It is not the Bible as such, as a book, primary source, or the like, that possesses authority, but rather its content, which overwhelms us and which we acknowledge as valid. Such an approach, however, presupposes that man is capable of recognizing and deferring to authoritative content as such. The approach thus rests on the prior knowledge and competence of man. It differs from an approach based on "experience" or "practical knowledge" in that it is more intellectually and argumentatively oriented.[48] The nature of this material content of which Elert speaks comes to the fore most sharply when there is need to bring the truth of Scripture and the truth of reason together. Thus, e.g., for Mosheim sin became irrationality; he attempted to lead persons to faith through proofs and reasons.[49] We said earlier that Mosheim is an extreme example. But he indicates the direction in which a "material" basis for scriptural authority leads. As important as the rational comprehension of Scripture's content is, just so little can the confirmation of this content through man serve to ground Scripture's authority. Reason is always at war. It cannot transmit the certainty that befits a genuine authority.

6. Basing the authority of Scripture on its *divine initiator* is a decisive step beyond the foundations explored thus far. Here Calvin comes first of all to mind. "The decisive ground for the authority of Scripture" is for him "that it is God who speaks there" ("Summa scripturae probatio a Dei loquentis persona sumitur").[50] Here it is no longer necessary to make the authority of Scripture depend on man. This authority rather rests in something extrinsic to us (*extra nos*) which can furnish certainty.

Calvin was not the only one to argue along this line. We find similar reflections much earlier in Tertullian.[51] Reformed and Lutheran Scholasticism follow the same path.[52] Calov calls Scripture the "very word of God" ("ipsissimum Dei verbum") and infers its authority from that fact.[53] For Gerhard and Hafenreffer the Scripture is a "letter from heaven" ("epistola coelestis").[54] From then on the analogy of a divine epistle remains an important element in establishing Scripture's authority; this may be seen in Spener and Bengel, among others.[55] In the heyday of Protestant Scholasticism the term *auctoritas causativa* was used, meaning the authority that is rooted in God who initiates and sustains it.[56] We could point to parallel statements from Catholic theologians.[57]

It makes no essential difference[58] if one speaks generally of the Divine Initiator/Author, or draws more particularly on inspiration as a basis. When, e.g., Dannhauer writes: "auctoritatem habet a theopneusei" ("[Scripture] derives authority from *theopneustos* [divine inspiration]"),[59] then he is saying that God speaks in the Bible, and this occurrence confers authority on the Bible.

Yet where do we get our knowledge that God is the originator of Scripture? To pose this simple question is at the same time to put a finger on a weak point of the argumentation just above. It is striking that none other than Calvin draws very strongly "on the hidden witness of the Spirit" ("testimonium spiritus sancti internum").[60] "The same Spirit, therefore, who spoke by the mouth of the prophets must pierce our hearts and makes us aware that they faithfully and accurately conveyed what God entrusted to them" (Inst I, 7, 4). But isn't this again to make man—not the natural, but the regenerate, yet still *man*—into the attesting authority of revelation's authority? Calvin and his successors largely neutralized this objection with a second line of argument that took the self-attesting quality of the Bible as its starting point. "Holy Scripture possesses its confirmation within itself, and its authority is not to be based on rational deductions but rather asserts itself by means of the Holy Spirit," says the *Institutes* (I, 7, 5).[61] This second line of argument frees Scripture from all human certification ("it would be a perverse starting point to want to urge the sure trustworthiness of the Bible on someone through disputation," I, 7, 4) and instead binds the Spirit's witness to the dynamic, transforming power of Scripture.[62]

7. In fact we cannot derive from either the "witness" of a spiritual person or from a pious-rational a priori that God is the originator of Scripture. We can only derive this from Scripture itself. So we come finally to the basis for scriptural authority in revelation itself.

## THE BASIS OF THE AUTHORITY OF SCRIPTURE
## IN REVELATION

Once more, then, we begin here with revelation itself. We do this not in isolation but in agreement with others who share the same conviction: "The authority of the Bible must . . . find its justification in the Bible itself."[63] We must "take our stand on the ground of the objective revelation of God."[64] Precisely here Luther's thesis must prove itself; he held that Scripture by itself is the ultimate source of certainty as "it proves, judges and illumines the words of all" (omnium omnia probens).[65]

1. In this regard Jesus' handling of the Old Testament is of central importance.[66] This handling is described by many as critical. Abraham claims that Jesus broke the Law; to an extent he uttered a no to the Old Testament. As a whole, the New Testament shows only the "traditional Jewish respect" for the Old Testament, nothing more.[67] Barr champions the same position.[68] Somewhat more cautious is P. Stuhlmacher,[69] who, however, likewise can speak of a "criticizing giant step" that Jesus took "beyond the wording of the Old Testament command."[70] The passages, however, that are supposed to typify Jesus' "critique" do not yield this picture. Mark 10:1ff./Matthew 19:1ff. are neither a break with the Law nor an "objection to Moses," but rather messianic unfolding of the original will of God. This will as expressed in Deuteronomy 24 is still circumscribed by its redemptive-pedagogical intent (see Gal 3:24); its full obligatory impact is made clear to man with the Messiah's advent.[71] In Mark 7:1ff./Matthew 15:1ff. Jesus does not oppose the Mosaic Torah but rather the Halacha (legal traditions) of the Pharisees. Still less can the Sermon on the Mount be cited to show an alleged critique of the Old Testament by Jesus. His messianic-divine "But I say to you" assumes as

its basis and starting point nothing other than the Mosaic Law. And once more Jesus unfolds the true will of God, which came to expression in the Old Testament only partially and in preparatory fashion (Gal 3:24), and presents it in its full compass (cf. Mt 5:17). Unfolding and application, therefore, not "antithesis,"[72] describe Jesus' relation to the so-called Old Testament.[73]

It is characteristic that Abraham, in order to justify his position at all, must represent Jesus as speaking ad hominem in John 10:35.[74] The overall context of the Gospels teaches us something different. For Jesus, as for his Jewish discussion partners, Scripture was the last court of appeal. Therefore, and only therefore, Jesus argued many times based on Scripture. "Have you not read?" "You know the commandments . . ." "What do you think about the Christ?" "If you believed Moses, you would believe me." "Is it not written . . . ?" These and similar turns of phrase are typical in discussion settings (cf. Mt 12:3ff.; Mk 10:19; Mt 22:42; Jn 5:46; 10:34). A lawbreaker could never have posed the question, "Which one of you can convict me of sin?" (Jn 8:46). Even the rankest chicanery would not have allowed the disciples of the Pharisees to say to a scofflaw rabbi: "You teach the way of God rightly" (Mt 22:16). Jesus' words should be taken seriously: "Do not think that I have come to set aside [katalusai] the Law or the Prophets" (Mt 5:17). This comports well with John 10:35: "The Scripture cannot be broken" (luthēnai). Jesus trusts the power of every letter of Scripture to be fulfilled, right down to the smallest part of the tiniest Hebrew letter (Mt 5:18). Genesis 2:24 and Exodus 3:6 are interpreted by him in a manner that presupposes literal and historical validity (Mt 19:4ff.; 22:31f.). Enough examples: there can just be no doubt that in Jesus' eyes the Holy Scriptures were accorded an incomparable authority. Anyone who finds "criticism" of the Old Testament by Jesus must turn things upside down to do so.

How can this authority be delineated more precisely? In Scripture the Creator and Father speaks (Mt 19:4f.; Jn 10:34ff.). His will is obligatory for Jesus and his disciples (Lk 24:44ff.). Moses and the prophets are mediators but not the originators of the Holy Scriptures (Jn 5:37ff.; 6:32f.). The Father illuminated the human authors by his Spirit (Mt 22:43). It is the Father who wills the fulfillment of the Scriptures (Mt 5:17; 26:39, 56), who has placed the power for fulfillment within it (Mt 5:18), and who opposes every human reduction or alteration of his will (Mt 5:19f.). Every human Halacha (oral legal tradition) and interpretation must defer to the clear wording of Scripture (Mk 7:9ff.). The true content of Scripture, however, is unfolded by Jesus as the Messiah and Son of God, who is even "Lord of the Sabbath" (Mk 2:28).

Certainly: Jesus' authority as the living Son of God is a higher authority than that of Scripture. To that extent it is Christologically justified that we see the fullness first of the New Testament and then read the Old in light of the New. Yet it is still the case that precisely this Messiah and Son of God attests to the reliability of the Scripture and gives this Scripture to us so that we might orient ourselves by what it says.[75] In that his statements and finally the entire Gospel of his words and deeds become Scripture[76] and "Scripture" thereby reaches its entirety, he encounters us today in it in trustworthy fashion. The living Christ, like the Father, has bound himself to the word of revelation and thereby makes good the promise of John 16:13 and Luke 10:16. This makes a well-known statement from Reformation times exegetically untenable: "If however the opponents press Scripture over against Christ, then we press Christ over against Scripture."[77] Only as a paradox of the impossible is the statement meaningful. For Jesus' praxis and doctrine do not permit us to pit Scripture and Christ against each other as opposites. On the contrary, Scripture is the gift and word of the crucified and exalted Christ who still makes people his disciples.

Biblical revelation's unique authority consists in its normative transmission of the word of the triune God. In any case, that is the claim that revelation itself makes. No other document, occurrence, or authority can occupy a position at its side.

2. What we have observed with respect to Jesus applies also to the rest of the New Testament. Characteristically, the two phrases "God

says" and "Scripture says" are interchangeable with each other (cf. Ro 9:15, 17).[78] God himself is the originator of Scripture and speaks in Scripture to us. It is he who "in various ways spoke through the prophets." It is he who "has spoken to us in these last days through his Son" (Heb 1:1f.). The epistle to the Hebrews, by placing the prophets and the Son, former times and the present, alongside each other, points to the basic principle of the Christian Bible, the principle that binds Old and New Testament together and unites them into a new unity. This unity is rooted in the *one* person who here makes his word known: God. Because he addresses us in Scripture, creating a living encounter, the formula "Scripture says" can justifiably be used (cf. Ro 4:3; Gal 4:30; 1Ti 5:18). The Scriptures of the so-called Old Testament and the words of the Lord Jesus are ultimate authorities and the foundation for claims and argument in the writings of Paul, Peter, John, and Hebrews (cf. 1Co 7:10ff.; 9:8ff.; 10:11; 1Pe 1:16; 2:21; 4:14; 2Pe 1:16ff.; 1Jn 1:1ff.; 3:5, 12, 17; Heb 1:5ff.; 2:1ff.; 3:1ff.; etc.).[79] Scripture comes about at God's prompting. True, it is men who write, but they speak "from God" (*apo theou*) and are "moved by the Holy Spirit" (2Ti 3:16; 2Pe 1:21). Already in 2 Peter 1:12–15[80] and 2 Peter 3:15[81] we can see that Petrine and Pauline doctrinal traditions themselves are regarded as Scripture. They accordingly partake of the authority of God-effected revelation.

3. Let us summarize the statements of revelation concerning the authority of Scripture. Our starting point has been that the final basis of this authority can only come about through biblical revelation itself.

Revelation claims to have issued forth from God's Spirit. This revelation, in the context furnished by both Old and New Testaments, is God's address to us. Whoever hears it is hearing first of all not the human authors and witnesses to faith but rather the triune God. Nowhere else can such a trustworthy and adequate message from this God be found. As unique speech from God, it has a unique, incomparable authority. God has bound himself to this word. He has determined that it is the location where he will encounter us. He will vindicate and fulfill this word in every way. The authority of Scripture is, fundamentally, the personal authority of the God who encounters us there.

It is just as possible to reject this claim of revelation as it is to affirm it. To affirm it is likely to call forth the objections that have echoed repeatedly since 1525 to protest a theology of *sola scriptura:* the Bible is being made a paper pope; "word idolaters," "Biblicists," "Scripturalists," "word-lackeys" are allegedly pursuing their evil ends.[82] In modern times philosophical idealism's disdain for the book—in contrast to the "living spirit"—may also play a role. Thus Wellhausen thought that the lamentable aspect of Josiah's reform was that "he based it on a book" (p. 135). Similarly, James Barr despises every "scriptural religion" (pp. 10ff.). For Wellhausen it is a negative outcome of Israelite history that "the people of the sacred word" were changed "into a people of the sacred writing."[83] Contra Wellhausen, however, Scripture is living word as well as "sacred word." It cannot be cast aside by men as a dead letter; it rather remains a means of encounter, a dynamic instrument of God in his search for persons. Therefore, it is important that we recognize its authority as the personal authority of the God who encounters us in it.

## EXTENT AND CONSEQUENCES OF THE AUTHORITY OF SCRIPTURE

### SCRIPTURE AS SOLE *NORMA NORMANS* (NORMATIVE STANDARD)

It has become clear that enscripturated revelation according to its own claims is the highest and ultimate authority, the highest and only normative standard for the fellowship of Jesus Christ. In other words: it is our sole *norma normans* (normative standard).

The Formula of Concord (1577) was right, therefore, in affirming: "Credimus, confitemur et docemus unicam regulam et normam, secundum quam omnia dogmata omnesque doctores aestimari et iudicari oporteat, nullam omnino aliam esse quam prophetica et apostolica scripta cum Veteris tum Novi Testamenti" ("We believe, confess, and teach that the only rule and norm according to which all doctrines and all church teachers ought to be evaluated and judged is nothing other than the prophetic and apostolic writings of the Old and New Testament").[84] Reformed confessions say nothing different. At this point, according to O. Weber, there are "no differences among Protestants."[85] Weber continues, "It is clear enough that here every other norm outside of Scripture is excluded. The Protestant church exists only where this exclusivity of the biblical witness reigns."[86]

A second authority, one in competition with the Bible or even restricting it, is accordingly excluded. This applies, e.g., to reason as it came to be lifted up as the rule for interpretation during the Enlightenment. According to Joh. Franz Buddeus, revelation could contain nothing that went against the doctrines of natural theology. Thus for him "reason is the authority in the light of which the truths of revelation must prove themselves."[87] The same move inevitably comes about in the later "historical-critically oriented scientific" theology that thinks it "is the ultimate judge in the battle over the meaning of Scripture."[88] The profile of a second authority comes into sharp focus in G. Ebeling's seminal article of 1950. He maintains that we are "obligated" "to do theology and interpret Scripture with the means, and in light of the problems, of modernity." Essential here is the "understanding of reality" that "the spirit of the modern age has adopted." The church "is not permitted" to "tamper with" this.[89] That is, a second authority in the form of historical-critical science is itself untouchable, but it "permits" itself and its intellectual presuppositions to place restrictions on the Bible and "tamper with" it. Like many others, E. B. Redlich also comes to the result: "The sound conclusions of modern science must be accepted and recognised."[90] We refrain from reciting further examples so as not to repeat what we have already said in part two of this chapter ("Normative Authorities Along with Scripture"). It should only be underscored that in erecting a second authority there is the tendency to abandon the *norma normans* and the authority of Scripture. Therefore we must abide by the principle that biblical revelation is "sole rule and standard."

## OUR OBEDIENCE AS THE GOAL OF SCRIPTURE

If we take it seriously that God has made Scripture the locus of encounter with him, and that Scripture's authority is rooted in the personal authority of the God who speaks, then an intellectualized acknowledgment of Scripture will not suffice. The goal of Scripture lies rather in our obedience. Just as Paul in his oral proclamation wished to establish the "obedience of faith" (Ro 1:5; 10:3), indeed as Christ himself seeks the obedience of the nations (Ro 15:18), so does enscripturated revelation seek the comprehensive trust and obedience of persons who are internally vanquished. True, this internal vanquished state comes, as Ricoeur has nicely put it, through a "nonviolent appeal."[91] True as well that in this state objections, doubts, and even complaints against God may have their place. To that extent revelation has the character of a conversation. Still: one can only speak of an actual "authority" of Scripture when from it flow obedience and grateful service to God.

To that extent scriptural authority and obedience are integrally linked. Dogmaticians of bygone years saw that clearly.[92] Especially instructive in this respect are Calvin's comments. He emphasizes that "the knowledge of God does not rest on cold thoughts. Such knowledge rather gives rise to the veneration he deserves."[93] The internally vanquished hearer of revelation ascertains "with full certainty that Holy Scripture, even if by human agency, has come to us from God's own mouth. In Scripture we see God himself standing before us, contemporary with us. We do not seek proofs or probabilities upon which we might rest our judgment, but we subordinate our judgment and our thinking to an incontrovertibly certain fact."[94] It was practical obedience, comprehensive and responsive to God's word, that animated not only Protestant orthodoxy but also the champions of scholarly Pietism. They saw points at which Scripture was subject to attack just as clearly as the approaching rationalism did. But because the authority that works through Scripture led them to obedience and grateful confession, the way they handled Scripture at its vulnerable points was entirely different. This comes out sharply in, e.g., Bengel when he would "rather do violence to secular history" than to Scripture in the event that "Scripture and history" contradict.[95] This is not a case of superficial *sacrificium intellectus* (sacrifice of intellect). For Bengel it is rather a matter of the choice that Scripture generates between a *praeiudicium auctoritatis propriae* (prejudice of one's own authority) and a *praeiudicium auctoritatis alienae* (prejudice of an alien authority, i.e., God's authority).[96] Here is a stark either-or. From the point of view of authority a decision must be reached wholly one way or the other.

## THE PERSPICUITY OF SCRIPTURE

The authority of Scripture cannot be maintained apart from reflection on its perspicuity. This matter too was comprehensively addressed in the age of the Reformation and Protestant Scholasticism. It is well known that Luther advocated with special emphasis the thesis of Scripture's clarity (*claritas scripturae*).[97] Two aspects of this issue must be distinguished. On the one hand the issue involves the internal and the external clarity of Scripture. The external, the understanding of the words, is accessible to every person. The internal "is resident in the knowledge of the heart" and is granted only by the Holy Spirit.[98] On the other hand the issue involves the comprehensibleness and unambiguousness of Scripture that are available to every Christian. It is most of all K. Holl who has brought out this second aspect. Without the "unambiguousness of the Bible" it would not be possible for someone to conform himself to it. Holl quotes Luther: "if however it is conceded that Scripture does not insist on one simple sense, it becomes an utterly ineffective weapon."[99] That is the point at which Luther and Schlatter agree. The insistence on the unambiguousness of Scripture is for Luther of a piece with emphasis on the literal sense; he refers to "the holy writer and speaker who is in heaven and on earth so that his words might have no more than one basic meaning."[100] The authority of Scripture can, practically speaking, prevail only if every plain Christian is in a position to gain a clear concept of Scripture's content. Here of course the knowledge of the languages is included as soon as questions arise concerning the meaning of the original text.

Against Jesuits and Socinians, Protestant Scholasticism defended the perspicuity of Scripture.[101] The former upheld the obscurity of Scripture in the sense that it required the interpretation of the church to give it clarity.[102] Against this, Lutheran dogmaticians took the position that the content of Scripture "is accessible to the understanding of every single person."[103] What about the undeniably difficult passages of Scripture, however?[104] Protestant Scholasticism answered first that everything necessary for salvation is clear (Quenstedt: "in illis quae ad salutem creditu sunt necessaria, clara est et perspicua" ["in those things which are necessary to be believed for salvation, Scripture is clear and perspicuous"]).[105] Here it was possible to appeal, e.g., to Augustine.[106] The second answer was that difficult passages were to be explained with reference to clear passages ("secundum analogiam fidei" ["according to the analogy of faith"]).[107] Here is where the Reformation interpretive principle that Scripture must be explained by Scripture ("scriptura sui ipsius interpres") proved itself.[108] Thomas Aquinas supported this view.[109] A third answer involved the attempt to explain the sense of obscure passages hermeneutically. Flacius thought that not God but man in his blindness was at fault in obscure passages.[110] A modern example of this approach is found in F. Pieper: difficult passages "serve to make us study Scripture all the more zealously as God's word, marveling worshipfully at the exalted majesty of him whose hidden heavenly wisdom shows up our spiritual ignorance, while in the bright and clear passages he points us the way to eternal life" (p. 156f.). We should, however, exercise caution at this point. All too quickly our explanations become ecclesiastical rationalism or verge on speculation.

It is more important to hark to the clarity of Scripture regarding revelation itself. It speaks of a message that is accessible to every person: "Now what I am commanding you today is not too difficult for you or beyond your reach. It is not up in heaven, so that you have to ask, 'Who will ascend into heaven to get it and proclaim it to us so we may obey it?' Nor is it beyond the sea, so that you have to ask, 'Who will cross the sea to get it and proclaim it to us so we may obey it?' No, the word is very near you; it is in your mouth and in your heart so you may obey it" (Dt 30:11–14 NIV). That Paul builds on this oracle (Ro 10:6ff.) only underscores the weight of this Old Testament declaration. Micah presupposes that God's message is generally understandable and unambiguous (6:8). Jesus could repeatedly pose the question, "Have you not read . . . ?" (Mt 12:3, 5; cf. 9:13; 24:14) only because he was convinced of the clarity of Holy Scripture. He himself formulated his statements in pedagogically reflected and easily remembered fashion in order to assure that their content would be grasped and his words retained.[111] Where doubts arose regarding Jesus' messiahship and the redemptive messianic event, the early Christians referred to the Scripture (cf. Jn 5:39; Ac 17:11). To summarize: enscripturated revelation maintains that it is accessible and sufficiently clear for every person to understand. True, it links comprehensive understanding and existential transformation to the gift of the Holy Spirit. But philological understanding and the essential content lie open to every person. The Christian community itself requires no special class of people "in the know" who alone are competent to open up Scripture's meaning to the rest. Therefore, we abide by the principle of the perspicuity of Scripture in the double sense alluded to above.

The protest against the perspicuity of Scripture has traditionally come from three quarters: from Gnosticism, from the champions of the Catholic teaching office, and from historical-critical theologians. The last-named group is abundantly aware that the principle "sacra scriptura sui ipsius interpres" (Sacred Scripture is its own interpreter) is only possible if (verbal) inspiration is presupposed.[112] But this will be taken up more fully later.

## SCRIPTURE SUFFICES FOR SALVATION

The authority of the Bible can be seriously maintained only if it is adequate for salvation. If other revelations were necessary to lead us into fellowship with God, then Scripture would have only relative authority. In no case could it then be regarded as *norma normans* (normative standard).

It is clear that especially the churches of the Reformation took keen interest in the matter of so-called *sufficienta* (sufficiency). They championed, after all, the motto *sola scriptura*. At the center of their concern stood the opposite affirmation, the principle of tradition of Tridentine Catholicism. The Roman church at the Council of Trent affirmed its commitment to treat Scripture *and* church tradition "pari pietatis affectu et reverentia" ("with an equal affection of piety and reverence").[113] There are, to be sure, precedents for this, such as Vincent of Lérins (d. fifth century).[114] But we also find lines of development of a quite different nature. Thus, e.g., Tertullian affirms the sufficiency of Scripture ("sufficit sibi").[115] So then, the Council of Trent marked the high point of the "tradition principle"; the counterpart to this was the "Scripture principle" of Protestant Scholasticism, the rejection of according extrabiblical tradition such lofty status.[116]

Protestant thinkers were conscious of the limits imposed on this position by the Scripture's central purpose. It sufficed for salvation. But it obviously possessed gaps that do not deal so directly with salvation. Calvin spoke of Scripture as a "school of the Holy Spirit, in which nothing is left out that is necessary and useful to know, and also nothing taught but what is expedient to know."[117] The "gaps" (lacunae) of Scripture extend in two directions: #1) Scripture is no "encyclopedia of general human knowledge" (Pieper, p. 151), and #2) "Scripture also does not reveal all spiritual matters" (ibid., p. 152).

Once again we inquire concerning the statements of revelation itself. Scripture is given to us "for deliverance" (*sotēria*, 2Ti 3:16). It serves the purpose of making us "people of God" (2Ti 3:16). It is light that shows us how to find God and then how to live in fellowship with him (Ps 119:105; 2Pe 1:19). Jesus himself is light, way, truth, and life, so that we may come to the Father through him (Jn 14:6). The Word is meant to bring us to an eschatological destination (Heb 2:1ff.). The divine Word is to be preserved as a witness for the world and as an essential binding tie to God till he one day judges the world (Rev 3:8ff.; 13:10; 14:12). In fact, everything centers around the concept "deliverance," "salvation" (*sotēria*). Holy Scripture is, then, according to its own statements a book with an expressed purpose. But that is not all: Hebrews 1:1ff. makes it clear that subsequent to the first advent of the Son—of Jesus and his apostles—no new revelation is to be expected. But that means that, already by that time, everything necessary for salvation stood revealed. The sufficient amount and scope of the revelation passed along to us in the Bible (see above) has its counterpart in the completion of revelation in the apostolic age. To embrace post- or extra-biblical traditions as *essential supplements* to Scripture would amount to a correction of salvation history.

Positively, we should now say that the original text of Scripture is preserved in ample measure. If the text were hopelessly corrupt, then its authority would also be undermined. Dogmaticians in previous eras realized this, asserting more than proving the text's good condition.[118] Today we can calmly state that the Bible is the most soundly attested book of antiquity. The Dead Sea Scrolls, e.g., as a whole demonstrate the stability of the Old Testament text. True, evaluation of the Septuagint is still an open problem. Yet the New Testament, in spite of its piecemeal preservation among more than six thousand handwritten documents, has turned out to be substantially unaltered from its original form.[119]

O. Weber rightly points out that there is also a "Protestant analogy to the (Roman Catholic) tradition principle." He discovers such a principle in Schleiermacher, who defined the church based on the "common spirit" that prevails within it, a spirit which finds "the same faith" in the Scripture as in the church. Here "the validity of Scripture" is made "dependent on faith."[120] Actually, in Schleiermacher the danger arises that the understanding of Scripture will become dependent on another entity, namely, the church, or the faith of the church. In that case, however, "there can finally be no more talk of the sufficiency of Scripture."[121] Beyond Weber's example, Scripture's sufficiency is also called in question where Scripture is subordinated to historical relativization or taken up as a self-contradictory witness to faith. In Girgensohn's experience, "for many the transition to radical historical contemplation of Scripture means at the same time the hopeless breakdown of any faith in the authority of Scripture."[122] This is relevant to the issue of Scripture's sufficiency in that Scripture alone no longer holds the answer to the question of what is required for the salvation of mankind. Rather, this answer must be found with the help of extrabiblical information. For this reason one should be cautious of speaking disparagingly of "the Bible's lowly form."[123] Others then too quickly become "lords" over this "lowly form." Where this leads can be seen, e.g., in the recent remarks of E. Grässer. He "refuses to tolerate a different governance" for modern-historical theology "than that which inheres in its own methodological principles. . . ." An understanding of the Bible is "absolutely impossible without content criticism [Sachkritik]."[124] Here, as in F. C. Baur, "the autonomy of the (human) subject"[125] has run its course. Here too there can simply be no more talk of a sufficiency of Scripture.

Against all these attempts to dissolve the sufficiency of Scripture in the sense of its determinative purpose, revelation itself maintains that it transmits to us all that is necessary for salvation. Its sufficiency is an indispensable consequence of its authority.

# CHAPTER TEN

# The Unity of Scripture

Today the notion is widely prevalent that biblical revelation exhibits *no* unity. Old and New Testament are said to be "everything but unified";[1] indeed, they "abound in contradictions."[2] This leads, on the one hand, to the rejection of "attempts at harmonization" and to disparagement of the "unfruitfulness" of such attempts.[3] On the other hand some go so far as to recommend a method of systematic dissent.[4] Rejection of Scripture's unity has made deep inroads as well into "positive" or "biblicistic" circles.[5] In this climate, anyone who advocates the unity of Scripture falls under suspicion of impermissible harmonization.

It was not always like this. The first ones to attack Scripture's unity, as far as we know, sallied forth from Gnosticism. Thus the Valentinian Ptolemy (second century A.D.) saw contradictions between the Sermon on the Mount and the Pentateuch.[6] Yet it was not until the Enlightenment, and in the years since, that the conviction of Scripture's unity was lost among many in Christian circles.[7]

## SURVEY OF CHURCH HISTORY

Let us once more sketch historical development in concise fashion:
Jewish interpreters of the first century A.D. were convinced of the unity of Scripture. Josephus made this a point of apologetic emphasis.[8]

For Philo it was a correlate of "the strictest verbal inspiration" and the multiple sense of every Scripture passage.[9]

The authors of the early church—with the exception of the Gnostics!—followed in the train of Jewish interpreters at this point.[10] According to Campenhausen, Justin Martyr presupposed the "seamless unity and freedom from contradiction of the divinely inspired Holy Scripture" (p. 120). Both Campenhausen and Chmiel quote from the *Dialog with Trypho* (65,2): "I am entirely convinced that no Scripture can contradict another, and I would admit rather that I do not understand what it says."[11] The situation is no different in Irenaeus, Tertullian, and Origen. "The indestructible unity and coherence of the Scriptures of the Old and New Testaments is the foundational biblical doctrine for Tertullian as for all the church fathers since Irenaeus in the battle against the Gnostics." Scripture's unity "was first seriously called in question with the advent of modern historical criticism."[12] Augustine defended the Gospels determinedly against the (pagan, Jewish, and heretical) objection that they contradict each other. In his *De consensu evangelistarum* (*On the Agreement of the Gospel Writers*) he calls this objection "the showpiece of their empty vanity" (1,7,10).[13]

Luther upheld the idea of Scripture's unity. His interpretive rule "was Christum treibet" ("what promotes Christ") is not a critical-historical principle of elimination but rather, as Scheel emphasizes, a religious principle of interpretation.[14] Kraus levels the charge against Calvin that he "was still bound and transfixed by a doctrinal mode of thinking based on the unity and harmony of Scripture."[15] The more that the Reformation took *sola scriptura* as its basis, the stronger its interest in the unity of Scripture had to be. That can be seen readily in Flacius and his Protestant Scholastic successors.[16] In this connection we note that already in Flacius the comparison between Scripture and an organism crops up, a comparison that would later be very important for Pietist interpreters.[17] For Bengel, Scripture is a perfect corpus.[18]

A break with the conception held earlier comes about with the Enlightenment. For Spinoza the Bible has lost its unity. It is contradictory, as can be seen e.g., from the opposition between Paul in Romans and James.[19] In subsequent decades historical criticism dissolves the unity of Scripture more and more.[20] This takes place, however, amid passionate battles. Thus Ernesti (1707–81) still disputes that Scripture contains contradictions.[21] Karl August Gottlieb Keil allows for contradictions, yet in his book on hermeneutics establishes the principle that one must first attempt to resolve such contradictions.[22] By today's standards, then, Keil would be a "harmonizer"! Similar views are found in Lücke.[23] The unity of Scripture was also a visceral concern for salvation-historical theologians. In Hofmann we repeatedly encounter the concept of a "unified whole."[24] In J. L. Samuel Lutz's *Biblische Hermeneutik* we read, "Hermeneutics must show precisely the unity of the whole Bible and its interpretation."[25] Older Lutheran dogmaticians vehemently rejected the "modern hunt for differences."[26] Someone like Philippi charged the Christian theologian with the "task of harmonization."[27] Even such a critical proponent as W. Wrede raises the question whether "the opposition to a dogmatically determined harmonization" were not "itself a form of dogmatism."[28]

If one surveys Protestant theology in more recent times, there are the following prominent currents that continue to insist on the unity of Scripture: first, theologians who continue to be strongly influenced by Lutheranism or Calvinism;[29] next, Pietist[30] and biblicistic theologians;[31] third, the wide spectrum of "evangelical" theology.[32] From this third group we encounter in renewed form the conception of Scripture as a "coherent organism"[33] along with the demand, "Our approach must be harmonistic," because God does not contradict himself.[34] In addition there is a fourth group, the proponents of "pneumatic exegesis." Here also the Scripture is conceived of as "a grand unified organism,"[35] and there is talk of an "inner unity of Scripture."[36] Here Girgensohn and Procksch wish to link their work with Hofmann and "the great old scholars of Württemberg."[37] Fifth, it should be noted that modern Old Testament scholars emphasize the unity of Old Testament and New

Testament, even if they are thoroughly committed to the presence of contradictions within this overall unified framework.[38]

## THE REVELATORY STARTING POINT

Amid the welter of human opinions, secure ground is also in this matter only to be gained from going back to revelation itself.

We observe first of all that the New Testament is able to summarize the entire enscripturated revelation of the old covenant under the rubric "the Scripture" (*hē graphē;* cf. Jn 7:38; Ro 4:3; 1Ti 5:18). Such summarization is only possible if a connection and unity between the individual writings in question is presupposed. The same applies to the summary formula "the Scriptures" (cf. Ro 1:2; 1Co 15:3f.). According to the gospel of John, Jesus himself spoke in the same sense of "the Scripture" and "the Scriptures" (Jn 5:39; 10:35). When the resurrected Christ in Luke's gospel spoke of the fulfillment "of everything . . . that is written in the Law of Moses, in the prophets, and in the Psalms," and when he in addition "opened" the disciples' understanding "to the Scriptures" (Lk 24:44f.; cf. 24:27), then it again indicates the view that the (Old Testament) Scripture is a unity. But it is also regarded as a unity in the apostolic tradition (*paradosis*). Acts 2:42 could otherwise never have been formulated. In the hour of martyrdom (Rev 3:10) the "word" (singular!) is an indissoluble unity (Rev 3:8); this already summarizes both the Old Testament and New Testament Word. The course of enscripturation of this apostolic *paradosis* can already be glimpsed in, e.g., 2 Peter 3:15.[39] Here it becomes clear that the idea of Scripture's unity is closely related to the idea of its authority.[40]

All in all we conclude that revelation of Old and New Testament affirms the unity of the message it contains.

It should be immediately granted that there are further and variegated assessments to be made here. We turn first, however, to the basis of this unity.

## THE BASIS OF THE UNITY OF SCRIPTURE

1. The unity of Scripture finds its most secure basis in the One who ultimately brought it forth: God. More specifically, it is God the Holy Spirit who permeates it and constitutes it as a unity (2Ti 3:16).[41] In fact, the case for contradictions in the Bible depends on making the human witnesses to faith the primary authors of Scripture and supplanting the Divine Author. The argument for such contradictions brings a contradiction into God himself—of whom, however, it's rightly said, "Unity is God's characteristic feature."[42]

2. The unity of Scripture is further grounded in the fact that all the books of the Bible summon to faith in one and the same God. The Father of Jesus Christ is none other than the God of Abraham. The nations receive no other God and no other Messiah than does Israel (cf. Ac 17:22ff.). Just as faith was reckoned to Abraham as righteousness, so it is to us (Ro 3 and 4). In Christ the barrier between Israel as God's chosen people and the nations is broken down (Eph 2:14). Gentile believers are grafted into the olive tree of the fellowship of faith of the old covenant (Ro 11:17ff.). Thus arose "the one holy Christian church" of all times and races—and on the basis of a unified message from the Bible. True, the unity of this fellowship is an article of faith. That is not expressive, however, of its deficient reality but rather of its deficient visibility. Bengel spoke rightly of the Bible as a unified "inventory catalog of the community of God's people in Old and New Testament."[43]

In this connection Schlatter's fetching remark comes to mind: "The unity of Scripture in its outcome corresponds to the unity it possesses at its basis" (Dogma, p. 371). By that he means that study of the Bible from any starting point leads into the entirety of Scripture. The "church . . . came to the clear realization that a genuine attachment to Scripture did not remain limited to one of its parts, just as deviation from one of its parts could not fail to become deviation from many more parts as well" (Dogma, pp. 371f.).[44] In other words, the community of believers owns the Bible as a unified plumb line—or it no longer owns any plumb line at all.

3. Along with Scripture's *one* ultimate source and *one* faith in this *one* God, there is a third basis for the unity of Scripture: the unity of the history created through God's Word. His Word lays out the present created order as the framework of history. As "the Word of God" Jesus is coming again to usher the present order into the new creation (Rev 19:13). In Jesus Christ this history has its unity.[45] He is the turning point of the times. In him time has its "fulfillment," and the "fullness" of time makes its appearance (Mk 1:15; Gal 4:4). He encompasses all "that is in heaven and on earth"; he repeats in his own person the history of mankind (Eph 1:10). Thus in Jesus, who is himself God's very "Word," all is summed up into one: creation, time and history, and the Word that is the basis for all that is. On that basis we are justified in speaking of the *one* salvation history. And the Word from which that history goes forth we rightly regard as *one*.

4. In addition to the three preceding arguments for Scripture's unity, there is a fourth, perhaps somewhat negative in nature. It is, like the others, contained in revelation itself. It runs: where the unity of Scripture is lost, the means to fight against heresy are also lost. The New Testament refers repeatedly to "sound" or "good" doctrine (e.g., 1Ti 1:10; 4:6; 2Ti 2:15; Tit 1:9; 2:1, 7f.). But if the New Testament were contradictory, how would it be in a position to offer "sound doctrine"? Without unity the Scripture can likewise no longer serve as "unica regula et norma" (unique rule and standard). Significantly, since the Enlightenment there has continued to be church discipline, but basically no longer any doctrinal discipline. E. Käsemann set forth the famous claim that the New Testament is not the basis for the church's unity but rather for the diversity of its confessions and Christologies—because of its own diversity and contradictoriness.[46] But if this diversity is actually a sound inference from the New Testament, where then is the "true" church to be found? Then all church orders and confessions as such are correct in principle, and truth is relativized. Taken seriously,

Käsemann's principle permits no more biblical distinguishing of the spirits, no more distinction between heresy and sound doctrine. This would be, however, to turn the New Testament on its head.[47]

Let us summarize: the one God, and therefore the one faith, the one salvation history, and the one binding doctrinal nexus are the basis for the unity of Scripture. Anyone who, in opposition to seventeen centuries of Christian conviction, denies the unity of Scripture must face the question of how his faith as a whole comports with that of all these previous generations. "If Scripture is to help us to our destination, it may not destroy its own word through contradictions and thereby be a source of discord among us."[48]

## UNITY AND THE PROGRESSIVE NATURE OF REVELATION

It is nonetheless impossible to present the unity of Scripture as an abstract doctrinal system. Scripture itself is, after all, not put together as an arrangement of proof texts. It rather gives a step-by-step description of God's activity in a historical progression. At each stage God reveals himself in the specific manner fitting for that time. We are dealing, then, with a "progressive revelation."

The concept "progressive revelation" is nonnegotiable because it arises from revelation itself. Not until Jesus' advent is the "full" interpretation of the so-called Old Testament manifest (Mt 5:17). Not until the apostles is the hidden truth proclaimed that "the Gentiles are heirs together with Israel" (Eph 3:6 NIV). Not until Jesus is "all the fullness of the Deity" present "in bodily form" (Col 2:9 NIV). Not until Christ's appearance is the deliverance revealed that the prophets announced (1 Pe 1:10ff.). Simultaneously, both the completion and the peak of God's revelation through history were realized when God "spoke to us in these last days by the Son" (Heb 1:2).

Consciousness of progressive revelation remains acute everywhere that salvation-historical thinking and interpretation prevails.[49] It should not be supposed, however, that this progression is unilinear. Rather, God awakens numerous witnesses with thoroughly diverse tasks in many respective times. Indeed, one and the same witness could be called to various ministries. Thus Jonah prophesied to Jereboam II (783–743 B.C.) the restoration of the Israelite kingdom, while he also moved the Assyrians, Israel's mortal enemies, to conversion by his call to repentance, which meant finally the renewal of Assyrian might (cf. 2Ki 14:25ff.). At first glance much seems to be contradictory. Yet it all dovetails into a unity after careful attention to the historical interconnections and the diverse workings of God. Knowledge of the progressive nature of revelation must, therefore, be supplemented by knowledge of the complexity of revelation.[50]

An example of this is furnished by H. E. Weber. Among the "antitheses" that he thinks he finds in the Bible he cites, e.g., "Esther and Mark or John, the genealogies and the Sermon on the Mount."[51] It is, however, quite unclear why "antitheses" should be said to be present here. Esther is an account of divine preservation. God's providence assures the survival of the people from whom redemption is to come. Without the Jews' survival, John 4:22 ("Salvation comes from the Jews") would never have been uttered, for example. When Jesus assures the continued existence of Israel (Mt 24:32ff.; also 23:39), what he says relates even to the divine act of preservation reported in Esther 4:14. And why should "the genealogies and the Sermon on the Mount" be antitheses? The genealogies are signs of the connection of human history, of a human race therefore that is invited to discipleship and eternal life in the Sermon on the Mount. Further, the genealogies point to the survival of Israel as it is preserved and led under God's providence. And finally, these genealogies integrate Jesus into mankind and uncover the fulfillment of the promises given long before to David and Abraham (Mt 1:1).

At the same time, however, we must take full cognizance of the complexity of these revelations. In Esther there is peace with the enemy only by the sword (9:16, 22). In the New Testament there is eschatological peace only for the one who dispenses with the sword where the faith is concerned (Mt 26:52ff.; Heb 4:1ff.). The salvation-historical epochs, therefore, are also varied, and revelation comports with this historical variability. Anyone who proceeds here on the basis of preconceived material criteria is most emphatically not interpreting historically but is committing to an abstract doctrinal norm.[52]

Observation of the progressiveness and complexity of revelation compels us finally to a salvation-historical interpretation.

## THE UNITY OF SCRIPTURE AND SALVATION-HISTORICAL INTERPRETATION

Salvation-historical interpretation has a threefold advantage over other interpretations: #1) it does the most justice to the historical structure of revelation; #2) at the same time it embraces the fullness of revelation, for history is always richer than an intellectualized systemization of history; and #3) it is best suited to express the unity of revelation in all its challenging complexity.

The New Testament itself has a "salvation historical outlook."[53] It concentrates at the point where the New Testament understands itself as the fulfillment of the Old Testament.[54] The salvation-historical conception is not extraneous to this; it cannot be dismissed or reinterpreted at our discretion. Rather "the Christian Bible has a . . . conception of salvation history as its abiding presupposition."[55] Justin, Irenaeus, Tertullian, and others confer normative importance on salvation-historical exegesis in the ancient church.[56] For Ticonius, the creator of Christendom's first hermeneutical handbook, the salvation-historical outlook numbers among the essential hermeneutical presuppositions.[57] The theological-historical scheme constructed by Joachim of Fiore (ca. 1135–1202) assumed a salvation-historical viewpoint.[58] The same viewpoint was determinative for many early Anabaptists.[59] Salvation history is fundamental to the work of Flacius,[60] to early covenant theology,[61] and to scholarly Pietism.[62] Salvation history exegesis of Scripture even became the central theme for the prophetic-salvation historical theology of the nineteenth century.[63] Biblicism, too, occasionally emphasized "the grand salvation historical context."[64] One of the champions of pneumatic exegesis inclined in the direction of Hofmann's salvation-historical interpretation.[65] Today evangelical theologians see themselves as standing within the salvation-historical tradition.[66] To the extent that critical researchers proceed from the basis of a connection between both testaments, interpreting the Old Testament–New Testament relationship as "promise-fulfilment,"[67] they too are making use of a salvation-historical understanding.

Before we sketch the various dimensions of a salvation historical interpretation, *a preliminary definition of "salvation history"* is called for. Salvation history denotes the activity of God, inseparably woven into history in its entirety, through which he effects his redeeming and perfecting saving will. The term *inseparable* does not mean "indistinguishable." Salvation history and history in its entirety can certainly be distinguished; they are, however, not separate. The opposite of "salvation history" is also not "secular history." For from the Bible's point of view there is no "secular," no God-less flow of history. All history rather receives impetus from, and is made possible by, God. There is, however, with and within history in its entirety a quite specific manifestation of God's salvific and perfecting will. History in its entirety and salvation history are, therefore, similarly related to each other as world order and God's particular ordering of his own people, as the people at large and the community of faith. Luther's depiction of the two spheres of God's ordering furnishes another illustration.

1. Salvation-historical interpretation is first of all *historical interpretation*. It is fundamentally independent of contemporary historical interest. Salvation-historical thinking practiced a "historical" approach to the Bible long before there was such a thing as "historical criticism." If interest in history were to wane in contemporary culture, it would not impair salvation-historical interpretation. At the most it would present a greater challenge for its justification. Because salvation-historical thought takes God's action as its point of departure, it is essentially con-

cerned to relate to and incorporate the universal cosmos, God's creation. That renders it a ready discussion partner with other sciences, most of all the so-called natural sciences, but also with historians, archaeologists, and anthropologists. To that extent it occupies an extreme opposite position compared to existential interpretation, for which discussion with the natural sciences increasingly broke off. One might compare here, e.g., the researches of Bengel, Ötinger, P. M. Hahn, M. Stifel, and K. Heim, all of whom took keen interest in relating their findings to the natural sciences, to creation and the environment, with the work of Bultmann. The latter's position, based on an irrational mathematical point of decision, met criticism from other sciences (Gödan, Gigon; cf. Schadewaldt's interaction with Käsemann).[68] It is indeed striking that so-called "conservative" (which, however, is not the same as "salvation-historical"!) theologians have been more competent in archaeology and historical science than leading historical-critical theologians!

Because salvation-historical theology takes God's action as its starting point, it will try to comprehend the *stages* of his work. There are various names for these stages: "covenants" (foedera), "divine economies" (oeconomiae divinae), "periods" (periodi), "states," "epochs," and so on. All of these originate in the common attempt to organize history under the rubric of revelation and to distill out what is distinct for each individual period. In this way a differentiated outlook becomes obligatory—again long before "historical criticism." The charge of reducing "everything in the Bible to the same level,"[69] which may justly be said of some approaches, does not apply to salvation-historical interpretation.

Because, however, these stages form an interconnected whole, and because God's revelation itself is goal-oriented and purposeful, every salvation-historical interpretation becomes teleological in scope. This explains the tendency to emphasize the *eschaton*. This emphasis comports with revelation to the extent that revelation does indeed impinge on man, beckons him and refers him to the consummation as a source of meaning for the present. It is true that salvation-historical interpretation must struggle with the danger of thinking only in terms of the *eschaton*, thereby impoverishing itself through fixation with eschatology alone. Its *teleological vision*, however, brings with it the further positive possibility of grasping *history as pedagogy*. In that way it can appeal to the *paidagogos*-statements of the New Testament (Gal 3:24; 4:2), as well as to the wisdom and Old Testament conceptual field of *musar* (instruction, reproof) and the basic relationship of believers, as God's children, to their heavenly Father. Constant attention to God's action protects salvation-historical interpretation from the misunderstanding of confusing salvation history with tradition history.

Further, the connection of the stages of God's action concretizes itself in the phenomenon of "types." Goppelt has nicely shown how important this concept is in the New Testament. He goes so far as to call *typology* the "pre-eminent and . . . characteristic mode of interpretation" of the New Testament.[70] In fact, the New Testament shows us the close connection between salvation-historical and typological understanding. Because God gives history a purpose, each individual event and its respective form lie in a more or less direct connection to that purpose. The purpose of events is not exhausted in their isolated occurrence; it rather reaches beyond them. The doctrine of the Bible relates more to the typology of the historical than to a didactic system of doctrinal concepts.

2. Salvation-historical interpretation is, second, an interpretation that is *open to the fullness of revelation*. It is noteworthy that this form of interpretation has no need for an elimination or qualitative rejection of certain biblical strata. This becomes most visible in comparison with the Enlightenment. Karl Aner once said in view of Neology: "The content of which Neology emptied the concept of revelation is the historical; the content with which Neology replaced it was rational in nature."[71] The moment that history is replaced with the rational, however, the Bible becomes a legalistic norm. It is thoroughly understandable that in the Enlightenment moral reason is elevated to the status of a dogmatic criterion, that concepts like morality and moral perfection hold sway, and

that Christianity is "transformed into ethics."[72] Thus arose an atmosphere in which Karl (Carl) Friedrich Bahrdt could translate Matthew 5:4: "Happy are those who prefer the sweet melancholies of virtue to the boisterous joys of vice."[73] The fullness of Scripture was bound to be impoverished by this "cult of virtue" (Aner, p. 164). Further, it is also understandable that sturdily historical books like Nehemiah, Esther, Chronicles, and Kings were set aside as unsuitable in terms of "virtue."[74]

Existential interpretation was also in no position to grasp the fullness of revelation in history. Bultmann believed that "the mythological garb" of the New Testament could be "stripped off." Then one could push through to the "understanding of existence" concealed beneath it.[75] Here Israel's history becomes meaningless for Christian faith.[76] In contrast to H.-D. Wendland, Bultmann does not wish to speak of "view of history and consciousness of history in the New Testament" but rather solely of a "historical mythology." His fateful conclusion: "precisely the events and persons that constitute salvation history are, in the New Testament sense, not historical but mythological phenomena."[77] This turns salvation history into a myth.

Salvation-historical interpretation can take quite a different tack. From the outset it can dispense with squeezing the fullness of biblical statements through the filter of a legalistic norm or some other set of principles. It will seek out historical connections but also allow that which is unconnected to stand in its historical diversity. It will be able to hear everything the Bible records—because that is just how it took place in the history that God has constituted and reigns over. It comes, therefore, in its own way to Ricoeur's basic principle: "The event is our master."[78]

Here it must acknowledge that the enscripturation of revelation presents a selection of events. The Bible has "*gaps.*"[79] The causal chains that we like to establish are often impossible to construct—with the one exception that a certain cause, the God who reveals himself, orchestrated the rise of all these reports. On the other hand we are dealing with a *dynamic fullness* which never becomes just "an empty oneness"

(Schlatter, Dogma, p. 369). A graphic example here are the resurrection reports. They have the "scent of truth" about them.[80] They have decisive importance for the New Testament. They furnish a dynamic entrée into and for subsequent church history. Yet to the present day there has been no convincing organization of these reports into a synopsis or a smooth chronological sequence.[81] Another example would be the accounts of Jews fleeing to Egypt during the time of Jeremiah. The trail of these fugitives dwindles into nothing within the Bible, as it does also for Jeremiah himself. Or to switch to another level: we know nothing very precise about the origin of Satan, despite his importance for the course of salvation history. We meet, then, with a dynamic fullness, not a seamless mosaic or perfectly pieced together puzzle. A flexible, open, salvation-historical interpretation corresponds most adequately to this situation.

Nevertheless, there are *tendencies and various levels of importance* within this dynamic fullness. The predominant tendency is doubtless the Christological. Two simple facts account for this. First, Christ is the central figure of the New Testament. Second, for its part the New Testament is the fulfillment, the goal, of the old covenant. The much-maligned Wilhelm Vischer, scorned for his Christological interpretation of the Old Testament, at least made the attempt to follow this predominant tendency, a tendency central to revelation.

Scripture reveals to us not only tendencies but also various levels of importance. In his rebuke of Israel's leaders Jesus says they had "neglected the more important matters of the law—justice, mercy and faithfulness" (Mt 23:23 NIV). As interesting as the Bible's genealogies are in their place, Paul nevertheless warns Timothy against devotion "to myths and endless genealogies" which "promote controversies rather than God's work . . ." (1Ti 1:4 NIV). Salvation-historical interpretation seeks to trace nothing other than "God's work." As it does this it also discovers "more important matters" in comparison to less important. It does this, however, in the course of study of the Bible and through inner-biblical standards, not with preconceived principles like "love," "justification," or the like. It thereby remains open to revelation insofar as it freely discusses the tendencies and levels of importance it discerns rather than apodictically setting them in concrete.[82]

3. Salvation-historical interpretation corresponds, third, to *the complex character of biblical revelation*. To depict this let us consider recent Protestant-Catholic dialogue. On the one hand E. Käsemann emphasized that Romans 4:5 was the Archimedean point of New Testament theology.[83] He wished to center the entire structure of New Testament theology on this point, the doctrine of justification. On the other hand Catholic theologians like H. Küng and W. Löser responded with the question whether an interpretation that was foresworn to uphold the doctrine of justification in this way could possibly be in a position to discern the entirety of the biblical message.[84] Their question cannot be facilely dismissed by referring to Catholicism's beloved "Complexio oppositorum" (integration of opposites). The New Testament message is not, in fact, exhausted in what it says about the justification of the ungodly. And the only way Käsemann could arrive at such a position was by combining a traditional (i.e., Lutheran) Paulinism with an exclusion of "early catholic," "inauthentic," and other elements that the New Testament contains.

The Jesus tradition alone gives abundant indication of just how complex the New Testament is. The same Jesus who referred to the nearness of the kingdom of God also founded the church (cf. Mt 4:17 with 16:18f.; 18:15ff.; 28:18ff.). The same Jesus who called for ongoing eschatological readiness also prepared his disciples for the unexpectedly long time until his return (cf. Mt 24:42ff. with 25:5, 19). The same Jesus for whom the righteousness of the Pharisees and scribes was insufficient also praised harlots (cf. Mt 5:20 with 21:32). Complexity was, however, already integral to the Old Testament. The same God who visits the guilt of the fathers on the children (Ex 20:5; Nu 14:18; Ex 34:7) also moves his prophets to say that the son does not have to bear the guilt of the father (Eze 18:20; cf. Jer 31:29f., but also Dt 24:16; 2Ki 14:6). In many passages the complexity is so profound that prima facie contradictions appear (cf. Ro 3:28 with Jas 2:24). Salvation-historical interpretation, by taking seriously the historical location and particular time of each individual witness, is not compelled to become referee or schoolmaster over revelation's various statements. It can accord to each statement its rightful place in the dynamic and contingent onrush of salvation history. Salvation history has no need, therefore, to slip into the garb of the censor, a garb readily donned by Enlightenment critics and criticism.

*Complexity is a hallmark of history itself* as we experience it. In certain of Jesus' teachings on discipleship (Mt 8:18–22/Lk 9:57–60), e.g., Jesus gives quite various instructions, which, however, fit into specific situations when applied with pastoral wisdom. Peter, who one minute wishes to fight and die for Jesus, denies Jesus shortly thereafter. Paul dogmatically rejects circumcision, yet practices it on missionary grounds (cf. Gal 5:1f. with Ac 16:3). The state can be called God's minister (Ro 13:4, 6), yet may transform itself into an anti-Christian structure (Rev 13).

No doctrinal system, however ingenious, is in a position to deal with this complexity of revelation. But *salvation-historical interpretation is sufficiently open and flexible to cope with it.* Recalling Bengel's hermeneutical principle "Distingue tempora, et concordabit Scriptura" ("Distinguish the times, and Scripture will agree"),[85] we thus see in salvation-historical interpretation the interpretive procedure that is most capable of doing justice to the unity of revelation.

## SCRIPTURE'S UNITY AND CENTER

It is difficult to speak of a "center" of Scripture today, because the rubric "center of Scripture" is often separated from the "unity of Scripture." While the two were closely identified at the time of the Reformation, the Enlightenment disengaged them. Indeed, the "center of Scripture" practically replaced the lost "unity of Scripture."

In discussion to date, the notions of "what promotes Christ" and "justification of the ungodly" play a central role.

It is undeniable that Luther's work exhibits a "christological concentration."[86] This same concentration is also present, however, as early as Irenaeus and other patristic interpreters as they construe the Old Testament as pointing to Christ.[87] It should not be forgotten that Luther's remark about what "promotes Christ" appears in a *specific* passage among a *specific* system of coordinates. The remark is #1) a "religious" principle[88] and is therefore to be used to exclude writings on critical grounds only with great caution; it relates #2) to a writing which Luther did not hold to be canonical;[89] and it is #3) indicative of a weighty subjectivity[90] that still remains all too virulent today. All in all, the Lutheran "what promotes Christ" is unsuited to replace the idea of the unity of Scripture.[91]

Still less can "justification" serve in this capacity.

Recently Werner Löser, a Catholic discussion partner in Protestant-Catholic dialogue, has again thrown open the question of how the determination that the doctrine of justification is the center of Scripture relates to the unity of Scripture. He calls for reflection here whether Protestants are "making just one particular segment of doctrine (doubtless important, but neither exhaustively nor exclusively adequate to convey the fulness of the biblical message) the key and standard for the whole."[92] His deliberations culminate in the pointed question: "Does Protestant theology really allow Scripture to serve as 'source and norm of proclamation'. . . when it makes an admittedly important but still partial aspect of Scripture the preeminent, central, and normative aspect of the entire Scripture?"[93] Löser thinks it rather imperative "to seek to determine Scripture's unity instead of its center."[94] It will be recalled that earlier H. Küng raised similar questions with Käsemann.[95] These questions cannot be pushed aside as confessional polemic. They are rather justified when the center of Scripture is pitted against the entirety and unity of Scripture.

Neither church history nor revelation permits us to pit Scripture's center against its unity in this way. That is obviously the reason why the young Karl Barth, of all people, heartily agreed with Catholic critics at this point. He rejected both Luther's "what promotes Christ" as well as other talk of the "center of Scripture" for the simple reason that the entirety of Scripture is, or ought to be, the center of focus.[96]

If, however, it is impossible to replace the unity of Scripture with its center, or to play the two off against each other, then the question becomes all the more pressing: assuming Scripture's unity, can we speak of a "center of Scripture"—and if so, how? In pondering these questions we are not in an *ab ovo* situation, i.e., starting from scratch, but can rather refer, e.g., to A. Schlatter and O. Weber for guidelines.

Schlatter at first endorses a "central point of Scripture."[97] He even wishes to formulate it as Luther did: "Whatever promotes Christ is canonical." He, then, however turns against the misuse of this formula, offering the following comments:

> That principle [i.e., "what promotes Christ"] would be misused if it were used to prove that only explicit proclamation of the Christ needs to be regarded as the divine word. It would be misused if taken to mean that the only thing important in the Old Testament were that which contains the messianic promise, and the only thing important in the New that which directly refers to Jesus. Thus conceived [Luther's] notion would approximate the idea of Christ's kingly office, understood in such a way that all other ideas of Christ are deprived of importance and dismissed—the Old Testament prophet becoming nothing unless he speaks directly of the kingly office, the New Testament apostle nothing unless he describes that office. This would be to replace the concrete unity of Scripture again with an empty, monotonous uniformity.

In other words, when "Christ the center" becomes "Christ the exclusive reigning principle," then Scripture is emptied and robbed of its fullness. The parallel here to W. Löser (above) is obvious. Schlatter's consistency here is why for him—as for Bengel!—even the epistle of James leads to Christ.[98]

O. Weber offers two further valuable thoughts. First, he urges us to consider that the center of Scripture "is not an idea but an event."[99] That means, however, that the center of Scripture is determined by a person. "Jesus Christ is . . . the center of the whole Scripture."[100]

Schlatter and Weber furnish usable starting points. Yet it must now be pointed out that revelation itself makes no mention of "the center of Scripture." That is in any case a warning to us lest we make such a "center" into a slogan or speak of it as a self-evident given. We also observe, nevertheless, that the Old Testament presses toward the figure of an eschatological redeemer, whether he be called "Son of Man" or "Messiah" or something else. We observe, further, that the New Testament recognized precisely this Messiah in Jesus (e.g., Jn 20:31) and that the New Testament derives from this redeemer. Undoubtedly, Jesus Christ is the turning point and central figure of both testaments.[101] It is possible to take a further step, following both Schlatter and Weber as well as early church and Reformation exegesis, in affirming that if Jesus is God's Son, then he cannot be fit neatly into our contemporary conceptions. For in that case he existed prior to Scripture, and he is, in Trinitarian unity with the Father and the Holy Spirit, also the author of Scripture.[102] What confronts us in both Old and New Testament is not a word ignorant or hostile to Christ but rather a word that is in the deepest sense "Christ"-ian. Christological interpretation of the Old Testament was, then, no mistake but rather a necessity for the church. To express it in Weber's apt formulation: the Old Testament "has its origin in the one who is also its destination."[103]

A "center of Scripture" can, then, only be spoken of in a revelationally sound way if its *threefold characteristic* is upheld: #1) The center can only be personal, as given in the person of Jesus, the Son of God and Messiah. Every attempt to determine this center materially, e.g., as the doctrine of justification or a *theologia crucis* (theology of the cross), goes astray.[104] #2) The center can only be *dynamic-historical* in nature, a center that stands in a living relation to the entirety of salvation history. Every attempt to distill this out as an isolated entity, or to formulate it as some binding doctrine, disrupts and destroys the continuity of salvation-historical revelation. The center and turning point that consists in the redemptive work of Christ Jesus is also given in dynamic-historical fashion.[105] #3) Finally, what is at issue is that the triune God speaks to us in the *entire Scripture*. We cannot merely declare Jesus to be the center of the New Testament. He is also responsible for the *authorship* of the Old Testament, in the same way that the Spirit who brought forth the New Testament is the Spirit of Christ, indeed the very "Lord" himself (2Co 3:17). Otherwise we receive two Bibles that are different from one another in principle, a Jewish and a Christian.

## UNITY AND HARMONIZATION

Finally we must once more take up the key word *harmonization*. What is the relation between "harmonization/harmonizing" and "unity of Scripture"? The opening of this chapter made clear that harmonizing attempts in scriptural interpretation often meet with strong, occasionally emotional resistance. In the history of theology, however, we find not even one "no!" to such attempts. We recall Pierre-Daniel Huet's *Demonstatio Evangelica* of 1679, which attempted to harmonize the witnesses of antiquity and the statements of the Bible.[106] We further recall the work, which we have already alluded to, of Karl August Gottlieb Keil (1810), who expressly charged criticism with the obligation first of all of trying to eliminate contradictions.[107] We found in W. Wrede the knowledge that "opposition to a dogmatically determined harmonization" is "itself of a dogmatic nature."[108] Based on all this it is understandable that interpreters who are convinced of inspiration speak quite openly of the "task of harmonization"[109] and distance themselves from a "modern quest to find differences."[110] They likewise regard "the method of harmonizing and integrating all that Scripture declares" as proper.[111] Quite recently Craig L. Blomberg has produced a thorough investigation of the justification and boundaries of harmonization. He concerns himself with, among other things, extracanonical literature. Blomberg shows that the attempt to harmonize can be a permissible, indeed proper method in the area of historical science.[112] Harmonization is also *an* "entirely legitimate" working possibility for the interpreter in the area of historical investigation of the Bible.[113]

We conclude that the history of theology and research forbid us to see only something negative in "harmonization." It is not necessarily the sign of a heretical *theologia gloriae* (theology of glory) when someone tries to iron out alleged discrepancies of Scripture.[114]

Revelation itself opens to us the proper, i.e., revelationally supported, path. If the statement is correct that God spoke by the prophets of the Old Testament, by his Son, and by the apostles (cf. Heb 1:1f.; 1Th 2:13); and if it is moreover true that revelation has God as its one de facto author (cf. 2Ti 3:16; 2Pe 1:21); then it is in fact the duty of the interpreter to do justice to *this* unity of the entire Bible.[115] That is, it is his duty to attempt to demonstrate as far as *possible* (see below) this unity in faith and the veracity that the Holy Spirit grants. We arrive here at a point, then, where we see that the inspiration and unity of Scripture, together with the interpreter's stand toward or against the faith, shape the direction that interpretation will take. But mark well: that person who cannot affirm the inspiration and unity of Scripture, who demands that the interpreter be an ostensibly "neutral" scientist who eschews the faith—that person likewise labors under factors that shape his interpretation! It should however be clear on all sides that "grotesque attempts at harmonization" and "gross artificialities" are not to be countenanced.[116] The Holy Spirit is no enemy of honesty.[117] That is why we emphasized "as far as *possible*" above; it was an implicit recognition that the human interpreter remains constantly fallible and limited—and that applies to the regenerate interpreter, too. It was also a recognition that Scripture, from a human viewpoint, evinces gaps and conveys a history, not a seamless doctrinal system. The question finally arises, then, whether the concepts "harmonization/harmonization methods" are really well-advised. It would be better to speak of a "convergence method." That would aptly express that the specific nature of salvation-historical events and statements are not all to be leveled or smoothed out but rather are to be related to each other in the light of the *one* human author. That would be to express, further, that the Bible aims at goals and a future and wishes to be understood along the broad lines of these purposes and future aims.

CHAPTER ELEVEN

# The Historical Nature (Historicality) of Scripture

## THE PROBLEM OF SCRIPTURE'S HISTORICAL NATURE (HISTORICALITY)

For many faithful churchgoers today, talk of the "historical nature of Holy Scripture" immediately conjures up the specter of biblical criticism. Why? Because in the past they repeatedly heard pastors, religious educators, professors, and church representatives—all convinced that historical criticism is essential—insist on the historical nature of the Bible so they could better show discrepancies and contradictions, cracks and flaws, mistakes and errors in the Bible. Such leaders urged that the Bible is an "earthen vessel"—a clever but ill-conceived twisting of 2 Corinthians 4:7—whose content has seeped out of its cracked container and is no longer recoverable. In this way Scripture as normative foundation for living was taken out of faithful churchgoers' hands.

Nevertheless, we must speak of the historical nature of Scripture.

Why? Because divine revelation entered into human history. And this entrance is unlike, say, what Islam claims for the Koran. Revelation rather took shape through a chain of events which in turn created new history (Heb 1:1f.). Revelation did not thereby become no more than a part of human history. But it is also not totally separate from that history. What took place was rather a form of progressive verbal fixing (*Inverbation*). Human ears, eyes, and hearts could grasp it. It is not true, as was ascribed to Philo for many years, that man received revelation "in an ecstatic state,"[1] that inspiration made man "completely unconscious."[2] What took place here was not the obliteration of consciousness but its expansion. Man is urged to the highest unfolding of his natural and spiritual gifts in order to understand God's revelation (exemplarily illustrated in Da 10:8-11).

God made the creation. God is the ultimate ground of history. God revealed himself in history in such a way that his revelation could be discerned even in the midst of a fallen human race. When we speak of the historical nature of the Bible, we have in mind precisely that crossover of the eternal divine revelation into the present space-time world (*transitio revelationis*). This crossover, in which the eternal enters the temporal and itself assumes the characteristics of a temporal phenomenon, is a mystery.[3]

This crossover confers on the Bible the features of a "history book."[4]

For those who are convinced of the reality of a self-revealing God and who encounter this God in Scripture as actually given, it is impossible to remain indifferent to history. Two rather divergent examples will serve as examples. The first is C. F. H. Henry. He points out that the "idea of history" itself stems from the Bible.[5] "God reveals himself . . . within this external history in unique saving acts."[6] Therefore, we must insist that "historical acts" belong inextricably to divine revelation. A consequence of this for Henry is that evangelical theology in particular must work and research within a historical framework.[7] The second example is W. Pannenberg. He defines "history" as "that occurrence that is suspended between promise and fulfillment, in that it receives through the promise an irrevocable orientation toward future fulfillment."[8] Then however he continues: "History is the most all-inclusive horizon of Christian theology."[9] This "historical quality of redemptive occurrence" must "today be championed in interaction with . . . the methodological principles of historical-critical research." Pannenberg's opponents are the existential "historicality" of Bultmann, the "metahistory" of Kähler, and the "primal history" of Barth.[10]

To summarize our initial conclusions: #1) God is the initiator and shaper of history. We can therefore agree to no concept of history that separates God from history. Christian theology would, e.g., have to reject as incompatible with revelation a "scientific" concept of history in Girgensohn's sense, one which regarded history as "always the human-earthly and not the divine-heavenly." For history is not the opposite of God.[11] #2) Because God via revelation projects himself into the history he creates, we must take history seriously and investigate the historical outworkings of revelation. Historical research, rightly understood, is no enemy of a theology of revelation; it rather follows from it.

Here, however, we encounter a whole series of questions and problems.

## THE RELATION OF FAITH AND HISTORY

First we inquire more precisely: What does biblical faith have to do with history? The answer emerges immediately if we make a comparison with extrabiblical religions, e.g., with Buddhism. For a Buddhist, no essential importance attaches to where Buddha was born or where and when he died. Indeed, the Buddhist would really feel no decisive loss if it turned out that Gautama Buddha had never lived at all. Buddha's eightfold path to virtue is basically true even if the historical person from which the path derives never existed. The situation is entirely different for the Christian. For him it is decisive whether Jesus was God's Son, came from David's lineage, and died on the cross of Golgotha.

Proof that Jesus did not die on the cross, that the tomb was not empty, would permanently shake his faith, alter it, eventually even terminate it. Biblical faith is actually quite closely bound to real history.

This also, however, weakens the Christian faith in the eyes of the world. If you remove the historical basis upon which it rests, you have in principle refuted it. Not until we grasp this do we begin to understand why there had to be such serious and dramatic debates over the historical nature of the biblical accounts. When we do grasp this, we see why H. E. Weber is justified in characterizing the relation of faith and history as "the theological central issue" of trust in the Bible. We also see why he states that faith "hinges on its historicity."[12] Even in the disputed area of Old Testament study, Otto Procksch once remarked, "If Abraham or Moses had to be given up as historical figures, then my faith, but with it also my status as a Christian, while not destroyed, would nevertheless be altered at this more or less decisive point."[13]

For clarification we must add that Procksch's statement touches on a problem not unique to academic theology. The same problem affects the so-called laity, too, because what Procksch calls his "status as a Christian" is ultimately the same for all.

We ask, therefore, "what actually happened,"[14] and in placing the question we do so consistent with revelation. Here we touch on the true "servant form" of Scripture: to the extent that its character is historical in nature, it is open to attack and to very different interpretations.

This weakness or "servant form" of Scripture emerges still more sharply when we clarify the tension between faith and history. For both belong quite closely together, yet also find themselves to a certain degree in conflict with each other. This tension shows itself on a number of levels.

First, faith is dependent on factual history: "without factual redemptive history evangelical faith would be null and void."[15] Indeed, faith "clings to" these God-furnished facts (words or deeds). Without a preceding event there is no faith. On the other hand, historical investigation cannot create faith.[16] Even a 100-percent convincing historical demonstration does not, of itself, necessarily lead to faith. Why? Because all historical events are only a means of encounter, and faith seeks fellowship with that one who encounters us through such events. Even the person who knows without question that God exists is not necessarily a believer. This is proved by Genesis 3 (cf. also Jas 2:19 with Heb 11:6). To that extent one can say the faith extends beyond history. Or to put it another way: the history God brings about is the presupposition, but not the source, of faith.

A second tension results from the peculiar nature of historical research. For historical judgments as such can never be more than judgments of probability.[17] The historian remains, therefore, ever unsure, tentative, hypothetical.[18] Faith, however, trusts entirely and unconditionally —although this is not to be confused with freedom from trials and temptation. Why? Because faith extends beyond the event to the person in whom the event has its origin. Faith binds itself to this person in a comprehensive sense, a sense that is not dependent on every detail of every event. Nevertheless, it also holds true here that the course of events can enable faith or destroy it. As strange as it sounds: historical investigation takes on more weight in destruction than in construction. That helps explain the apologetic interest of theologians. In this connection the interaction between Siegmund Jacob Baumgarten (1706–57) and Johann Martin Chladenius in the eighteenth century is of interest. In contrast to Chladenius, Baumgarten held that a verdict of probability was sufficient in the area of historical investigation of the Bible. Probability judgments developed "into the chief form of historical verification."[19] For Chladenius, however, there was "in principle no way from probability to certainty."[20] Clearly Baumgarten stood closer to the truth. It is not possible to elevate historical judgments to judgments of certainty. In the historical dimension we must content ourselves, then, with a judgment of probability.

We would be giving short shrift, however, to the tension between the judgment of probability of historical research and the judgment of certainty of faith if we did not also point to a solution. #1) A solution emerges, first, through noting that by far most acts in human life are based on judgments of mere probability. When I walk to the train or bus each morning, it is "probable" that it will run as scheduled. But it does run (as a rule)! This is, then, a parallel to the statistical probability of the "laws of nature"—which actually work! To the extent that historical investigation is a part of normal life and of human history, we may not erect higher demands than we do elsewhere in the framework of life as God establishes it. #2) Historical research, however, is only a partial aspect of biblical interpretation. It is embedded in a larger and comprehensive encounter with revelation, an encounter which in turn flows into an encounter with the One from whom revelation issues (see chaps. 5 and 6 above). It would be erroneous to want to do away with historical research. It would also be erroneous, however, to isolate historical research from its larger connections with revelation and encounter, and even more mistaken to want to burden it with the entire responsibility for deciding yes or no. The kernel of truth in the view that wants to dissolve ties between faith and history lies here: historical research overwhelms, indeed becomes a form of antitheology, when it is said to be the sole deciding factor in deciding the faith question. The tragedy of those who champion the absolute freedom of historical criticism from church dogma lies not least in the fact that they make this erroneous move. Instead, faith in the self-revealing God and trust in his revelation must be underway before we tackle historical investigation of the Bible. Such investigation is, therefore, actually the outcome and not the presupposition of a theology of revelation.

But doesn't that mean that those persons are right who raise the objection that theologians who believe in revelation are not really working "historically," that they are convinced in advance that "the Bible is always right"? The answer to this can be given in a pair of statements. #1) Like every other act in life, historical investigation entails the danger that the interpreter's faith will be changed or even destroyed. To that extent, then, historical work is not undertaken as a game but as a serious risk—just like every other step in faithful discipleship. #2) As long as the interpreter, however, trusts God and his Word, he will agree with revelation also at those points where it stands in tension with or contradiction to other sciences and life experiences. Revelatory truth possesses a higher worth for him than any "truth" outside of revelation. Examples of this are found in Luther and Bengel, who would have "rather [done] violence to secular history" than give up the preeminence of Scripture.[21] It is, to be sure, an article of honesty to lay such tensions on the table openly, neither concealing them through cosmetic measures nor denying their existence.

## THE ATTEMPT TO SEPARATE FAITH AND HISTORY

Based on the previous section, it is a mistake to want to dissolve the tie between biblical faith and history. Attempts in this direction have taken various forms.

The roots of such attempts may possibly stretch back to the occasional remarks of Martin Luther. In his study of Luther, Heinrich Bornkamm cites such an utterance: "better that we lacked world and history than the word and doctrine."[22] True, Luther did not let go of history. But his placing of the Pauline Epistles ahead of the Gospels, a move closely related[23] to the quotation just given, signals the possibility of a distance between the two, even in relation to salvation history. As soon as doctrine is absolutized, such tendencies can become dangerous. This is observable in the Enlightenment in pronounced measure. To cite Karl Aner's well-known formula once more: "The content of which Neology emptied the concept of revelation is the historical; the content with which they refilled it was rational."[24] Rationality therefore came to take history's place to a great extent. Lessing valued "truths of reason" higher than "truths of history." Semler rejected most of all the Old Testament historical books (Judges, Ruth, Samuel, Kings, Chronicles, Ezra, Nehemiah, Esther) because he found "absolutely no trace of God's word" in them.[25] In 1803 Gottlieb Wilhelm Meyer hurled the charge at Luther that the latter still took the Old Testament as history.[26] Once historical criticism had cast doubt on the historical substance of Scripture, it began to yearn for the "absolute," which at the same time had to be "super-historical." The "tendency to detach religion from history"[27] had a twofold effect: in the "historical" is seen only the "relative," and then historical investigation is deprived of the "absolute" that is a necessity for religion. History withers to mere "appearance" of the "super-historical."[28] This historical skepticism spilled over and influenced biblicism, even Kähler.[29]

It is almost reminiscent of W. Bousset when Girgensohn states that "the super-historical . . . only glimmers through the earthly-human shell."[30] Essence is discovered beyond the historical realm, for "essence is . . . that which is super-human, super-historical."[31] The historical becomes merely a vehicle of eternal ideas. What harm can historical criticism do? "The vast sweep of eternity alone is decisive, the great, eternally unchanging spirit of the whole. This frees us from the details of the unholy guerrilla war [that history comprises]."[32] But at what price! The history that God has brought about, the world that saw his mighty acts (Ac 2:11), is reduced to an insignificant "guerrilla war." Indeed, history is ultimately excluded totally from the work of redemption: "That which is historical cannot redeem mankind."[33] Gottlob Schrenk (1952) likewise takes his stand on the "super-historical, the absolute," which remains inaccessible to historical research and untouchable by criticism, while the historical events of revelation are handed over totally to criticism.[34]

History becomes radically distant in the "dialectical theology" of Emil Brunner. "History or Revelation?" is the provocative question that served as title of an impressive article he penned. It sounds like an echo of Girgensohn, among others, when Brunner states, "Faith deals with the absolute. Therefore it is not directed toward history but toward the end of history." Then still more sharply: "History" is "that from which revelation in Christ . . . redeems us."[35] It is, then, "in principle totally irrelevant when, under what temporal circumstances, in which historical context, Christ lived and what preceded him and what 'conditioned' him."[36] The Platonism that vitiates this Protestant theology of history finally confirms its own crass character when Brunner defines history as "recognition that only the entirely other is the actually self-existent."[37] In the final analysis this means that we can "not take both God and history seriously."[38]

Oepke (1947) perceived this Platonism, which Barth and Tillich could also be charged with,[39] and refused to accept an only "tangential" contact with history.[40] He saw, however, "nearly insurmountable difficulties" when it came to "the problem [of] faith and history."[41] He felt these difficulties could be overcome by supplementing historical interpretation with a superhistorical pneumatic interpretation, which he described as "metahistorical exegesis."[42]

All these developments give us opportunity to become acquainted with the importance of a positive relation between faith and history from the reverse direction, so to speak. Where history is dismissed, close connection to the Word is extinguished. A process repeats itself that is similar to what we can observe among the Radical Reformation, namely, recourse to a spirit that is greater and different from the Word of revelation. This ultimately incomprehensible spirit also appears to animate J. Wellhausen's words: "In the core of my soul I make contact with eternity," and God stands "behind and beyond the mechanism of the world."[43] Where Protestant theology took up the retreat from history, even declaring that faith having a historical component is damaging, an idealistic spirit-religion with Platonic features streamed into the vacuum. People thought they could acquire a deeper vision elsewhere than that afforded by the Word. The claim to know "the actual" was made. In this way Protestant theology became an advocate of historical skepticism.

The protest of evangelical[44] and Catholic theologians was not lacking.[45] A clarification of the historicality of faith is, in fact, essential.

## THE REVELATORY STARTING POINT

Such a clarification can only be carried out working from the basis of revelation. One of the key passages for faith is Exodus 14:31. We read of the people of Israel after they passed through the Red Sea and were delivered from the Egyptians: "And when the Israelites saw the great power the LORD displayed against the Egyptians, the people feared the LORD and put their trust in him and in Moses his servant" (NIV). The faith that arises here attaches itself (this is the likely the root meaning of the Hebrew *'mn* in the Hiphil) to the mighty act of the Lord. Faith's object and trust in the Lord do not, however, require a miracle. A word, a promise, can also suffice, as Genesis 15:6 shows. In any case, word and deed are brought together into one entity in the Hebrew concept *dabar*.

The true prophetic word is recognized by its coming to pass, i.e., by its historical realization (Dt 18:20ff.; cf. 1Pe 1:10ff.; 2Pe 1:16ff.). There is also the reverse possibility, e.g., in Numbers 16:28ff., where there is a "preliminary discrediting"[46] of a contingency (the natural death of Korah and others) that does not come to pass. Here a word from the Lord receives the status of a "sign" whose existence could vouchsafe the word. Indeed, the very word that God spoke creates history:

> ". . . so is my word that goes out from my mouth:
> It will not return to me empty,
> but will accomplish what I desire
> and achieve the purpose for which I sent it."
> (Isa 55:11 NIV)

Out of this came Israel's education in reality, an education with no genuine parallel elsewhere. While the Greek world was for the most part content with concordance of thought, with its logical system, Jews sought transformed reality. No better characterization of the two outlooks exists than that offered by Paul: "Jews demand miraculous signs and Greeks look for wisdom" (1Co 1:22 NIV).

The actual root of the concept of history is the promise. Promise confers a connectedness on the course of events associated with it. Promise creates consciousness of the progress and outcome of occurrences. It makes observers pay attention to the fate that the word of promise enjoys. History is thus born, in the actual sense of the word, through divine revelation. "History" is not the discovery or exclusive province of modern man. Moderns are able to pursue history only because biblical revelation teaches them what it is. Later we will return to this point.

We can measure the above observations against the faith that becomes visible in the New Testament. The disciples' faith begins as they respond to the promise-laden allusion of John the Baptist (Jn 1:35ff.) and to the invitation "Come . . . and you will see" (Jn 1:39 NIV). Peter's faith reaches new heights when he casts the net at Jesus' command and takes the promised catch (Lk 5:1ff.). The publican Zacchaeus finds his way to faith when he climbs a tree "to see who Jesus was" (Lk 19:3 NIV). Confession of Jesus as God's Son arises through the Jesus who actually and historically encounters those seeking him (Mt 14:33; 16:13ff. par.), not through the speculation of a theological expert. Certainty regarding the One who was resurrected takes shape in the literal "tangible" encounter with him (Lk 24:13ff.; Jn 20:14, 19–21). Apostles must have been members of the group "who have been with us the whole time the Lord Jesus went in and out among us" (Ac 1:21 NIV). We will not even recount here the "sign" that Jesus intended to be of assistance in coming to faith (e.g., Jn 10:38). Nor will we take up discussion of the faith that God proffered through resurrecting Jesus, according to the Areopagus address (Ac 17:31), or other similar incidents. In any case this much has become clear: faith can only arise where God has previously—not thought, but acted. That is, it arises as biblical faith only in the realm of biblical revelation whose occurrence has extended itself into history.

Whoever separates faith and history, therefore, contradicts revelation. And at the same time we recognize that we must bring a concept of history derived from, not autonomous from, revelation itself into connection with revelation. Thurneysen called starting from a "modern" concept of history "fanaticism."[47]

## THE ATTEMPT TO DISSOLVE FAITH INTO HISTORY

There is, however, another error that must be rejected: the attempt to dissolve God and revelation into history. This path has been tried more seldom, perhaps, than the opposite one of trying to emancipate faith from history. Yet we encounter a quite serious challenge here, too.

In view of F. C. Baur, Geiger came to this conclusion: "Baur's life work consisted . . . in the dissolution of theology into history."[48] Once again everything depends on the concept of history that is assumed. Under Hegel's influence Baur regarded history as "self-unfolding of the spirit,"[49] and that means the human spirit. Accordingly, it is also true that "Christianity is nothing supernatural and above reason," but the "inherent possession of the human spirit . . . not something that comes into it from without."[50] With such presuppositions the dissolution of theology into history entails two corollaries. First, a second source of revelation is opened up in the form of Baur's "speculative" (intellectualized) history. Second, revelation is ultimately robbed of its divine origin beyond the realm and ken of mankind.

Hegel's influence, combined with ideas from romanticism, is also present in Gunkel.[51] The bearers of the history of religion become the "great men who were touched by God's spirit." For in Gunkel's view theology is now "history of religion,"[52] and the concept of development plays a decisive role. Gunkel glimpses, to be sure, in this development the "hand of higher reason"[53] and can therefore maintain a thoroughgoing grasp on the absolute validity of Christianity. But it is precisely history that leads to the result that we find today in the form of the Bible. To that extent one is quite justified in speaking of a "faith in the revelatory character of history"[54] in Gunkel's case.

These examples could easily be multiplied. Whether we are dealing with the claim that "after Auschwitz" theology can no longer be done as previously; whether the assertion is made that only "the poor" understand the Bible aright, so that we must first all become existentially poor; whether the subject is a true theology of the people,[55] to be pitted against the false theology of former times; whether the demand is that the Bible must be composed entirely anew for our time—in all such approaches the presupposition is present, implicit or explicit, that biblical revelation must be supplemented by "history."

This always, however, means *interpreted* history. The one who interprets it is, in all these cases, man himself. He lacks the authoritative divine Word, so all that meets him from out of history is that same human word that he brings to it. Precisely for that reason, however, God is not to be identified with history, and revelation is not to be dissolved into history.

## REVELATION AND BARE FACT

The connection between revelation and history leads us to a further precise question: What role do bare facts play here? Behind us lies an era of existential interpretation which taught us to view "bare facts" negatively. A distinction was made between bare facts (*Fakten*) and "meaningful facts" (*Tatsachen*), on the one hand, and "historicality," on the other. Not until existential relation was present did facts become positive "historical" phenomena: "facts of the past do not become historical phenomena until they become meaningful for a subject who himself stands in that history and participates in it. They become historical phenomena when they speak."[56]

The connection here in the history of ideas with Kierkegaard, for whom "truth" was only that which "is true for me,"[57] is obvious. Another important link, however, is to German idealist historiography. A historian like Johann Gustav Droysen made a sharp distinction between "reality" and "truth." The history that we study is the "actualization" of moral forces.[58] What occurs and is externally discernible is only the outward appearance of the moral world from which history grows. The moral world has "truth"; the outward appearance, "reality." To think historically, then, means "to see this truth in these realities."[59] This furnishes the historian his task: "The idea (or complex of ideas) which an interpretation highlights in its overall account is in our view the truth of the overall account. This overall account is in our view the reality, the outward appearance, of this idea."[60] However: this by no means suggests that the "real" overall account loses its significance. For interpretation is only successful if the prominent presence of the bare fact remains preserved. Droysen opens up the question: "Is there a truth without being right about the facts?"—and answers in the negative.[61]

But precisely this basic characteristic of the historian, which itself determined his standpoint "between theology and philology,"[62] was widely abandoned by those engaged in existential interpretation. Discussion in German-speaking circles bit especially hard on concepts like "truth" and "reality," "significance" and "bare fact."[63] For example, in 1967 Edwin E. Schneider proceeds from the assumption of an antithesis between truth and reality. While natural scientists decipher only reality, truth is a "central concept of theology."[64] E. Fuchs rejects an identification of "true" and "real" on the grounds that this would lead to a "sovereignty of what is factually established."[65] In remarks of another student of Bultmann, E. Dinkler, the consequence of this line of thought emerges. He thinks that "the truth of faith in Christ is not dependent on the correctness of historical-critical elucidations."[66] While for Droysen in the nineteenth century, therefore, there was no truth without factual correctness, now the theologian dispenses with such correctness in order to live on the basis of the "pure truth."[67] It is intriguing here to recall that S. J. Baumgarten, theological ancestor of German Enlightenment theology, shared Bolingbroke's stand on the "facts" and thus "related" Christianity "indissolubly to historical facts."[68]

Understandably, protest arose from theological,[69] historical, and philosophical quarters against this isolation of fact from meaning and against a one-sided preference for "significance." Theologically we may note that there can be no more talk of "redemptive facts" if all that lay behind these were significance.[70] Among the best-known protesters was E. Betti. He did not share Bultmann's skepticism, according to which an "objective knowledge" was impossible, and he insisted against

Gadamer and Bultmann that not only the "meaning" but also the "events" themselves must be the "object of historical understanding."[71] So much for theological objections; philosophical protest assumed its fullest form in P. Ricoeur. His "hermeneutics of testimony" is directed against the theological separation between "witness of facts and confessing of truth."[72] He finds in the Bible a thoroughgoing "strict union" of report ("narrative kernel") and "confession of faith."[73] Here he refers to von Rad and the historical credo of Deuteronomy 26:5–9.[74] What simple church folk had already urged in the debate surrounding existential interpretation is confirmed for them by Ricoeur (appealing to Ex 20:2!): "It is not possible to testify for a meaning without testifying that something has happened which signifies this meaning."[75] Every testimony has two "poles": the "confessional" and the "narrative."[76] This is especially true for the Bible. In Hebrew, indeed, "the event and its meaning closely" coincide.[77] Ricoeur simply uses the term *event-signs*.[78]

It makes sense here to check extrabiblical and biblical-historical sources. In his introduction to Herodotus's *Histories*, W. F. Otto underscores the pains taken by the Greek historian to give "reliable factual reports." What was true already of Herodotus[79] is all the more true for Thucydides.[80] The reader should "recognize . . . how it truly was."[81] Thucydides, according to his own introduction to his work, had *to alēthes* (the real truth) and *to saphēs* (the clear truth) in view. They were his first priorities. Personal testimony and careful sifting of the testimony of others come together.[82] Along with the concept of *alethes*, with which also Herodotus was familiar,[83] Thucydides also mentions *akribeia*, which means something like scientific exactness, as the ideal for which he strives.[84] Here it is worth noting that this guiding motif of Greek history writers remains constant in spite of the switch from myth to the exclusion of myth.

We immediately feel reminded of this guiding motif when we turn to Josephus, the great Jewish historian of the first century A.D. He, too, wishes to furnish an "exact [*akribes*] historical presentation."[85] He, too, places high value on "truth" and "precision" or "careful accuracy" (*alēthes, akribeia*).[86] Yet he emphasizes "facts" or "things that took place" (*pragmata*) much more strongly.[87] True, the simultaneous presence of both *logoi* and *pragmata* (words and deeds), which according to Schadewaldt characterized ancient historiography,[88] can likewise be discovered in Josephus.[89] But the latter (*pragmata*, "deeds") were stressed, in conscious distinction from Greek authors.[90] This stress on *pragmata* begs to be brought into connection with the Jewish instruction in reality of which we spoke earlier.

The Roman historian Livius, in opening remarks to his *Ad urbe condita*, likewise set forth a few basic tenets of his procedure. He distinguishes between "more poetically adorned tales" (*poeticae magis decora fabulae*) and "unimpeachable historical reports" (*incorrupta rerum gestarum monumenta*).[91] Both, however, are employed for an overarching goal: Livius shows "exemplary models" suited to learn lessons from (*inde capias*)[92]—history as educator!

Luke bears thorough comparison with the examples mentioned above. Sneen compares him especially with Thucydides and Polybius.[93] Doubtless, however, Josephus's preface to *De Bello Judaico* (*Jewish Wars*) yields the next parallels. Luke has numerous key terms in common with Josephus. Among the most important are "events" (*pragmata*), "report" (*diēgēsis*), and "carefully" (*akribōs*).[94] Sneen comes to the conclusion that Luke 1:1–4 strives for both "historical reflection" and "kerygmatic testimony." Sneed formulates a fundamental Lucan conviction as follows: "sound history is an indispensable foundation for faith."[95]

The result of the soundings into ancient historians above is this: bare fact and proclamation, event and meaning, do not admit of separation.[96] "Historicality" without foundation in the factual is an ahistorical construct. "Existential interpretation," then, to a very considerable degree has withdrawn from history and from communication with historians.

As far as we can survey from Greek, Roman, Jewish, but also Christian historiography, we are dealing everywhere with interpreted history. Without the interpreting word, the fact never becomes known as the truth. Without the fact, the interpreting word becomes myth or fable. As far as we can speak of history writing at all, we can only receive fact and proclamation as a tightly interlocked whole—or receive neither one or the other.

The task of theologians who work with an eye toward history, therefore, does not consist in purifying faith of the greatest part of its "factual" component. Their task is rather what Nabert and Ricoeur have characterized as "the criteriology of the divine."[97] More simply: we must find the correctly interpreted history! Or to formulate it still differently: we are not consigned to digging out some existentially determined "significance"; our task is rather to select the correct history from among the various "kinds" of interpreted history.

Precisely at this juncture we encounter biblical revelation anew. It sets forth the claim to be "testimony"—"and we know that this testimony is true" (Jn 21:24). It reports, e.g., of that "which Jesus did" (Jn 20:30; 21:25) or, to be concise, of "the factual." (Interestingly, the Greek *poiein*, "to do," as in "what Jesus did," is equivalent to the Latin *facere*, "to do," from which our word *fact* derives.) But at the same time it gives the true meaning. That is why for Luke, in contrast to the Greek writers, "eyewitnesses" in general do not suffice. Rather, they must be eyewitnesses who are at the same time "servants of the Word" (Lk 1:2). For only such persons can rightly interpret what has taken place. The "correct" interpretation of the occurrences is also furnished by the passion story, by the story recounted through Hebrew and Jewish history in response to the child's question at the Passover meal (Ex 12:26f.),[98] and by the historical credo of Deuteronomy 26:5ff. Regarding the last passage G. von Rad spoke of "redemptive acts" and "redemptive history," indeed even of a "designation of the most essential brute facts."[99] And to return to the Gospels, Martin Dibelius's judgment here is very clear: "The Gospel . . . encompasses, then, two elements from the very outset: . . . accomplished and interpreted history."[100]

The interpreter seeking to work in the light of revelation, then, will also note that he can never have the kerygma, the proclamation, without the fact, and never have the fact without the kerygma. He will turn to both dimensions with equally scrupulous care. The "servant form" of revelation does not consist only in its historical vulnerability and its susceptibility to false interpretations. It also consists in this: that revelation has entered into the link between the kerygmatic and the factual, a link that characterizes all human history writing. This mystery alone explains how someone could accuse revelation of historical indifference or even historical error because it is a "faith testimony," and conversely could be content with a *fides historica* (assent to the veracity of historical facts) and in that way evade revelation's demand for trust. Revelation itself, however, forbids that we play off "faith testimony" and "historical reliability" against each other.

## REVELATION AND MIRACLE

Questions surrounding the factual reach their peak once more in the problematic of miracle. H. E. Weber did not err in seeing the touchstone of the problem of "faith and history" in the "question of miracle."[101]

In Christian theology miracle has suffered a strange fate. Christian apologists in the early years of the church battled pagan miracle stories because they were scientifically untenable.[102] Their own (Christian) miracles stories, however, they held to be capable of withstanding any investigation. For Melanchthon and Flacius, miracle was the basis for the Bible's authority.[103] This viewpoint extended into the earlier period of the Enlightenment. Even the *Institutiones Theologiae dogmaticae* of Joh. Franz Buddeus (1723) used miracle and prophecy as pillars of biblical authority.[104]

Then there came one of the most radical upheavals in the history of theology. In 1670 B. Spinoza in his *Tractatus theologico-politicus* had given "compelling" proof of "the impossibility of miracle."[105] With the help of pantheism Spinoza was able to "include" God himself in his system.[106] If God's will was congruent with nature as perceived by reason, then a miracle that violated the natural order was impossible. Indeed, it was an abasement of God. Only what reason can understand and justify can demand our recognition.[107] The speed with which Spinoza's ideas spread is proven by the anonymous work that appeared in Holland in 1683: *Miracles No Violations of the Laws of Nature.*[108] Alongside of Spinoza arose the influential movement of English Deism. The question of miracle occupied a central place in its discussions. David Hume, e.g., would later write his famous essay "Of Miracles," while somewhat earlier the English Deist Thomas Woolston (1670–1731) wrote "Six Discourses on the Miracles of Our Saviour."[109] The basic drift in Woolston: "Miracles, which in the new 'scientific age' can be shown never to have happened, are inappropriate faith convictions."[110]

Discussion turned on the question whether "such a thing [as miracles] has actually taken place."[111] In the eighteenth century German theology opened itself up to English Deism on a broad front.[112] Even conservative interpreters like Joh. Franz Buddeus or Chr. Matth. Pfaff, who basically would have liked to hold fast to miracles,[113] effect a stark rationalization in exegeting the miracle accounts. Pfaff, e.g., interprets the book of Jonah to say that Jonah was picked up by a ship bearing the name "Great Fish"; in Joshua 10:12ff. the sun's movement did not cease, nevertheless its rays continued to shine; Samson did not execute his deeds alone but was the leader of a large band; etc.[114] This creates a pattern that shows up elsewhere with innumerable modifications.[115] Johann Friedrich Gruner (1777) is already a breakthrough in the direction of Schleiermacher as the former deprives miracle of its objective character and declares it to be "inconceivable for us."[116]

Schleiermacher procured widespead recognition for this view. His interpretation of miracles can perhaps be summed up in one sentence: the "wondrous" replaces the "miraculous."[117] Anything that the religious heart apprehends with awe as flowing from God is a miracle. When, however, all religious experience is made to become miracle in this way, the biblical and classical concept of miracle is abandoned. In view of the historical reports Schleiermacher and his students hold to the rationalistic outlook that actual miracles are impossible.[118] Basically, all nineteenth century theology in Germany, to the extent that it relates to historical-critical research, shares the opinion that today we can no longer believe in miracles.[119] E.g., K. A. G. Keil in his hermeneutics book of 1810 rules out all "that can surely not have been fact" (p. 131). Baur (1855) writes to Karl Hase that "there is no absolute miracle"; "Lazarus can thus not really have been dead."[120] Baur's student D. F. Strauss, in a letter to Baur (19 August 1836) appeals to the "unthinkable nature of the thing itself."[121]

Indeed, even twentieth-century criticism is still dominated by the idea that miracles are unhistorical—at least those miracles that one does not understand! Healings and exorcisms remain because they are thought to be understandable by psychological means (power of suggestion, psychosomatic considerations). But the so-called nature miracle—which indeed cannot serve as a sober genre-historical concept!—has found recognition only in evangelical and biblicistic circles of Protestant theology.[122] It should, nevertheless, be expressly mentioned that the papal Bible commission in its "Instructio" of 1964 underscored "the incursion, which occurred by revelation in the strong sense, of the personal God in the world, as well as the possibility and factuality of miracles and prophecies." It also upheld that the disciples "rightly understood the miracles as [real] deeds" (*recte tanquam facta*).[123]

We have thus been reminded once again of the concept of the factual. If the connection between fact and proclamation is recognized, then the two cannot be detached from each other in the area of miracle. The interpreter of the Bible must here, too, take his stand against the critical dogmatician who sees no "objective place" for miracle and narrows the "concept of miracle" to a purely "subjective" notion.[124]

Revelation indisputably proclaims that the miracles it relates actually took place. What kind of God would it be, anyway, who did not really bring forth the created world (Ge 1 and 2); whose "right hand" did not "shatter the enemy" at the Red Sea (Ex 15:6); who did not "do miracles before your fathers in Egypt" (Ps 78:12); who did not fulfill his promises to Joshua and his fighting men so that it could be said, "Not one of all the LORD's good promises to the house of Israel failed; every one was fulfilled" (Jos 21:45 NIV)! Had Jesus not worked actual miracles, then the likes of John 10:38; 20:30f.; 21:35; etc., are completely unthinkable. Then the early Christian sermon to Israel about Jesus, "accredited by God to you by miracles, wonders and signs, which God did among you" (Ac 2:22 NIV) would never have taken place. With what determination the Bible proclaims that miracles actually occurred is seen in the reportage of the Jewish explanation of the empty tomb in Matthew 28:11f., in the arraying of witnesses in 1 Corinthians 15:5ff., and in the depictions of various encounters with the resurrected Jesus. Revelation tolerates objections (e.g.: Did it really happen? Did it happen that way? Isn't it all "empty talk" [*lēros*; Lk 24:1]?) and answers them (cf. Mt 28:17; Lk 24:11, 34, 38ff.; Jn 20:24ff.; Ac 17:32ff.). Miracles cannot be relegated to a secondary level of the Gospels, as if the oldest level knew nothing of them. Nor can the New Testament be sliced up into miracle-friendly and miracle-hostile currents, as Schmithals, among others, attempted.[125] Miracle belongs to the most ancient content. Without miracle there would be neither the Gospels nor Old Testament revelation, apart from a few wisdom sayings perhaps. Not even the reports of what Jesus' opponents said would have been possible unless he had done miracles.[126]

The interpreter who works in the light of revelation will therefore resist the temptation to distill from the miracle reports merely that which pertains to the proclamation. He will rather exercise utmost care here, too, in giving due consideration to both dimensions, the factual and the kerygmatic. The pure proclaimer thinks ahistorically in principle. Against this, our task is to engage in interpretation of miracles and make it fruitful. They are, namely, attesting signs, mediating occurrences, that point to the one who works them. They belong, therefore, in the revelatory sense to the encounter that God seeks with the person he addresses. They lose their purpose when this encounter does not take place.

Schlatter commented that "miracle does not endanger the idea of causality"; it rather "confirms" it: "for by miracle we do not imagine an effect without an effecter. We rather expressly apply the idea of causality since we recognize God as the miracle worker in the miracle."[127] Schlatter notes further that "nature" gives us no "cause to declare miracle impossible." For nature receives its definition from God and thus becomes an attesting sign pointing to the greater Person that gave it its definition.[128] In fact, the human judgment of "possible" or "impossible" high-handedly displaces the content of revelation. God then becomes an idol which human thought brought forth. And conversely: it is a constituent part of grace that God reveals himself in miracle—in his own time!

## REVELATION AND PROPHECY

The problem of prophecy has always been closely linked with the problem of miracle. This connection can be readily explained in that true prophecy is itself a miracle.

It is sufficient to say here in summary that the Bible's fulfilled prophecy was one of the stoutest pillars of Christian proclamation through seventeen centuries.[129] It was held to be sufficiently convincing to furnish the basis for the authority of Scripture.[130] The first handbook of biblical hermeneutics that we know of in Christendom, Ticonius's *Liber Regularum* (ca. A.D. 382), originated in interaction with prophecy.[131] Otherwise, prophecy also formed the root of hermeneutics for the Qumran Essenes.[132] Joachim of Fiore, Joachimism, the anabaptist movements, covenant theology, Pietism, nineteenth-century salvation-history theology—these all used prophecy as normative basis. This assessment of prophecy endures in many segments of Christendom still today. In Catholicism the "Instructio" of the papal Bible commission (1964), which we have already mentioned a number of times, defended "the possibility and actuality of prophecies" (*prophetiarum possibilitatem et existentiam*).[133] For evangelicals such a position is self-evident.[134]

To what extent may one speak, then, of a "problem" of prophecy? It becomes a problem at the moment that human reason and science become the standard for what is possible. That takes place, notoriously, in the Enlightenment. English Deism, which sees itself as the embodiment of the new scientific age, takes up the question, "How likely is it that such a thing has actually taken place?" and takes offense at supernatural prophecies.[135] In addition, the Enlightenment glimpsed the goal of history in the perfectibility of mankind. Here Lessing ventured a prophecy of his own: "It will certainly come"—"the time of perfection."[136] A corresponding view from the Christian side saw the goal of history to be the responsible (in the deepest sense), "moral" Christian. The Latitudinarian J. Locke put it this way for us: "These two, faith and repentance, i.e., believing Jesus to be the Messiah and a good life, are the indispensable conditions of the new covenant."[137] But if salvation is a matter of the moral perfection of man, then the Bible's prophecy is no longer needed, at least not so urgently. J. J. Mosheim (1755) demonstrated this. He regarded as essential only those truths of the Bible necessary for salvation. On the other hand, he continued, prophecies and histories are nonessential.[138] Among those following Semler's line of thought the verdict was more stringent. F. A. Stroth (1771) is totally frank: "What good would it be to us to know that in a hundred years Islam and Judaism will cease to exist?" "Would that make us more perfect or virtuous and more skillful in all good works?"[139] Corrodi of Zürich argues (1781) along the same line: religion serves to further "the enlightenment of human understanding and the perfection of mankind."[140] Transcendentally derived prophecy has no more place in the context of "reasonable" and "true" understanding. Corrodi puts it this way: "Faith in the gift of prophecy" is for the present time "extinguished."[141] Thus it became necessary to understand that which the prophet spoke in the name of God as simply the message of the prophet himself. That comes to expression in virtually classic form in J. Wellhausen, who once remarked of Isaiah, "When he spoke in the name of Yahweh he proved to have an acute grasp of mankind and of the human condition."[142]

The appeal to Yahweh, then, was a means to an end, and the "acute grasp" does not come from God but from man. But if prophecy is simply human utterance, then it may be critiqued with impunity. Thus Wellhausen charges that Ezekiel "lived in reminiscences and phantasies."[143] In Wellhausen's view there was no such thing as God-given prophecy about the future. The passion predictions in the Gospels are therefore "inauthentic," secondary: "Jesus' disciples were in no way prepared in advance for Jesus' death."[144] The question of the extent to which God divulged the future also caused severe reverberations in "positive" theology, which tried to oppose Enlightenment "critical" theology by pressing its critical tools and methods into the service of traditional Christian theology. E.g., O. Zöckler regarded such detailed predictions as Daniel 11 to be impossible.[145] The temptations of the era come brilliantly to light in the work of Franz Delitzsch (1813–90). In his introduction to the third edition of his Isaiah commentary (1879), he describes the relation of the critic to prophecy with these words:

> For critics it is impossible that in Hezekiah's time Isaiah predicted the universal dominance of Babylon and its fall to the Medes and Persians. Hitzig affirms plainly that the very same *caligo futuri* [dimness regarding the future] that was the bane of the human race during the time of the oracle at Delphi also covered the eyes of the Old Testament prophets in general. Ewald speaks of the prophets with incomparably more optimism, but for him the prophetic state is still nothing more than the flaming-up of the natural spark that slumbers in every person. The modern critic finds himself squeezed between a pair of pre-judgments: there is no genuine prophecy, and there are no actual miracles.[146]

It cannot be said that these two prejudgments have vanished in recent times. For F. Hesse (1966), e.g., only the "basic promise" of the Old Testament ("I will be your God; you shall be my people") is the "divine word." All else is purely human "concretization" of that "basic promise."[147] From that starting point Hesse explains the concrete "prophecies" of the Old Testament as human; prophecy is "capable of error" and also "factually proven to be erroneous"; it "could not prophesy" the fact of Christ.[148] If the New and Old Testament are compared, the New Testament salvation event "simply cannot be squared with the Old Testament prophecies."[149] In concrete terms, then, the prophecies were false. This outlook makes its presence felt in modern dogmatics as well.[150] F. Hesse also serves to show how the critique of prophecy is of a piece with the critique of revelation in general. For at the most basic level Hesse says of the biblical statements according to which God allegedly revealed himself to Moses and to the patriarchs: "It is clear to us that we cannot believe these stories as they stand."[151] But if Old Testament prophecy fails the truth test through the fact of Christ, then it is no longer credible regarding the future, either. Hesse even says that the future announced in the Old Testament will "never become fact."[152]

In spite of all this, many remain aware that the Old Testament prophet understands himself as a prophet and traces his message "expressly and unambiguously back to entirely definite objective revelations."[153]

Two chief currents, then, were important for the dismantling of the earlier conception of prophecy. One, rooted in a particular view of the world, saw no more possibility for "supernatural" prophecy given the framework of a natural and rational causal nexus. The second, rooted in an ideal for mankind, saw no more necessity of such prophecy given the ultimate goal of human perfectibility.

We are now in position to clarify the problem of prophecy through more precise reflection. Leading questions are: Just what is "prophecy"? What is the nature of its relation to the causal nexus as we understand it? To what extent is it necessary for revelation and for Christian proclamation? How do Old Testament prophecy and New Testament fulfillment relate to one another? What about Bible prophecies that have yet to be fulfilled?

From the purely human standpoint nothing definitive can be said about the possibility, the necessity, or the essential nature of prophecy in itself. It could indeed be the case that we are dealing here with a sharply pointed instance of something "entirely different." If anywhere, then it would be fitting here to query "revelation" carefully as to the claims that it makes.

Prophecy in the broader sense is the passing along of God's utterances through persons. "Let the one who has my word speak it faithfully" (Jer 23:28 NIV)—those are the instructions for a true prophet. Isaiah and Amos take their stand entirely on this basis: "I tell you what I have heard / from the LORD Almighty, / from the God of Israel" (Isa 21:10 NIV; cf. Am 3:8).

The formula "thus says the Lord" (*coh 'amar Yahweh*) refers repeatedly to this basic structure. God assures hesitant chosen prophets, "Behold, I place my words in your mouth" (Ex 4:12; Jer 1:9). If the word is passed along, then it is not actually the word of Jeremiah or some other prophet himself; it rather remains the word of the Lord (Isa 55:10f.; Mt 1:22, among other fulfillment citations). It is not arbitrary to be reminded here of Paul Ricoeur's judgment, based on Jeremiah 2:1, that the idea of revelation comes out most pristinely in prophecy.[154] Here there must be a sharp distinction between what the prophet passes on "in truth" (Jer 23:28) and the self-understanding of the prophet. The prophet may feel his office to be a burden (Jer 15:10ff.). He may deny it for a time (Jonah). He may understand what is said only with great difficulty (Da 7:15ff.). He may even sin and be lost (Balaam, the prophet in 1Ki 13:11f.). None of this affects the fact that God spoke through their mediation (cf. in the New Testament Jn 11:51f.). What characterizes the prophet is not "his human, prophetic, and authorial stature,"[155] as German idealism falsely thought. It is rather the "truly" given commission that makes him a mediator of God's revelation. It is the "illumination" through which God transmits to him what he has in mind. This basic structure may be traced right into the New Testament, where Jesus, taking up the Old Testament "servant of God" and "friend of God" motifs, calls his disciples "friends" and justifies his act by saying, "For everything that I learned from my Father I have made known to you" (Jn 15:15 NIV). Under this broadened concept there is profound homogeneity shared among Moses, other prophets of the old covenant, and the prophets and apostles of the new covenant.

In a narrower sense, prophecy is the conveying of divine predictions of the future. As with prophecy in the more general sense, so also here the distinction between true and false prophecy arises. It is interesting to note that the common conviction of several prophets is not a standard of truth. Quite often the true prophet stands alone against an entire council of false prophets (e.g., Nu 16; 1Ki 22; Jer 23:9ff.). Revelation takes up the question of the standard of distinction. God's people need orientation points and should not remain in darkness. One of the most ancient standards is the attesting sign. In order to refute the charge that "the LORD did not appear to you" (Ex 4:1), Moses receives the power to effect such signs. They accompany the entire Exodus. Moses himself can demonstrate his authenticity through special signs. At the rebellion of many Levites, Moses says in almost "Johannine" language, "This is how you will know that the LORD has sent me . . . : If these men die a natural death . . . then the LORD has not sent me" (Nu 16:28f. NIV). To the question "How can we know when a message has not been spoken by the LORD?", the answer is that the word of the Lord comes to pass; it comes true (Dt 18:21f.). And what if even bogus predictions come to pass? What if false prophets imitate those who are truly from God, the only One who can announce the future according to Isaiah 41:22ff.; 42:9; 43:9ff.? Then revelation holds a further standard in reserve. According to Deuteronomy 13:2ff., the false prophet whose predictions come true is not to be heeded as soon as it becomes clear that he is promoting idolatry.[156] Yet what is it that unmasks him as an idolater? The context of Deuteronomy 13:1 permits only one answer: his breach of the previously revealed divine word.

It is easy to document the same structure in the New Testament. Among other roles, Jesus fills that of a prophet (Mt 16:14; 24:1ff.; Jn 2:18ff.; 4:19; 6:14; 9:17; Lk 24:19). Immediately the question of his legitimacy arises. Is he a true or false prophet (i.e., a deceiver)? A sign is demanded of him (Mt 12:38; 16:1; Jn 2:18). Jesus gives to both his opposition and his disciples the requested signs (Mt 12:39; 14:33; 16:4; Lk 11:20; Jn 7:17; 10:38).[157] Even his opponents must acknowledge the realization of certain signs (Jn 3:2; 11:47; Mt 12:22f.).[158] After Jesus passed the test of Deuteronomy 18:20ff., the only possibility remaining was to try him according to Deuteronomy 13:2ff. The majority of the Jewish leaders, after initial wavering, opted for this procedure. Jesus was executed on the cross as a "deceiver" (Mt 27:63; cf. Jn 8:48). The Talmud confirms this with the frank statement: "Because he practiced magic and enticed and stampeded Israel," "they hanged Jesus on the evening before the passover feast."[159] After his resurrection, however, the disciples made use of the basis which even their opponents could not dispute, namely, that of Deuteronomy 18:20ff. They proclaimed Jesus, who was "accredited by God to you by miracles, wonders and signs" (Ac 2:22 NIV; 10:38). They broadened this basis, however, using two essential elements. One was the constant reference to God, who by Jesus' resurrection had shown that Jesus was truly sent from God, so that Deuteronomy 13:2ff. could not be applied to him (Ac 2:24ff.; 3:13ff.; 4:10ff.; 10:40ff.). The second element was the proof that in Jesus Old Testament prophecy was fulfilled, even down to predictions of his suffering (Ac 2:25ff.; 3:21ff.). Stephen went a step farther and charged that Israel's leaders consistently persecuted the prophets, so that Jesus' persecution was practically an attesting sign of his legitimacy (Ac 7:51ff.; cf. however also Mt 23:29ff., 37ff.).

Can, then, the thesis that the New Testament cannot be squared with the prophecy of the Old Testament continue to be affirmed so facilely? Not when it is considered that the above claims were not bits of Gentile Christian artfulness but rather modes of argumentation applied by Jews, some rabbinically educated—their line continues as late as the Palestine-born Justin (d. ca. A.D. 165)—with thoroughgoing success.

This is the point where we must once more return to the New Testament. We discover first that Jesus understood himself as an Israelite, a Jew. "Only ahistorical fantasy affirms that Jesus separated himself from Israel."[160] That means, however, that when he appeared he must have clarified his relation to prophecy and to the entire "Old Testament." It would be fair to surmise this even if we knew nothing about it in particular. But we do: the Gospels give us just information enough. Like other teachers of Israel, Jesus acknowledged the Holy Scriptures without modification (Mt 5:17ff.; Jn 10:35). What he disputed was the Jewish Halacha (interpretative tradition). And even that he did not reject in an undifferentiated fashion, as Matthew 23:2f. shows.[161] Schlatter rightly emphasized that one cannot begin here with isolated proofs. Jesus establishes "the connection between his and Israel's Scripture not only through individual words . . . but he relates the entire history and Scripture of Israel to himself and his office."[162] Therefore he assumes the title of the messianic redeemer, like Messiah, Son of David, Son of Man, and makes Scripture the standard rather than the Halacha (Mt 9:13; 12:3, 5; 15:3ff.; 21:12ff.; 22:23–46; Jn 3:13ff.; 5:39; 10:34ff.). From Scripture, not from nationalistic expectation, he derives his suffering and resurrection (Mt 12:40; 16:21ff.; 21:42; 26:56; Lk 24:25ff., 44ff.; Jn 3:13ff.; 13:18). Now, with his coming, the time is fulfilled which the fathers and the prophets yearned for as the time of redemption (Jn 8:56; Lk 4:16ff.; Mt 9:15ff.; 13:16f.). No wonder that all the New Testament writers—nearly all Jews!—glimpsed in Jesus the prophesied Messiah.[163] We find here no trace of that opinion that the so-called Christ fact does not correspond to prophecy, or that the prophecy turns out to be false even respecting concrete fact. Should someone, however, regard all these statements by New Testament authors as fictions, as attempts to show correspondence where none actually exists, then the words of Joh. Dav. Michaelis (1717–91) should be recalled. Michaelis characterized the situation of Jesus' disciples among their contemporaries as follows:

> It would be a totally unbelievable impudence for someone who had formerly spent time with people to write to them later, 'I did miracles in your presence; indeed, you received ability from me to do miracles and to speak in strange tongues,' if nothing of the sort had occurred. Such impudence would bring its perpetrator into immediate disgrace in the eyes of his correspondents, and eventually in the eyes of the whole world—especially if those to whom he wrote had doubts about his teaching or were prejudiced against him.[164]

Revelation does not therefore deny us an answer to the question before us. It defines prophecy for us as the passing on of divine utterances. It shows us the prophet as the essential mediator of this divine revelation. Obviously prophecy, as mediator "between the secret and the revealed,"[165] cannot be dismissed without revelation as factually entrusted to us collapsing like a house of cards. With Schlatter and Ricoeur we do not hesitate to characterize the occurrence of this prophecy as "supranatural."[166] Such prophecy itself determines the conditions of its manifestation.

In view of the causal nexus, the same can be said here as was said about miracles. It is not feasible to argue based on the created order against the Creator who brings about that order. Whoever judges prophecy as questionable or even impossible based on a humanly established notion of a closed causal nexus is proceeding rashly. The dogmatic notion of the *creatio continua* (continuity of creation) is helpful here in that it takes account of the Creator's continuing activity. Creation came to be through the word (Heb 11:3). Who wishes to banish this word from creation? God has rather granted to creation the ongoing reception of his word (Isa 55:10f.). Only an atheistic causal nexus would be an opponent of prophecy.

Also prophecy in the narrower sense, i.e., the announcement of things to come, may not be excluded by appeal to what is allegedly "possible" or "impossible." God places the prophet on his watchtower (cf. Hab 2:1), where there is neither a forgotten past nor an unknown future. Where God is, our time comes to an end. What is future—in human understanding—is seen and taken up by the prophet as present. He who can alter "times and seasons" (Da 2:21), who shortens the days for the sake of his elect (Mt 24:22), who created time (Ge 1:14) and will one day terminate it (Rev 10:6), is not bound by our time (Ps 90:4; 2Pe 3:8). He is eternal (Ps 90:2). "Tomorrow" is within reach of him "today"—humanly speaking (1Ki 22:19ff.)! The prophet draws this "future"—again speaking humanly—into the present of the people of God (Rev 1:1–3—3:19). And in that this future is manifested in the present, it begins to leave its impress on the present. This announcement of the future remains, however, strictly connected to the self-revealing God. Prophecy is not about our perfection but about God's plan coming to pass and about God's honor. That is why both are closely bound together in Isaiah 42:8f.: God will not give his honor to another, and he proclaims that which is new. Humanism feels that divine prophecy is an enemy of human autonomy and therefore rejects it.

On the other hand, there is prophecy that vouchsafes itself with signs. It becomes a sign for us itself. Jesus says repeatedly to his disciples: "I am telling you now before it happens, so that when it does happen you will believe that I am He" (Jn 13:19 NIV; cf. Mt 24:25; Jn 14:29; 16:1, 4). Predictive prophecy, therefore, is a handmaiden of faith. Its fulfillment confirms the truth of the divine message. That applies first to the relation of New and Old Testament. That also applies, however, in view of the occurrences that Jesus prophesied. The statement of Hesse[167] must, therefore, be totally inverted: because Old Testament prophecy became "fact" according to the testimony of the New Testament, prophecy that is not yet fulfilled—of both the Old and New Testament!—will also become a "fact."

But that is not yet the whole story. We must rather fill out the picture through a look at the pedagogical role played precisely by predictive prophecy. Without its warning the Christian community could not withstand the battle with false teaching, could not see through contemporary ideological currents, could not formulate confessions. Such prophecy also leaves an essential impress on the unfolding of doctrine. And most of all: it gives firm ground for hope. For hardly anything is more dangerous than for hope to become abstract and bloodless. As one of the most important pedagogues, predictive prophecy—so often ridiculed as "eschatological roadmap," "apocalyptic fantasy," or a pitiable literary genre—sees to it that God's people can take sure steps into the future. When the heavenly jubilation of the redeemed breaks out (Rev 7:9ff.; 19:1ff.), then thanksgiving for that jubilation's harbinger and precedent, prophecy, will receive its due.

## REVELATION, CHRONOLOGY, AND NUMBERS

Chronology and numbers are an unmistakable indication of the historical nature of the Bible. At the same time they point to the ongoing nature of revelation, or "progressive revelation."

In his 1956 Jordan Lectures David Daube mentioned a rabbinic rule: "There is no before and after in Scripture."[168] He used Exodus 15 as an illustrative example of this rule, where the death of the enemy is reported first and then later what the enemy said (cf. Ex 15:9 with 15:4ff.). Another example is Ezekiel 2, which chronologically must come before Ezekiel 1.[169] Daube suspects that that the Gospel writers may possibly have taken up this rabbinic rule.[170]

Careful investigation of the Lucan prologue (Lk 1:1–4) gives additional pointers in this direction. The two terms *akribōs* and *kathechēs* in Luke 1:3 do not necessarily refer to chronological arrangement, as Sneen demonstrates.[171] Even if *kathechēs* does connote "in order,"[172]

which is not yet established,[173] it is still possible that "order of significance"[174] is what the author intended, an arrangement appropriate to the
significance of the events and not to their chronological order. Blomberg
has underscored this "topical" rather than "temporal sequence."[175]
Blomberg draws the conclusion that it is therefore "methodologically
inconsistent to infer chronology from mere narrative sequence, even
where no potential conflicts with parallels arise."[176] Interestingly,
Augustine was also convinced that the Gospels do not always report
chronologically.[177]

On the other hand, we observe that the Bible has an uncommon
interest in chronological determination, which typically distinguishes it
from other "religious" literature, even, e.g., from the Koran.

This chronological organization begins already with the structure
of the canon. The postexilic writings do not stand at the beginning of
the so-called Old Testament but rather primarily at the end. And in the
Pentateuch it is precisely not the patriarchal narratives or the Exodus that
stands at the start but the report of the beginnings of creation and of history. This corresponds to what we find in the New Testament. It is the
story of Jesus that forms the beginning of the New Testament, not the
temporally later event, presumably circa A.D. 95, of the vision received
on Patmos. The Spirit who created this entire work of revelation followed, then, the idea of a principally historical-chronological order.
What that means just for the history of ideas can hardly be measured.

From this starting point we can follow the chronological organization right down into individual groups of texts. A classic example is
again the Pentateuch. It originates with the origin of life, depicts the
course of primal history (cf. the genealogies), follows the course of the
patriarchal history, and finally, from Exodus to Deuteronomy, sketches
the history of Israel down to the death of Moses. The enormous mass of
commandments contained in the Pentateuch did not destroy this chronological structure. Just how important the idea of a chronologically
ordered sequence is may be seen in Deuteronomy 26:5ff. This credo
became a central component of Israel's confession of faith.

A second, no less impressive classic example is the innumerable references to dates in the prophetic books. The Old Testament contains the genre "prophetic narrative." That is, the historical activity and suffering of a prophet (Elijah, Elisha, etc.) is set forth in an approximate chronological framework. Where entire books bear the name of a prophet one finds both direct and indirect, approximate and exact, references to dates (to cite just a few examples: Isa 1:1; 2:1; 6:1; 7:1; 14:28; 20:1; 36:1; 39:1). We encounter nothing different in the New Testament. The story of Jesus can be synchronized and thus dated in relation to Herod, the Baptist, and Pilate (cf. Mt 2:1, 19; 3:1; 27:2; Lk 1:5; 2:1f.; 3:1ff.; 23:1ff., 7ff.), even if an uncertainty of three years remains regarding the exact time of Jesus' death (A.D. 30? Or A.D. 33?). The book of Acts again shows a basically chronological construction and permits a rough dating of Paul's activity (especially Ac 18:12ff.). Paul's letters can be divided into Prison Epistles and epistles whose setting is prior to his imprisonment. A comparison with Acts aids, e.g., in establishing 1 Thessalonians as one of the earliest, if not the very earliest, letter of Paul.

Other observations, however, appear to contradict the chronological interest of revelation as we have just sketched it. This may be said, first, of the structure within larger groups of texts. Thus the Minor Prophet corpus (twelve prophets in all) unites prophets from three centuries, from Hosea (ca. 750 B.C.) to Malachi (ca. 480–450 B.C.). True, it appears to follow a chronological order within itself. But it came to stand after Ezekiel because it was placed into the sequence of prophetic books according to its closing portion, the book of Malachi. That means that within the Hebrew canon Hosea, which may be placed in the mid-eighth century B.C., follows Ezekiel, who prophesied in the sixth century. Here thematic organization ("twelve minor prophets") takes precedence over chronological considerations (Hosea actually prophesied before Ezekiel). The same applies to the Pauline corpus. It is obviously not arranged chronologically. Otherwise, as far as we know, 1 Thessalonians would have to come first, with Acts immediately after it. Instead thematic considerations reign. They dictate that the letters addressed to congregations be grouped together (Romans through Thessalonians), and that the longest come first within this division.

What we see within the larger text-groups is repeated in the smaller ones. Thus we find in the Gospels certain arrangements that are clearly thematic. Parables of Jesus, e.g., are brought together in special parable chapters (Mt 13; Mk 4). Or to cite a further well known example: what Matthew presented in one individual context as the Sermon on the Mount, Luke presented over the course of several chapters. The Gospel writers felt a freedom, therefore, to work within thematic rather than chronological parameters. This observation agrees with what we said above regarding the rabbis. It is interesting that students of the apostles related that Mark did not give a chronologically ordered presentation.[178] Because chronological and thematic viewpoints stand side by side, it is difficult for us to determine whether John 2:13ff. pictures a second temple cleansing, or whether John placed the incident at the beginning of his gospel for thematic reasons. We can also observe within an individual pericope that it is not temporal succession but thematic interest that determines and organizes the story. In Jonah 3, e.g., one can see that it is the command of the king, serving in his role as priest, that effected the general repentance of the inhabitants of Nineveh. Chronologically, then, the events of Jonah 3:6–9 predate those of Jonah 3:5. Also in Jonah: The third clause of 1:10 temporally precedes the second, and the second for its part precedes the first. Jonah conveys a message, the sailors gain awareness thereby resulting in fear and interrogation. Here scholars speak of a "backward facing style" of the Hebrew language. If this peculiarity is noticed, then there can be no more talk of contradiction because of the sequence of events on the stormy lake (Mt 8:23ff.; Mk 4:35ff.). True, Matthew first records the question about "little faith" (8:26), then the stilling of the storm, while Mark's order is opposite: first the quieting of the storm (4:39), then the question to the disciples about their deficient faith. If, however, one or even both of the Gospel writers were working from a primarily thematic basis, then we should not expect chronological precision in the depiction of the course of events![179] Now we understand better why some rabbis said that in Scripture there is no "before" and no "after."

We must therefore proceed from the fact that chronological *and* thematic viewpoints *together* determine the arrangement of biblical statements. What are the consequences of this? #1) First, it is still true that overall the chronologically ordered course of occurrences is predominant. Scripture is rooted in the origins of creation and leads to the prophetically manifested goal of salvation history. #2) Further, Scripture's references to dates are not to be moved about at will. Where such references show up, they are a part of revelation that is to be taken seriously. #3) Nevertheless, within Scripture's overall chronological scaffolding there are numerous cases in which arrangement is thematic, not chronological. This becomes clear in view of the Gospel narratives. In all four New Testament Gospels we find an unalterable fivefold framework: introduction (e.g., John the Baptist), early days of Jesus' ministry, interactions and disputes, passion, resurrection. This comprises the skeletal structure of the overall report. But within the individual categories the Gospel writer is free to organize material either chronologically or thematically. #4) A fourth consequence is that we must exercise utmost caution in attempting to establish dates where the Bible itself gives no precise information. Precisely, New Testament research has taught us to handle individual pericopes first of all as small discrete units. #5) In agreement with Blomberg[180] we must emphasize that no contradiction is to be deduced from varying arrangements of events or accounts. Talk of "contradictions" thereby loses considerable foundation just in view of the different narrative possibilities of Scripture.

Concerning *numbers* in the Bible, their significance is generally hotly disputed. Here we can set aside chronological information, which we have already discussed. It will suffice to glean some wisdom from church history, in particular a few of J. A. Bengel's infelicitous calculations. Bengel regarded the Bible's numbers as its skeleton in a quite literal sense: "I think that . . . what the skeletal system is to anatomy, biblical chronology is for the knowledge of redemptive truth."[181] When Bengel set Jesus' return at

1836, he overstepped the biblical boundaries set for us by Matthew 24:36 and Acts 1:7. This boundary is not to be dismissed with the explanation that the earthly Jesus did not know the time and hour, while the exalted Jesus did know them and passed them along to the prophet who wrote the book of Revelation. The chronology of the Bible cannot facilely be extended into the *eschaton*. Nor can it, however, be facilely projected back into the mists of temporal origins. What lies back beyond the Fall eludes all description from the side of fallen mankind. Therefore we no longer know the age of the world, the first dates of creation and of history.

What about symbolic numbers? Here too the boundaries of interpretation are discernible. One boundary is the fact that the Bible doubtless makes use of such numbers, e.g., at Matthew 1:17, and very probably also at John 21:11. Few will doubt that the number 7 contains and expresses spiritual import. A second boundary is cautionary: the danger of speculation regarding such numbers is especially great. That goes for liberal interpretation just as much as for conservative. Between these two boundaries lies a great host of cases where various views are plausible even within the church itself. Context is often useful in arriving at a resolution. Thus the number 2 in Zechariah 4:14, or 7 in Zechariah 4:10 and Revelation 1:20, is explained more fully. Other numbers are intentionally not explained. E.g., we are not certain to this very day what 666 in Revelation 13:18 means. Overall, strict restraint should be exercised in the interpretation of symbolic or allegedly symbolic numbers when a supporting contextual basis is absent.

## IN WHAT SENSE IS THE BIBLE HISTORICAL?

It is worthwhile to restate a few basic thoughts.

1. We started with the *mysterium* of the *transitio revelationis*, i.e., the mystery of the transition of divine revelation into human history. This secret is not to be resolved by taking a stand on either end of two extremes. Some do this from the human side, seeing in the Bible a mere document of history, a book with errors and contradictions, or even a

book just like any other. Some do this from the divine side, regarding the Bible as the product of spiritual ecstasy, an esoteric document for a few specially qualified persons, or a message originating beyond history.

2. As revelation thoroughly integrated into history, the Bible challenges us to historical investigation and interpretation. Broad stretches of it are patent of historical verification. The advantages of historical investigation of the Bible lie in the expansion of our cognitive understanding, in apologetic as well as missionary conviction of its reliability, in the methodological accessibility of a doctrinal consensus, in a conveying of its content in pedagogically effective ways, and in the correction of mistaken paths that appear through a primarily dynamic-direct or even spiritual application of the Bible.

3. The historical nature of the Bible means, moreover, that it mirrors in itself a historical progression. It reveals to us, so to speak, the steps that God's self-revelation has taken in the course of earthly history. It possesses an unimpeachable chronological structure. It thereby forces us to distinguish that which is distinct to each given specific temporal zone of God's activity. Whoever mixes statements of revelation from the various ages is sure to arrive at mistaken interpretations.

4. The transition from eternity to temporality also means, however, that revelation appears ambivalent and can be interpreted variously. It can be rejected and accepted, rightly and wrongly understood. In this essential ambivalence lies its servant form. This servant form does not, as is often claimed, consist in some necessary proneness to error and mistake. It would however be disastrous if we nullified God's decision in favor of this ambivalence and sought to flee to a storm-free world beyond history and historical research.[182]

5. Finally, as symbolic numbers showed us, the historical meaning of a biblical statement presents no impediment to a *sensus plenior* (deeper meaning).[183] Historical and spiritual interpretation condition and supplement each other. Anyone who makes monopolistic use of the historical, or any other sole interpretative approach, subjects revelation to a restriction that is quite foreign to it.

# CHAPTER TWELVE

# Revelation
# and Criticism

## DEFINING HISTORICAL CRITICISM

In an inaugural lecture (published in 1984) in Basel, Switzerland, Joachim Latacz recounted the highlights of a famous debate in classical scholarship dealing with the ancient Greek poet Homer.[1] It all started, Latacz reports, when in 1795 Friedrich August Wolf asked, "Can the two great early Greek epics the *Iliad* and the *Odyssey*—the first about 16,000, the second about 12,000 hexameters in length—have come from one author each, or one author only? Wolf and his students answered: no. Two considerations speak against it. First, the works exhibit logical and stylistic contradictions in their structure and narrative form. Second, their authorship cannot have succeeded with the aid of writing, because at that time writing did not exist." The *Iliad* and the *Odyssey* "were rather pieced together by a number of poets in the course of a long tradition process." Soon the work of from two to twenty hands was discerned—"depending on the ingenuity of the scholar making the analysis." "The outcome: from Friedrich August Wolf to Gottfried Hermann, Karl Lachmann, Ulrich von Wilamowitz-Moellendorff,

Wolfgang Schadewaldt, and Karl Reinhardt, to many others right down to Peter Von der Mühll, there came to be as many Homers as there were Homer experts. The public . . . was helpless. It no longer knew what it was reading: where Homer was speaking in the *Iliad*, where other bards—earlier, later, contemporary—where the hands of poetasters, interpolaters, would-be poets were in evidence. And then: was Wilamowitz's Homer the real one? Or how about the Homer of Von der Mühll? Or did the real truth lie in the view that objective criteria of differentiation were demonstrably mistaken because of the failure of all those analysts to come to a consensus? Was the whole controversy just a tiresome game?"

If we replace the name "Homer" with "Moses," the title *Odyssey* with "Pentateuch," and the names of Homer scholars with Pentateuch critics, then we have a fairly precise picture of the course of historical criticism as applied to the Bible, which has run parallel to Homer research in the last two hundred years in astonishing fashion.[2]

This criticism, which characterizes itself as "historical criticism" or "historical-critical investigation" or "historical-critical method(s)," today dominates Western and ecumenical theology. Moreover, it is commended to us as the best, most appropriate, and most promising means of opening up the meaning of the Gospel.

If we desire to enter a discussion on this subject that extends beyond the German-speaking realm, we must first touch on the *problem of definition* with which especially English-language usage presents us. Conservative, even fundamentalist theologians defend "historical criticism." "Historical criticism" serves as a bulwark against obscurantism, subjectivism, and inappropriate allegorization.[3] The demand therefore arises: "[T]he Christian cannot deny the legitimacy of historical criticism"[4]—"historical criticism . . . should be supported and encouraged."[5] Characteristic here is Clark Pinnock's *The Scripture Principle* (1984). Pinnock defends the inspiration and authority of Scripture and likewise its "inerrancy."[6] At the same time, however, he casts his vote for "positive criticism."[7] In all these uses "criticism" means careful scientific investigation. "Historical criticism" amounts to "historical research." But that is not what the German theologian, influenced by his own peculiar history, denotes when he speaks of "historical criticism." The concepts "historical" and "critical" are not, therefore, simply congruent. This shows itself in the concern some express to distance "historical criticism" from "radical criticism" or "German rationalism."[8]

In what follows we proceed from that form of "historical criticism" that developed before and during the Enlightenment into a fundamental theological *modus operandi.*

## AN "INTELLECTUAL DESTINY"?

Emanuel Hirsch thought that the rise of historical criticism was our *"intellectual destiny."*[9] It was inevitable. The view that "we can no longer go back to being without it" is one of the most broadly held opinions, also among so-called evangelical theologians.[10] This furnishes a basis from which the theological right to apply historical criticism is derived. Richter could still write in 1971: "The right to make use of historical criticism is today . . . undisputed in the area of theological thought."[11] Here is it clear on all sides that "criticism" entails not only the (self-evident!) task of differentiation but also a "critical" judgment of the biblical statements. This "criticism" affirms or rejects those statements; in a word, it is content criticism (*Sachkritik*) of the Bible.[12] Some authors go as far as E. Käsemann and E. Grässer, who hold that the historical-critical method "factually" divides science from speculation or primitivism.[13] More conservative interpreters content themselves with mentioning that the "historical-critical outlook" (almost always in the singular!) has "its entirely definite boundaries."[14] We will have to pose the question, therefore, whether this criticism of revelation is actually an intellectual destiny—or rather a disaster. Yet we may not stop with this question, which can be finessed, but must push ahead to the ultimately decisive question of whether and how criticism actually relates to revelation.

## THE DANGER OF MORALISTIC JUDGMENTS

The discussion to be taken up here is not only burdened with problems concerning definition. Moral judgments and objections also pose difficulties. Many advocates of historical criticism emphasize their love of truth and feel themselves "obligated solely to knowledge of the truth."[15] True, we seldom encounter any more the overblown eulogies once heaped on D. F. Strauss for his "thirst for truth, love for truth, devotion to truth," "his uprightness," and "his morality."[16] It is nevertheless striking that students of A. Jülicher (1857–1934) honored him as the model "educator . . . for strict veracity and objectivity,"[17] and that Bultmann by his own admission "encountered the seriousness of radical veracity in liberal theology."[18] Thus even conservative researchers arrived at the conviction that "historical critical research . . . fulfills . . . a simple obligation to truth."[19]

Those not embracing historical criticism were seen as less than objective and truthful. D. F. Strauss, caught up, it is true, in polemical language more common in the nineteenth century, accused the conservative scholar Hengstenberg "of pious vileness."[20] Strauss regarded him as "outside the pale of science" while at the same time according "moral dignity" to himself and his teacher F. C. Baur.[21] Even harder blows were aimed at A. Schlatter, who was cannily wary of historical criticism, by E. v. Dobschütz in 1927: Schlatter's "interpretive ideal . . . is dilettantish."[22] And more bitter still was G. Ebeling's blast leveled at Hans Asmussen (1950) when Asmussen defended the unity of the book of Isaiah (Ebeling was not an Old Testament scholar): "This primitively dogmatic argumentation, which in general does not even betray a precise knowledge of the general opinion of the Old Testament research that it battles against, is not only bereft of sober exegetical labor. It also tacitly incorporates a fundamental No to the historical-critical method."[23] Later in the same article Ebeling called opponents of historical criticism "internally untruthful"; they work "to say the least in an unreflected, inconsistent fashion."[24] We have seen the outcry against "primitivism" directed against the opponents of historical criticism again in 1980 by E. Grässer.[25]

The other side certainly did not take all this lying down. Both sides inflicted wounds. But because of the influence and dominance that historical criticism had won in the nineteenth century, the verdict of dishonest, ignorant, and unscientific hung over all who opposed it, generating fear. In any case this conflict, waged on a moral and injurious level, shows that historical criticism by no means involves mere technicalities and procedural issues. It rather touches "the deepest foundations and most difficult connections of theological thought and ecclesiastical existence."[26] To that extent G. Ebeling proved to be correct.

## THE HISTORY OF HISTORICAL CRITICISM

The history of historical criticism reveals to us the basic tenets of this mighty movement. Many volumes have been written about this history. In the scope of our presentation we can attempt no more than a few sketchy and quite condensed remarks.[27]

In 1966 Klaus Scholder offered the following summary of his investigation of biblical criticism's origins: "The development of historical-critical theology—doubtless one of the most important events in recent theological history—has until now never been presented in context."[28] It is an "event of inestimable import."[29] Many agree with this judgment. Thus, e.g., Ebeling spoke of a hermeneutical "turning point."[30]

It is sometimes supposed that natural scientists brought things to this turning point. That is true, if at all, only in a very limited sense. Galileo, e.g., explained in 1615 (writing to Christine von Toscana) that the Scripture is free of error when interpreted according to its own sense. It appears that many natural scientists saw a long-term solution in some form of accommodation theory.[31]

Le Brun, however, cited three different causes for historical criticism: #1) Catholic skepticism, #2) application of reason to the Bible (rationalism), and #3) a "novel Protestant theology."[32]

Doubtless, the Catholic skepticism arose not from some craze to criticize but rather from love for the (Catholic) Church. W. G. Kümmel begins his book on the history of New Testament research[33] with Richard Simon (1638–1712). Simon himself explains he will "take sides only with the truth" and at the same time faithfully "follow the Catholic faith."[34] The "truth of religion" does not, however, lie in the Bible but "in the church."[35] The "extensive alterations that were made to the biblical text," many of which he detected and investigated, "completely destroy," he thinks, "the [Scripture] principle of Protestant and Socinian alike, who focus exclusively on just these manuscripts of the Bible."[36] The Protestant insistence that "Scripture is clear in the light of itself" can no longer be sustained.[37] Simon thus pushed aside the Scripture principle (*sola scriptura*) of the Reformation. He stands firmly within the tradition of Catholic Tridentine theology, which had consistently contested the sufficiency and clarity of Scripture as interpreted with reference to itself. Others in the same tradition are e.g., Montaigne, Charon (1594), Magni (1628), and Morin (1591–1659).[38] Simon was applauded by J. S. Semler and Joh. Dav. Michaelis[39] and is praised right up to the present day by Protestant historical-critical interpreters.[40] In any case historical criticism fought the Reformation Scripture principle.

As far as we can determine, the Socinians (Sozzini, Crellius, Ruard, among others) were the first sizable Protestant group to place Scripture and reason on the same level and thereby elevate *sana ratio* (sound reason) to the ultimate norm.[41] From the standpoint of philosophy the reign of rationalism begins with René Descartes (whose famous *Discours de la méthode* appeared in 1637). The human "I" "moves into the center of the universe."[42] It becomes "the foundation of all human knowledge."[43] Since Descartes it is philosophically impossible to prove one's case on the basis of authorities—e.g., church tradition—other than reason.[44] A second consequence of the Cartesian revolution is the "absolute priority" now accorded to man in the former triad God/world/man.[45]

As an example of "novel Protestant theology," Le Brun cites the academy of Saumur, where Louis Cappel, the author of *Critica Sacra*, maintains that Hebrew is inherently unclear. It requires, he argued, illumination by other Semitic languages.[46] Whether such theological views played as great a role as Le Brun thinks is an open question. It appears, however, that Catholic skepticism and burgeoning rationalism gave primary impetus to the new development.

The point at which rationalism managed to breach the wall of Protestant theology was in the area of the first article of the Apostles' Creed, the theology of creation ("We believe in one God, the Father Almighty, *creator* . . ."). Protestantism in the form of a "Cartesian middle party"[47] came up with an intellectual construct that enjoyed lasting popularity, according to which God was said to have created both revelation and reason—and then the inference was drawn that God "must have created them both without essential contradiction to each other."[48] Since it was easier, even for the theologian, to determine the content of his reason than the content of revelation, the latter had little chance to exert decisive influence. It was reason which gradually acquired leverage over revelation. Now what if Picht is right in his claim that "reason, as understood in Europe through Kant and beyond, is nothing other than an idol"?[49] In any case "reason" or its equivalent now became the authority that along with Scripture called the theologian to account.

Various impulses, not only Descartes or Spinoza, played a part in the formation of full-blown Enlightenment theology. The influence of English Deism is widely recognized, embodied by the likes of the Latitudinarian John Locke (1632–1704), John Toland (1670–1722), Matthew Tindal (1657–1733), and Thomas Clubb (1679–1747).[50] Still in 1809 Gottlieb Wilhelm Meyer appealed to Bolingbroke, Chubb, Collins, Hume, Morgan, Tindal, and Woolston.[51] A strong historical interest makes itself felt, e.g., in Baumgarten, but this interest did not yet by that fact lead to historical-critical theology.[52] Also making itself felt was the decisive will to shake off church dogma as a representation of slavish conditions. It was thought that this would effect an essential liberation of theology.[53] To be "dogmatic" became a sharp reproach.[54] By fighting dogmatic restrictions, one contributed simultaneously to human freedom, to the progress and improvement of mankind. Some theologians described this as practically a fight "with superstition" or even as a "fight between light and darkness," between "insight and ignorance," between "wisdom and error."[55] What took place prior to Luther was "darkness."[56] The consciousness of liberation led to the praise of Erasmus[57] and to contact with the Renaissance, so that one could occasionally speak of "impulses of the Greek spirit."[58] Luther, on the other hand, had to accept considerable censure.[59] The "happy revolution" that took place here according to G. W. Meyer (V, p. 4) was described by Schöffler in slightly baroque terms. Schöffler says it was a time in which the "upper levels of our culture sailed out away from the sweet stream of faith, which flowed securely between the stalwart banks of dogma, into the brackish waters of rationalistic Protestant Scholasticism, and then into the waters of Enlightenment rationalism, so that in a short time they were finally driven onto the bitter sea of unbelief with its storms and shipwrecks."[60]

Sociologically speaking, it is significant that Enlightenment literature was widely produced by "theologians and sons of theologians."[61] Participation by children of the manse was uncannily extensive.[62] Out of this grew a movement of "pastoral Enlightenment advocates" who sought "to spread sound reason everywhere and to enlighten religious sentiments."[63] It was therefore more a "revolution" of the upper class, behind which stood "no very considerable army of laypersons," according to Aner.[64] We often encounter cases in which theologians of the Enlightenment distance themselves from dogmatically strict figures, e.g., J. A. Turretin (1671–1737), the son of a strict Calvinist,[65] or J. S. Semler, who hailed from "strongly Pietistic circles."[66] Historical criticism as established in the eighteenth century is the undisputed offspring of the Enlightenment.[67] It was itself conscious that it advocated something new and that it would bring about profound change in the history of theology.[68] Its "dogmatic foundation" lay in the "Enlightenment's faith in reason," as Gadamer termed it.[69] This foundation no longer supported traditional dogma.[70] What was rejected was, e.g., the doctrine of original sin. Lessing saw mankind "in the first and lowest stage" as simply incapable of following "moral laws."[71] Instead of sin, therefore, the problem is weakness! Man was basically good. The doctrine of propitiary atonement also fell into disfavor.[72] So did most supernatural aspects of the Christian conception of faith. Thus, e.g., Johann Joachim Spalding (1714–1804) demanded that "the doctrines of the trinity, of reconciliation, and of justification be abolished from preaching" on the ground that they are "theoretical religious doctrines."[73] Early in the history of these developments the doctrine of inspiration was restricted to inspiration of the person, as seen, e.g., in Chr. Matth. Pfaff.[74]

Exegesis at that time had already long been called "grammatical-historical interpretation" of Scripture.[75] But soon this became "historical" or "biblical criticism."[76] Historical understanding received enormous emphasis, even if, e.g., Baumgarten still left room for a "sensus mysticus."[77] Nevertheless, if one scrutinizes more closely, the individual steps in the new method were not so revolutionary after all. Pfaff—like Bengel before him!—made use of philology, history, classical studies, geography, chronology, and rabbinic witnesses for his interpretation.[78] Baumgarten—like Rambach before him!—wished to investigate the "historical circumstances" as precisely as possible and took special note of the author of a Scripture passage, the addressees, the time and place of writing, and why it was written.[79]

We must once more concur with G. Ebeling when he sees the "truly decisive and revolutionary aspect" of the historical-critical method in this: "all sources of the past"—even the Bible!—moved into "the light of the new presumed certainties."[80] That is, it was not the discovery of new, heretofore unknown means of investigation or methodological procedures that fomented the radical changes. It was rather the principally skeptical handling of Scripture, which was now "to be interpreted like, say, a text from Plato."[81] Thus we once more run up against the basic question: Exactly how does (historical) criticism relate to revelation?

## CRITICISM OF CRITICISM

It would be an inexcusable gap in even a sketch of the history of historical criticism if we made no mention of the criticism of criticism. We will discover that the judgment of Gustav Schulze (1891), which is representative of a whole other side of opinion, contains at least a grain of truth: "The history of criticism is the judge of criticism."[82]

Not long ago (1977) J. van den Berg impressively stated the burden of the decisions that need to be made here: "The question of the legitimacy of historical criticism brings all sorts of questions along with it: not only the question of what the Bible says, but also the question of the world view, the view of God, the manner of revelation, the value or lack of value of the metaphysical thought. All the great theological problems are wrapped up in it."[83]

Following is a thematic, not chronological, list of points at which criticism has been questioned.

1. The complaint about the *destabilization of faith* would not go away. The fear of departure from the most ancient, received Christian faith formed, e.g., an element in the bitter opposition faced by D. F. Strauss in Würrtemberg and Zürich.[84] In 1926 Girgensohn registered the experience of many: "When young theologians enter church work with their historical conception, they find mostly strong resistance to the way they regard Scripture."[85] Theology students themselves were in the front lines of those affected. Characteristic is an invitation sent out to a pastor's prayer fellowship (Zentrale Arbeitskreis der Pfarrergebetsbruderschaft) on January 18, 1961, announcing the first seminar of the new term: "In increasing measure we are unsettled that theology students go astray in their faith, no longer reading their Bibles personally and unable to pray." The invitation goes on to pose the question of "what is wrong with the basic approach of present critical work" and asks "whether the way future pastors are educated might not be in need of reform."[86]

2. The concern with *technical scientific problems* often distanced academic theology from the church and its practical problems—even if

this distance fluctuated and, e.g., after World War I was especially strongly felt;[87] and even if every form of theology (not just practical) was threatened by such idiotically specialized one-sidedness. The complaint remains that due to the combination of destabilization of faith and specialization, a structural alienation arose between large segments of congregations and historical-critical professors. Here we stumble against a sort of prolongation of the Enlightenment tradition with its one-sided domination by an educationally privileged citizenry.

3. Historical criticism saw in historical explanation of the Bible the sole scientific way. This meant a monopoly by the historical-critical method. The conviction was, in Childs' words, "that only the historical method has a validity for biblical studies."[88] Protest arose against this one-sided, historicizing focus, which wanted absolutely nothing to do with other approaches.[89]

4. A special problem involved the *virtually unlimited plurality of hypotheses*. Already in 1927 R. Seeberg reported that historical-critical exegesis was being reproached for leaving behind a "field of wreckage."[90] Criticism is too uncritical about this plurality, the protest ran. E. Güttgemanns spoke, e.g., in 1970 of "an uncritical exuberance in hypothesis formation."[91]

5. Historical criticism had once been developed to comport with the philosophy of the Enlightenment. It had drawn its cogency not least from this agreement with the general cultural and intellectual climate of its day. Now, however, it must hear the charge that *it simply accommodates itself to modern man*. E. Fascher even cited Nietzsche in this connection in speaking of "temporally fashionable triviality."[92] From the opposite side arose the complaint that historical criticism finds itself in a "psychological vicious circle of scientific methods and findings"; it often betrays "a scholastic attachment to a particular line of thought."[93]

6. Still more profound was the charge that *faith can find no footing on the hypotheses of historical criticism*. It is surprising to find Martin Dibelius, a historical critic, voicing this sentiment in 1925: "Faith, however, cannot be built on a foundation that must be replaced

every ten years in keeping with the state of research."[94] He speaks of the virtual demise of historical research of the Bible: "It has not fulfilled the religious mission of passing on a unified and unshakable ground for faith."[95] Dibelius therefore sought refuge in the "suprahistorical."[96] F. Beisser in 1973 voiced a similar charge: "An absolutely established critical consciousness means the replacement of truth with hypothesis. This would be the end of faith."[97]

7. One of the essential presuppositions of historical criticism is placed in question by the insistence that *authority can also be based outside of reason*. It should be noted here that philosophy is witnessing a stocktaking of the history of the Enlightenment. The assessment is in part highly critical. Three names come to mind. Gadamer starts with the Enlightenment's quest to arrive at "the subjection of all authority to reason."[98] Gadamer wishes, on the other hand, to show that authority as such can also "be a source of truth." The Enlightenment erred in "simply defaming all authority."[99] A second and more expansively critical voice is that of Ricoeur. He battles Descartes and his starting point in the reflective human subject. Instead, Ricoeur sees every consciousness as being determined by an event. At this point the concept "revelation" receives a new significance. To the extent that revelation precedes consciousness and shapes it, it can no longer be derived from consciousness. And to the extent that historical revelation is involved, we must reckon with the "priority of historical testimony over self-consciousness."[100] Consequently Ricoeur fights the "idea of the autonomy" of consciousness.[101] His "concept of revelation," or "hermeneutic of revelation," reminds us of Schelling's "philosophy of revelation."[102] In addition to Gadamer and Ricoeur we may mention G. Picht. He sees "the act of questioning" as the "fundamental impulse of thought."[103] "Perhaps the question to be answered is what form of the knowledge [*Erkenntnis*] of the truth accounts for all possible knowing [*Wissen*]."[104] Such openness to questioning, however, shatters the current prevailing construct of human reflection as the basis of knowledge. For who is the "I"? What is "thinking"? Picht clearly follows Schelling in no longer regarding sub-

jectivity as the "foundation of our knowledge of the world."[105] But that also calls in question a starting point in human reason. At the same time, this openness to questioning wins back the possibility of receiving answers from outside the ego. Picht addresses the question of how truth and knowledge can come to us: it must be the "task of theology . . . to call the sciences of this world in question and to test them by standards that are not discoverable by scientific-immanent means"—namely, on the basis of the Gospel.[106]

8. A further criticism of historical criticism involved its *elimination of the supernatural*. "A new scientific spirit developed," says Girgensohn in his treatise on the proof of Scripture, "the spirit of heedless historical criticism over against all supernatural constituents of tradition."[107]

9. The same author, Girgensohn, lamented the "historical *distance*" that historical criticism placed *"between the word of Scripture and its contemporary reader."*[108]

10. Yet not only this distance, but also the *elevation of the theologian* over the Bible draws fire from critics of the historical-critical method. The way of dealing with the Bible chosen by historical criticism "means . . . that I place myself and my scientific judgment above the material: I possess some kind of standards that I regard as scientific and by which I measure the object under scrutiny. Or to put it differently: as scientific subject I am judge of what truth of Scripture is valid and what is not."[109]

11. From this follows that *"the autonomous thinking subject"* is *"the ultimate deciding authority* in resolving all scientific questions"—"the critically thinking person becomes the measure of all things."[110]

12. Distance, elevation, autonomy of the subject—so runs a further objection—have called the biblical tradition in doubt. As the decisive entity of the Bible, Jesus has often been made the standard of what being Christian means. But what do we know of Jesus if the tradition is unreliable? O. Procksch comments, "If we call the [apostolic] procla-

mation in doubt, *we also give up the only historical tradition* that exists about him."[111]

13. With dogged consistency the criticism of historical criticism culminates in the *demand that the historical-critical method be given up*. The point was long since reached, critics say, "when its [i.e., historical criticism's] work seemed to produce more negative than positive results."[112] Now there is need to reestablish connection with "precritical interpretation."[113]

The above points of criticism sharpen the question of how revelation and criticism relate to each other. Yet, just what do we mean by "criticism"?

## THE CRITICAL ELEMENT

In all the above the concept of "criticism" is accorded considerable weight. Strangely, we typically find an entirely uncritical confusion in the various conceptions of "criticism." We find only a few reflections on possible usage. In addition to this, there are the problems of definition in various languages to which we have already alluded. Generally appeal is made to the Greek *krinein*, which occurs in the New Testament, to justify "criticism" of the New and Old Testaments. Occasionally such appeals tend to present the "harmlessness" of biblical criticism.

The Greek word *krinein* contains two chief meanings: #1) discerning comprehension, and #2) willful negative judgment. If the first meaning is intended, Greek usage often adds a *dia* prefix: *dia-krinein* (verb), *dia-krisis* (noun). This comprehension is related to the Hebrew *biynah* (understanding), according to which one must stand "between" in order to gain insight. The Hebrew word, however, carries a stronger connotation of personal relationship.

If we turn to the concept of criticism that we encounter in revelation, we see that it is foremost God—and not man—who is critic. It is God who justly "judges," comprehends, assesses; God acquits man or damns him (Ro 2:1ff.). God already exercises his "criticism" today, especially through his word: "It judges the thoughts and attitudes of the heart" (Heb 4:12 NIV; the Greek text contains the word *kritikos*, "able to judge"). God is the One to whom we must give account (*logos*), must answer to (Heb 4:13). It is man, then, who stands in question. Since the Fall he has neither sufficient redemptive knowledge nor the sovereignty to make a decisive judgment—insofar as concerns the relationship to God that decides his life's fate. Certainly, within man's internal creaturely existence, comprehension and judgment are ongoing activities; they are essential and appropriate. In that sense the critical faculty practically amounts to a good gift of the creator. Indeed, Schlatter rightly calls it "our duty . . . to be critical, i.e., to be analyzing [*zerbrechen*, "break into pieces"] both our own thoughts and those of others."[114] But note carefully that he speaks of "our" thoughts—human "thoughts"! To apply such a procedure to revelation would be perverse. Contrariwise, it is first revelation that makes theological-intellectual distinctions possible, so that we are able to comprehend what is really before us, able to assess and to judge. But this only takes place after *we* are judged, after we are known (cf. 1Co 13:12).

Everything hinges on the priority of revelation. True, revelation as such can be rejected or affirmed, for it involves a "nonviolent appeal" (Ricoeur). It can, however, be neither confirmed nor "criticized." For man possesses neither the standpoint, nor the knowledge, nor the might, to ground the justification of revelation on human confirmation or make revelation dependent on human opinion. The *praeiudicum* (prior judgment)[115] of God went forth long before man set out with his "criticism." Only when he assumes the status of one "criticized" by God can he be critically active in the space God's "criticism" allots to him.

We arrive at the following preliminary major features of the relation between revelation and criticism:

1. As "discerning comprehension" (see above), "criticism" is possible and essential. This is true in two respects. First, it involves a creaturely perception that distinguishes the entire form of divine revelation on the level of what occurs within created humanity from other forms

and occurrences. Just as the human ear could understand the speech of the prophets and was in a position to distinguish that speech from others, we today hear or read the "book of books" in distinction to others. This creaturely, "critical" perception involves, e.g., the locating and determining of the text, commonly called "textual criticism." To infer "content criticism" (*Sachkritik*) from this "textual criticism" is diabolically wrongheaded. Just as one cannot well argue that Jesus, in calling listeners to heed his words by the Sea of Galilee, was inviting them to a content-critical (*Sachkritische*) exercise, so one cannot legitimate content criticism by appealing to the philological, literary, or historical means by which we discerningly comprehend the text.

Second, "criticism" in the form of discerning comprehension is likewise offered and made possible by revelation by virtue of its particular contents. Its sequence and its interrelatedness, its similarity and dissimilarity should be pondered. This is already inherent in its history-book character, which is how the Bible *also* encounters us. We have already seen how closely such work is connected with salvation-historical interpretation. This discerning comprehension is, however, as an *interpretive* procedure bound as much to the spiritual renewal of the interpreter as are other steps in that interpretive process. That means that this area involves not only a *creaturely* but a *new-creaturely* level (cf. 2Co 5:17).

Those researchers who have understood their task to involve this kind of spiritual discernment and comprehension have described it as *crisis sacra*, "holy criticism."[116] To make an Enlightenment "content criticism" out of this "holy criticism" is once again a historical miscue.

2. Revelation in its entirety presents itself to "willful negative judgment" (see above) in its servant form, i.e., through the mystery of its transition into human history. It can be accepted or rejected. It can be obeyed, or obedience can be denied it. On this level of encounter, then, "criticism" is permitted to man. But note well: "Criticism" in this sense is tantamount to denial. It is impossible to change the Gospel into an "other Gospel" (1Co 15:11; Gal 1:6ff.)—the "other Gospel" is no longer

a revealed Gospel. And the Law can be observed or broken only as a whole (Mt 5:19; Gal 5:3; Jas 2:10).

3. "Willful negative judgment" in the sense that man decides what is revelation and what is not, is impossible for us on two counts. First, it is impossible on the created level because man lacks the prior knowledge and certainty of what is and can be revelation. Both knowledge and certainty first arise in encounter with God—which is to say, through the revelation of God himself, not, however, detached from it. Second, it is impossible because, on the spiritual level, the level of the new creation, both revelation itself and the Holy Spirit testify to the genuineness and completeness of revelation in the Christian community. "Content criticism" is at best an attempt using unsuitable means on an unsuited object; at worst it is human autonomy creating revelation for itself. "Theological content criticism" is, therefore, a contradiction in terms.

Again, the notion of criticism in general comes in for discussion when its historical right is argued for by appeal to Jesus or to the Reformation.

The relation of Jesus to the Old Testament has already come under consideration (cf. chaps. 7 and 9 above). We restrict ourselves here, then, to the most needful.

Both liberals and biblicists have maintained that Jesus exhibited "freedom" in his use of the Old Testament, that he acknowledged errors in the Old Testament, that he even used "incisive criticism": "He does not hesitate to criticize scripture."[117]

As an example the Sermon on the Mount is commonly adduced due to its so-called antitheses.[118] This example carries weight, however, only if Matthew 5:17ff. is eliminated. For there Jesus lays down a strong confession of trust in the Old Testament: "Do not think that I have come to abolish the Law or the Prophets [= the Old Testament!] . . . not one jot or tittle will disappear from the Law until everything takes place." Jesus does not, then, employ criticism on the Old Testament; he rather unfolds its purpose statements in messianic-divine power.[119]

A similar case can be made regarding the divorce passage,

Matthew 19:1ff. par., which is also often cited.[120] We search this passage in vain, however, for any reproach of Moses. What is reproached is Israel's hard-heartedness. The Mosaic divorce permission (Dt 24:1) had its place. Now, however, the time of pedagogical permission has passed. From now on God's original will in its full extent applies.

Matthew 7:1–23 is said to furnish another example of how Jesus applied criticism to the Old Testament.[121] What is denied there, however, is the Jewish Halacha. Jesus insisted on the validity of the biblical commandments! That a time will come when external food laws will no longer apply because the new covenant displaces the old—that is an entirely different matter. The Old Testament itself refers to this new covenant with its obedience from the heart (cf. Jer 31:31ff.; Eze 36:27).

Jesus' statements regarding *oaths* have also been used to prove his "content criticism" (*Sachkritik*) of the Old Testament.[122] This is another example of the salvation-historical and pedagogical aspects of revelation being ignored. While the Old Testament regulations sought to insure that the *oath* was carried out, Jesus seeks to insure that all our speech squares with what we do. What is latent in the Old Testament is, then, unfolded and brought to fruition—exactly like the commentary that Jesus himself appended to his statements in Matthew 5:17. Not criticism but affirmation and further application of the Old Testament characterize Jesus' teaching on the Old Testament.

Jesus' alleged breaking of the Sabbath can also not be used as evidence that Jesus took a critical stance toward the Old Testament. This is shown by the fact that Sabbath healings in Israel were a thoroughly debatable subject. Jesus was not crucified for breaking the Sabbath. His saying that the Son of Man (Da 7) is "Lord also of the Sabbath" (Mk 2:28) does not do away with the Sabbath but gives its content. The content, however, is given by the one who, as the heavenly Messiah, proclaims and interprets the Torah: he is the Lord of the Torah!

Occasionally one hears that Jesus "critically" judged the temple tax and temple rituals.[123] There is a sense in which this applies, if "critically" be taken to mean "prophetically." It cannot be concealed, however, that the temple was given over to the enemy because of Israel's sin, and that according to God's will the outer temple was only a temporary measure (cf. Da 9:24ff.; Mt 21:12ff., 18ff., 33ff.; 24:1ff.; Ac 7:47ff.). Anyway, Jesus paid the temple tax (Mt 17:24ff.).

It is unnecessary to take up more individual passages here. What is important is that Jesus derived his being sent out and his going forth from the Scripture (Mt 12:40; 21:33ff.; 22:23ff.; Jn 3:14ff.; 5:39), that he clearly placed the Scripture above the Halacha (Mt 15:1ff. par.), that he rooted his actions in the Scripture (Mt 12:1ff.), that he led his disciples into study of the Scripture (Mt 24:15), and that he regarded the Scripture as irrevocable (Mt 5:17ff.; Jn 10:35). How could he—just looking at it from the human standpoint—as Messiah "criticize Scripture"? Jesus did not criticize the Scripture; he "did" it (Jn 4:34; 6:38; Lk 4:21; Mt 5:17–20). Marcion and Mohammed applied criticism to the Bible; Jesus did not.[124]

While it is totally illegitimate to appeal to Jesus in defense of modern "content criticism" (*Sachkritik*), the appeal to Luther appears to hold brighter prospects.

J. S. Semler wanted to associate his views with Luther.[125] Neology clearly felt that an all too critical break with all tradition would not be advisable. So he attempted to enlist the Reformers as fathers of later historical-critical developments. Later this attempt is pursued further. Moldaenke mentions that in Gustav Frank's doctoral dissertation (1859) Luther is regarded as a direct *praecursor rationalismi* (forerunner of rationalism).[126] In 1926 Frick wrote: "The first and sharpest Bible 'critic' on Protestant soil was—Luther."[127] Such claims heighten in the middle of the twentieth century. Thus according to Dinkler the rise of Christianity involved a "reformation" that was "quite essentially" concerned with "the right of biblical criticism" (referring to Jesus and Paul!).[128] On the one hand, Ebeling spoke carefully of "principles" of historical-critical theology among the Reformers and recognized "certain inner material connections."[129] On the other hand, he glimpsed practically the perfecting of the Reformation in the historical-critical method. Protestantism's decision "for the historical-critical method" is said to have "upheld and confirmed the decision made in the 16th century with the Reformation."[130]

What can be said for this view? There are mainly two arguments. The first consists in the Christological concentration that Luther carried out in his Bible interpretation. We find the most pointed formulation of this in WA 39, I, 47, where Luther's forty-ninth thesis, *de fide* (on faith), on the occasion of the disputation of September 9, 1535, says: "If however the opponents promote the Scripture against Christ, then we promote Christ against the Scripture (urgemus Christum contra scripturam)."[131] Both, however, are paradoxical moves. *In point of fact* Scripture cannot be urged against Christ; *in point of fact*, then, there is also no need to urge Christ against Scripture. Those who want to press the words of this disputation easily forget Luther's continuation of this series of theses: "All prophets and fathers," in the Spirit of Christ, "spoke all that stands in Scripture" (fifty-seventh thesis). "All apostles" were "sent as infallible teachers" to us by God's counsel and thus could not err (fifty-ninth and sixtieth theses).[132] The appeal to "we promote Christ against the Scripture (urgemus Christum contra scripturam)" is therefore unfortunate.

The second argument consists in the "content critical [*sachkritischen*] viewpoints" that Luther is said to have used in his forewords to the Bible (WADB 7, 344f.).[133] Yes: Luther spoke content-critically. But: this content criticism had nothing to do with what he took to be the canonical books but rather with the noncanonical. With Philippi one can "doubt that he would have ventured such bold statements in the case of writings recognized unanimously as canonical by the ancient church."[134]

Therefore, Luther research throws up a defense against the rationalists who "in peculiar blindness" wished to see "in Luther a forerunner of their conception of Scripture."[135] It would be farfetched "to want to make [Luther] the father of modern historical-critical scientific study of the Bible."[136] I. Lönning raises the charge against advocates of historical criticism that they worked with "formulas that are in part not found in Luther's time"; they interpret Luther "from the standpoint of a later set of problems."[137] R. Bring is another who sees Luther as standing in opposition to historical criticism, which "is absolutely incapable of reckoning with God."[138] O. Scheel and F. Beisser indicate that Luther hung on every individual word of the Bible and reproached statements that contradicted the Gospel.[139] Scholder does discover a "critical principle" in Luther, but he thinks it is "gleaned from Scripture itself," whereas the Enlightenment mode of posing questions was "dictated from without."[140]

Luther may not, then, be regarded as the source of anything more than weak "principles" or "starting points" for historical criticism. Even his statements that can be construed that way result from abrupt formulations that threaten to transform Scripture into principles ("Law," "Christ," "Gospel"), or from critical but distinctly personal assessments of certain biblical writings.[141]

Overall, however, the Enlightenment had no right to appeal to Luther. Its connection to Luther (and Calvin) amounts to a rupture, not continuity. Most of all, historical criticism developed into opposition to the conception of Scripture of Jesus, the apostles, and the Reformers. We see that clearly once more when we ponder the "tendencies" that Ebeling noted in the hermeneutical "turn to modern times": "abandonment of the doctrine of inspiration"; "distinction between Bible . . . and God's Word"; "autonomy of exegesis from dogmatic (confessional) regulating"; "equating in principle of the Bible with other literature"; "application of the various modes of historical criticism."[142]

Historical criticism possesses, therefore, no *historical* right that it could derive from the origins of Christianity or the Reformation. It is and remains a child of the autonomous spirit of modernity.

## THE HISTORICAL ELEMENT

Till now we have scrutinized but one element of the historical-critical method, the "critical" element. We now turn to the second component, the "historical."

*How "historical" is historical criticism?* To raise this question is to stumble on one of the most astonishing discrepancies in the history of theology.

Doubtless it was historical interest—in evidence since at least the time of Baumgarten—that Enlightenment theologians sought to establish as the leading impulse of their interpretation. Well into the nineteenth century it was even thought possible to comprehend documents of the past, e.g., the Bible, "objectively" in their existence and givenness. Illustrative here is F. C. Baur's treatise *An Herrn Dr. Karl Hase* (*To Mr. Dr. Karl Hase*) in 1855. Baur states that this "is the actual task of criticism: to produce the original facts of the case; to see a thing as it really is, based on its existence; to let oneself be deterred by nothing in clearing away all that hinders us from apprehending a thing in its pure objectivity."[143]

Of this very same Baur,[144] however, H. Liebing shows how criticism and reconstruction were constantly intertwined in his work.[145] Baur very probably let himself be deterred from "pure objectivity," namely, through the effort to see history à la Hegel as "an interconnected entirety."[146] Observations made about the New Testament were pressed into the framework of the Hegelian system. But where philosophical conviction determines the shape of the framework, it is historical *construction* and no longer the historical as such that has the last word. We discover, then, that the historical interest of so-called historical criticism was a *limited* interest.

We encounter the same thing in the case of D. F. Strauss, probably the most famous student of Baur. Schleiermacher and Hegel determined his thinking, and later Feuerbach (from 1839 on?).[147] For him "speculative thought" is the decisive factor if one wishes to interpret the Bible aright.[148] For the essential content of the Bible consists in the early Christian ideas that are contained in it. We must therefore push through from the idea to the concept.[149] He subjected ideas to the sharpest of criticism. But now we must make a peculiar observation. In his *Das Leben Jesu kritisch bearbeitet* (*The Life of Jesus Critically*

*Examined*; 1835/1836, 2 vols.), Strauss states clearly the conviction that his historical criticism is of utterly no concern to the core of the Christian faith: "The author [i.e., Strauss] knows the inner core of the Christian faith to be completely independent of his critical investigations. Christ's supernatural command, his miracles, his resurrection and ascension, remain eternal truths, however much doubt may plague their reality as historical facts [*historische Fakta*]. Only the certainty of this can give calmness and value to our criticism."[150] The consequences of this conception are obvious. A distinction is introduced between "truth" and "reality" ("Fakta"). The "historical" comes to be tantamount to the factual. It is by no means any longer the decisive factor. The decisive factor is rather a "core" that is inaccessible to historical investigation. Criticism can only destroy the "outer shell," not the core. Faith, however, involves the core that is impervious to critical attack. That is, its certainty lies beyond the historical realm. Faith and history are separated from each other. To sum up: the passionately pursued historical research of the Bible no longer deals with the "core" of the Christian faith. Historical criticism basically cultivates an ahistorical faith.

One might think that this is an extreme view, limited to the likes of a radical like Strauss. But we find the same view—at least in part—already in the air much earlier. In circles close to Spinoza there appeared in 1666 a work called *Philosophia sacrae scripturae interpres*.[151] It shows a way to interpret Scripture by use of reason. This way consists in—allegorization![152] If one chooses this way, then in any case historical events are not the main thing but rather certain material statements of Scripture which (in best allegorical style!) are no longer dependent on history.

In his remarks "On the Proof of the Spirit and of Power" Lessing pitted "facts of history" over against "truths of reason" and declared the latter to be fundamentally independent of the former: "Contingent facts of history can never become proof of necessary truths of reason."[153] Insofar as faith is "reasonable," then, it requires in principle no historical basis. Already here, long before Strauss, the "core of faith" is removed from history. What historical criticism undertakes no longer affects this core.

Lessing's approach is carried further by Semler: "The only proof that entirely suffices for the circumspect reader is the inner conviction through truths which are encountered in this Holy Scripture (but not in all parts and individual books)."[154] "Moral truths" are what Semler seeks. He has an aversion to historical books, which do not serve "the betterment of mankind."[155] We may recall once more Aner's verdict that Neology "emptied the concept of revelation" of the "historical . . . in order to replace it instead with a rationalistic content."[156]

These lines of thought can be traced right into present times. For Wellhausen the subjective experience of faith was decisive, not the historical fact: "Jesus was dead. Christ lived."[157] Jesus' preaching involved "the highest ethical conceptuality."[158] This cannot be destroyed through historical criticism. We have basis for faith beyond the realm of history: "In the core of my soul I lay hold of eternity."[159]

M. Dibelius, influenced by Kant,[160] likewise distinguishes "the historical garb" from the core, from the "suprahistorical."[161] Faith must culminate in this suprahistorical realm and become independent of historical research and indeed of history itself.[162] Thus factual matters become secondary. Easter, Dibelius remarks, calls for "presenting the events, not as the disciples . . . experienced them at the time, but as those events later appeared to those who became clearsighted through Easter faith."[163] Easter faith is accordingly more important than Easter fact. This preference for the suprahistorical marks a renewed emergence of historical criticism's bias toward an ahistorical faith.[164]

In some measure historical criticism confronts us with a "docetism from the other side," since in this criticism the historically legendary— to put it bluntly, the historically untrue—is called on to ground faith and commitment. Once again there is a working distinction between "truth" and "reality," a distinction we have already explored repeatedly (cf. chap. 9). W. Joest states, e.g., that "something can be legendary as a historical description, yet true as believing understanding of the reality of Jesus."[165] It may be that doubt concerning the hypothesis jungle of historical-critical exegesis has tempted a systematician like Joest to come up with such a solution. He, too, is concerned to incorporate the "material" that withers under historical scrutiny into his edifice of faith: "a legendary (by historical standards) feature of the reports can very well express something by the content of its theological statements that decidedly belongs to that which pertains to who Christ is."[166] However: here again truth has been emancipated from reality, faith from history. Historical criticism, pursued in this fashion, becomes prelude to an ahistorical faith.

An index of this tendency is the treatment of external criteria in the overall scope of historical criticism. H. Frei observed that already in the eighteenth century, German Enlightenment theology, in contradistinction to theology in England, preferred "internal evidence" to "external evidence."[167] In his treatise on form criticism L. J. McGinley raised similar objections especially against Dibelius and Bultmann. Both neglected the external witnesses of church history.[168] Both are ruled by a prejudice against "the historical value of the whole Gospel story."[169] Indeed, McGinley even comes to the conclusion: "Historical testimony . . . is totally neglected."[170] Even if this judgment is too severe in individual cases, the neglect of "external criteria" by Continental historical criticism is undeniable. This obviously has inner connections with what we have already shown regarding the way the "historical" is handled.[171]

The discrepancy of which we spoke above can be delineated more precisely. It lies between the emphasis on historical biblical exegesis, on the one hand, and the dogmatic move to break free of what is historical, on the other. In terms of their faith, most historical-critical proponents are unhistorical. To put it more sharply: the very historical-theological movement that wanted to claim to be the most "historical" has done the most to devalue history.

## THE SOURCES OF HISTORICAL CRITICISM

To inquire about the sources of historical criticism means more than enjoying a historical reminiscence. Since it comprises the most influential "critical" movement within Christian theology, the question about sources is tied to the hope of coming up with prototypical insights into the relation of criticism and revelation.

Among historical criticism's proponents there exists, first, an astonishing agreement that this criticism is "a child of the Enlightenment."[172] This lineage determines it down to the present day.[173]

This expresses the dominant role that reason plays. Until Descartes philosophy had to answer to theology. After Descartes the relation reversed: theology had to answer to philosophy—as the Enlightenment consciousness saw things, anyway.[174] When we speak here of reason, we are dealing with the reason of the "natural," not the regenerate person. On this Picht remarked: "here, then, the metaphysical discipline of the 'psychologia rationalis,' i.e., man, receives an absolute priority."[175] But this is only one aspect of the new situation. Another becomes clear in observing that this "reason" possesses no neutrality in terms of its worldview. On the contrary, it is a *religiously determined entity*. To cite Picht again: "'Reason' in European thought is, as a projection of the god of Greek philosophy, saturated with myth right down to its innermost components. It is a sign of deficient enlightenment if we do not know this. From this point of view new light falls on the tension between faith and reason, but also on the unfortunate love of theologians for this very 'reason.'"[176] That means that the contact of theology with Enlightenment philosophy and the development of a biblical science that answered to reason was emphatically not a matter of method in the neutral sense.[177] It rather involved religious contamination.

But such contamination was not merely a feature of criticism's beginnings. Rather, historical criticism of the nineteenth century developed in such a way that Grant spoke of theology being shaped by "philosophical presuppositions."[178]

The new situation, through which such application of criticism arose, must clearly be characterized as a break with preceding Christian history. Schwaiger spoke here of a "new establishing of theology,"[179] Westermann of the "opening up of a new dimension,"[180] Ebeling of a "revolution in the history of ideas."[181] Such comments could be multiplied. This revolution marked a collapse of sacred hermeneutics (*hermeneutica sacra*).[182] Metaphysics and the supernatural became dubious.[183]

Yet in recent times this determinative "reorientation" through the "spirit of modernity" has been passionately defended. G. Ebeling explicitly criticizes Fichte, who had seen the Enlightenment as the age of perfected inquiry.[184] Ebeling rather explains that historical criticism is "only the reverse side of assurance of salvation sola fide [by faith alone]," because historical criticism "totally smashes all presumed historical assurances that make the decision of faith less than necessary" and thereby "lies on the same plane" as the battle against the redemptive significance of good works.[185]

Claim is laid here not only to the heritage of the Reformation. Claim is also laid to a missiological outworking for historical criticism. This criticism makes it possible "to address the modern person."[186] It guarantees the "connection to the thought of the age."[187] In the interest of contemporaneity it behooves "to let burn whatever will burn."[188] Let us presuppose that a missionary impulse was a factor in the development of historical criticism. The result can nevertheless not be characterized as the attainment of missionary goals. For an entire branch of historical criticism, existential interpretation, almost totally broke off discussion with the natural sciences. Even at that point where discussion must at all events be pursued, namely, the doctrine of faith, it most commonly did not take place. Symptomatic here is Trillhaas' presentation of Christian eschatology. He totally excludes a cosmological eschatology and in the process remarks: "Duration of the world and future destiny of the earth are questions for the natural sciences and as such should be dismissed as beyond the competence of theology."[189] The demarcation from the natural sciences could not be sharper. Of model significance here is also Wolfgang Schadewaldt's interaction with the Tübingen critical school represented by E. Käsemann, but also by R. Bultmann. Schadewaldt criticized their "hypercriticism."[190] After reading Bultmann's *Geschichte der synoptischen Tradition* (*History of the Synoptic Tradition*) he formulated his reaction in the following words: "I experienced a tremendous disappointment, indeed desperation. Upon reading this book I felt somehow robbed." At that point he drew the analogy to Homer research (cited at the beginning of this chapter) and saw in comparing the two "certain perhaps not incidental similarities."[191] Schadewaldt was not the only classical philologist that was able to make little sense of critical synoptic research.[192]

As far as missionary impulse in the narrower sense is concerned, the deficient missionary penetration of historical criticism can be traced to the simple fact that with one exception[193] not one significant German missionary society was founded by liberal-critical theologians or circles. The idea of standing condemned in God's judgment was felt by many, as it was by Semler, as "horrid, monstrous doctrine."[194] The impetus to labor for the salvation of other persons remained weak, then, even if the pathos of Enlightenment care of souls and liberation was present.

What is the result of these observations? To deny the missionary impulse totally would be unjust. It may not even be denied of a Harnack, who in the dispute with Barth protested against changing "the theological teaching chair into a pulpit for preaching."[195] It must, however, be unambiguously stated that mission was not the decisive motivation for the development of historical criticism.

To the contrary, individualism is what historical criticism has nurtured since its earliest days. Just consider how G. E. Lessing in his quintessential "Against Herr Pastor Goeze in Hamburg" defended heart and soul as sources of knowledge. Lessing distinguishes here expressly between religion and Bible, basing the former in that which the Christian "*feels.*"[196] It is self-evident that this "feeling" demands that the individual hark to his own personal sense of responsibility, not to something outside that sense. The true Christian takes up the "doctrinal concept" that has been "drawn from the Bible," and he holds "this doctrinal concept to be true, not because he has drawn it from the Bible, but because he perceives that it is more appropriate to God and more beneficial to the human race than the doctrinal concepts of all other religions—because he *feels* that this Christian doctrinal concept gives him peace."[197] The "I," made the foundation of every decision by Descartes, makes the decision regarding true and untrue. The "I" makes this decision by itself. As Lessing put it, under the "banner" of that which the "I" holds to be true, "only an individual person has room for religion in the heart."[198] It is no accident that "psychology" gains a central place in the Enlightenment.[199] "Being determined by what the soul requires is typical for the neological stage of the German Enlightenment," wrote Aner.[200]

This was not the case in the same manner along every stretch of road that historical criticism opened up. Yet historical criticism did tilt steeply toward individualism. Most of all it gave the religion of German individualism renewed impetus in this direction. Paradigmatic here is Wellhausen's conviction that the Gospel preaches "the most noble individualism," "the liberty of the children of God."[201] The same tendency has an effect when D. F. Strauss characterizes the Protestant principle as "letting nothing be prescribed as necessary to believe, but only believing that which one experiences oneself in one's own inner person."[202] The contact with existentialism, which went forth from Kierkegaard, likewise brought an intensification of individualistic tendencies with it. One of the most far-reaching principles of Kierkegaard was that relevant truth was only that which "is truth for me."[203] It is well known that R. Bultmann and his students drew on this heavily. This is again exemplified well by W. Trillhaas, who says in his introduction,[204] we can "no longer let history answer for us, but we must answer ourselves."[205] Did Strauss not tender a similar argument? In view of his "modern knowledge of truth" Trillhaas can no longer accept responsibility for speaking of a "cosmological eschatology." As a result it is rejected.[206] What remains is individual eschatology: "Salvation is my salvation, or it does not exist."[207] The content of that which remains is the personal, eternal, continual existence after death: "Eternal life . . . is the actual and ultimate goal and epitome of the Christian [!] hope."[208]

We conclude that next to faith in reason, individualism is one of the strongest motives of historical criticism. Both together, however, do not suffice to explain the genesis and shape of historical criticism; they do not yet afford a grasp of historical criticism's ethos. This criticism views itself as a defender of the truth and of freedom. Along with the Enlightenment it wages the "war of light against the darkness."[209]

Its final source lies in the renaissance of the non-Christian Western man.[210] Kant's formulation retains pioneering importance for our understanding: in the Enlightenment there occurs "man's exit from his self-imposed immaturity."[211] Man is dependent on neither revelation nor the church. Not on revelation, because—according to a famous dictum of Lessing—it can give man nothing "at which human reason left to itself would not also arrive."[212] Not on the church, because everything depends on "the internal conviction of truths,"[213] while nothing depends on the authority of the church. Man is basically good, and he has the capacity to order and shape his life according to his knowledge. He tests everything that claims to further his welfare, or transmit knowledge, by his own sense of responsibility. If he confirms the "internal truth" of what he encounters, then there is no further need "of external verification."[214] Thus he has left behind immaturity and attained his maturity. This renaissance of non-Christian Western man is not to be confused with absence of faith. A religious longing quite definitely lies in it, a longing that leads it to "religion," if not necessarily to the "Bible."[215] Aner spoke here of a "religion of humanity."[216]

It is the peculiar feature of historical criticism that it emerges from a concept of personhood as religious, yet wanting to be autonomous—all the while wishing to hold on to Christianity as the true religion. In this combination lies its character. That is why it can regard itself simultaneously as the heir of both Luther and Erasmus, of both Reformation and humanism, of both the Bible rightly understood and naturalistic Deism, of both classical antiquity and of the apostles, of both reason and revelation.

This can be exemplified again by consulting the *Biblical Theology* of that theologian whose heyday marked the moment when the concept of "historical-critical method" "became common coin in New Testament research,"[217] Georg Lorenz Bauer (1755–1806). We will add a few citations here from the beginning of Bauer's four-volume work:[218]

> How could we then work towards this separation of truth from error more confidently; how could we endeavor on our part to get closer to an answer to the question that interests many thousands of well-disposed people, the question, namely, whether Christianity is a rational and divine religion which deserves to be respected, believed, and followed by the learned and unlearned; how better could we do this than, from the records of the Christian religion, the writings of the New Testament, quite impartially, without predilection for them or bias against them, and with the preliminary knowledge necessary to their proper understanding, to seek to present what the Christian theory of religion actually is; how Jesus wishes himself to be regarded; and for what reasons he demands that we believe in him? For only after having honorably carried out such research can one who accepts nothing without first having tested it, but who at the same time also keeps his ear open to the voice of truth, determine whether to accept or reject Christianity.

All the essential markers that determine the character of historical criticism find expression in Bauer's words. It is man who does the testing. It is religious man who "is ever ready to hear the voice of truth." The battle being waged here involves the "truth." If the scientific "prior knowledge" is present, then man is eminently well situated to wage that battle. Claim is laid to an objectivity that flows from the fundamental autonomy of man. A plea is made for Christianity. But the plea seeks to show both its rationality and its divinity—this too is only thinkable from the position of autonomy. Man makes his own decision for a doctrine ("theory," "Christianity"). And all this is done "honestly," in the freedom of the autonomous person who no longer lives in subjection to conventional dogma.

Autonomy, faith in reason, individualism, Christianity—if these are the primary sources of historical criticism, it is imperative to make clear what possibilities there are for distinguishing each in the collective image they project. The answer has been arbitrary from critic to critic—any of these four sources could be modified or even excluded. Instead of autonomy, faith could be demanded as facilitating interpretative presupposition. Or at least a dialogue could be called for between the Bible and modern consciousness of truth, a dialogue that calls one's own prejudgments in question. Instead of faith in reason, sciences of experience (psychology) or new paradigms could be introduced. Instead of individualism social consciousness could be trusted, as e.g., in the modern "ethnic" theologies. Even Christianity could be replaced, e.g., with the radical skepticism of a Franz Oberbeck (1837–1905).[219] A comprehensive critique in modern times is rare to say the least. Yet the four fundamental components cited above appear to be normative for historical criticism in terms of the "big picture." It is here that discussion must begin if we wish to determine the relation of revelation and criticism.

Revelation knows "autonomous" man only as "lost" man. Jesus' parable of the prodigal son (Lk 15:11–32) conveys this way of viewing things in a concentrated form. The younger son gains a certain—not *full*—measure of autonomy *from the father*, suggestive of a cutting loose from God. This autonomy "suffers" under two limitations. #1) It cannot thwart the reign and love of the father. #2) It cannot assure that forces other than the father will not exert their power over the son during his sojourn in a strange land. His life becomes debt-ridden; he falls into dependence. The once free son becomes a slave (cf. *pepramenos*, "sold" in Ro 7:14). From the very start his autonomy was a utopian illusion, a path into slavery, indeed very nearly a course leading to total destruction.

Revelation knows of human reason that also endures beyond the Fall. But it does not call this reason the light of man. It does not go beyond asserting the human capacity to hear. *What* is heard, however, varies. In his lost condition and apart from God's Word, man hears the seductive whisper of his sin and of evil, thereby becoming—even if he is an Israelite, one of God's own!—a "child of evil and of darkness" (Jn 8:49; Eph 5:1ff.). Reason is, then, an organ of reception, not a source of revelation. It depends on its sources of intake, on the content of the diet on which it is nourished. Apart from the Word of God it lacks the capacity to discern in the spiritual realm. No doubt it possesses a notion of God through the work of creation (Ro 1:19ff.) and through the question of the meaning of life. It suspects that a God could exist, that man may not be pleasing to God, and that man may have to give an account of himself to God at the end. But it lacks certainty. Certainty, the capacity to discern, spiritual insight—all these it receives for the first time through relationship with God. Here the seminal principle of the Bible applies: "The fear of the LORD is the beginning of knowledge" (Pr 1:7; 9:10; WS 1:1ff.). The Enlightenment faith in reason, then, committed a twofold error: it forgot that reason, too, was perverted by the Fall; and it confused the primary receiving and duplicating function of reason with content acquired independently.

As for the third component of historical criticism, revelation also knows certain forms of individualism. Among these is, e.g., personal responsibility before God that cannot be transferred to someone else: "Each shall die for his own sin" (Dt 24:16; 2Ki 14:6; Eze 18:1ff.). There is also each individual's confession of guilt: "I have sinned against you"

(Ps 51:4; cf. 2Sa 12:7). There is also personal faith (Jn 11:26) and other individual aspects of life and belief. Revelation constantly reminds, however, of that fellowship with God that is requisite for the individual to unfold the full extent of his potential. In addition, individualism as revelation views it involves fellowship with other believers and with those whom each person may be given to serve (from Ge 2:18ff. onward). God's saving plan ultimately encompasses the entire creation (cf. Rev 20–22). An "individual" in the literal sense, i.e., an isolated human entity not participating in life as constituted and granted by God, does not exist as far as revelation is concerned. The Trinity itself contradicts the classical concept of the individual.

The concept of "Christianity" is foreign to revelation, although theology uses it as an abbreviation and perhaps has no choice but to do so. Yet the question should constantly be posed to the user: what does the term mean? Undeniably, intrinsic to being a Christian belongs a certain body of doctrine that is (and must be) fleshed out as tradition and a system. The New Testament speaks of such doctrine or *paradosis* rather often (Ac 2:42; 1Co 11:2; 1Th 4:1f.; 2Th 2:15; 3:6; 1Ti 6:1, 3). Yet, still more fundamental, soteriologically speaking, is faith and personal devotion to Christ (cf. Ac 9:2; 19:23; 22:4; 24:14, 24:22 on the "way" of the Christian sect; also Ac 16:31; etc.). Personal categories are more important than formal ones in defining what being Christian means. A formal category can also more easily be corrupted than a personal relation. On the whole one suspects that the fundamental component "Christianity" is diverse in meaning and often ambiguous.

If one reflects carefully on historical criticism's normative quadriga of autonomy,[220] faith in reason,[221] individualism, and Christianity, then it becomes clear that it cannot be brought into harmony with revelation at decisive points. Biblical revelation rather characterizes man in his actual state with terms like lostness, dependence on God's Word, orientation toward social relations, and personal devotion to Christ. Revelation's concept of spiritual rebirth is utterly opposed to the concept widespread in Western Renaissance thought. Historical criticism, which rose "out of the spirit of the Enlightenment,"[222] must inevitably miss revelation.

## THE STARTING POINT OF HISTORICAL CRITICISM

*Skepticism* and *doubt* are the starting points of classic "historical criticism."

To this very day the German theology student in his first seminar learns that the point of departure for New Testament research generally is "scientific doubt."[223] This doubt in many cases becomes constitutive for his theological and spiritual existence.

To this day he can find commendation of methods that advocate dissent. This commendation may take the form of warnings against harmonization and emphasis on divergences rather than unity.[224]

Doubt has been sown and cultivated in the course of a lengthy history. Here we refer once more to Klaus Scholder. He sees "the principle of universal doubt" as being introduced into modern thought by Descartes.[225] The Enlightenment extended this principle into "critical" theology, so that Karl Lehmann can state: "In the Enlightenment era systematic doubt, according to which the reports of Scripture could possibly obscure actual understanding, came to assume total dominance as the fundamental presupposition of historical criticism of the Bible."[226] Stephen Neill concurs; since the Enlightenment in Germany "nothing was to be taken for granted."[227]

One of the most far-reaching consequences involves the burden of proof in historical investigation. It shifted to the one who wished to advocate the authority of biblical statements. Now it was no longer doubt but confidence and trust that required justification. If the justification is not forthcoming, then the statement in question remains simply unjustified and therefore nonbinding: "Lack of justification, using Enlightenment reasoning, does not open up room for other means of certainty. It rather means that the judgment in question has no ground in the thing itself and is 'unjustified.' That is a typical conclusion where the spirit of rationalism holds sway."[228] We encounter this demand for proof, which is now laid upon theologians, in crass form with Lessing: "If no historical truth can be demonstrated, then nothing can be demonstrated through historical truths."[229] The theological echo, so to speak, of Lessing is found in Johann Philipp Gabler (1753–1826). He admits that with grammatical interpretation, the explanation of that which the biblical writers meant in their time, interpretation has only reached a first stage: "But in our day little is gained if one knows only the grammatical sense of a biblical passage. Now it is historical and philosophical criticism's turn, which subjects the biblical passage to its sharp scrutiny." That is called "the enlightenment of the thing itself."[230] Here reason decides based on the analogy of contemporary experience and knowledge. Applying his principles to the Gospel narratives about Jesus' temptation, Gabler accordingly places the question: "*Can* the devil have tempted Jesus in such a personal manner? *Can* Jesus have followed the devil everywhere so good-naturedly . . . ?—anyway, the Jewish devil is, in fact . . . a Persian and Chaldean product which the Jews first encountered in the exile: how can he then be accepted here as actually existing?"[231] The answer: he can't. The modern knowledge of the truth of reason speaks against it.

Let no one say that is an outmoded point of view. In E. Hirsch's judgment the Bible has no "authority that a priori excludes doubt and contradiction."[232] If one takes J. Barr's line (1983), then it is essential for both scientist and pastor "to know that there is a question about it, that it is at least possible, perhaps likely, that such and such a sentence was not spoken by that person."[233] All that remains here is skepticism; it becomes the hallmark of theology. Right down to the present, K. Lehmann describes this basic tendency: "The truth and historical originality of what the Bible claims cannot simply be presupposed but must first of all be established."[234]

To be sure, we should not overlook the uneasiness afoot recently[235] among critical theologians who distance themselves from a "radical historical skepticism."[236] Examples are M. Hengel and P. Stuhlmacher.

Hengel observes that "radical criticism" too, with its skepticism, "has no less often led to uncritical speculations during its two hundred year history than apologetic-fundamentalist defensiveness."[237] Particularly in view of Acts research Hengel presses, e.g., for more trust regarding the historical work of Luke: "Luke takes a back seat to no other ancient history writer when it comes to trustworthiness."[238]

If we can speak here of a tentative return of trust, the basic question nevertheless remains: how does faith awakened by revelation relate to the doubt of historical-critical criticism? Reinhold Seeberg long ago indicated the direction in which the answer lies: in his view a "believing criticism" is simply no longer "criticism"![239] It is really "urgently necessary" that historical criticism "earnestly question its presuppositions, which are still very much an Enlightenment legacy."[240]

Here it is essential to note the basic movement of revelation. In it God seeks to win people's trust. That is why the promise is older than the Law (Ro 4:13ff.; Gal 3:15ff.). That is why the Beatitudes stand at the head of Jesus' teaching (Mt 5). That is why the history of human survival after the Genesis flood begins with a covenant rich in promise (Ge 9:1ff.). That is why the story of the patriarchs is introduced by the approval of and promises to Abraham (Ge 12:1ff.). Even historical reminiscence serves to strengthen trust in the self-revealing God (cf. Dt 32:7; Pss 71:17ff.; 106:1ff.). It should also be noted how Jesus structures the first encounters with his disciples in such a way that trust can arise (Jn 1:35ff.). Right into the wisdom tradition, the plea for trust plays a central role: "My son, give me your heart / and let your eyes keep to my ways" (Pr 23:26).

An encounter with revelation that makes skepticism and doubt a guiding principle amounts to a brusque no to revelation's concern to elicit trust. Psychologically and existentially the most hostile position that an interpreter can occupy is one of systematic doubt. In addition, this doubt is not restricted to the small sphere of the theological study but has become a scientific identification card. The so-called conservatives (who occupy the middle ground between fundamentalist anti-intellectualism and liberal hypercriticism) are also affected by this. What else explains how a theologian highly respected in Bible-believing circles could write, "If any of the Gospels merits mistrust, it is most likely Matthew . . . it reports . . . much that could absolutely never have come from the mouth of Jesus."[241] In a lecture at a Stuttgart parliament building the usually very sober M. Hengel found in the same gospel of Matthew a "tendency" "to heighten the sharpness of the imperative and sanctions of punishment for pedagogical and catechetical purposes" (on 9 November 1982).[242] These examples from Matthew interpretation can be quickly extended to the rest of the Gospels and to the entire New Testament. Doubt and skepticism are at times influenced by cultural currents and stirred up anew. Thus a pastor in 1981 reveals, attempting to rethink the relation to Israel: "I want to learn to understand Bible texts that in the history of interpretation have been used anti-Semitically, and I want to pass them on with only critical comment."[243] The questions we raise here about how critical attitudes affect preaching and the teaching of pastoral ministry have been raised regarding academic interpretation in a similar manner by U. Luz in his Matthew commentary.[244]

We conclude that the impulse to mistrust that is inherent in historical criticism is found in its unabashed divergence and dissociation from revelation's concern to elicit trust. This mistrust hampers the openness necessary for interpretation—and hampers even more the prior extension of trust which theology owes to revelation based on the history of its effects.

## THE LOSS OF THE BIBLE'S AUTHORITY IN HISTORICAL CRITICISM

Where doubt and skepticism reign, there can be no talk of biblical authority, at least not in the classic sense.

Once more it is Klaus Scholder who has seen things rightly. He characterizes the development of historical-critical theology as a "process at whose end stands the toppling of the Bible as the authoritative source of all human knowledge and critical understanding."[245] And once more we must return to the development's point of departure in order to grasp the process that unfolds here.

The luminaries of greatest importance are three in number: Spinoza, Lessing, and Kant. Spinoza regarded the Bible as a human book. As a result he refused to accept the view "that reason must subordinate itself to the revelation, laid down in Scripture, that transcends reason."[246] If one begins with human autonomy, then Spinoza's conclusion is actually entirely logical. For Lessing, truth, as "reason" perceived it, stood above religion. One of his theses in the *Axiomata* runs, "Religion is not true because the Gospels and the apostles teach it, but they taught it because it is true."[247] Indeed, he puts an even finer point on it: "Even that which God teaches is not true because God wants to teach it, but God teaches it because it is true."[248] Accordingly it is truth that is accorded actual authority, not the Bible as a book. It is a material truth that Lessing speaks of, not a personal truth which is bound to the person of God. Finally, in Kant we encounter a "fundamental integration of revelation into reason."[249]

We must concede that according to the Enlightenment's own consciousness, loss of *biblical authority* was by no means harmful. For reason was just as valid a source of truth as the Bible, and biblical revelation could not convey anything fundamentally new. "Therefore," says Lessing,[250] "revelation gives nothing to the human race at which human reason, left to itself, would not also arrive. Revelation just gave and gives the important things earlier."

That is, to be sure, a standpoint diametrically opposed to Luther and Calvin.[251] That, however, is totally beside the point, says W. Schmidt in 1968. "The Bible as understood in Protestant orthodoxy has not worked out. To appeal to it as the Reformers did is today no longer possible."[252] Entirely in agreement with Ebeling, Schmidt likens his position to the "outcomes of Luther's ninety-five theses."[253] This is an extreme position. But the position is illustrative of a tendency that we can trace from Lessing and Kant right down to the present hour. W. Hermann was in any case not all too different from Lessing in declaring the Bible to be "servant and not Lord" in a Christian congregation; Scripture's function is only the clarification of faith.[254] We are reminded again of E. Hirsch, who in the Bible saw "writings of human origin" which make "human life lived out before God visible." Hirsch also disputed the Bible's "divine authority."[255] On the whole, E. Dinkler in his treatise on "The Authority of the Bible and Biblical Criticism" framed the problem of historical-critical, scientific investigation of the Bible this way: the question is "whether it [i.e., historical-critical, scientific investigation of the Bible] has not led and even must lead to the weakening of biblical authority, to the disintegration of biblical authority, actually to its denial; i.e., whether scientific investigation of the Bible does not finally lead to its own self-nullification."[256]

We have consciously cited here only theologians who understand themselves as critical theologians. We are saying nothing of the charges of their opponents. There can accordingly be no doubt that historical criticism as such denies authority to the entire "Bible"-book. Anyone who considers a return to the authority of the Bible within historical criticism[257] has already departed from its classic framework.

Characteristic of how the Bible is handled where its authority is not recognized is the demand that it be treated as "a book like any other." The trail of this view can also be traced to Spinoza. He wanted "basically no other rules" to apply "for the interpretation of Scripture . . . than for the interpretation of any other book."[258] The prior assumption here—and Spinoza, unlike many others, made his view quite clear—is that Scripture is not revealed but is rather a purely human book.[259] Jean Alphonse Turretin (1671–1737) procured room for this conception among theologians. In *De Sacrae Scripturae interpretandae methodo tractatus bipartitus* (1728) he championed the view "that the Holy Scriptures are to be explained in no other manner than are other books."[260] Here, however, the theologian's intention in questioning undergoes a fateful shift. Instead of asking about the will of the Divine Author, now the question involves the intention of the human writers.

Consequently Turretin states: "We must see which [ideas] could arise in the souls who lived at that time."[261] In short, we read the Bible "just like the letters of Cicero, Pliny, and others."[262] K. A. G. Keil in his hermeneutics textbook (1810) could already appeal to Semler, Herder, Turretin, and others when he remarked that one must explain "the books of the New Testament in terms of just those basic principles . . . according to which any other book written by men must be explained."[263] Critical theology sticks to this viewpoint, which gained ascendancy by about 1800.[264] With few divergences we find this same view in R. Bultmann and the entire theological enterprise of which he is representative.[265] Ebeling emphasizes (against Schlatter?) that the Bible "is to be interpreted like, e.g., a Plato text."[266] Salvation history and Sacred Scripture are thereby done away with.[267] The Bible is precisely no longer "Holy Scripture" in the former sense but only a "historical object." And "the historical-critical method" cannot be curtailed in its application to any historical object.[268] That means that biblical authority is sacrificed to historical criticism. It is interesting that modern authors attempt to switch to other methods of interpretation as soon as they conclude that "the Bible is a quite different case from all other books of the world."[269] An example here would be Girgensohn's move to pneumatic exegesis. Such dissenting authors confirm from the opposite point of view that historical criticism as such actually destroys biblical authority.

It is too little noted that we are not dealing here with merely a loss of "formal" biblical authority. It is rather the case that far-reaching "material" forfeiture is underway. In any event distinction between "formal" and "material" biblical authority can only take place if objective categories are employed. As soon as one takes as basis the overwhelmingly personal categories that mark revelation in the encounter of God and man, this distinction fades away. It should nevertheless be observed that "materially" speaking even the central figure of Scripture, Jesus Christ, ceases to be an absolutely superior authority for us as soon as we hear in the Bible nothing more than ordinary people. This can be seen in the history of theology in the work of, e.g., Johann Gottfried

Herder (1744–1803). Herder defined "the Gospel" "in the Gospels" as "the teaching and character of Jesus and his work."[270] This all pointed to a continuation in mankind. Jesus established an example that now guides contemporary man. The result: "The so-called *religion based on Jesus* must necessarily, unnoticeably, and inexorably alter to a *religion like Jesus' religion* in the course of time. His God our God, his Father our Father!"[271] This is reminiscent of the modern formula "believe like Jesus" rather than "believe on Jesus." In any case it is clear that Jesus can no *longer* claim authority since he is no more than a thoroughly human example. Jesus, too, becomes prone to error.[272]

With the demise of biblical authority the possibility also vanishes of deriving from Scripture "eternally valid norms" that are understandable to all.[273]

We have already spoken of the authority with which revelation, according to its own statements, confronts us (chap. 9). Openness, willingness to risk faith, and obedience are appropriate responses from the human side. There is therefore no need to set forth yet again why the loss of biblical authority militates against revelation. We should, however, indicate that this loss was reflected even in the sphere of historical-critical research. Already in 1950 E. Dinkler wrote, "To possess a divine revelation means to possess a revelation of the divine will, and to believe this revelation means to obey this will."[274] R. Bultmann was also conscious of the lofty demand of revelation.[275] Appealing to Augustine's "You have made us for yourself," he invalidated that demand.[276] More recently the so-called positive criticism seeks to win back the biblical authority that has been lost by, e.g., speaking of Scripture's "lead" respecting "truth."[277] It is vehemently attacked by more radical critics for its views.[278] At the end of the day all these attempts just go to show that the *essence* of historical criticism stands in an irreconcilable contradiction to the authority of the Bible. Whoever wants to unite both the authority of revelation and historical criticism falls into an intolerable tension which in the end must give way to one side or the other.

## THE LOSS OF THE DOCTRINE OF INSPIRATION
## IN HISTORICAL CRITICISM

The authority of Scripture would not have been dismantled to such a great extent if the *conviction of the inspiration of the biblical writings* had not *increasingly diminished.*

One of the striking features, however, of the process of historical criticism is that the conception of inspiration proves more tenacious than faith in the authority of Scripture. Johann August Ernesti (1707–81) could simply assume that "Holy Scripture was written by inspired men."[279] Semler and Michaelis likewise did not deny the authority of Scripture as such.[280] Yet a twofold movement takes place here. First verbal inspiration is given up in favor of inspiration of content or personal inspiration. Then inspiration is characterized as no longer so crucial. It is clear that, e.g., Johann David Michaelis (1717–91) ranks the question of genuineness above inspiration: "The question whether the books of the New Testament were prompted by God is not of such central importance to the Christian religion as the prior question of whether they are genuine."[281] Johann Philipp Gabler wanted first "entirely to skip over" the "doctrine of inspiration" and "not until later" consider it "when we treat the dogmatic use of biblical conceptions."[282] That means that inspiration is meaningless for exegesis. Then, however, it was only a matter of time until it was basically shut out of interpretation. W. Gass (1867) shows us the change that took place. According to his remarks "inspiration and confessional standard" serve only "a practical function of authority"; but "scientific theology in the more recent sense can and may not be subordinate to them. Scientific theology's sure possession is its elevation above these norms."[283] Historical criticism has freed itself from the chains of the traditional conception of inspiration. Thirty years later (1897) W. Wrede remarks in passing that "we cross out the doctrine of inspiration,"[284] and shortly thereafter (1914) H. Gunkel says that the doctrine of inspiration is "in principle long since collapsed or radically reconstructed."[285]

Here is the late fruit of Deism. Among statements made in 1730 by M. Tindal, in a foundational publication called "The Bible of the Deists,"[286] is his remark that as a starting point one must assume that the contents of the apostolic writings were "not inspired by God."[287] At about the same time Th. Morgan deduced from the conflict between Paul and Peter the impossibility "that they all should have been inspired or stood under the infallible leading of the Holy Spirit."[288]

Regarding the modern situation E. Dinkler states that "there can be no talk of inspiration,"[289] while Amberg lends Dinkler aid with the judgment, "The rejection of the old Protestant scholastic doctrine of inspiration is nearly unanimous."[290] Nor did K. Barth make a return to it![291]

Most recently we observe beginnings of a return to the biblical understanding of inspiration. This is true, e.g., of P. Stuhlmacher. He does not wish to put up with the situation as it exists in Protestantism that threatens to wreck the doctrine of inspiration. Yet so far he has not gone beyond an understanding of revelation as personal.[292]

An almost self-evident outcome of the abandonment of the biblical-Reformation doctrine of inspiration was the *secularization of the interpretation of the Bible*. Even for "positive" theologians it holds true that scientific investigation of the Bible must proceed "according to the general basic principles of historical work."[293]

A second, almost equally self-evident outcome was the *forceful rise of immanentism*. Explanation of revelation restricted itself—more on this below—to immanent modes of understanding, e.g., analogy. Even if E. Troeltsch with his systemization of the "historical method" be regarded as an extreme position, it is nonetheless true that since Lessing[294] the dominant view of history's terrain is the one that starts with the present possibilities of man and therefore builds on conclusions based on analogy. H. E. Weber rightly speaks of the "spell of the idea of immanence"[295] under which scientific-critical investigation of the Bible operates. Acknowledgment of inspiration had broadened the view for transcendence. Now a restriction to the temporal and humanly possible entered in, reminiscent of Lessing's critique of miracles: "There are those miracles that I see with my eyes and have opportunity to test myself, and there are those miracles of which I have only historical knowledge of, which others claim to have seen and tested."[296] At times immanentism goes so far as to characterize the entire content of Christianity as "not transcendent but immanent."[297]

Where the inspiration of the Bible falls away, where immanentist understanding reigns, the human authors must be reevaluated in ways hitherto undreamt of. Already in S. J. Baumgarten the "humanity of the Bible" along with historical interest moved to center stage.[298] His student J. S. Semler regards the human authors as "the actual originators" of Scripture.[299] They are to receive all the attention. "Material explanation" for G. L. Bauer (1755–1806) means to explain the "ideas" presented in the Bible "based on the customs and form of interpretation of the [human!] writer himself and his age, his nation, sect, religion, etc."[300] This established a pattern that proved momentous for the future. Modern refinement of that pattern may be observed in, e.g., E. Basil Redlich, who finds the truth of the Bible precisely in the human viewpoints that are presented there: The Bible is "true, in that it gives us a true account of the beliefs and views held by the writers."[301] Close nearby stands the statement that verbal inspiration "is a pure invention."[302]

The demise of biblical inspiration opens the way to discover *errors in the Bible* and to interpret the Bible in the light of these errors. We sketched earlier (chaps. 7 and 9) the development that attended acceptance of errors in Scripture. This acceptance led from the Catholic critics of the *sola scriptura* principle[303] into the circle of "conservative" or "positive" Protestants.[304] Today it is commonly accepted that Scripture may err. According to E. Dinkler, an essential outcome of the historical-critical method is that Scripture contains that which is false and "unhistorical" and is "by no means free of error."[305] In a generally moderate essay, E. Schweizer arrives at the same position: "An 'infallible' Scripture exists just as little as an 'infallible' church teaching office."[306] Dogmaticians follow this same line for the most part.[307] Assessments of the New Testament writings such as "they contain much unhistorical" or "legendary features" or "It may be that words were put into Jesus' mouth here"[308] are also not foreign to the Anglo-Saxon realm and are just as prevalent in Old Testament research.[309]

There is no need to furnish more citations showing that the demise of the doctrine of inspiration effected the *dissolution* of one of the strongest ties holding Scripture together as a unity (cf. above chap. 10). Since Thomas Morgan it has been possible to build understanding of the New Testament on the thesis that there are irreconcilable contradictions in Scripture.[310] The opinion that Scripture lacks unity found the same wide distribution as the view that it contained errors.[311] A measure of how wide is indicated when Dinkler declares it to be the logical consequence of the historical-critical method.[312] Most of all with respect to the relationship between Old and New Testaments, the widely held notion of Scripture's contradictoriness had disastrous effects. In spite of much effort, e.g., by H. Gese, to show a unity between the two testaments, the mainstream of historical criticism steadfastly maintains that such unity between Old Testament and New Testament does not exist.[313] As a result, parts of the Bible are classified as "running contrary to the true will of God."[314] Even in the newest branch of "positive criticism," which is excoriated by "radicals," it is still regarded as given that the Bible is at least partially "contradictory."[315]

An understanding of Scripture that annuls such fundamental claims of revelation as its inspiration, unity, and coherence is no longer suited for encounter with this revelation. Historical criticism finds itself, therefore, in substantial contradiction to revelation.

## HISTORICAL CRITICISM'S MISTRUST OF THE SUPERNATURAL

If inspiration and authority fade and immanence assumes a dominant role, then *all that is supernatural is jeopardized.*

The repression of the supernatural in historical criticism runs parallel to some extent to the "destruction of metaphysics" in philosophy since Kant.[316] W. Schulz has indicated, however, that metaphysics did not simply go under, but, e.g., through Heidegger experienced a revival.[317]

The supernatural became suspicious in the eyes of theology at that moment when it committed itself to a tension-free depiction of reason and revelation.[318] Aner produced an impressive summary of those points that have been attacked or denied since the rise of Neology: e.g., the divinity of Christ,[319] the existence of the Devil,[320] the death of Jesus Christ as satisfaction for the penalty of sin,[321] supernatural working of grace,[322] the Trinity,[323] and everlasting punishment in hell.[324] Gottsched said, "I stick to what is most certain, which is what the pure light of reason teaches me about God and my actions." This describes the undergirding stance of Neology, out of which historical criticism arose.[325]

Still today F. Beisser sees science as a cause of the "destruction of the metaphysical."[326] In fact, traces of the traditional, historical-critical antisupernaturalism are still visible. One notes, e.g., A. Oepke's definition of "revelation," in which he remarks that it is "not transmission of supernatural knowledge."[327] On the other hand it must be expressed with all clarity that at one decisive point historical criticism holds fast to supernaturalism: in its talk of God. Why should this talk not thrive on "transmission of supernatural knowledge"? Only occasionally have any gone as far as F. C. Baur, who could no longer conceive God as a personal being but only as "thought itself."[328] Typical of ongoing wrestling with talk of God is the solution of Bultmann's renowned demythologization lecture. In plain terms Bultmann there admits that he must let the "myth" of God stand. Ebeling therefore displayed well-founded caution when, regarding the characteristics of historical criticism, he spoke not of an exclusion of the metaphysical but only of an "exclusion of all metaphysical statements from the realm of the self-evident."[329] It is indeed also curious that historical criticism continually betrays a tendency to anchor faith "beyond science,"[330] somewhere or other in an eternal, suprahistorical, or metahistorical sphere.

At the point of supernaturalism, then, one can only say that historical criticism represents repression, mistrust, and threat.

This mistrust was at least so great that prophecy and miracle—as already shown above—were widely eliminated.[331] And on the other hand the tendency toward antisupernaturalism was so strong that historical criticism landed itself in the prison of a naturalistic causal nexus. Still today one encounters such statements as: "The historian can presuppose a suprahistorical incursion into the causal nexus as foundation of his work just as little as the interpreter of the Bible can presuppose the Holy Spirit"; otherwise we would succumb to a "revelation docetism."[332] The counterquestion to this is simply: what if revelation itself—in prayer, miracle, prophecy, and so forth—constantly and unconditionally presupposes such suprahistorical incursions?

A consequence of the aversion to supernatural statements with far- and deep-reaching consequences for the life of the church was the *enmity against the dogmas* of the church.[333] The substance of these doctrines was for the most part supernatural, and not just in such areas as doctrine of God, creation, and eschatology. Baur posed the provocative question, "If we [i.e., historical critics] too do only that which Christendom did in ages past, why open critical questions?"[334] We leave out of consideration here the voices of those who want to do away with dogma totally.[335] We mention only Gunkel's aim "to clear dogmatic prejudgments out of the way and lead theology into the freedom of historical thinking."[336] All in all, E. Esking's judgment, made in conjunction with his Lohmeyer investigation (1951), is amply confirmed: "often an outspoken loathing of all dogmatic Christian conceptions" has ruled liberal exegesis.[337] Recently, moderate criticism has attempted to exert a corrective influence at this point.[338]

## THE PREEMINENCE OF HUMAN JUDGMENT IN HISTORICAL CRITICISM

Historical criticism has not only pushed the human authors into the foreground, contrary to the structure of revelation; it has also attempted *to subordinate* revelation *to ordinary human judgment.*

In this way it has built up a number of bastions.

1. One of the first of these bastions consists in the *doctrine of man's goodness.* The quality of being human is held to include that the will is guided by reason. Man thereby acquires the capability of doing good. In Gottsched's words, "Our will always directs itself according to reason."[339] Lessing called it "blasphemy" to deny that the human race would attain the "highest stage of enlightenment and purity."[340] The mind must be exercised until it "makes us capable of loving virtue for its own sake."[341] The time will come—Lessing could call it the "time of a new eternal Gospel"—in which man "will do what is good because it is the good, not because arbitrary rewards are attached to doing it."[342] In Neology the "doctrine of the moral nature of man" becomes part of theology.[343] Jerome and Augustine are condemned "because they often did injustice to Pelagius."[344] The doctrines of original sin and Christ's atoning death vanish; the way of salvation becomes "synergistic."[345] A "cult of virtue" arises;[346] instruction and appeal dominate church life.

Baur still prized Pelagius.[347] His student Strauss leveled the most vehement criticism against Luther for thinking "that he and all men . . . were subject to eternal damnation, out of which they could be redeemed only through the blood of Christ and their faith in its power." To Strauss that was "so repugnant that there could never be any talk of sympathy between him and me [i.e., between Luther and Strauss]."[348]

This doctrine of human goodness was not embraced where consciousness of the Reformation was cultivated and honored, in dialectical theology, in biblicism, and similar quarters. Yet Neology's optimism drags on right up through the most recent times of recent church history and crops up again, e.g., in modern liberation theology.[349] In any case it should be noted that the origin of historical criticism is closely linked with the doctrine of human goodness.

2. A consistent component of the entire course of historical criti-

cism is the view *that man must decide regarding the truth content of revelation.*

K. Lehmann described the state of affairs this way: "Through the formal 'critical' intention . . . the truth content of the biblical Scriptures has factually always been measured by one's own understanding of self and world and thereby also limited by one's own ability to believe."[350]

This "one's own ability to believe" depends in turn on the philosophical, religious, or psychological presuppositions of each researcher.[351] Two principles apply across the board: #1) "There is no presuppositionless understanding"[352] (Bernard Lonergan calls presuppositionless exegesis "the principle of the empty head");[353] and #2) one's own understanding of man decides what revelation is—then in innumerable cases the prior character of man takes precedence over the new insights of revelation. Unalterable grids of understanding arise. Whether as for Bultmann the connection with Heidegger,[354] or as for Baur the appropriation of Hegelian thought,[355] or as for Gunkel "the idealist tradition of the 19th century" and "the spirit of romanticism,"[356] or as for Jülicher the influence of Herder[357]—again and again the tendency arises to subordinate revelation to established prejudice.

Yet in the same breath there is polemic against the "revival preachers," "who rely on their own understanding of the Bible and establish their own authority."[358] The polemic arises, however, not because such preachers subject Scripture to a *human* prejudgment but because they subject it to a *false*, uncritical prejudgment: "they . . . lack the knowledge of criticism and the categories necessary to understand it; they live precritically. . . ."[359] One recalls that during the Enlightenment's full flower the terms *pietistic, mystical, fanatical,* and *extremist* were also all lumped together.[360]

3. Whoever wishes to determine the truth content of revelation needs certain *criteria* to do so. Let us return for a moment to Adolf Jülicher (1857–1934). Jülicher applied the following criteria of authenticity to the Jesus tradition: "Not capable of being invented"; "out of the ordinary"; having the "magic of fresh life"; religious "depth and

warmth."[361] It is not hard to detect the influence of Herder here. The number of such examples is practically boundless.[362] All these categories confirm once more that historical criticism in its basic principles remains captive to a humanly prescribed grid of understanding.

But shouldn't our pattern for understanding be determined by revelation itself? Once more "positive criticism" is moving cautiously in this direction, as when, e.g., it speaks of the "head start" that Holy Scripture has in the realm of truth.[363]

4. Without question historical criticism requires a *prior knowledge* "regarding what religion and revelation are, or what they should be,"[364] if they want to make a decision about the truth content of revelation.

This prior knowledge has been expressly defended by Bultmann against Barth.[365]

This prior knowledge must at the same time also amount to additional knowledge, indeed at times *presumption*. "The modern historian," says Ebeling, meaning the historical critic as well, "is rightly convinced that he knows certain things better."[366] Otherwise, how would it be possible that he "tests" "the substance of the facts reported"?[367] In contrast to laypersons, who are left to engage in "the simple hearing of the Word,"[368] the historical critic possesses "competence."[369] The modern critic ought not, in Barr's opinion, question how we understand God's Word for today. He ought rather ask, "How is that hearing to be modified, refined, and clarified through our knowledge of the actual character of the biblical text as mediated through critical, historical, and other sorts of knowledge?"[370] Since he is, therefore, in the position "to penetrate behind the texts,"[371] he is concerned with the giant task of first producing the true content of revelation. The critic proceeds here "according to the laws of historical probability,"[372] which he knows.

At this point there is nothing more to say about the roots of this conception in Descartes, Spinoza,[373] and Kant.[374] It should, however, be remarked that it has become dominant in dogmatics right down to the doctrine of Scripture itself. According to Trillhaas, e.g., historical criticism sets forth "facts of history over against illusions. Only the person whose eyes are closed could hold to the orthodox doctrine of Holy Scripture."[375] It is clear: man is the one who believes he is, based on his abilities, competent to recognize truth and to distinguish revelation from what is not revelation.

Before we attempt to assess this procedure, we must follow its *modus operandi* just a little bit farther.

## THE SEPARATION OF SCRIPTURE AND REVELATION IN HISTORICAL CRITICISM

Fundamental to the historical-critical work is the separation of Scripture from revelation, or of the Bible and Word of God. For historical criticism the two are by no means identical.

J. S. Semler's principles in this regard have come to be practically the critical creed: "Holy Scripture and Word of God are very much to be distinguished, because we know the difference; just because someone has not previously seen that difference, that is no prohibition against us seeing it."[376] The contents of this creed are: Scripture *contains* God's Word. That is its value and irreplaceable significance. Scripture, however, *is* not God's Word. For it contains a good deal else that is not God's Word at all.[377] This "good deal else" can be separated out through man's critical competence. As a result Semler goes so far as to say that he felt a critically constructed *condensation* of the Bible would be possible and desirable, a version that would consists only of God's Word.[378] This would suffice for our salvation. Once more Semler's implicit claim is that man is in the position to undertake such an operation "because we know the difference." Semler just as clearly states that such a procedure is thinkable only since the rise of the Enlightenment. For "previously"—i.e., prior to the Enlightenment—this "difference" was "not seen." Semler's remark is correct. To take an illustrative example, for Luther the Bible was "actually the Word of God itself."[379] And old Protestant Scholasticism ruled out the "difference" spoken of by Semler, because in its view reason could not judge faith (and with it revelation).[380] Semler and other theologians of his stripe, however, want a new theology, one that no longer takes its cue from Protestant orthodoxy.

In this Semler and others enjoy the support of Lessing, who in the conflict with Goeze sets forth the thesis: "The Bible obviously contains more than what belongs to religion."[381] He states this in direct opposition to the thesis "the Bible *is* religion."[382] Engaging in wordplay with Goeze, who was a pastor in the Hanseatic trading center of Hamburg, Lessing exclaims: "Surely there will be no dispute in Hamburg over the difference between 'gross' and 'net.' In a city where so many wares have their respective tares [weight deduction from gross weight of a substance and its container, made in allowance for the weight of the container], will no one permit me to allow for tare in such a precious ware as Holy Scripture?"[383] By "tare" Lessing means, e.g., "David's Cherethites and Paltites," i.e., all the obscure tribal names that seem irrelevant to the modern reader, or "the cloak that Paul forgot at Troas."[384] But what is to be done with such things that seem so irrelevant to religion? Lessing likens them to the bag in which a doctor carries medications and asks, "Is no one healthy except the person who swallows not only the medication but also the bag along with it?"[385]

This is a graphic picture of the "husk and kernel," an image used with great relish by theologians in subsequent years regardless of their origin. A few examples will suffice here. Notoriously, D. F. Strauss saw "the inner kernel of the Christian faith" as unaffected by criticism.[386] Harnack spoke of the "kernel" and "husk" and sought the former in the "Gospel in the Gospel."[387] Dibelius wanted to separate the temporally conditioned "garb" from the eternal and suprahistorical.[388] Dobschütz, too, wanted to distill "timeless foundational ideas" out of the Bible.[389] Further examples could be cited.

This image rests on an axiomatic presupposition. This presupposition "says that God divulges himself as God in these texts [= the Bible] *not directly.*"[390] Revelation, then, is something other than the Bible. This axiom is determinative for historical criticism to the present hour and is one of its definitive features. Gottlob Wilhelm Meyer (1802) could, e.g., characterize it as superstitious to want "to seek high divine wisdom in every individual word [of the Bible]."[391] True, at first this referred to the search for multiple meaning in Scripture. Nevertheless, a fundamental attitude expresses itself here, an attitude that weighs even the words of the Bible to see whether and how, if at all, they set forth that which partakes of the divine.

The divine and the human are, then, separated.[392] J. Weiss desires "to teach clearly and forcefully that the New Testament is not only something eternal and divine; it also has a human, a historical character."[393] The so-called positive theologians at the onset of the twentieth century, who fought for the genuineness of biblical statements, still admitted, "Word of God and Scripture, however, are indeed not congruent."[394] In the same vein we may understand the conception that the Bible is *witness* to revelation but not revelation itself. Ebeling makes this clear in his characteristically lucid diction: "Revelation denotes not so much . . . or at least not in the first place the Holy Scripture"; revelation is rather "the event attested to in Holy Scripture."[395]

Consequently it turns out—for K. Barth too, by the way[396]—that the Bible is fallible; infallibility can be predicated only of the divine Word that stands behind the Bible.

From that point it is but a small step to the further resulting view that the "human," the purely "historical" parts of the Bible no longer apply to us. Thus F. Hesse in 1966 came to the conclusion "that there are lengthy chapters and sequences of chapters, indeed even whole books of the Old Testament, that are obviously bereft of any significance for us under even the best-intentioned consideration."[397] He cites here Leviticus, Esther, Song of Solomon, Chronicles—following much the same line as Semler.

With this separation of Scripture and revelation historical criticism cleared the way to make its own decisions about the truth content of the Bible. It thereby consciously gave up the Reformation Scripture principle that was the foundation of the Protestant churches at that time, as R.

Simon knew very well. Even a Girgensohn, who wanted to return to Reformation principles, faulted the "exaggeration of the Scripture principle" in the Reformation.[398] In 1924 Thurneysen wrote: "we also know that modern thought has taken so much offence at no other point of theology than precisely this one"[399]—i.e., the Scripture principle. Thurneysen's statement is no less true today.

Historical criticism's manner of approach did not, however, destroy only the Reformation foundation of *sola scriptura*. The further question arises whether it did not thereby attack the very foundation of being Christian itself. This question has been asked before. It would have to be answered affirmatively if Esking were correct in saying: "It may be impossible to deny that the so-called historical-critical method carries with it a series of motives that are alien and unnatural, or even dangerous, to the conception of Christianity."[400]

Prior to an ultimate answer, however, we need to reflect on a final point.

## HISTORICAL CRITICISM AS CONTENT CRITICISM

Historical criticism is, right to the present hour, intended to be criticism of the content of the Bible.

"Content criticism of the biblical texts is a non-negotiable element of all theological interpretation," says P. Stuhlmacher, who embodies the attempt to bring historical criticism into conformity with the Bible.[401]

Such concord is impossible. Stuhlmacher himself testifies to this in deliberations from 1986: "According to a widespread (mis)conception, spiritual interpretation is incompatible with criticism of Holy Scripture. That seems evident at first glance. How can we approach God's revelation as a gift, as proffered boon, and at the same time take a critical stance toward it!"[402] But now we see the effect of separating Scripture and revelation. For Stuhlmacher remarks, "What stands in Holy Scripture from Old and New Testament is not all Gospel."[403] There is then, already in the Bible, true and false proclamation. Therefore he arrives at a conclusion that is "at first glance" surprising: We are "obligated to criticism" also "within . . . the Scripture."[404]

What the "first glance" reveals is correct. Hearing that transforms the listener occurs only where the entire biblical Word is heard in actual *openness*. But every content-critical approach must proceed from a prejudgment of which it cannot turn loose. The necessary openness is, therefore, no longer present in principle. If that prejudgment were laid aside, then criticism could only arise where revelation led us to it. That occurs, however, only with respect to the prejudgment of the interpreter—and precisely not "within the Scripture." Guidance from Scripture that denies Scripture by Scripture (which is what the term *content criticism* indeed implies) is found nowhere in Scripture.

Theological "content criticism" is by its very nature "distinction between time-conditioned statements and what is abidingly valid"[405] within the Bible. The time-conditioned does not bind and obligate us. The abidingly valid lays binding obligation on us. We have already become familiar with how this distinction is made (see "The Separation of Scripture and Revelation in Historical Criticism" above). How content criticism works can be characterized in another, simpler fashion: biblical statements that are unambiguous from a grammatical-historical viewpoint are entirely or partially rejected. Every content-critical reading of the Bible therefore sacrifices part of what it contains.

Various time-conditioned or personal fluctuations determined which statements were denied by historical criticism in the course of history.[406] For Hermann Samuel Reimarus (1694–1768) "the resurrection of Christ" was "a fabrication of the disciples" and a miracle that was impossible.[407] For J. Wellhausen (1844–1918) Jewish eschatology was "utopian" and its God "the God of wishes and illusions."[408] For Stuhlmacher "God in Christ" "transcends" Hebrews 6:4, which accordingly is theologically untrue.[409] The countless fluctuations to which content criticism has been subject in the last three hundred years expressly refute the contention that Scripture furnishes the resources from itself to facilitate such content criticism.

Nevertheless, precisely in the last years and decades the need for content criticism has received striking emphasis. In his criticism of Barth, e.g., Bultmann insists that the "real content" (*Sache*) of the New Testament that is accessible to the modern exegete "is more weighty than even Paul" and must be used critically even against Paul. Paul becomes the moving force of Pauline criticism.[410] Ebeling, who also on this topic produced the "leading essay,"[411] enjoins the modern researcher who makes use of the historical-critical method to content criticism as a matter of principle: "It [i.e., the historical-critical method] is not only present where it perhaps oversteps its legitimate boundaries; it is also essentially bound up with content criticism."[412]

Emphasis on content criticism takes on the features of an established dogma. Thus for E. Grässer (1980) it amounts to a "debasing" of exegesis if it "forbids itself from engaging in content criticism."[413] And Robert Funk, in tallying up the history of historical criticism, arrives at the finding that it has become less and less critical of itself and "thereby increasingly more dogmatic."[414]

## THE INCOMPATIBILITY OF HISTORICAL CRITICISM AND REVELATION

Early in this chapter we stated that the decisive question is: how, as a matter of principle, does criticism relate to revelation?

In view of the considerations laid out above the answer must be: *historical criticism is utterly incompatible with enscripturated revelation*—and if it is made compatible then it ceases to be "historical-critical."

If "unrestricted trust" is "the basic occurrence between man and God,"[415] then what God says can and may not be bracketed out of this "basic occurrence." According to the Bible's self-testimony God speaks—and this is *the same* God!—reliably in the *entire* Scripture. Historical criticism contradicts this self-testimony to the extent that it disputes that God speaks in parts of the Scripture.[416]

According to the Bible's self-testimony there is no further or other revelation outside the Scripture. There is none, also not in the sense that actual revelation "is" "there behind the letters."[417] The historically transmitted, contingent Bible *is* the revelation. *Thus*—and not otherwise—God intended to speak to us. Historical criticism contradicts this self-testimony to the extent that it believes it is privy to an "actual" revelation that entered Scripture only in broken form.

According to the Bible's self-testimony God revealed himself through this enscripturated revelation. Apart from it man does not know what God, what revelation, what faith is. Historical criticism, however, believes it knows what the true God, what genuine Word of God, and what true faith are. With this foreknowledge and corresponding prejudgments it casts a pall over Scripture. It cultivates the legacy of a "religion of reason,"[418] while it lives in essential contradiction to the "theology of revelation" that has been entrusted to us.[419]

According to the Bible's self-testimony God's revelation is directed at our openness, our trust, our obedience. Historical criticism exempts itself from this intention. Instead of being open, it defends the "frontier fortresses"[420] of the customary, of that which has already been considered, and presses revelation through these grids of the customary, the long known and accepted. Instead of trust in the biblical texts it leads to distance from the biblical texts.[421] Instead of obedience it exercises content criticism where it thinks it needs to do so.

It was, among others, Ernst Fuchs who appealed to the thesis: "every science orients itself according to its object."[422] Biblical science must accordingly construct itself out of what God says. It must be willing to allow its certainties and positions to be given it from revelation itself. The origin of historical criticism, however, lies in the self-assurance of autonomous man; it lies outside of God's self-disclosure and its enscripturated revelation. This alien origin is what inspires its sinister arrogance. One must not succumb here to the misunderstanding that this arrogance is to be ascribed to the personalities of historical-critical researchers. The historical-critical researcher too wants to be humble.

The arrogance is rather of a structural nature. Over 150 years ago Friedrich Lücke (1791–1854) warned that "historical criticism" in Germany had "worked itself up to such a lofty position that it must necessarily annihilate itself, if it does not, commensurate with its highest ideal, again humbly subordinate itself to the synthesis [that it labors to understand]."[423] In view of the expanses of scientific ruins it has left behind and its missionary unsuitability, it appears that historical criticism justifies Lücke's prophecy to some extent.

With Ebeling we must insist that here we touch on "the deepest foundations and the most difficult connections of theological thought and church existence."[424] There is no question of a "compromise" between historical criticism and "believing the Bible," contrary to the suggestion of, e.g., H. E. Weber (1914).[425]

The only question surrounds how to seek a new way for more suitable interpretation to take place.

The objection will immediately arise that such a renewal of biblical hermeneutics and biblical exegetical methods is not possible. For #1) we cannot turn back the clock to a day before historical criticism;[426] #2) historical criticism is relatively speaking the best interpretive procedure;[427] #3) the only scientific thinking is critical thinking.[428]

Objection #1) is already questionable because, first of all, in individual areas thoroughly new methods are being demanded and applied. An example here would be so-called Pentateuchal criticism, in which Childs, Rendtorff, and H. H. Schmid, among others, call for "new, adequate methods."[429] What applies in individual areas must also hold true for the whole discipline. Second, it would be blind, then, for us to overlook that historical criticism since its onset was constantly accompanied by other, indeed antithetical procedures. We speak here not only of loners like J. T. Beck or A. Schlatter but also of broad, church-steering currents like the so-called evangelicals or—to a still greater degree—traditional Catholic theology. Third, the reforming of methods and the rejection of historical criticism have been underway for a long time and along a broad front. We refer here to, e.g., theologians of the

"Third World."[430] We refer also however to contemporary evangelicals. The declaration of "bankrupt" against historical criticism even sounds from within depth-psychology interpretation (E. Drewermann, W. Wink).[431] Fourth, historical criticism itself came to life as a radical break with the acknowledged orthodoxy. How can it now seek refuge in a monopoly of its seniority? Fifth, however, and this is the decisive argument, it wrongs its "object." Instead of adjusting the "object"—biblical revelation—to false method, we have to correct the method in keeping with this "object."

Regarding objection #2) above, we first of all concede that remarkable results were attained even under the lordship of historical criticism. We are also by no means about to give up the advantages of a *historical* (not: historical-critical) study of Scripture. In view of historical criticism's past failures, however, it cannot be maintained that historical criticism is relatively speaking the best interpretive procedure. And what is best for the future remains to be seen.

Objection #3) contains a kernel of truth: Every science thrives on "painstaking scrutiny," which can also be described as "critical investigation."[432] In addition, we have ascertained in this chapter that "criticism" in the sense of discriminating apprehension (*crisis sacra!*—sacred judgment!) most definitely belongs to the duties of the Christian interpreter. In this realm critical thinking is, then, undisputedly required. But anyone who wants to make of this a manifesto for historical criticism and theological science acts in an untrustworthy fashion. It holds true at this point too that revelation (the "object") must determine the method and not vice versa. Should historical criticism turn out to be in contradiction to revelation, then it can no longer be peddled as "the" scientific method.

As soon as it is recognized that historical criticism stands in contradiction to revelation, it can no longer obligate us to regard it as "intellectual destiny." The need is for a newer, more suitable way to interpret the Bible.

# CHAPTER THIRTEEN

# Revelation and Method

## TWO IRRECONCILABLE ENTITIES?

At first glance the concepts "revelation" and "method" appear to bounce off each other like a pair of billiard balls. For what human method can comport with the sovereign acts by which God's Spirit divulged something of the "depths of God" (1Co 2:10 RSV)? And conversely, should the elemental power of encounter with God admit of reduction to rational, even juridical formulas?

It should not amaze us if Christians have repeatedly *rejected every use of method*. Such a rejection—albeit heretical in nature—cropped up already with the "pneumatics" Paul addressed in 1 Corinthians, who resembled children in their thinking (14:20), confused the Spirit of God with "disorder" (14:33), and believed themselves to be mindless instruments of the divine spirit, who strummed them like a harp to produce sound. Yet Paul saw things quite differently. His counsel was, "The spirits of prophets are subject to the control of prophets" (14:33 NIV; cf. 14:7). The pneumatics' line of rejection continues in the *unio mystica* (mystical union) of the Middle Ages, which sought encounter with God in unification of the soul with God. This was obviously in contrast to the path of Scholasticism followed by many others. The same line appears with the spiritualists among the Anabaptists, who despised the external Word, doctrine, and the sacraments and yearned to follow only the inner light of the Spirit.

In citing these examples it immediately becomes clear that the majority of Christians have not gone along with such total rejection of doctrinally appropriate method. Why not? Without anticipating too much of what follows, we can already give a few reasons: Jesus and the apostles were teachers of the Scripture and of God's will—and they performed their exegesis in a manner that was thoroughly methodical and reflected.[1] In Israel high status was accorded to the sages and scribes who worked with methodological awareness. Their status was so high that the charge of a "book religion" has occasionally been heard.[2] After the death of the apostles the genuine tradition had to be cultivated, guarded, and thoughtfully appropriated.[3] This finally led to the catechetical schools, e.g., those of Alexandria. In addition there was the necessity of answering for the Christian faith in the sense of 1 Peter 3:15 in the midst of a non-Christian environment (cf. the early Christian apologists). Ultimately Christian mission itself was, since the time of Paul, dependent on the *nous* (reason; cf. 1Co 14:19ff.). Although reason cannot bring forth faith (in the sense of *fides qua creditur*, personal trust in Christ), it can nevertheless set forth what must be believed (*fides quae creditur*, the objective content of Christian doctrine; cf. Heb 11:6). It can also deal with real or imagined objections to the Christian faith.

The majority of Christians, then, never embraced the notion that the fact of a divine revelation must exclude methodologically aware reflection on revelation.

## KEY QUESTIONS OF PNEUMATIC EXEGESIS

### STARTING POINTS OF PNEUMATIC EXEGESIS

On another level we find *objections* to methodologically rigorous interpretation *raised from the side of "pneumatic exegesis."*

The program of pneumatic exegesis arose at the end of the nine-teenth and beginning of the twentieth centuries. Two basic considera-tions stand behind it: #1) realization of the necessity to engage in spiritual interpretation of a spiritual message, and #2) knowledge that atheistic methods were working incalculable woe in both academic the-ology and the church.

Some well-known sentences from Friedrich v. Bodelschwingh document the problem: "An inexorable flood of unbelieving and impi-ous criticism flows from the theological professors of our German uni-versities, inundating our hapless young people in theological training and shaking the foundation of our faith, which is the Holy Scripture. . . . They enter the university secure in their faith and come back with faith destroyed."[4] Such laments were not, however, confined to the university. They also arose in response, e.g., to religious instruction, "where those theologians who were all too liberal for service in the church gladly became religion teachers in the secondary schools,"[5] to quote a remark made by Hermann Diem in 1950. Bodelschwingh's opinions find their critical counterpart in Karl Girgensohn. He noted an "embittered battle in the church against the historical-critical understanding of Scripture" and admitted: "It was . . . a correct instinct when they sensed, 'Your basic presupposition partakes of an entirely different spirit.'"[6] Girgensohn surely speaks from experience as he went on to write that "for many the transition to a radical historical consideration of Scripture means at once the hopeless collapse of any belief in the authority of Scripture." Historical interpretation kills "any reverence for Christianity."[7] As a result "Protestant theology . . . has fallen into a grave internal crisis that has lasted a century and a half now."[8] If one sets alongside of this Adolf Schlatter's battle with Paul Jäger (1905) against "Atheistic Methods in Theology,"[9] then it is clear that a program of spiritual biblical interpre-tation is a virtual necessity given such a situation.

Theology has been reminded constantly that the Bible seeks to be more than a document subject to historical-critical testing. But at the end of the nineteenth century this awareness sharpened. The history-of-religions school was not the least of the contributing factors. This school of thought posited a deep ditch, indeed an antithesis, between Jesus and our present world. Jesus is quite alien to contemporary times. It even became problematic whether one could speak of "New Testament theology." Wrede demanded, e.g., that it be renamed "early Christian *Religionsgeschichte* [history of religion]" or "history of early Christian religion and theology."[10] Additionally, in liberal exegesis the last bastion of the Gospels' reliability had fallen with recent investigations of the (presumably earliest synoptic) gospel of Mark. For Wrede in his book *The Messianic Secret in Mark* (1901) had shown that Mark, too, was steered by doctrinal interests that led him to distort historical matters for the sake of the theology he sought to spread. But did that mean the Bible's contents were reduced to historical accuracies, or inaccuracies, as the case might be? M. Kähler called Jesus research of that area a "dead-end street."[11] This ushered in a search for what transcends history; there was new openness toward the pneumatic character of Scripture. The line of this reorientation can be traced down to Barth, who rejected liberal interpretation with the charge that it had lost the ability to penetrate "into the spirit of the Bible."[12]

These developments need to be pondered if we hope to understand the concern and approach of pneumatic (or neo-orthodox) exegesis.

In this reorientation mentioned above the *influence of Johann Tobias Beck* (1804–78) plays a leading role. He was, besides much else, one of M. Kähler's teachers. From 1838 on Beck strove for a pneumatic interpretation of the Bible.[13] Such interpretation presupposes, first, the spiritual rebirth or regeneration of the interpreter. The interpreter may allow for "distribution" of the "Holy Spirit."[14] The Holy Spirit drives him to praxis: "Go forth and do what your conscience becomes aware of as the will of God."[15] Thus arises the unity of doctrine and life. And precisely through his praxis the interpreter finds "that Scripture is God's Word."[16] God's Word proves itself "in your conscience" itself.[17] The old basic principles of the *testimonium Spiritus Sancti internum* (inner witness of the Holy Spirit), of the unity of Scripture, and of the equivalence of Scripture and Word of God are therefore taken up by Beck and continued. In doing so Beck regards Scripture as a doctrinal system that must also be systematically unfolded. For Beck, then, pneumatic exegesis is nothing arbitrary. It rather means the doctrinal unfolding of the pneumatically generated Scripture through the regenerate (pneumatic) interpreter.[18]

It may be mentioned that the "pneumatic state" of the interpreter was also an essential point for Johann Ludwig Samuel Lutz (1849) in his *Biblische Hermeneutik*.[19]

## PNEUMATIC EXEGESIS' UNFOLDING IN KARL GIRGENSOHN

*Karl Girgensohn* (1875–1925), like Kähler, followed J. T. Beck.[20] Girgensohn also appealed to Hamann,[21] Hofmann, E. Schrenk, and "the grand old practical biblicists of Württemberg."[22] Yet he himself did not wish to be a biblicist.[23]

Girgensohn recognized that the usual historical-critical method of Scripture interpretation did justice to neither the church nor the saving faith of the individual Christian—and certainly not to the Bible. It did injustice to the church because "deriving eternally valid norms from Scripture" was becoming more and more difficult, yet "the Protestant church" could "not exist as a Protestant-Christian church without such norms."[24] It did injustice to the saving faith of the individual Christian because historical criticism set its doubt over against "all supernatural components" of the faith.[25] It did injustice to the Bible because "the autonomy of human reason," "the principle of immanent explanation," and "the bias toward a mechanistic-causal explanation of reality," all characteristic of modern scientific thought, stand "in direct contradiction" to the Bible.[26]

Girgensohn sought a way out of this crisis in a synthesis. He wished to combine "the strength and depth of the biblicists with the critical sharpness of today's science."[27] To make this synthesis possible, a "practical-edifying understanding of Scripture" must first be developed alongside the historical-critical understanding.[28] Here 1 Corinthians 2:4ff. assumes central importance.[29] In the practical-edifying interpretation of Scripture the "submission of one's own self to the will of God" takes place[30]—in direct contradiction to the autonomous reason of criticism. Through prayer and listening to the text there must next follow the "application of the Bible's word to one's own self." Girgensohn here appeals to Bengel's "Te totum applica ad textum, rem totam applica ad te" ("Apply yourself wholly to the text; apply the text wholly to yourself").[31] By this means we open up "the suprahistorical revelatory content" of Scripture.[32] Girgensohn also describes the suprahistorical as the "imperishable" and "eternal."[33] It is first at this level that man's redemption can be spoken of. For "the historical . . . can not redeem man.[34] . . . Only the grand course of eternity decides."[35] Along with all this, however, the historical-critical approach remains in force. Without it pneumatic exegesis would "steadily somehow" become "a form of spiritual fanaticism."[36] Both modes of procedure, the practical-edifying and the historical-critical, stand alongside one another equally justified, both autonomous, both mirroring "two quite different stages of the process of knowing."[37] Girgensohn tested these two levels with his students for five semesters and at the end of the experiment detected a "form of bilingualism."[38] What was viewed as synthesis turned out to be mutual supplementation of two different, indeed contrasting ways of interpretation that remained basically independent.

Anyone concerned with hermeneutics cannot ignore Girgensohn. How did theology respond to him at the time?

Girgensohn's ideas were almost unanimously rejected. This rejection was sometimes quite blunt. In the pages of the journal *Theological Blätter* R. Bultmann wished that the "chatter about pneumatic exegesis might soon cease."[39] Like Bultmann, F. Torm likewise found the notion of a "pneumatic exegesis" to be "detestable."[40] R. Seeberg, in contrast to a pneumatic exegesis, set forth the "demand for a theological [!] exegesis."[41] The repeatedly expressed fear was that Girgensohn's approach would end in eisegesis and subjectivity. At the same time, with incredible naiveté, many felt that their own historical-critical method could "cause only what has objective validity to surface."[42] E. Fascher sounded the alarm that "Girgensohn's ideal view" was "a scientifically refined" version of what Elias Schrenk represented;[43] Fascher finally concluded that all exegetes would reject Girgensohn.

In critiquing Girgensohn's proposals we must first point to their positive content. Girgensohn wanted "to hear" in the Bible "not only a historical human word about God, but also the voice of the living God."[44] Doubtless Girgensohn grasped the intention of the Bible better at this point than his opponents did. For Girgensohn it follows that there must be a special theological hermeneutic.[45] And the reason for this is that Girgensohn, like Beck, regarded a *theologia regenitorum* (theology of regeneration) as necessary: "The divine spirit of prayer is the best leader to the divine spirit of Scripture . . . ultimately the Holy Spirit himself must lead and illumine us if we wish to arrive at an actual pneumatic understanding of Scripture."[46] In this way theology becomes a science having a form of its own. It must think through its foundations anew. Girgensohn is aware of this task, for he asks "under which presuppositions the pneumatic understanding of Scripture can be scientifically constructed, once the limitations of the Enlightenment concept of science are removed."[47] It is interesting that in all events Girgensohn holds to the scientific character of theology and does not simply give it up.[48] In his new concept of science, reason, i.e., reason "led by the Spirit of God," is accorded a central role.[49] This reason fits in well with meditation, which is today being expressly called for once again.[50] "If it is to yield its deep truths," states Girgensohn, "the scriptural word calls for meditation in quiet and inner concentration under the influence of an attitude of prayer." It is necessary "that we let Scripture work on us, as we pray and continually reflect, with open hearts and in living obedience."[51] This is reminiscent of J. T. Beck's stress on the importance of the interpreter's practice of the faith he sought to articulate. It also seems natural to call attention here to Planck's *Kleines Homiletisches Testament*, where these words were written at about the same time that Girgensohn framed his views: "How great are the demands of understanding! Standing; standing still; standing within; standing against."[52] Another positive aspect of Girgensohn's approach, finally, is that it grants appropriate importance to the unity of Scripture. A "canon within the canon" appears impossible to him.[53]

Other aspects of Girgensohn's approach have rightly drawn criticism's fire. Even sympathetic consideration cannot avoid the realization that Girgensohn did not arrive at the synthesis toward which he strove.[54] Pneumatic-edifying and historical-critical interpretation are wed with each other only through the person of the interpreter. Otherwise the two modes of consideration remain unrelated, almost autonomous, alongside each other. Indeed, the reciprocal principles contradict each other. While the historical-critical mode of consideration is steered by autonomous reason, the pneumatic approach evades this autonomous reason and gives itself captive to the Spirit of God. The "felicitous complementing of each approach's strengths by the other's" spoken of by Girgensohn[55] does not come about. A result of this is that historical criticism remains untouched by it all. It is as little corrected in Girgensohn as in Karl Barth.[56] But what happens when the two interpretive approaches contradict each other? Girgensohn repeatedly explains that in such cases the pneumatic conception of Scripture can "thus" trim back "some of the excesses" of historical criticism. It can set limits to criticism's "naive hypothesis-spinning" and "never push so far the customary fragmentation of the Bible into the smallest possible particles."[57] Pneumatic interpretation's role, then, is one of offsetting excesses—not exactly resounding success! The development of this exegesis showed that pneumatic method was by no means the way to overcome historical criticism's excesses. The restorative power of this pneumatic exegesis, then, remained quite negligible. At the spiritual level, however, Girgensohn pressed forward to a notable position. That is, he arrived at the view that historical criticism could "possibly amount to sinful guilt and rebellion against the revelation of the divine."[58] Later H. Frey took up this impulse, which we will consider more closely below. Criticism raised a further problem: does such a thing as a "pneumatic method" even exist? Isn't there really only the "pneumatic interpreter"?[59] The Spirit's dynamic working through the Word does in fact elude reduction to some set method. Therefore "something tentative, ambiguous"[60] clings to Girgensohn's study. And precisely because pneumatic apprehension of Scripture cannot be transformed satisfactorily into a method, historical-critical method, which seems more illuminating because it is more "methodical," remains the victor in interpretation.

Girgensohn's "two-stage" hermeneutic, then, is ultimately unsuitable. It basically runs aground on its own inability to come to grips satisfactorily with the two authorities of the Enlightenment, reason *and* revelation.

## CONTINUANCE OF PNEUMATIC EXEGESIS IN PROCKSCH AND OEPKE

What we have said of Girgensohn must likewise be said of Otto Procksch and Albrecht Oepke. They are also representatives of a pneumatic exegesis, though in a modified form and manner.

In his 1925 essay "Über pneumatische Exegese" ("On Pneumatic Exegesis"), *Otto Procksch* consciously related his work to that of Beck and Girgensohn.[61] The proper theme of the Bible, he argues, is the battle between God and (sinful) man.[62] "No man can project himself into the mind of this God; one can only subject oneself to him."[63] "Faith in Christ" thus remains the only way to an adequate understanding of the Bible.[64] Yet Procksch denies the notion that there could be a "pneumatic method." "What is distinctive," he states, "lies not in a method of research but in the pneumatic points that confer initial life on the whole."[65] In his Old Testament theology (*Theologie des Alten Testaments*, 1949) the principle of pneumatic exegesis continues to shine through. Theology must demand "recognition of revelation," which on the other hand makes faith a necessity.[66] "Complete knowledge" of the Bible is "impossible" in the presence of "exclusion of the concept of revelation in the sense of divine self-disclosure and exercise of faith."[67] That basically includes the demand for a special biblical hermeneutic—and at the same time presupposes a *theologia regenitorum* (theology of regeneration). Girgensohn's two steps are still recognizable, even if in weaker form, when Procksch writes, "As the literal sense opens up the forms of history, a history that must face unfettered research of its sources, so the pneumatic sense opens up its ultimate content."[68] Full "unfettered" freedom is, then, necessary for historical criticism. It is however at the same time restricted to the "literal sense." The "ultimate," the "complete," is the peculiar province of the pneumatic interpreter. Yet it is an open question what this ultimate consists in. A genuine synthesis between the pneumatic and the historical-critical is not, then, reached here either.

Albrecht Oepke (1947) pleaded expressly for a "two-stage approach" in interpretation.[69] Historical and suprahistorical interpretation of Scripture are both simultaneously required by scientific exegesis.[70] Historical interpretation is steered by the question, "What did the Word say back then?"[71] Here it is clear "that . . . criticism must be used; that is a fundamental given."[72] The basic principle applies: "We cannot go back to the time before Semler."[73] Suprahistorical interpretation is steered by the question, "What does the Word say now?"[74] In this "metahistorical exegesis" there is even allowance for multiple meaning in Scripture.[75] Which interpretive possibility should assume prominence is left open by Oepke. One is left with the impression that Oepke assumed some kind of basic adding together of the results of the two approaches, but he apparently did not think this through.

## THE PNEUMATIC EXEGESIS OF HELLMUTH FREY

Finally, Hellmuth Frey is still another who made an impressive attempt to furnish a new foundation for theological work understood as pneumatic exegesis.

In this Frey is aware of standing in the Girgensohn-Procksch line.[76]

But at the same time he appeals to, among others, Luther, Bengel, Schlatter,[77] and—understandably for an Old Testament scholar!—Franz Delitzsch, who "realized most purely"[78] the elusive intention that Frey sought to achieve.

Frey's central concern is that we get free of "the autonomy of the human spirit."[79] This autonomy has squeezed all "results of theological research into" a "preconstructed framework."[80] It decides what is historically possible and impossible and thereby gives up, e.g., the possibility of miracles.[81] Frey has in mind, of course, autonomy in the sense common to Enlightenment reason.

Such freeing from autonomy, however, does not only mean that we must ponder new ways of reflection. It rather confronts us with a spiritual turning point. We recall that Girgensohn had already spoken of the "sinful guilt and rebellion" of historical criticism. Now Frey speaks increasingly of the necessary "submission to judgment . . . which in the cross extends also over the knowledge we gain through research."[82] We must repent of the sin of self-sovereign autonomy which we use, precisely in our roles as theologians of the Word of God, to empower ourselves.[83] Such a call to repentance was seldom ever heard before in theological circles—and it remained largely unheeded.

The positive, new possibility that we have is to engage in a "surrender . . . to the leading of the Spirit."[84] He is the real interpreter of Scripture. Frey's understanding of Scripture pushes 1 Corinthians 2:6–16 onto center stage.[85] Frey states, among much else, that every "possibility of man using Scripture to empower himself" is "condemned" by 1 Corinthians 2:9ff.; "every method's absolute claims are relativized and referred back . . . to the servant role" it ought to perform. "Autonomous man is even dethroned from his role as interpreter."[86] With this a *theologia regenitorum* becomes unavoidable.[87] As we already expect from his connection with Bengel and Delitzsch, Frey opts for a salvation-historical understanding of Scripture.[88] Frey likewise affirms the unity of Scripture, pointing to the "unity of truth and reality in the Old Testament concept of *'emet* [truth]."[89] Furthermore, Frey conceives of theology as a service rendered within the Christian community. The interpreter must "have grown into the church of God and the fellowship of his children." That also means "contact with the constellation of proven interpreters of the past," among whom Frey numbers Schlatter, Delitzsch, Bezzel, Bengel, Calvin, Luther, and others.[90]

Regarding the question of how this new way of interpretation should look in specifics, Frey went considerably beyond Girgensohn. He insists that in interpreting the Bible "the divine and the human" may not be "divided" from one another.[91] Girgensohn still distinguished sharply between a divine and a human factor in Scripture. Frey, on the other hand, draws a parallel between Scripture and Chalcedon's affirmation regarding Christ: "The 'unmingled' and 'undivided' [both applied to the full union of both human and divine natures in Christ] applies to Scripture as well."[92] Accordingly, Frey upholds—again in distinction to Girgensohn—the "doctrine of the total and verbal inspiration of all of Scripture."[93] Yet he separates himself "from the mechanical theories of inspiration of fundamentalism and Protestant Scholasticism."[94] Actually Frey appears as an outspoken enemy of fundamentalism.[95] The Bible is inerrant only in the mediation of "salvation."[96]

Yet at this point—and this point possesses decisive weight—Frey remains indebted to the heritage of Girgensohn: at individual points of exegesis there is very little difference. True, one can sense how Frey has wrestled with this matter and achieved more and more distance from everyday historical criticism. Nevertheless: he does not overcome historical criticism at the level of exegesis of individual passages. Still in 1963 he emphasized that there is no need "to ban the rational methods of research in themselves."[97] He has no desire to see "a new course of research or knowledge" be added "to philological, literary critical, comparative religious, historical, and traditio-historical interrogation of the texts."[98] That means that Frey leaves research in the same place he found it! This same position can be detected in his collection of lectures *Krise der Theologie* (*Crisis in Theology*) in 1971,[99] even if he takes more pains there regarding renewal in exegesis of individual passages.

At the end, therefore, Frey is left standing before two levels of interpretation. True, these are no more the historical-critical and the pneumatic-edifying, as they were for Girgensohn. They are rather the rudimentary, acritical, pneumatic level, on the one hand, and the rational-critical in particular application. But the unifying of the schema is just as little achieved as in Girgensohn's case. The unfortunate two-tiered character clings, therefore, to pneumatic exegesis across the board.

In Frey's *Krise der Theologie* he finally draws out a line that he had already mentioned in the Otto Michel Festschrift of 1963. He wished, namely, to dispense, decisively and radically, with *every* method. Every method, whether pious or critical, has as ultimate effect the manipulation of the Holy Spirit by man. So every method, in whatever form, finally becomes sin for us. The exception is exegesis of individual passages, where methodological procedure is to be followed—and here we see continuance of the double-thinking, two-staged approach, doggedly defended no matter how bleak its prospects. The organic connection between methodologically reflected individual exegetical steps on the one hand and a reflected whole, on the other, is, however, strongly denied.[100]

Frey had given us, then, a trio of points to ponder: a call for theology to repent, counsel to pay attention to the role of the interpreter, and the unresolved problem of a pneumatic exegesis conducted on two levels that never meet.

If we survey the pains taken by pneumatic exegesis, we arrive at a surprising conclusion: methodological interpretation of Scripture itself has come to be regarded as questionable. Frey said that every method amounts to sinful manipulation. Does that mean there should be no method? Or to put the question differently: *Do we even need a method for the interpretation of Scripture?*

To shed light on this question our first move will be to call attention to the criticisms of method being debated today.

## PRESENT CRITICISMS OF METHOD

The *general admissibility of criticism of method* must without question be granted its right to exist, if one is convinced of possible progress in science. The due place of such criticism is repeatedly conceded. Even Wolfgang Richter, who could still write in 1971 that "[t]he right to apply the historical-critical method is today . . . uncontested,"[101] emphasized on the other hand that there "can . . . be no ultimate doctrine of methods; such doctrine corresponds rather to whatever state of research prevails at a given time."[102] "To that extent," criticism of method is for Richter an "inherent component of scientific progress."[103] Hans Walter Wolff speaks along the same lines. He rejects every interpretive methodology "that uses some principle to set itself up as Lord over the text and its context instead of laboring in its service."[104] In the most general form the admissibility of criticism of method is set forth by Otto Merk in his TRE article on scientific study of the New Testament. At the end of it he writes that "New Testament science . . . remains critical regarding its proposed solutions and open regarding the raising and framing of new questions."[105]

The danger of such assurances lies in their platitudinal nature. As soon as the right of historical criticism is questioned, there is an immediate change of tone. A. H. Gunneweg (1976) is no exceptional case at this point when he writes that the historical-critical method is the sole "scientifically proven method."[106] Nevertheless, we stand by our insistence that criticism of method is no sacrilege but rather a nonnegotiable essential in the science of interpretation.

Wolfgang Richter goes a step farther in his already mentioned 1971 treatise "Exegese als Literaturwissenschaft" ("Exegesis as Literary Science"). He pleads for the necessity of a *"pluralism of method."*[107] Pluralism of method is, therefore, receiving attention at the present time. General "acceptance" has not yet arisen. And we should be careful with this; for in handling the Bible we are faced with the matter of "truth." And where "truth" is merely negotiated, boundless pluralism is not exactly likely to be the best method to recommend. We are reminded that pneumatic exegesis, discussed just above, wished to make use of two entirely different approaches alongside each other and in that sense implied a plurality of methods.

Criticism of method appears de facto in many forms. Basically it is already underway where *religious feeling is preferred to doctrine*. Sometimes Pietism displays this tendency. Philippi felt compelled to complain that in Pietism he confronted "a relative disdain for the integrity and purity of Protestant doctrine."[108] B. Ramm repeated this lament in 1956 as he placed Pietism in the category of "Devotional Schools" of interpretive thought.[109] Against this, however, it must be noted that Pietism as found in Spener, Francke, Bengel, and others began as a scientifically serious movement. This should not make us blind to the dangers of a later overemphasis on pious feeling which had no compunction about applying even critical methods. Romanticism and idealism could also be filled with contempt for theological methods. We may point here to a shift made by Goethe as an example. He expressed himself in favor of comprehending the Bible emotionally and didactically, not dogmatically and fancifully.[110] This basic posture did not hinder him from authoring a historical-critical poetic essay in 1797 in which he calculated the wilderness-wandering at two rather than forty years.[111] We observe therefore also in Goethe a combination of deep feeling, moral purpose, and critical theories—a parallel that is not so very far removed from modern pietistic movements.[112] Here, then, the method of interpretation is relativized at the outset through a prevailing tone of feeling.

Another form of criticism of method confronts us where the *Bible* is conceived *as something prefatory*, as a phenomenon of an ineffable truth, as an obscure transmission of a revelation, as a stained-glass window of light that eludes our grasp. When "the actual subject matter" lies beyond the Bible in this way, the method of interpretation of the Word is likewise only something preliminary, prefatory. It never arrives at the real truth. The method can then be unabashedly critical. It takes on a jaunty air. But this itself is a weighty form of criticism: method is stripped of ultimate relevance. One recalls the charges that were hurled at Karl Barth in this regard. His exegesis was said to be "fanatical";[113] he was said to make the text into a "mouthpiece for his own prophetic utterance."[114] We find the conviction in M. Dibelius (1925) that the "revelation of the unconditioned was given" to us "in historically conditioned form."[115] The parallel to Barth is obvious. All methods grasp, then, only as far as the historically conditioned, while the revelation of the unconditioned remains ultimately inaccessible to them. Faith becomes a courageous act that transcends the historical, the outward shell. Or as M. Dibelius himself put it: "In the final step of faith time extends itself upward into eternity."[116] It is then not so bad if "the suitability of the method" cannot be "ascertained."[117]

The conviction that the concrete word of the Bible is only a penultimate word, and that the ultimate word must be discovered out somewhere beyond it, assumes a number of forms. E. Lohmeyer is another who wrestled with "the problem of revelation in history." In 1951 Erik Esking examined Lohmeyer's theological exegesis and found there "intellectual mysticism and scientific passion" alongside each other[118]—a syndrome we have already encountered above. At this point a glance beyond the confines of theology is warranted. August Boeckh, author of the foundational *Encyclopädie und Methodologie der philologischen Wissenschaften* (*Encyclopedia and Methodology of the Philological Sciences*) that appeared in 1877, restricted the possibility of a scientific hermeneutic to the realm of the human. In view of the Bible he expressed this judgment: "[I]f it is a divine book, then it is raised beyond all hermeneutics and cannot be grasped through the art of understanding, but only through divine spiritual influence."[119] Yet man is capable of even this "divine spiritual influence," for the human spirit "is indeed of divine origin."[120] It would not be far wrong to detect the basic outlook of German idealism in such utterances. No method reaches the divine, which is the real subject matter of the Bible. From that point on methods were given free, even critical leeway. In recent times talk of the eternal or the divine has receded. What has not receded, however, is that inner distance of the exegete from the raw material of his work. The exegete is conscious of making contact only with the prefatory through his historical methods. There also continues to be present the yearning to attain a deeper understanding of the Bible beyond that offered by the usual historical work. H. W. Wolff formulated that "border-consciousness" of the critical exegete in this way: "No methodology can replace the Spirit of the living God as the actual interpreter of the text."[121] And in 1987 P. Stuhlmacher warned that "the historical-critical method must not simply be elevated without scrutiny to a theological method."[122] A "theological method," in his view, also presupposes a *theologia regenitorum* (theology of regeneration): "Only the person who participates in the faith and life of the Christian community gains access to the inner clarity of the biblical testimony to the Gospel."[123] Although it remains unclear what this "inner clarity" amounts to, and although Stuhlmacher still calls for theological method to work "critical of the content of its subject matter" ("sachkritisch"),[124] it is nevertheless obvious that "historical-critical method" and "theological method" stand alongside each other as respectively contrasting entities. But that is to declare the historical-critical method as insufficient. By itself it cannot achieve theological understanding. In this way too the method as usually practiced meets with criticism.

A further form of criticism of method is found where *supporting pillars of historical criticism are subjected to reconstruction*. Currently this is taking place with form criticism. Uneasiness about form criticism has been around for a long time, especially in terms of its development in German theology.[125] Already in 1927 no less clear-sighted a researcher than E. v. Dobschütz termed the "application of Greek terms" to Palestinian traditions "wrong."[126] He was not pleased that actual history was receiving too little regard. The "decisive question" would be: "History of Jesus or history of the Christian community?"[127] Thirty years later (1957) H. Riesenfeld subjected form criticism as it existed at the time to fundamental criticism.[128] The Jesus tradition was preserved and cultivated from Jesus' time onward in a manner with analogies in Judaism, which was the soil in which Jesus and his followers were rooted. Jesus, like a Jewish rabbi, had his disciples commit his words to memory.[129] In their epistles Paul and James presuppose familiarity with the Jesus traditions in the congregations to whom they write.[130] Riesenfeld rejected as "romantic" the established form-critical scenario of the Gospels arising out of "free formations" or "inventions" by pneumatic Christians.[131] Three years later (1960) the German Heinz Schürmann wrote on "The Pre-Easter Beginnings of the Sayings Tradition." Along with sharp attacks on form criticism—which he reproached for "blindness" and "shortsightedness"[132]—and appealing to Soiron, Riesenfeld, and others,[133] Schürmann conceived of "Jesus as teacher,"[134] who "formed his sayings consciously and passed them along to the disciples."[135] The New Testament has as its basis, then, "a cultivated continuum of tradition."[136] Later (1973) in "A Method-Critical Meditation"[137] Schürmann directed remarks against Bultmann and his followers; Schürmann went beyond the problems of form criticism to state: The "mechanisms" of critical method are "too narrowly focused."[138] Then in 1970 Erhardt Güttgemanns published "Open Questions about Form Criticism of the Gospels." He pointed to a long list of researchers (among others E. Fascher, H. Riesenfeld, V. Taylor, B. S. Easton, E. B. Redlich, G. Schille).[139] "Uncritical dabbling in hypotheses," "scholastic attachment to a certain direction" of analysis, and the assumption of a literarily productive "collective" community had hindered more fruitful results.[140] In 1979 Hubert Frankemölle, like Schürmann above, authored "A Method-Critical Meditation,"[141] in which he opposed "a traditional, anti-individually oriented form criticism, with the exaggerated role it ascribes to the community." The upshot: "The acceptance of a creative production by anonymous, collective communities . . . is to be rejected. Individual bearers and sculptors of tradition . . . are the creative producers of the texts."[142] Here traditional form criticism is overcome by criticism of method. The tradition of a method itself is subject to question and if necessary thoroughgoing replacement.

We turn now from criticism of particular areas of the historical-critical method to *fundamental criticism of the historical-critical method*. The diversity of this criticism is surprising. Wolfgang Richter (1971), e.g., is of the opinion "that the term 'historical-critical science' no longer be utilized." Why not? Because the enemy, i.e., "systematic" or dogmatic theology, is dead![143] With the end of the battle the end of the victor has arrived, too. N. Yri (1978) speaks quite differently. He wishes to continue orthodox Lutheranism's understanding of Scripture, most of all on the basis of inspiration and the authority of Scripture. History, he thinks, has practically disappeared in historical criticism. For in its reading of the Bible it sees there only "interpreted history." So he demands a suitable "historical-theological method" instead of the historical-critical method.[144] B. S. *Childs* sets his "canonical interpretation" of the Bible alongside more traditional criticism. By "canonical interpretation" he means that the biblical text is to be interpreted #1) based on its "final shape" and #2) based on its position in the canon of the Jewish, or Christian, community of faith ("canonical shape").[145] Since Childs practices both interpretive methods alongside each other—the historical-critical and the canonical—he falls prey to the same two-stage dilemma as Girgensohn once did.

Walter Wink counts as one of the most pronounced representatives of a "psychological interpretation" of Scripture. He speaks unabashedly of a "bankruptcy" of the historical-critical method (1975).[146] The reason it must be declared bankrupt lies in its abstractness and alien relation to life. It can no longer aid man in his existence. It must, therefore, be "brought over" into helping and healing action. Under closer scrutiny one discovers a two-stage problem in Wink, too, one that is structurally reminiscent of both Childs and Girgensohn. In a first pass Wink interprets material in an entirely conventional historical-critical manner. After that his psychological-therapeutic model comes into play.

A witness to how resilient and many-sided this two-stage model is may be seen not least in the materialistic biblical exegesis of M. Clévenot. Here as well the presupposition remains that in the first pass a historical-critical exegesis is produced. After that the result gleaned from the first pass is situated in a materialistically understood life context—which however now sovereignly determines the sense of the text.

All the forms of fundamental criticism of method that we have just touched on show commonality: they regard the historical-critical method as insufficient. Historical criticism does not achieve that which an interpretation of the Bible ought to.

At the beginning we posed the question: do we even need a method? To find an answer we wanted to listen to current criticism of method. We have come to see the shape of this criticism of method, even if only by some examples. What we see is this: even the most radical form of the criticism of method assumes that we do need a method. No one in the discussion above has called for a fundamental renunciation of it.[147]

We are aware that we have not thereby answered the question of whether we even need a method for interpretation of Scripture. What we have done is establish a *fact* that needs to be taken into account. But we must now take up the question of what the voices of earlier and earliest Christians have to add to our search for an answer.

## METHODICAL INTERPRETATION OF SCRIPTURE IN JESUS AND THE EARLY CHURCH

We begin this overview with *Jesus' interpretation of Scripture*. Research has learned more and more that it needs to pay heed to Jesus as teacher.

Let us state at the outset that Judaism at the dawn of the common era experienced a flowering of scriptural interpretation. Jews were truly a "people of the book." And more: there was, as G. Vermes emphasized, a fundamental unity in the exegetical tradition of the time[148]—regardless of whether we speak of Pharisee, Qumran, or Jewish Christian interpretation. Richard N. Longenecker, in striking parallel to L. Goppelt, has worked out four kinds of interpretation common in Jewish exegesis of the first century A.D.: "literalist," "midrashic," "typological," and "allegorical" (Goppelt's categories were: "literal," "symbolic," "typological," and "allegorical").[149] This exegetical tradition rested on two basic pillars: #1) the starting point of inspired words, and #2) the acceptance of a multiple sense of meaning in Scripture, which in turn was made possible by the conception of inspiration.[150]

Today there is widespread agreement that both basic pillars of all four kinds of interpretation listed above were part of Jesus' use of Scripture.[151] That is even true of "literal" exegesis.[152] Here see Matthew 5:18; 22:31f. Jesus even makes use of a few scribal interpretive rules, like the much-favored reasoning from the lesser to the greater (*kal wahomer*). Examples would be Matthew 7:11; Luke 12:28; John 7:23; 10:34–36.[153] Inference in the opposite direction, from the greater to the lesser, is also present (e.g., Mt 10:25). In other places one gets the impression that Jesus, similar to the rabbis, used a doubled proof from Scripture, adducing support from, say, the Torah and the Prophets (cf. Mt 12:3–5). The phrase "again it is written" as employed by Jesus in Matthew 4:7 points to the desire to avoid contradictions in Scripture.[154] The common question "Have you not read . . . ?" (RSV), or the presupposition of "reading" in Scripture, again shows Jesus' involvement in the scribal, thoroughly methodical interpretation of his time (cf. Mt 12:3, 5; 19:4; 21:16, 42; 22:31; 24:15; Lk 10:26). Especially weighty is the observation that Jesus taught his disciples like a Jewish rabbi would teach his.[155] In any case a portion of his sayings were consciously formed so as to be suited for memorization (cf. Mt 6:9; 28:20; Lk 11:1f.). Someone proceeding in this fashion is thinking methodically.

To summarize: Jesus certainly prescribed no binding "method" for his followers. But still less did he forbid them to employ methodical interpretation of Scripture. He rather encouraged them by the example of his earthly activity to regard Scripture in a methodical-didactic manner.

The example of the apostles points in the same direction. Once again we find in the writings of the New Testament many established rules and ways of interpreting that were current in Jewish circles.[156] Most of all we can point here to typological interpretation.[157] That is part and parcel of the prevalent stress on salvation history in the New Testament, as New Testament figures understood themselves and their times as the fulfillment of that which was proclaimed in the Old Testament (cf. e.g., 1Pe 1:10–12). Paul furnishes us with especially rich illustrative material. For "literalistic exegesis" one may note e.g., Galatians 3:16, where the exegesis is rabbinic in principle.[158] We encounter typological exegesis, basically similar to that used at times by the rabbis, in, e.g., 1 Corinthians 10:1ff.; 2 Corinthians 3:14ff.[159] (Note *tupoi*, "types," in 1Co 10:6 and *tupikōs*, "typologically," in 10:11.) First Corinthians 9:9f. offers an example of pesher method (as well as a *kal wahomer* inference?). So does Galatians 4:25. Paul also makes use of allegory, e.g., in Galatians 4:21ff.[160]

Inspiration; multiple sense of Scripture; literal, typological, and allegorical interpretation—these all remained *principles of the early church*.[161] Irenaeus[162] and Augustine are, moreover, impressive advocates of salvation-historical schemas proceeding from a carefully reflected hermeneutic. If one goes on to ponder the Scripture interpretation of the medieval church; of Luther and Calvin; of a Flacius and Protestant Scholasticism; of scholarly Pietism as typified, say, in Francke, who could write the essay "On the Definition of Method in the Study of Theology,"[163] or of a Bengel and the preface to his *Gnomon*—then it becomes clear that a methodical interpretation of Scripture has been present consistently among Jesus' followers.

From a historical point of view, then, we can only issue a decisive yes to the question: "Do we even need a method?"

## INNER REASONS FOR THE NECESSITY OF A METHOD

It is not only the *imitatio Christi* (imitation of Christ) or consideration of church history that pushes us toward a method-driven interpretation of Scripture. *Inner reasons* come into play, as well.

One of these reasons involves *testing*, an ongoing necessity in the midst of the real conditions of this world. Genuine and false prophecy required constant testing and differentiation already in Old Testament times. The instructions given in this regard (e.g., Dt 13:2ff.; 18:20ff.) demand what we might call a "sanctified rationality." While false prophecy often makes its appearance in the garb of ecstasy (e.g., Isa 28:9ff.) and indulges in signs (cf. 1Ki 22:10ff.; Mt 24:24; 2Th 2:9ff.; Rev 13:11ff.), the necessary testing does not take place in ecstasy. It rather makes use of observation, of reflection, of deductions. Thus, e.g., it is striking that Jesus often proposed a procedure for arriving at a conclusion so that his opponents might gain clarity about his origin and purpose (cf. Mt 7:16ff.; 11:2ff.; 12:25ff.; 16:1ff.; 22:41ff.). As the phenomenon of prophecy required testing, so much more did the phenomenon of messiahship. Who is the true Messiah? Jesus appealed to Scripture to decide this question and to enable Israel to give an answer (cf. Mt 4:4, 7, 10; 5:17ff.; 9:11ff.; 12:1ff.; 15:1ff.; 21:16; 22:41ff.; Jn 5:39; 7:19ff.; 10:34ff.). Precisely in this connection the searching of Scripture receives high praise from Jesus (Jn 5:39). It should also be noted here that the investigation of Scripture also gained decisive importance for understanding Jesus' suffering and resurrection (Lk 24:25–27, 44–47; Jn 20:9; 1Co 15:3ff.). And so, as the presence of the Messiah becomes certainty through testing by the Scripture, insight into the future of the world and the Lord require testing by Old Testament Scripture, or by words of Jesus placed on par with Scripture. (Here cf. Mt 24:15 and Jesus' eschatological discourses, on the one hand, and 1Th 4:15ff.; 2Th 2:1ff.; 1Ti 4:1ff.; 2Pe 3:2; Jas 5:7ff., on the other.) Not only eschatology but also ethics must constantly draw its necessary leading lines from interpretation of the divine Word. First Corinthians 7 is the star example, but so are Romans 13:1ff. and 1 Peter 2:18–25. Indeed, even the contemporary proclamation of Christ in the earliest churches still had to be Scripture-tested as it went forth (1Th 5:21; 1Co 14:29; cf. Ac 17:11). Early Christianity even set up the office of "teacher" in order to take over at least a portion of the necessary testing. These teachers owe their origin to appointments made by Jesus himself (Mt 23:34; 28:20). They played a decisive role in the Palestinian churches (Jas 3:1ff.). They also quickly came to occupy a leading place in the oldest churches outside of Palestine, augmenting the authority of the apostles and prophets (Ac 13:1; 1Co 12:28ff.; Eph 4:11). Discussion about women's participation in this instruction (1Co 14:33ff.; 1Ti 2:12ff.; Tit 2:3ff.) makes sense only if teaching and testing of teaching were central concerns. At the same time the New Testament makes clear that Christianity is obligated to abide by the apostolic doctrine (Ac 2:42; 1Co 15:11; Gal 1:6ff.; 2Pe 1:12ff.; 2:1ff.; 3:1ff.; 2Jn 9). This ability to "abide" presupposes testing. All in all we may say that the testing demanded by the Bible itself necessitates an intellectually ordered interpretation of Scripture, or more precisely a methodologically responsible interpretation of Scripture. We could also speak of *methodeiai tou diabolou*, evil and subversive methods (Eph 6:11); but that is another subject.

A further reason lies in the need to *pass along the message*. What the medieval church sought to vouchsafe as *successio* (succession) was actually the unfalsified *traditio* (tradition). This concern needs to be taken seriously. Today we would say that the concern is the *passing along of evangelical doctrine*. This is thinkable only in close relation to Scripture. That is to say that evangelical doctrine is biblically grounded and biblically regulated doctrine. Yet even what Scripture says and the contents of its statements must be opened up through pondering the biblical writers' thoughts in their train and implementing the biblical directives as laid down. This is not a call to an ecstatic state or response any more than the call to repentance is. It is rather a call for employing Spirit-directed reason. This too is part of "reasonable service of worship." For good reason the following three key expressions crop up directly after one another (in Ro 12:1f.), serving as the heading of a section on the grace gifts: "test" or "prove" (*dokimazein*), "renewing of the mind," and "reasonable service of worship" (*logikē latreia*). The teaching office is replete with *diakonia* (service) and *paraklesis* (encouragement), with *logos* (word, instruction), *sophia* (wisdom), and *gnōsis* (knowledge) (Ro 12:7f.; 1Co 12:8; Jas 3:13ff.) but not with visions and ecstasy or direct inspiration. In Philippians 4:8f. the teaching and tradition process is connected to both reflection (*logizesthai*) and to praxis (*prassein*). Observation also plays a central role. In 2 Peter 1:12–15 remembrance and memory (*hypomimneskein, mnēmē*) are decisive for the future of doctrine. All of this amounts to a prescription for ordered reflection, or what we in modern times call "method."

*Method* is a term that points to a means that others can make use of, too. If my method is to be usable by others, I must #1) realize and #2) make clear to others the path I am claiming to follow. By the way, the latter step (making clear to others) is the original sense of the Greek word *hermeneia*, from which our word *hermeneutic* derives, according to A. Boeckh.[164] But how can I make my interpretation clear to others if my interpretation did not follow a certain order of thoughts—if it had no "method"? How can others follow along if the steps I took to arrive at my interpretation reflect no certain connections and therefore cannot be reconstructed by someone seeking to follow the course my mind took? Precisely because it is biblical-evangelical doctrine, Christian doctrine is not possible without method.

A third reason for method lies in the realm of *mission*. It is worth pointing out that the missionary sermons in the book of Acts were thought through intensively (Ac 2:14ff.; 3:12ff.; 10:34ff.; 13:16ff.; 17:22ff.). These sermons arrest the hearers in their real situation. They convey the reasons for the message that are understandable to the hearers. They make use of the data that are available to the hearers, whether this is Scripture citations or a line of poetry (Ac 17:28 quotes Aratus).[165] Without a certain doctrinal development, for which there was of course already a precedent in Judaism, such missions proclamation would have been unthinkable. Mission in the New Testament sense is more than an excitement-filled testimony. It is most of all intellectual mission. The root of this form of Christian mission is Jesus. His solicitation of Israel did not consist of emotional or suggestive speeches but in teaching and proclamation (Mt 4:23; 9:35). He appealed more to the will and the understanding than to feeling and sense of excitement (cf. Lk 11:27f.; 12:20f.; 23:27–31). Early Christian mission tended heavily in the direction of a doctrinal evangelism. The mission command of Matthew 28:19f. stands out as both typical and impressive. Mission activity following that command requires teaching that is methodologically ordered.

A fourth reason for method involves *apologetics*. The term *apology* and its related verb play a surprisingly positive role in the New Testament. Leaving aside for the moment certain examples Paul affords (cf. Acts; 2Ti 4:16), we find elsewhere an entire group of statements by Jesus (Lk 12:11; 21:14), Paul (1Co 9:3; 2Co 7:11; Php 1:7, 16), and Peter (1Pe 3:15f.). These statements bear common features. The best known is 1 Peter 3:15: "Always be ready to give an answer [*pros apologian*] to every person who demands an account from you. . . ." Since this is to take place "with humility" (v. 16), and since humility is a central component in all New Testament doctrine (Mt 11:29; Jas 3:13ff.), such "apology" does not consist in outbursts or juristic tactics. The form is rather suited to the doctrine. It is most surprising, to be sure, that the New Testament does not prescribe silence in the face of persecution, interrogation, trial, and the like—Jesus' behavior in Matthew 26:63; 27:12, 14 (cf. 1Pe 2:23!) might have at least suggested this—but rather missionary witness! That is what Jesus himself intended (Mt 10:18ff.; Lk 12:11f.; 21:12f.). That is what the resurrected One announced to Saul in Damascus (Ac 9:15f.). Later that is how Paul made sense of his Roman imprisonment (Php 1:7, 16). Peter makes this an obligation of Christian congregations (1Pe 3:15). "Apology" in the New Testament, then, is not a shameful occasion, not a defensive lashing out. It is carried out with devotion, trusting in the leading of the Spirit, as an excellent chance for witness. This outlook makes correct understanding of passages like Acts 22:1; 24:10; 25:8, 16; 26:1f., 24 possible. The distinctiveness of this testimony lies not only in the unusual nature of the listeners, which included the representative of earthly government and therefore afforded what we might call official publicity for Paul's message. Its distinctiveness also consists in its exposure of the reasons for unbelief. Ultimately it is participation in the trial carried on by the Holy Spirit with the world (Jn 16:8ff.). Since churches in the West have long been relatively untouched by persecution, and since apologetics is virtually in ruins there as a result of ecclesiastical relativism, we have a hard time dealing with such matters today. But that does not change the biblical task of apologetics. And apologetics is another area that cannot move forward without methodological interpretation of Scripture.

So, along with historical reasons, a whole series of other reasons (testing, doctrine, mission, apologetics) arise that *make a method of interpreting Scripture necessary*. Reflection to this point has already turned up a number of substantive elements that belong to such a "method": ordered thought, a connection of intellectual steps (coherence), an understandable presentation, testability, feasibility, Spirit-guided rationality ("reason"), confutation of the reasons for unbelief—and all this in a unity of pondering the biblical writers' thoughts in their train and implementing the biblical directives as laid down, i.e., a unity of reflection and praxis.[166]

Speaking in concrete terms now, however, what kind of method?

## POSSIBILITIES OF A METHODICAL INTERPRETATION OF SCRIPTURE

### PRECRITICAL SCRIPTURE INTERPRETATION

One of the surprising developments in more recent hermeneutical discussion is the discovery of the positive aspects of precritical method(s). Childs, e.g., has raised the demand that we rediscover the "precritical" tradition.[167] Even where the indispensability of modern historical criticism is emphasized, as in the work of G. Strecker,[168] the advantages of earlier exegesis still come into view.[169]

What is behind this new trend? One motive is certainly the distance that modern exegesis has gained from the battles of the eighteenth century. This distance, together with much dedicated work in the area of church history, makes possible a less biased assessment of precritical interpretive science. A second motive lies in the awareness that since the eighteenth century we have failed to solve quite a number of important problems. Among these "unsolved basic hermeneutical problems" K. Lehmann finds e.g., "reason and revelation," the "right of a theological exegesis," "insight into one's own contingence," and the "ministry of the interpretation of Scripture."[170]

A third motive is the awareness of failure to fulfill our own demands. This is true, e.g., with respect to the objectivity of research. Thus F. C. Baur wanted to "apprehend" the state of affairs given to us in the Bible in its "pure objectiveness."[171] Similarly W. Wrede wished to work "as objectively . . . as possible."[172] Since that time we have come to realize that such "objective," presuppositionless exegesis is not possible. The same goes for overcoming a "dogmatic conception of Christianity."[173] In recent decades we have come to understand that a new "critical orthodoxy" has arisen that simply refuses to countenance anything that runs against its "critical conclusions."[174] This orthodoxy undertakes to label rival conceptions (salvation history, covenant theology, etc.) as not "dogmatically legitimate."[175]

A fourth motive consists in uncertainty that the progress being sought outweighs the damage caused by bidding farewell to precritical conditions. Even A. Gunneweg, who declared the historical-critical method to be the only "scientifically proven method," admits that in the use of that method "the fundamental and essential importance of the Bible, as upheld in the ancient church and—elsewhere—in the Reformation, was not preserved."[176] G. Strecker cited "three factors" favoring precritical "biblical theology": #1) "the material unity of Old and New Testament," #2) "the integrity of the biblical canon," and #3) "the identity of Scriptural doctrine and systematic theology." Strecker then continued: "The history of New Testament theology" has been the "history of the criticism and dissolution of the concept of 'biblical theology.'"[177] What sense can such a "history" make?

Down as far as B. Baumgarten, hermeneutics encompassed practical application.[178] Since then, however, exegesis has been emancipated from practical application. There was a time when the "solution to the hermeneutical problem" was foreseen as coming through the historical-critical method.[179] Now, however, we languish rather in a "methodological crisis."[180] No wonder there is renewed attention and openness to precritical, pre-Enlightenment exegesis.

Entirely apart from such references to the value of precritical exegesis, we will have to investigate carefully the extent to which an acceptance of certain elements of this precritical interpretation of Scripture may be feasible for us.

What was distinctive about it? H. W. Frei describes it this way: "Western Christian reading of the Bible in the days before the rise of historical criticism . . . was usually strongly realistic, i.e., at once literal and historical."[181] Based on that, we could characterize precritical exegesis as "literal-historical." We are reminded that both these qualities, literalistic and historical, can be shown to have been present in the exegesis of ancient Judaism, the New Testament, and the early church. Materially we are also not so very far removed from the "historical-grammatical interpretive method" of Theodore of Mopsuestia.[182] If one reflects on Bengel's occasional definition, according to which theology is "grammatica in spiritus sancti verbis occupata" ("philology concentrated on the words of the Holy Spirit"),[183] then the designation "grammatical-historical" does not appear to be too unsuitable. On the other hand Ernesti and his school selected precisely the term *grammatical-historical* to characterize their form of Scripture interpretation.[184] In 1810 Karl August Gottlieb Keil of Leipzig made the words "basic principles of grammatical-historical interpretation" part of the title of his *Handbook of Hermeneutics*. He emphatically championed the necessity of "grammatical-historical" interpretation.[185] In view of the fact that a segment of early historical-critical criticism wanted to use "grammatical-historical" to designate its work, this designation is not suitable to characterize *precritical* exegesis. Frei proposed that we speak of a "precritical realistic reading."[186] In any case we must be aware that it would be misleading to speak of a "literalistic" interpretation of Scripture. For in spite of widespread stress on the *sensus literalis* (literal sense), there was also openness to a spiritual meaning in Scripture, however halting that openness might have been. In this connection it is clearly pietistic exegesis that favors the multiple meaning of Scripture. By way of preliminary summary we may say at this point that precritical exegesis sought to work with philological precision, historical realism, and multidimensionality as a result of its conviction regarding inspiration.

Now let us look at a few examples of how evangelical exegesis from the Reformation to the Enlightenment has taken shape.

Matthias Flacius' *Clavis Scripturae* of 1567 is foundational. Dilthey called it the "first significant, and perhaps most profound, of these [hermeneutical] writings."[187] Flacius avoids applying a universal doctrine of understanding to the Bible. He rather unfolds a biblical hermeneutic, forged in dialogue with Scripture, that can serve as the starting point for a general hermeneutic.[188] Flacius belongs, then, among the fathers of a *hermeneutica sacra* (sacred hermeneutic). God is the originator of Scripture. Holy Scripture as a whole is inspired and created by God.[189] It is therefore not permissible to introduce principles that are alien to the Bible for the interpretation of the Bible.[190] Flacius does not forget that the Bible is largely determined by its purpose. It is an "instrument unto eternal life."[191] It should lay hold of man for this saving purpose and transform him accordingly.[192] By means of this instrument God establishes a relationship with man. The amount of space that Flacius devotes to reflections on the interpreter is astounding. Humanism and the Enlightenment demand of the interpreter most of all erudition (*eruditio*).[193] For Flacius, man is first blind and dumb before the Word of God.[194] Inherent in his present nature is also doubt of the truth of the Word.[195] It is first the power of the Word, which is also the power of the Spirit, that renders him capable of hearing and seeing. In this encounter with God through the Word, illumination (*illuminatio*) takes place by the Holy Spirit, along with restoration (*restitutio*) to the image of God (*imago Dei*) and spiritual rebirth.[196] Once again: only the transformed person can understand. Therefore the interpreter must be a "renewed person" (*renatus*).[197] Flacius follows the "I believe in order to understand" (*credo, ut intelligam*) confession of Augustine and Anselm.[198] What we require is not hermeneutical aptitude (*aptitudo*) and erudition (*eruditio*), not congeniality (*Kongenialität*) in the sense intended by those who favor that term, but the Holy Spirit and in that sense inspiration.[199] We must first, therefore, in God-granted contrition (*rebus divinis*) forsake trust in our own intellect.[200] The Christian interpreter cannot, however, dispense with Christian experience (*experientia*).[201] One notes that there is a coherent line from Luther's *tentatio-oratio-meditatio* (struggle-prayer-reflection) to the *experientia* of Flacius and stress on the practical piety (*praxis pietatis*) in the theology of Pietism right down to the praxis-centeredness of the interpreter in J. T. Beck. Not until the interpreter experiences unconditioned alteration through Scripture does knowledge of the real take place and have its due impact on interpretation.[202]

Even judged by today's standards, Flacius' exegetical procedure is impressively careful. Interpretation proceeds in three great stages: #1) *grammatica intellectio*, i.e., philological understanding, the apprehension of individual words and of the context; #2) *theologica tractatio*, i.e., theological preparation, or apprehension of the theological intention of the speaker; #3) *cognitio practica*, i.e., practical knowledge, understanding of the text for our Christian life.[203] It is not difficult to find here steps that are still recognized as requisite today: opening up of the text— theological interpretation—meditation or homiletical sketch. The numerous *individual steps* which must be pondered in the course of *grammatica intellectio* or *theologica tractatio* feel familiar to us. Along with investigation of the words and grammar, Flacius places questions concerning author, recipients, object, reason for writing, background, conditions, literary genre, structure, context, inner-biblical comparisons, and major point.[204] Here is the point where historical lore is brought in, e.g., concerning natural science, ancient crafts and trades, topography, anthropology, astronomy, meteorology, wild animal life, legal and political life, economy, trade, geography, ethnology. And then most of all Palestine's flora and fauna are to be factored in along with the customs of the people and the country, and indeed those of the entire ancient Near East. Obviously the whole scope of history generally is also brought to bear. Here we find help through use of ancient authors like Appian, Didorus Siculus, Strabo, Pliny, Aristotle, Dioskur, and Josephus.[205] Moldaenke declares: "This interest in concrete historical material . . . is thoroughly characteristic of Flacius."[206] Flacius' interest in chronology is well known. Already for Flacius—Bengel is not the pioneer here—biblical chronology furnishes "the scaffolding" for the entire world-historical outline.[207] Flacius wishes to contain the subjectivity of the interpreter by means of the *analogia fidei* (analogy of faith).[208]

Flacius provided a basis for evangelical Scripture interpretation that endured for centuries. If we compare his work to the exegesis that is dominant today, we are struck by the following. First, comparatively little has changed in the individual steps. Almost all procedures of modern text analysis are also present in Flacius, at least in principle: philological-grammatical investigation, structure, context, comparison with contemporary history of the time, history of the literary forms (form criticism), redaction criticism, tradition criticism, indeed history-of-religions comparison, scope. Literary criticism could be characterized as a modern achievement. Second, an eminent historical interest must be acknowledged to be present in Flacius' work. Third, Flacius makes visible in rigorous fashion the conditions of understanding. But it is precisely at this point that the differences between Flacius and modern exegesis come into view. Not only does Flacius give positive consideration to the *analogia fidei* (analogy of faith); he also demands an *interpretatio fidei* (interpretation in keeping with faith). This documents a hermeneutical bond with the fellowship of faith of the church. It is no "coincidence" that his third main interpretive step is the *cognitio practica* (practical understanding), which amounts to the transition to preaching and instruction. This third step then was lost at the Enlightenment, a consequence of its emancipation from the church. Finally, we discover two further decisive differences. One is rooted in Flacius' interest in real biblical history, which compels him to adopt a *salvation-historical interpretation.* The Enlightenment, in contrast, replaced history with morality. The other difference is rooted in an understanding of Scripture for which biblical answers to fundamental theological questions were normative; for Flacius this understanding assumed the unity and inspiration of the Word of God. The Enlightenment could accept none of these pillars of Flacius' understanding of Scripture.

In Flacius' wake there was at first no revolutionary renewal of evangelical Scripture interpretation. The "hermeneutical revolution"[209] of the Enlightenment preempted any such development. In the two centuries or so after Flacius there was only shifting of emphasis, with first one concern and then another receiving attention within a framework like Flacius drew up.

Old Protestant Scholasticism at the time of a Colovius, König, Hollaz, and Quenstedt devoted itself most of all to the doctrine of Scripture.[210] The differences between Lutherans and the Reformed were held within bounds.[211]

Hermeneutics experienced a revival through covenant theology, which was pursued most of all by Reformed thinkers. It stressed the historical side of the Bible. Chronology and prophecy came in for renewed scrutiny; the special character of the respective salvation-historical epochs was worked out; the proof-text approach to dogmatics was called into question to some extent. This did not, however, lead to biblical criticism in the modern sense.[212]

A comprehensive hermeneutical interest then awoke within Pietism. It recognized the challenge posed by rationalism and the Enlightenment and opted to face up to it. Various accents and outlooks came to the surface as the challenge was answered. To speak summarily of "Pietism" in the singular is therefore just as risky as summarizations of other theological trends. A. H. Francke and his school directed special attention to the person of the interpreter. Scripture interpretation and theological science were conceived as a part of the Christian life. As a result, Francke saw in theology a "means of furthering the kingdom of God under the leading of the Holy Spirit."[213] Francke's student Johann Jakob Rambach emphasized that the exegete must be illumined by the Holy Spirit and led by love to Jesus and his Word.[214] As for Pietism elsewhere, the necessity of a *theologia regenitorum* (theology done by regenerate persons) remained uncontested.[215] A second stress in Francke was on *applicatio* (application). He demanded of his students that they "become more pious through the reading of Scripture."[216] The *collegia biblica* (Bible college) was to serve that end; it was not necessary to be a theologian to attend it. Ongoing prayer was essential as well. In Francke's own words: "No theology lecture is held that does not appeal to the heart and that does not attempt to pierce the soul of every hearer."[217] Without the transition into Christian praxis, all remains dead orthodoxy. Here there is in principle no separation between the preacher's pulpit and the professor's podium. Pietism, centered in Halle, therefore responds to the flood of rationalism in its self-proclaimed emancipation from the church by extending church to the lecture hall. Over against emphasis on reason Francke states: "Everything depends, however, on reason subordinating itself to the faith."[218] Francke escapes the danger of superficiality that can easily arise through such theological evangelism. Like Bengel he devotes himself to the original text and seeks to improve Luther's translation of the Bible.[219] Both Francke's *Praelectiones hermeneuticae* (1717) and J. J. Rambach's *Institutiones hermeneuticae sacrae* (1724) attest to the seriousness of Pietism's hermeneutical-theological effort.

*Applicatio* (application) certainly possessed high value for J. A. Bengel, as well. But he was far more concerned than Francke with the content of revelation as such. It is not insignificant that attention to the text is mentioned first in Bengel's famous aphorism "Te totum applica ad textum—rem totam applica ad te" ("Apply yourself wholly to the text—apply the text wholly to yourself"). Bengel was among the founders of the discipline now called "textual criticism."[220] Well schooled in Cicero, he pursued investigation of the original text in exquisite detail, leaving no stones unturned and following every possible lead to its end. Bengel was in reality a biblical theologian. The comments in his *Gnomon* are still worth reading for the exegete today. Along with philological work, Bengel's second point of emphasis was the salvation-historical conception of the content of revelation. His sometimes peculiar chronological outlines serve this salvation-historical conception and open up the Bible's contents. In all this Bengel believed he was being guided by Scripture itself. His primary historical interest moved him to make distinctions that were almost suspect for Protestant Scholasticism of his day. Thus he distinguished, in a way similar to Theodore of Mopsuestia,[221] various forms and degrees of inspiration.[222] Like Augustine he could in principle view an apostolic lapse of memory as possible. On the other hand Bengel advocated the principle of taking Scripture in its entirety. He distanced himself from the "degenerate disciples" of Luther who disputed the theological integrity of the book of James. The book of Revelation, which Protestant Scholasticism occasionally ranked as "deuterocanonical," was for Bengel the indispensable touchstone of the entire Bible. In sharp distinction to rationalism, with which he was acquainted especially through interaction with Spinoza, he rejected the *praeiudicium proprium* (innate prejudgment) of human reason in order to place himself fully under the *praeiudicium* (prejudgment) of God in his revelation. Revelation and Scripture were identical for him—a position that he championed not least against the pneumatics and prophets of separatistic sects of his day. Part of Bengel's basic approach also included giving an account of a methodological way to do exegesis. His ideal here was a "suitably precise investigation." He held the following to be imperative: philological investigation right down to emphasis and effect of the biblical writers; attention to context and ancient history as well as other religions; relation to other statements in the Bible, i.e., inner-biblical comparison; integration into the appropriate portion of the salvation-historical economy; and the most precise possible conception of intent. For support he adduced ancient literature such as Josephus or Philo. For theological interpretation he pondered patristic interpretation as well as that of older church history. Following this came homiletical application. In short, Bengel's procedure in its individual parts points to painstaking care very much similar to that seen in Flacius. He passed along this carefulness to the school of thought that followed him. Frei's assessment about Protestant Scholasticism and Pietism is justified, at least when applied to Bengel: "They followed the Reformers and a large consensus of Western Christendom from earliest times."[223]

All stages of precritical evangelical exegesis between Flacius and Pietism showed the following five characteristics: #1) The *unity of Scripture and revelation* was foundational. The result of this was the exclusive normativity of Scripture. No other authority could rival Scripture. The formula *sola scriptura* was upheld right down to the time of Pietism. It included the unity and inspiration of Scripture. #2) Love for *philologically exact work on the text* was also characteristic. No wonder that so-called textual criticism arose in precritical exegesis and was not a child of the Enlightenment. This in no way shook the primacy of the *sensus literalis* (literal sense). Yet in virtually all cases, though in varying measures, a multiple meaning of Scripture was assumed. This too mirrored the conviction that God is the real originator of Scripture. #3) The *renewal of the Christian interpreter* through the Holy Spirit was constantly presupposed. Without exception the interpretation of Scripture was integrated into the life of the church. There should be no disjunction between life and doctrine in the interpreter. Interpretation aims ultimately at preaching and instruction. #4) A special *historical interest* grows out of interchange with the history-laden biblical texts. Prior to the Enlightenment this interest is overwhelmingly salvation-historical in nature. In this understanding the historical is at the same time the ultimately real. The more salvation-historical, the more real! Veering off into purely thematic categories or into a purely static scriptural mean was thereby precluded. #5) We find everywhere a *methodologically reflected interpretation*. All the essential elements of a method worthy of the name are present: self-awareness of one's own procedure, the coherence of each individual step, testability, feasibility (given certain presuppositions), understandable and learnable presentation, striving for unity between reflection and praxis.

If one's starting point is biblical revelation, then none of the characteristics cited above can be denied or dismissed as false. Then why not take up precritical, philological-theological methodology once more? The modern outcry that to do this makes one a "fundamentalist" is in any case not a cogent argument against such a reclamation.

There are, however, other reasons that hinder facile return to the earlier approach. In "Inner Reasons for the Necessity of a Method" above, we pressed for the necessity of methodological interpretation of Scripture. Here both testing and apologetics were accorded an important role. Both, testing and apologetics, deal with questions that hearers of the message pose to the Christian community and its proclamation. These questions are colored by the respective times in which they arise. This alters the way that the Christian message is unfolded. Interpretation is concerned to facilitate a focused and timely unfolding of this message. Therefore, it cannot simply duplicate earlier modes of approach or ignore the history that has transpired since earlier methods saw their own heyday. To that extent we cannot get outside of the history that theology has undergone since the time of precritical, philological-theological methods. However—and here we differ radically from historical criticism—we also do not make this history and its Enlightenment agenda into a second authority alongside of Scripture. The essential testing and apologetic functions forbid, however, a facile return to precritical exegesis as if nothing has happened in the intervening generations.

In view of shifts in outlook that have come about, two factors stand above all others in essential importance. #1) The first consists in the enormously *heightened historical consciousness*. Before our eyes lie entire causal chains that we use to explain the psyche and the course of an individual's life, the developments of political and economic history, and indeed the progress of the whole cosmos to an astonishing degree. Mystery has receded to the margin of the cosmos and in part even vanished from the margin altogether. From this starting point texts of the past have now been read "historically" for decades and centuries. This particular way of assessing history, or what is called history, is therefore very much more pronounced than in the precritical era. #2) The second factor consists in an enormously heightened *consciousness of autonomy*. Kant, in whom the Enlightenment was fully embodied, still acknowledged the necessity for thought to take God into account.[224] In modern times autonomous man does, following Kant, think of a God, but mostly due to anxiety *etsi deus daretur* (that God might exist). Modern man does not *want* to take account of him, however, because by his own estimation he has arrived at a point where he no longer needs a God. The question, How do I stay healthy? is more important today than the question, How do I receive a gracious God? The God who for Kant was still guarantor of the good, and was necessary for the good to come about, becomes guarantor of the good person under the banner of the "new religiosity"[225] which promises man security for man's own sake.

Given the prevalence of the stress on historicality and advanced sense of autonomy of man, a simplistic repristination of precritical exegesis is not possible. This insight leads to three essential points of orientation: #1) we need to seek out helpful examples of postcritical interpretation of Scripture; #2) we need to conceive a method that is suited to the skewed cultural outlook of our day; #3) we need to make concrete the nonnegotiable insights of precritical methods, even today.

## J. G. HAMANN

No orientation regarding a viable hermeneutical outline can afford to overlook *Johann Georg Hamann* (1730–88).

While as early as 1949 "the name J. G. Hamann" was "suddenly in the air once more,"[226] interest in this author has grown to such an extent in recent decades that one can almost speak of a Hamann-Renaissance. One notable indicator here is P. Stuhlmacher's hermeneutics book *Grundrissen zum Neuen Testament*. While the first edition (1979) did not even mention Hamann in the index, the second edition (1986) contained a special section on Hamann (pp. 140ff.). Occasionally "Luther, Calvin, and Hamann" are even placed alongside each other.[227]

Hamann possessed nearly encyclopedic knowledge. After his conversion in London on March 31, 1758, he placed this knowledge in the service of his redeemer Jesus Christ: "The small stream of my written works flowed out toward this King whose name, like his praise, is great and unrecognized."[228] With polished literary weapons he fought against the reign of the Enlightenment as the "sage of the North" (he hailed from Königsburg, a northern German region). Contemporaries reproached "the chaotic opacity of his writings";[229] he referred to himself apostrophically as "le Sophiste arctique" (the sophist of the north) in his "Letzen Blatt."

Hamann sought quite consciously to hold high the banner of Christianity and of Lutheranism.[230] At the same time, while sharing all "commitment to the concerns of Protestant Scholastic conceptions of Scripture," he "pointed ahead to the more recent historically oriented scientific study of the Bible."[231]

On a closer look at his view of the Bible, striking at the outset is his love for the Bible as a book. For him the Bible is "the book of God" and a "means of grace."[232] "Scripture, the Word of God, the Bible," is more glorious and perfect than nature.[233] It gives us—this was his own experience—God's "saving word" which is "the dearest gift of divine grace."[234] He speaks, clearly, of the form of Scripture as given. In this connection Hamann used the well-known formulation "God an author!"[235] He praised the fact "that the Holy Spirit set forth for us a book to convey his Word," and he called this book "the charter of our faith."[236] Yet with the same force he maintained that the enscripturation of divine revelation was the result of divine "condescension."[237] The Holy

Spirit surrendered himself to this humiliation when he created this book. Seen from the outside, Scripture is comparable to the "old rags" used to haul Jeremiah out of the cistern.[238] He regarded the unadorned Greek of the New Testament as a virtual proof of earliest Christian, authentic provenance: "the Oriental aspects of our pulpit style lead us back to the cradle of our race and our religion."[239] He emphasized that the New Testament confronts us with "historical writings with genuine understanding."[240]

How does the humble form of Scripture and its historical character, on the one hand, relate to its divine character, on the other hand? It would be tempting to relegate the divine aspect to some "real" revelation lying beyond Scripture's humble form, and to regard the humble form as a human testimony, full of errors and requiring our critical analysis. As we know, this is the path that theological hermeneutics has often traveled. Yet in Hamann we encounter a different solution. Hamann is able to hold the human and divine dimensions of Scripture together by conceiving them as arising from God's gracious condescension.[241] God wanted us to have Scripture in *just* the form that it lies before us today. It therefore remains a unified whole.

This view of Scripture held by Hamann stands up splendidly in interaction with Moses Mendelssohn and Gotthold Ephraim Lessing. Obviously in conscious opposition to Lessing Hamann says (in "Golgatha und Scheblimini") that he knows "of no eternal truths but the incessantly temporal."[242] That means that God speaks nowhere else but in the historical biblical revelation. Anyone who, like Lessing, wishes to seek eternal truths beyond or off to the side of the historical presented by the Bible presumes to enter "into the inner counsels of the divine understanding."[243] On the other hand it should be said that "without authority the truth of history" vanishes "with what has taken place itself."[244] God reveals himself in historical truths. Here we stand once more before the mystery of God, who as the Holy Spirit and for the sake of our redemption "humbles himself" in that he "has become a history writer of the most trivial, the most contemptible, the most insignificant incidents on earth."[245]

From all this it is clear that Hamann's starting point is the inspiration of the Bible. According to 2 Peter 1:21, God's Spirit "moved" the authors of the Bible.[246] In language much like that of Protestant Scholasticism, Hamann states that "the Holy Spirit" revealed himself "through the human pens of holy men that were impelled by him."[247] Here Hamann even draws a parallel between the incarnation of God's Son and the enscripturation of revelation by the Holy Spirit. The "servant form" of both leads, however—in stark contrast to Enlightenment and modern dogmatics—not to a deficiency but to encounter of God with man and to salvation. Hamann's view has rightly been called verbal inspiration.[248]

The result of the inspiration of the entire Scripture is the "unity of the divine revelation."[249] The result of its character of divine revelation is its exclusive normativity for faith: "Christianity's faith does not rest in the doctrinal opinions of philosophy."[250] Moreover, it would be an insult to God's redemptive self-humiliation if "man used the book of God as an object for criticism and philosophizing." Hamann therefore consciously excludes any content criticism of the Bible.[251]

Scripture's inspiration implies the necessity of interpreting it under the leading of the Holy Spirit. Hamann states explicitly that "understanding this book [= the Bible]" "cannot be attained by any means other than the same Spirit who moved the authors of this book."[252] For knowledge of the divine Word Hamann viewed himself as requiring "precisely the presence [of that Holy Spirit] by whom the Word has been written." He is "the only way to the understanding of Scripture."[253] The Spirit's leading does not bring about some ecstatic condition but rather love for, humility before, and trust in Scripture. "Humility of heart," says Hamann, "is the only state of mind proper to reading the Bible, and it is the indispensable preparation for such reading."[254] In order to know the divine Friend through Scripture's servant form, one needs the "illumined, aroused, jealous eyes of a friend, a confidant, a lover."[255] It is therefore admissible to see Hamann as still another proponent of a *theologia regenitorum* (theology of regeneration).[256]

The person who venerates the miracle of divine condescension can only be critical of the deification of reason in the so-called Enlightenment. How arrogant, that it viewed truth as resting in itself, that it set itself on the same level as the divine—even if it was by means of indirect revelation in the form of abstractions and concepts. Hamann asked, "For what is much-vaunted reason with its universality, infallibility, exuberance, certainty, and evidence? An *ens rationis* (mental construct), a chimera, to which the raucous superstition of irrationality ascribes divine attributes."[257] Reason, superstitiously aggrandized, is in fact the reason possessed by unredeemed sinners, who live on the basis of their own righteousness. "Tremble!" cries Hamann, "Woe to you misled mortals, who make the nobility of your intentions your righteousness!" And to those who seek to measure the miracles of the Bible by their own standards Hamann offers this food for thought: "The system of this current year, which excuses you from furnishing proof for your first principles, will someday be a fairy tale." "Let us please not assess the truth of things according to how easy we find it to imagine them to ourselves in a certain fashion."[258]

Hamann's grasp of the humble form of Scripture is distinct in itself when compared to the then-reigning Protestant Scholastic views. But there are additional principles that also go beyond Protestant Scholasticism. One of these principles is that Hamann sees use of the Bible as the decisive means to acquiring knowledge. In the well-known analogy to Jeremiah, in which Hamann compares the Bible to the old rags that could be used to pull Jeremiah out of the cistern, Hamann states: "Not their [i.e., the rags'] appearance but the service they rendered him, and the use that he made of them, redeemed him from mortal danger. Jer XXXVIII 11–13."[259] Naturally Hamann did not mean that the Bible became Word of God only as and when use was made of it. It is God's Word even apart from its use. But to encounter it aright, to experience its power and essence, one must put it into practice. That is the way that Joh. Tobias Beck was later to emphasize. A second principle that goes beyond Protestant Scholasticism lies in Hamann's reading of the Bible, which was simultaneously literal and typological.[260] Restriction to the *sensus literalis* (literal sense) does not take place: "Every stone [of Scripture] on which the Christian lays his head has its ladder, like the one Jacob saw in a dream [as he slept on a stone]."[261] For that very reason Hamann read the Old Testament like his "own life story." He could identify himself as Cain and as Christ's murderer, and he could make identifications between these two.[262] Hamann comes very close to a pietistic hermeneutic with his Scripture-bound reclamation of the *sensus literalis* (literal sense) and his use of typology.[263]

In summarizing J. G. Hamann's hermeneutical insights, one is astounded by the clarity and force with which Hamann critically engaged the criticism of the Enlightenment. "Our age is the real age of criticism, which must subordinate everything to itself," explained I. Kant in his *Kritik der reinen Vernunft* (*Critique of Pure Reason*). Hamann divested reason thus conceived of its arrogant self-proclaimed worth.[264] He called man to the "service of God rendered by those who listen."[265] Indeed, one could justifiably dub his a "hermeneutic of listening." Showing points of similarity to Protestant Scholasticism and to Pietism, and making both revelation and his personal experience a point of departure for his argumentation, Hamann championed the interpenetration of Word of God and word of man, the inspiration of the whole of Scripture, the unity of Scripture, the identification of revelation with the Bible, the exclusive authority of Scripture, the necessity of a *theologia regenitorum* (theology of regeneration), and the proving of Scripture by practice of it. The basic lines of the biblical-Reformation understanding of Scripture are maintained.

At the same time Hamann frees himself from the artificial arguments of Protestant Scholasticism that threaten to crowd the human and historical out of Scripture. Hamann is free to "acknowledge the humanity of the Bible."[266] From that starting point Hamann opens the possibility of historical labor[267] on the Bible, a labor that essentially coincides with his conception of inspiration because it originates in the condescension of God. If Hamann had been listened to here, the ditch between the idea of inspiration, on the one hand, and historical biblical exegesis, on the other, need never have arisen.[268]

In sum, Hamann is very much more helpful than e.g., today's "moderate criticism" (see "So-called Moderate Criticism" below). Yet we cannot neglect to make a few cautionary comments. One is the fundamental fact that Hamann was a *homme de lettres* (man of letters)[269]— not a theologian or exegete. We cannot expect from him either systematic-theological formulations or even the unfolding of hermeneutical consequences.[270] He leaves us with scanty allusions and with witty statements that are then almost monotonously cited in the literature. Occasionally more weight is placed on them than they can bear. Not clarified, e.g., is the relation between condescension and inspiration. That becomes somewhat clear in the tiff between Hempelmann and Lindner over the terms *condescension* and *accommodation* in Hamann's usage.[271] Certainly Hamann does not wish God's "self-lowering" to be understood as some departure from divine truth. Yet there are open questions here, especially regarding the historical conditionedness of Scripture.[272] Also not thoroughly clear is the relation of the "old rags" in the form of Scripture to the historical reliability of the Bible. Kähler could draw this inference from the "old rags" figure: "Apparently it would not have bothered him [Hamann] to read today's theories of the composition and redaction of the biblical books."[273] But that is just the question: would he indeed not have been "bothered" by current theories about "community formation," "secondary expansion," "pseudepigraphy in the New Testament," "sources," and the like? Likewise, we must ask to what extent Lindner actually betrays Hamann's "spirit" with his judgment: "Something of Hamann's spirit shows itself in Schniewind's willingness to engage in critical investigation of the New Testament without any dogmatic bias."[274] But precisely such questions and judgments show that Hamann is of limited value as a guide into the thickets of historical investigation. Added to this is the passion of the literary artist. It is well known that Hamann could write of the Bible that in it the Holy Spirit, "like someone foolish and daft, indeed like an unholy and impure spirit of our proud reason, made fables, small despicable incidents, into the history of heaven and of God."[275] Anyone who takes up this view of "history" in Hamann without careful attention to the context can easily twist Hamann into the posture of endorsing historical-critical interpretation of Scripture.[276]

J. G. Hamann remains a witness to hermeneutical truths that we cannot give up. But he beckons us to improve our own hermeneutical strategy more than he encourages us to replace ours with his.

## J. L. S. LUTZ AND J. T. BECK

J. L. Samuel Lutz (1785–1844) and Johann Tobias Beck (1804–78) are among the first to be commended as helpful examples of noncritical interpretation of Scripture. Both could be called fathers of "pneumatic interpretation."[277] It was Beck, however, who exerted the greater influence. Both show essential features of precritical interpretation and attempt to hold fast to them in the present situation. Thus Lutz emphasizes the suitability of a "historical-grammatical interpretation."[278] Thus Beck stresses that Scripture is *norma normans* (normative standard) and proceeds from the assumption of Scripture's unity and unified character. In this he is reminiscent of Bengel.[279] Yet for both Lutz and Beck the "pneumatic state" of the interpreter is much more at the forefront than it was for Protestant Scholasticism.[280] Lutz's view is summed up in the aphorism "Spirit seeks the spirit."[281] The Holy Spirit lets our "eyes . . . be healthy" and equips for knowledge of the "inner unity" of Scripture.[284] Therefore both Lutz and Beck underscore the necessity of the interpreter's spiritual rebirth.[283] J. Wach characterizes Beck with the statement that he strove for a "believing-scientific" interpretive method.[284] In this connection Wach also points out that for Lutz "interest in life" and for Beck practical application possess high hermeneutical rank.[285] The value they place on the person of the interpreter becomes more understandable in view of numerous biographies of "young theologians who then for inner reasons avoid the pulpit."[286]

It is doubtless fruitful to follow Lutz and Beck today in some respects. What they wished to preserve, we must also preserve. Yet they did not always succeed at transferring biblical foundations into their own present era. One deficiency, e.g., is a certain heedlessness of the historical. Precisely this absence of sufficient historical rigor—one could also term it a tendency to take a stand above history—later helped cause supporters of pneumatic exegesis like Girgensohn to remain hanging in a two-stage procedure. Where the independence of the Spirit is stressed too much, the result is what A. Schlatter called the "severing of Scripture from history."[287] The result of such severing is a vacuum, into which a historically oriented interpretation streams without sufficient control. Overemphasis of the pneumatic, i.e., elevating the pneumatic alone to the normative, becomes all the more dangerous today in the presence of the current "new religiosity." In this movement, does not everyone claim to speak "in the Spirit"? Nevertheless, it should not be said that Lutz or Beck themselves were not sober interpreters. But we can recognize the starting points of tendencies that we cannot make our own.

## ADOLF SCHLATTER

Another *helpful example of noncritical interpretation of Scripture* is Adolf *Schlatter* (1852–1938).

The fact that we are currently enjoying a Schlatter-Renaissance is all the more commendation of his example. Hasel calls him "a giant."[288] Others called him "unprofessional."[289]

First, there are impressive points of contact between Beck and his student Schlatter. Both distance themselves consciously and decisively from historical criticism.[290] Both stress the unity of Scripture. Schlatter's well-known line is worth citing: "Unity is necessary for Scripture so that it may be recognizable and of service to us as God's Word."[291] Both affirm the inspiration of the entire Scripture.[292] Both proceed from the assumption of Scripture's authority in the sense of *norma normans* (normative standard).[293] Both also possess a strong interest in praxis. Characteristic for Schlatter here is the tight relationship between belief, thought, and will. He states that "our will belongs to the conditions upon which the success of our thinking is dependent."[294] On the other hand faith becomes "the director of our will."[295] For Schlatter theology is finally an "act of worship to God"[296] and therefore wrapped up in the ministry of the Christian community.

Yet Schlatter's work comprises a "sui generis."[297] His difference from Beck is already recognizable in the manner in which Schlatter determines the way to knowledge. All human thinking follows a "law that we must honor as God's gracious will."[298] The intellectual work of theologians is fundamentally no different from intellectual work in the other sciences. "The knowing and proving work of the theologian is formally completely similar to that of the natural and historical researcher."[299] Why? Because every science is determined by the data with which it has to deal. The first and foundational act of becoming familiar with the facts and interacting with them he calls "perceiving." Perceiving, in turn, expresses what it knows in concepts.[300] Human thought is therefore basically a receptive process—"first reception, then production."[301] "The formations that fill us in the form of conceptions and ideas arise in us according to an ordered process that is implanted in us. In these formations we are the receivers. Where reception fails, our ability to produce goes under as well."[302] These statements by Schlatter force us to recall Ricoeur's "The event is our master." The fundamentally receptive form of thought conditions the central role of concepts like "perception," "observation," "seeing," "act of seeing," "hearing."[303] Can, however, God be "perceived"? And can *every* person in principle perceive him? Schlatter answers yes. He maintains that the idea of God is "unavoidable" on the basis of the facts that surround us.[304] Our own "vitality" and nature itself show us unambiguously that there is a personal God.[305] There is no knowledge of God only for those "who cannot make up their minds to be man."[306] In this view of things atheism becomes flight from perception; it even becomes ethically "abominable" at the point where "we evade the summons to faith that has become evident to us."[307] Conversely, theology's primary task is to unfold the states of affairs of which it has caught sight. Dogmatic work thus calls for "perceiving, and nothing but perceiving."[308] Perceiving occurs as commitment.[309] It requires courage: we must "have the courage to see what we see."[310]

Where Beck would have spoken of *pneuma* (Spirit), Schlatter therefore speaks of courage. Where Beck would have spoken of the *theologia regenitorum* (theology of regeneration), Schlatter speaks of the perception that is accessible to every person. Where Beck spoke of "entering into" "the entirety of divine truth," in the sense of theocentric, indeed even Bible-centric, thinking,[311] Schlatter's starting point is quite consciously "anthropocentric." That extends to the point that Schlatter handles special theology in the framework of anthropology(!).[312] To quote Schlatter once again: "All theological labor submits to the same rule that all other scientific work must obey, and obeys willingly. It does this, if it truly has its object in God and only in God, precisely as it remains anthropocentric, because its standpoint is not beyond but in man."[313]

As we saw, Beck and Schlatter differ in the way that Beck sharply separates theological work from other science, views the knowledge of God and his Word as possible only through the *pneuma* (Spirit), and thereby arouses the suspicion that he fragments unified processes of knowledge. Schlatter, on the other hand, views all of this as false. They also differ in the way they regard history. Beck treated the Bible most of all as revelation of normative doctrine and kept his distance from historical research. But Schlatter arrived at the content of biblical statements primarily through his historical investigation. True, both agree that history "has its unity in Christ."[314] But Beck would have greeted with reservation, if at all, Schlatter's disputing of "an antithesis between history and the work of the Spirit" and Schlatter's insistence that "Correct pneumatology and correct historiography [are] two sides of the same coin."[315] We discover, then, the sharpest hermeneutical difference between Beck and Schlatter in their views of the Spirit and of history.

There is much to be learned from Schlatter still today. His affirmation of the inspiration of all of Scripture, Scripture's unity, its exclusive authority, its infallibility as regards its divinely intended purpose, its perspicuity, and the rejection of a canon within a canon[316]—all this preserves essential basic hermeneutical principles of precritical Reformation interpretation of Scripture. Schlatter's position is, further, miles removed from "moderate criticism" (see "So-called Moderate Criticism" below), which would so gladly lay claim to Schlatter as its forerunner. In addition, Schlatter's positive assessment of history overcame a decided deficiency in Beck's hermeneutic.

Why not, then, simply revive Schlatter's position? If one compares it with biblical revelation, at least three considerations give us pause. First, the New Testament binds knowledge of God and his revelation not to Romans 1 (knowledge of God through nature) but to discipleship (knowledge of God through following Christ; cf. Mt 13:11f.; Jn 6:69; 1Co 2:6ff.; 2Co 3:14). Schlatter has moved too close to an illegitimate "natural theology" when he in principle grants to every person the possibility of "perceiving" God and his revelation. If Beck perhaps overstressed the role of the Spirit, Schlatter rather underemphasized it. Where do theological differences stem from, anyway? Is it merely a matter of the "eye"? The battle between the institutional critical enterprise and Reformation-biblical interpretation of Scripture can in any case not be fought out only in the area of "observation," "the act of seeing," and "listening." Second, Schlatter's position occasionally implies criticism of Scripture. He regarded the pietistic trust in Scripture as at times too "servile"[317] and allowed for false statements in the Bible. It is well known that he rejected 2 Peter as inauthentic and accepted that miracles could have been "embellished" by the early church.[318] It remains unclear where such critical results, where such "dislocations and obscurations" can rightly be detected in the biblical tradition[319]—and where not. Since Schlatter tended to carry on hermeneutical interaction only implicitly and not with open naming of friend and foe, both critics and Pietists gained the impression that they were justified in claiming him for their camp. Third, Schlatter's anthropological starting point has an incriminating effect. True, for Schlatter man never assumes highest rank. Like few others, Schlatter kept God's glory at the center of all he did. Man never assumes first place, not even in research and knowledge. For the "fact" of the living and life-giving God precedes every act of knowing. Our knowledge is indeed characterized precisely by the fact that it is fundamentally a receptive act. But Schlatter's decision to start theologically with *man* creates a dilemma. For in practical terms it is man as believer with whom he must start. Only the believer evinces the "consciousness" that Schlatter stakes out as the theological thinker's "sphere of labor."[320] Schlatter's approach makes it difficult for the unbeliever to enter the discussion, and at the same time Christian apologetics become problematic. Further, in the course of theological work it is by no means so easy to accord primacy to revelation, especially when it seems foreign to us, when the starting point is anthropological in nature.

Two specific examples are instructive here. First, on the opening page of Schlatter's dogmatics he formulates the leading question of "where and how we experience the processes that become the revelation of God to us." He also sets forth the dogmatic proof, the proof of God, as "consisting in this: that we indicate the events through which our consciousness of God arises and receives its content."[321] Such dogmatic proof, however, cannot be sustained without a prior knowledge of revelation and without having already integrated revelation into human consciousness. Otherwise—and this is just what Schlatter wishes to prevent—our consciousness of God becomes a filter that either affirms or denies given statements of Scripture. Second, the anthropological starting point, in which consciousness of God plays an eminent role, becomes questionable at the key point of testing for all hermeneutical concepts: eschatology. Here Schlatter openly acknowledges the difficulties of his outlook: "Methodological considerations could make it seem advisable to end a theology before treating eschatology" (in

Schlatter's dogmatics eschatology is the final section). Why? "Observation fails us when it comes to those thoughts that draw their content from our future hope."[322] But Schlatter could have gone farther; in fact, neither the doctrine of first things (protology) nor the doctrine of last things (eschatology) nor even prophecy can be derived from human consciousness. They are from the outset inaccessible to the "act of seeing," "perception," "observation," and like functions that play a similar role for Schlatter. They can no longer be justified anthropocentrically but only theocentrically. Schlatter's eschatology is weaker than any other part of his theology. Beck's eschatology was stronger. Given his theocentric starting point, Beck did not have the problems here that Schlatter had.

Much argues in favor of affirming and learning from the many positive aspects of Schlatter's approach and findings. But the above reflections on Schlatter's epistemology, criticism, and anthropocentricity compel us to avoid simply making his hermeneutical position our own.

## J. C. K. VON HOFMANN

Another commendable *example of noncritical Scripture interpretation* is the hermeneutics of the so-called Erlangen school, especially that of Hofmann.

Johann Christian Konrad von *Hofmann* (1810–77), the head of the so-called Erlangen school, belonged to the prophetic-salvation historical direction of nineteenth-century theology.[323] He had a strong hermeneutical interest that comes to light, e.g., in his 1863 essay on "Die Aufgabe der biblischen Hermeneutik" ("The Task of Biblical Hermeneutics") and in his book *Biblische Hermeneutik* (1880).[324]

The decisive starting point for Hofmann is the Christian self-consciousness.[325] "I, the Christian, am for me, the theologian, the most fundamental subject of my science."[326] But whoever approaches the Bible as a Christian brings his own dogmatic presuppositions with him anyway.

Hofmann by no means denies this. He calls attention to the fact that everyone—Christian or not, adherent to this or to that particular branch of the faith—inherently possesses dogmatic presuppositions. There is no presuppositionless exegesis.[327] The only question is *which* presuppositions are the most appropriate when it come to the Bible. And there Hofmann calls for "trust" in its message. Interpretation must begin "with trust, not with doubt and criticism."[328] It is as if Hofmann glimpsed in advance the next 125 years of theological and hermeneutical developments. Trust is a positive regard for Scripture in the whole of one's life. Is that not a burden, an encumbrance, a hindrance for the interpreter? By no means, answered Hofmann. On the contrary, the person who is allegedly unpartisan is actually indifferent and is not suited for the interpretive task.[329] Thus Hofmann arrives at a firm affirmation of a *theologia regenitorum* (theology of regeneration).[330] Now an additional result of Christian consciousness is that Scripture presents "a different object" than the one seen by "the profane researcher." Hofmann therefore rejects Semler's procedure of handling the Bible just like any other book.[331]

In the following areas Hofmann takes up essential elements of reformational-precritical interpretation and continues them into his own day: in his stress on trust, emphasis on *theologia regenitorum* (theology of regeneration), affirmation of inspiration, acknowledgment of genuine predictive prophecy, conception of the Bible as an object sui generis along with his salvation-historical interest,[332] and his unified view of both testaments. Moreover, with his *Verheissung und Erfüllung* (*Prophecy and Fulfilment* [2 vols., 1841, 1844]) he succeeded in renewing widespread interest in a salvation-historical conception. He also took up, to an extent, the modern demand for historical explanation.

Yet a foundational objection remains. It is not unjustified that J. Wach termed Hofmann the "great advocate of Schleiermacher's theology of religious experience."[333] In Hofmann what we really find is a theology of experience in one of its most impressive forms. But there can be no doubt that the apostles did not take their self-consciousness as their starting point; they rather took Jesus' words (Jn 6:68f.) and the

Word of Holy Scripture. The resurrected Jesus himself opened up the Scripture to them (Lk 24:27ff.)—he did not confer spiritual experiences upon them. Even the Holy Spirit himself brings about understanding of Scripture and of Jesus' words (Ac 2:16ff.; Jn 14:26; 16:13f.; 2:22; 18:9, 32). The apostles were, then, theologians of revelation and not theologians of experience. This, combined with the tragic history of mankind—even pious mankind—when he makes himself his own starting point, forbids us to take up Hofmann's position. We need a starting point in revelation itself.

## PNEUMATIC EXEGESIS

In a way *pneumatic exegesis* too, as it has existed since Girgensohn's proposals, belongs among the *examples of noncritical Scripture interpretation*. From "Key Questions of Pneumatic Exegesis" above, it is evident that we cannot locate our standpoint in the sphere of pneumatic exegesis. Yet it will be worthwhile to summarize again the major relevant considerations at this juncture.

"Pneumatic exegesis" is to be affirmed as far as its intention to renew church-centered and reformational interpretation in contradistinction to the abortive development of critical interpretation. We also agree that the spiritual condition of the interpreter is of great importance. A third similarity we have with pneumatic exegesis is the refusal simply to identify "historical investigation of the Bible" with "scientific" exegesis. Finally, along with pneumatic exegesis we emphasize that we must win back a suitable doctrine of inspiration.

Weighty considerations, however, arise against pneumatic exegesis as championed from Girgensohn to Frey. There is first the fact that it never found its way out of a two-tiered dualism between the historical and superhistorical, the critical and the pneumatic. The two levels remain fundamentally unrelated. Disparate, even antithetical standpoints are both found in the single person of the interpreter, who is at once both enlightened critic and pneumatic hearer. A perhaps even more dangerous consequence is the threat of the "spiritual" message being separated from the written word of the Bible. But the greater the rift between historical, critical exegesis and spiritual exegesis that recognizes the authority of the Bible, the more easily this rift becomes haven for a pious, "pneumatic" subjectivism which does not admit of correction and which also can no longer make itself understandable. A final consequence might be that the theology of revelation that was actually being striven for reverts into a pneumatic-esoteric theology of experience. But that would be to fail at two points: deleterious "historical" thinking as it has arisen through the cultural dislocations of modern centuries would not be overcome; and—even more seriously—revelation would not receive its due. We cannot follow an exegetical method that does not have the strength to stand its ground as a theology of revelation on the field of history. The greatest weakness of pneumatic exegesis lies in its failure to acknowledge the indispensable priority of divine revelation over all experience, including pneumatic.

## SCHOLARLY FUNDAMENTALISM

*Scholarly fundamentalism* also most certainly belongs among a list of examples of noncritical Scripture interpretation.

It is essential that we seriously investigate the interpretive possibility that this approach offers. In continental Europe, however, there are many who disagree.

Difficulties already arise with the *term*. As W. Joest in his article "Fundamentalismus" in TRE puts it, the term *fundamentalism* is "often used somewhat vaguely in German ecclesiastical and theological parlance . . . to characterize religiosity that is strictly conservative, Bible-oriented, and influenced by the Pietist tradition."[334] Joest himself warns against "a vague extension [of the term] that makes 'fundamentalistic' more or less identical with 'evangelical' or even 'pietistic.'"[335] Such an extension is ruled out from the outset by the single observation that fundamentalism is "not an organizationally unified, defined group."[336]

Difficulties continue due to the common polemic against fundamentalism that prevails in this country (Germany). Gordon J. Wenham (1989), though writing from England, vividly describes the situation:

> I suspect that if either you [a student] or your lecturers discover during your study that you are a Sabellian montanist or semipelagian gnostic, it will not cause over-much excitement. Such deviants are commonplace today and in this pluralistic society are usually accepted without much fuss. However should you be diagnosed as a fundamentalist your fate may be very different. In the modern theology faculty fundamentalism is the great heresy. It is regarded as nearly as dangerous as the HIV virus and is treated with similar fervour but with rather less tact and sympathy. Fundamentalists will find themselves denounced in lectures and tutorials, and doubtless will be encouraged to read James Barr's book on the subject.[337]

How supercilious I. Lönning was when he described J. I. Packer as "pathetic"![338] Polemic is a notorious hindrance to discussion and serious interaction. So chances are slim that Joest's warnings will be heeded or that appropriate means of communication will be established. The same problems are illustrated, for that matter, in long-standing difficulties that have become commonplace in interreligious dialogue.[339]

It is necessary to keep its history firmly in mind if one hopes to arrive at an understanding of the term *fundamentalism*. Beginning in 1909 in the United States, a total of twelve volumes entitled *The Fundamentals* appeared. Theologians like G. Campbell Morgan, H. C. G. Moule, James Orr, A. T. Pierson, R. A. Torrey, and B. B. Warfield were among the contributors. They were involved in a deeply concerned effort to prevent the spread of historical-critical research, as pursued most of all in Europe, to North American theology and North American theological training centers. Thus themes like the inspiration and authority of Scripture, miracles, redemptive facts, eschatology, prayer, and evangelization occupied center stage.[340] Not until 1920 was the term *fundamentalist* coined, and that was in the Baptist periodical *Watchman-Examiner*, which referred to "those who mean to do battle royal for the fundamentals."[341]

Four observations arise from the history of the use of the term. First, the fundamentalist movement, even if it found strong support among laypersons and in revivalist circles, was from the very beginning a scholarly movement. Second, it is typical of the history of theology in America and indeed partially even of the intellectual interchange between North America and Europe. Third, it was an act of defense and therefore possessed a basically defensive character. Fourth, it worked mainly on systematic-theological premises and therefore inclined toward deductive procedure.

Today, if one wishes to speak in a suitable manner of scholarly fundamentalism, it is best to think in terms of a broad theological current that in some way harks back to those fundamentals, and that still today emphasizes the inspiration of all of Scripture ("plenary inspiration") and Scripture's inerrancy. One or more of the basic features cited in the previous paragraph come into play as explanatory of its origin and nature. In this way one may work with a *suitable and practical term*.

Within the broad framework of this scholarly fundamentalism we encounter a pronounced *link with the Reformation*. Perhaps it could even be said that here we find the most persistent surviving example of reformational-precritical Scripture interpretation. To cite W. Joest once more: the hermeneutic of fundamentalism "was once a self-evident component of even Catholic doctrinal tradition and then most of all of old Protestant theology, Lutheran and Reformed alike."[342] Fundamentalism's hermeneutic "in its basic features" involves "upholding Reformation tradition in its old Protestant or Protestant Scholastic form."[343] Fundamentalists also continually appeal to Jesus, the apostles, and the ancient church as sources of correct knowledge which they wish to preserve.[344]

From this posture there follows first the doctrine that the Bible is inspired, literally and in its entirety. J. Gresham Machen, one of the leading champions of fundamentalism,[345] put it this way: "It is necessary to add to the Christian doctrine of revelation the Christian doctrine of inspiration."[346] Again and again we run up against terms like "plenary inspiration,"[347] "divine inspiration,"[348] "wholly and verbally God-given,"[349] and more rarely "verbal inspiration."[350]

In all this the human side of Scripture is indeed recognized, even made into a theme. Machen repudiates those "who do ignore the human characteristics of the Biblical writers."[351] In this connection fundamentalism variously rejects a mechanistic doctrine of inspiration. Machen protested, e.g, against the "misrepresentation" that a concept of comprehensive biblical inspiration "involved a mechanical theory."[352] Indeed, precisely in the area of the doctrine of inspiration we arrive at the concept of a "concursus," in which God and man are conceived as actual participants in the event of inspiration. As we understand it, Benjamin Breckinridge Warfield set forth this concept as early as 1894 in his essay "The Divine and Human in the Bible." A result of this concursus is that the Bible is "a divine-human book in which every word is at once divine and human . . . so that the Scriptures are the joint product of divine and human activities."[353] J. I. Packer (1958) and I. H. Marshall (1982) have again taken up this notion of a "concursive action." They understand it as involving complementarity. Thus one and the same event can be traced back to the working of God's Spirit and at the same time to the working of human factors. It can be explained purely in terms of human considerations or also in the sense of the classic doctrine of inspiration.[354]

Obviously, in describing such concepts we must at the same time register a certain shift within fundamentalism. The older fundamentalism placed the accent—despite attention to the human side of inspiration—clearly on the divine activity. Newer fundamentalism leaves more

room for human participation—evidently under pressure from historical investigation. In view of this shift alone, facile talk of "fundamentalism" as a monolith is scientifically negligent.

From the doctrine of inspiration follows the idea of the inerrancy
of Scripture. Because the Holy Spirit led the human authors of the Bible,
they were kept from error. God's Spirit, who is God himself, can, after
all, not lie. Thus Machen says, "The God whom Christianity worships
is a God of truth."[355] And N. Geisler states that the Bible in keeping with
its own claim "is absolutely true since it is given by the Holy Spirit from
the mouth of God, who cannot lie."[356] Similarly, the opening section of
the Chicago Statement on Biblical Inerrancy begins with the words
"God, who is Himself Truth and speaks truth only, has inspired Holy
Scripture . . . ," etc. Against the diverse historical-critical voices who
charge the Bible with contradictions, errors, and mistakes, large segments of fundamentalism come together around the affirmation of
Scripture's "inerrancy."[357] This inerrancy is in principle extended to the
entire Scripture.[358] But not all go as far as N. Geisler in saying that "The
Bible is as perfect as God is."[359] Overall it should not be overlooked that
some arguments follow the line that because God gave the Bible, and
because God does not lie, the Bible is free of error. Here a strong incli-
nation toward deductive-rational reasoning is evident.

If one examines these statements from the standpoint of historical
theology, it is first undeniable that even the doctrine of inerrancy is
firmly rooted in the Reformation. According to F. Kropatscheck, even
medieval Scholasticism was convinced "of the absolute infallibility of
the Bible."[360] In contradistinction to the Socinians, who viewed the Bible
as fallible and erroneous, the representatives of Protestant Scholasticism
likewise insisted on the inerrancy of Scripture. Colovius, e.g., stated categorically: "Nullus error . . . nedum mendacium ullum locum habere
potest in universa Scriptura S" ("No uncertainty . . . much less falsehood
can have any place in the whole of sacred Scripture").[361] Hülsemann
("extra omne erroris periculum" ["beyond all danger of error"]), Baier,
or König ("Quidquid scriptura sacra docet, divinitus inspiratum adeoque

infallibiter verum est" ["Having been divinely and infallibly inspired, whatever sacred Scripture teaches is true"]) argued no differently.[362] No less clearly since the time of Flacius[363] we find traces of thinking marked with deductive and rational features. Whoever condemns fundamentalism on these points, then, also condemns old Protestant doctrine.

On the other side it cannot be overlooked that developments have taken place within fundamentalism that lead to stark differences. Already with B. B. Warfield one can observe that terms like *trustworthiness* or *truthfulness* are occasionally preferred to the term *inerrancy*.[364] Subsequently there are attempts, e.g., by D. A. Carson and B. Ramm, to emphasize an inductive procedure.[365] Moreover, J. I. Packer indicates that the statement, the Bible is God's Word, remains a matter of faith; it is not rationally demonstrable.[366] Also of interest are the clarifications included in the Chicago Statement of October 1978. Among other things, article 14 states that Scripture still contains unsolved "alleged errors and discrepancies." This frees the interpreter from the compulsion of having to furnish a solution for every problem. The statement also affirms that confession of inerrancy is not a redemptive necessity: "We deny that such confession is necessary for salvation" (art. 19).

Finally the statement takes astonishingly precise notice of the biblical data. We cite here somewhat more fully from article 13: "We deny that it is proper to evaluate Scripture according to standards of truth and error that are alien to its usage and purpose. We further deny that inerrancy is negated by Biblical phenomena such as a lack of modern technical precision, irregularities of grammar or spelling, observational descriptions of nature, the reporting of falsehoods, the use of hyperbole and round numbers . . . variant selection of material in parallel accounts, or the use of free citations." If we ponder these statements about "lack," "irregularities," "hyperbole," "selections," and the like, then one can easily arrive at the conclusion that I. H. Marshall does regarding inerrancy: "It needs so much qualification, even by its defenders, that it is in danger of dying the death of a thousand qualifications."[367] In any case it is no longer possible to charge fundamentalism with working without historical consciousness. In our view, there also seems to be a tendency at work to replace the term *inerrancy* with *entire trustworthiness* or an equivalent.[368]

We have dwelt at some length on the two points of inspiration and inerrancy because they comprise the hermeneutical cornerstones of scholarly fundamentalism. Now we must also note that other fundamental convictions of Protestant orthodoxy are no less present. Among these is the view that the entire Bible is God's Word.[369] A "canon in the canon" approach is unthinkable here. We also find emphasis on the unity of Scripture.[370] Occasionally there is even talk of Scripture as an "organism."[371] Together with the concept of ongoing or "progressive"[372] revelation, this amounts to continuation of the interpretive model of reformational Scripture interpretation. Such a salvation-historical interpretation rules out the possibility of placing everything in the Bible on just the same level. In addition, fundamentalism is aware that the Bible has a "center" and a "heart."[373]

All of this is bound up with an unambiguous yes to historical investigation of the Bible. It defies understanding how W. Joest could come to the conclusion that in fundamentalism the biblical canon is "cordoned off from the marks of human authorship that arise through historical connections and that are conditioned by individual distinctives and limitation" (TRE, p. 735). Machen, e.g., is just as loathe as the Protestant Scholastics to "deny the individuality of the Biblical writers." Indeed, he emphasizes that careful attention to "the historical situations which gave rise to the Biblical books" is essential.[374] For "Christianity depends . . . upon the narration of an event."[375] The Chicago Statement focuses attention on "the various personalities and literary styles of the writers" and on the "literary forms and peculiarities" of the text.[376] However: historical investigation of the Bible may not convict the Bible of untruth. As in Luther and Bengel the predominance of the Bible over history, or over currently ascendent historical opinion, remains firmly in place.

If then essential basic features of the Reformation's understanding of Scripture remain preserved in fundamentalism, and if claims that the Scripture makes about itself are variously taken up—why not adopt this form of Scripture interpretation? Certainly we can gratefully affirm much that we find here. Certainly there also exists a tight connection between a "fundamentalist" and a—as we say in Germany—"pietistic" hermeneutic. In no case will we be able to agree with those who dismiss something merely because it is "fundamentalistic."

Yet there are four reasons why we cannot join in with the understanding of Scripture of scholarly fundamentalism as sketched above.

There is first of all the simple fact that we in Germany have a different history. This diverse historical origin alone rules out wholesale adoption of fundamentalism's hermeneutic. J. G. Hamann once read the history of Cain and Abel as his "own life story." He thereby created the possibility of identification with the narrative. As German Pietists, however, we do not read our "own life story" in fundamentalism. Thus an identification is not possible. Fundamentalism has its own unmistakably distinct character from the point of view of church history and cultural history as well as in terms of historical theology and the history of piety from which it arose.

Moreover, a defensive character continues to attach to fundamentalism. The catchword "inerrancy" is nothing but a defensive word answering to the challenge that the Bible is errant. Because of this defensive character the defender of inerrancy is constantly required to assume the burden of proof. He must at least show that the Bible is not necessarily in error. He can fall prey to suspicion that he is inhibited. But even apart from individual terms like *inerrancy*, a biblical hermeneutic can never center on mounting a defensive; it must rather center on the offensive encounter of God and man through enscripturated revelation.

Third, it must be said that fundamentalism, like Protestant Scholasticism, bears strong deductive features. Precisely because it is concerned with the defense of God's revelation, it builds its conception of the Bible almost imperceptibly from its image of God. But the question must be raised whether an inductive procedure, a hermeneutic of encounter, would not be more appropriate to the essence of revelation as a mediation of the encounter between God and man. *Doctrina* (doctrine) is the result of *communicatio* (communication) and not vice versa. From that point of view historical investigation of the Bible could be integrated into a comprehensive biblical hermeneutic more organically than occurs in fundamentalism.

The fourth reason is closely related to the third. In fundamentalism arguments often run more along logical-rational instead of biblical-exegetical lines. That can be shown by an example related to inerrancy. C. F. H. Henry, who has written one of the most impressive works on God and revelation, does not fail to notice that *inerrancy* is not a biblical term and that it is taught only indirectly in the Bible ("implicitly taught"). But, he continues, "inerrancy . . . is logically deducible."[377] At such a decisive juncture, however, biblical language and conceptuality would be preferable to a logical-rational argument.

In sum we must carefully factor scholarly fundamentalism into our deliberations. Yet the challenge to arrive at our own hermeneutical approach remains.

## SO-CALLED MODERATE CRITICISM

By virtue of its name, at least, so-called moderate criticism[378] with its "post-critical Scripture interpretation"[379] deserves to be included in our deliberations.[380] R. Smend spoke, e.g., of a "positive criticism" and pleaded with K. Barth (KD IV, 2, p. 542) for a "tested, critical naivete." The task is to break through to this "second naivete," to a "post-critical posture."[381]

In the approximately twenty years since Smend's essay, moderate criticism has made repeated calls for a revision of radical criticism and sought a new hermeneutical position.[382] It sees its task in light of the fact that historical-critical work "is today being probingly questioned more than ever before." It wishes to remain "critical over against its [historical criticism's] own solutions and open to new ways of placing questions."[383] And it is not difficult to tally up examples of such openness. Thus, e.g., H. M. Barth has recently attempted to make positive use of E. Drewermann's depth-psychological interpretation of the Bible.[384] Many voices counsel us to adopt the hermeneutical decisions of moderate criticism as these have thus far taken shape.

Shouldn't this be possible? We find here, indeed, an acute consciousness of the deficiencies of classical historical criticism. As H. M. Barth declared in his recent essay (1988): "Christendom's dealings with the Bible are mired in crisis"; "Historical criticism is unable to furnish a remedy here."[385] The realization grows that "Holy Scripture is to be interpreted in just the same Spirit by which it was authored."[386] That is, the interpreter requires the Holy Spirit. It is also being recognized that we need to rediscover texts like 1 Corinthians 1:18–2:16.[387] Biblical inspiration must be rescued from the disrepute in which it has languished and once again made fruitful.[388] Further, "the necessity of expansive, spiritual-theological interpretation of Scripture" is being proposed "over against a restrictive, purely historically-critically argued exegesis."[389] For Christians the Gospel becomes a given "by which and on the basis of which they must orient themselves."[390] The faith of the exegete, a positive practical orientation toward Scripture, and discussion with the Christian community as well as between exegetes and dogmaticians are being recognized as helpful and attainable.[391] Repeatedly, the concern is expressed to continue Reformation interpretation of Scripture, albeit with the modifications that the history of theology requires.[392]

Moderate criticism's hermeneutical attempt is to an extent sharply attacked by radical critics.[393] In an obstinate move to repristinate dead slogans they trudge along the path blazed decades ago by Ebeling, repeating his insistence that historical criticism serves the faith by obliterating its historical supports.[394] To this may be added the peculiar founding of historical criticism on the first article of the Apostles' Creed: "I believe in God the Father Almighty. . . ." In this view God, in whom the creed affirms faith, has "forced" us to a historical-critical understanding of the Bible through the event of the Enlightenment.[395]

It is not our task here to refute positions that are obviously outdated. Far more pressing is critical interaction with the hermeneutical proposals of moderate criticism.

First, the question arises whether a movement so deeply stamped by history as historical criticism can really be overcome by a "moderate" revision. If it is true that "historical-critical theology" is "a singular phenomenon from the historical-theological and church-historical viewpoint";[396] if it is true that it displayed a "tremendous intellectual- and church-historical effect";[397] if it is true that since Kant we are dealing with the "fundamental integration of revelation into reason"[398]— then little can be expected to come of any "moderate" modifying measures. And if, in addition, O. Merk is correct with his thesis, "Hermeneutics is the mother of New Testament science in the 18th century,"[399] then a fundamentally new conception of hermeneutics is all the more advisable.

On the other hand it strikes one as odd when H. M. Barth first states, "Historical criticism is unable to furnish a remedy here," yet in conclusion writes, "Historical criticism in its classic form will . . . remain obligatory."[400] P. Stuhlmacher strikes us the same way. At the end of his essay on the hermeneutical guidance given by 1 Corinthians 2:6–16 he surprisingly declares: "Historical criticism retains validity because and insofar as it is the best means to open up the original sense of the biblical witness to Scripture" (p. 156). How is that any different from G. Strecker, a radical critic, who maintains that historical criticism confers "on the text what belongs to the text."[401] And when even Stuhlmacher sets forth the thesis that "critical historical work on the Holy Scripture" is "absolutely essential,"[402] indeed that "theological thinking" must "be and remain content-critical [*sachkritisches*] thinking,"[403] how is he to be distinguished in this connection from C. Hartlich, who tells us: "the historical-critical method is the only one possible"?[404]

Along with the basic question whether modifications and revisions suffice to overcome a false fundamental starting point, other questions arise. As we saw, the inspiration of Scripture is being pondered anew in moderate criticism. Evidently this amounts to a break with radical criticism, which to this day disputes that the biblical writers possessed a "higher capacity of knowing."[405] Moderate criticism, however, does not go beyond personal inspiration (see chap. 7 above). That is, it speaks of the "empowering" of the biblical authors to be God's witnesses.[406] But the content of biblical statements remains quite decidedly subordinate to content criticism (*Sachkritik*).[407] We find, then, a peculiar combination of spiritual understanding of Scripture and content-critical science, of elect witnesses of God and fallible biblical writers who stand to gain by instruction from modern knowledge and who in fact require correction. Once more we are overcome by the suspicion that no convincing answer to the hermeneutical challenge is forthcoming from this kind of mediating and eclectic theology.

Another question remains: wherein does such a doctrine of personal inspiration differ, e.g., from J. Blank, who demands that the concept of inspiration must "today be modified and rethought" so that it conforms "to the historical and material diversity of the New Testament texts."[408] That, however, simply means that modern criticism draws the permissible parameters for the concept of inspiration. Or again: how is moderate criticism different from the social-historical interpretation of L. Schottroff, who derives the Pauline idea of human sinfulness from the "experiences of powerlessness of the Roman empire's little people"?[409] Paul shows up here as a witness to Schottroff's theory, indeed as a star witness. But he must be roundly corrected. If his chosen status extends only to his own person, if he is only "personally" inspired, and if this inspiration does not at the same time extend to his message, then such personal inspiration is little help against "modern" corrections.

With that we run up against the subsequent question of what "authority" such "correction" should assume. Even if we think that Paul himself summons us to content criticism of the Bible,[410] we must still furnish an answer to the question: *which* of the conflicting statements found in the Bible are justified? Since the Enlightenment the answer has been clear: it is reason that makes the decision here. Already in 1906 Reinhard spoke of a plurality of "authorities of truth" that arise after the Enlightenment.[411] Here we must consider that other entities, too, and not just reason, are cited, among them "experiential connection," coherence and analogy,[412] scientific character, the avoidance of *sacrificium intellectus* (sacrifice of intellect),[413] the new understanding of reality, the current consciousness of truth,[414] and "liberating praxis."[415] In any case Scripture is no longer the sole normative authority here. Since the Enlightenment we are rather dealing in principle with *two* authorities: reason and revelation.[416] Occasionally there are variations. Thus R. Rothe's (1799–1867) two authorities are called "piety" and "Scripture."[417] But overall it holds true that the Bible is no longer "the— exclusive—source of knowledge of Christian truth."[418] Unfortunately, "moderate criticism" has yet to find its way out of such two-authority thinking. Because and insofar as it exercises content criticism, it cannot dispense with a second authority alongside of Scripture.

It is clear that where content criticism is regarded as necessary, the unity of Scripture is lost. True, in moderate criticism there is no longer that "dismembered use of the Word of God" that Beck once lamented.[419] But that fact remains that moderate criticism, too, speaks of the contradictoriness of the Bible[420] and in principle denies its unity.[421]

Who says, however, that contradictions are purely "rationally" determined, explained, settled? From the Enlightenment onward, for many years it was believed that *ratio* (reason), and indeed a *ratio* with high moral qualities, was key here. Today we have shed this moralistic superstition. We are discovering that the separation of Scripture from revelation, the separation of the acceptable from the nonacceptable in the Bible, can itself give rise to an authority of a different description: to opinion or feeling, to sentiment that is not always rational. At this point we can envision sermonic meditations that begin, "What I like is . . ."[422] Here the text is weighed and assessed negatively because of contents that are allegedly culpable; next, speculation is proffered, e.g., that Genesis 3 has "contributed to the denigration of woman in church and society."[423] Or by social class analysis along with personal experience one learns that participation "in an affluent industrial society" necessarily generates a certain theology.[424] How can moderate criticism, caught up in affirming two authorities and the Bible's self-contradictoriness, hinder the burgeoning of such a theology of experience?

With all due respect for the efforts of moderate criticism, a seven-layered wall separates us from its hermeneutical position as currently articulated. First, there is their basic refusal to give up the dogma of historical criticism. As a mediating theology it contents itself with revisions—even if these are sometimes striking—where a fundamental new beginning would be necessary. Second, instead of regarding *Scripture* as inspired (2Ti 3:16), it does not go beyond affirmation of an inspiration of the biblical *writers*. Third, it remains captive to the Enlightenment in that it must posit a second authority along with Scripture to which the interpreter is responsible. As a result it cannot uphold the Reformation outlook of the Bible as the sole *norma normans* (normative standard). Fourth, it demands content criticism of the Bible. Without content criticism there would be no theology as science, as moderate criticism sees it. Fifth, it gives up the unity of Scripture—in contrast to reformational-precritical Scripture interpretation, but also in contrast to Beck and Schlatter. Sixth, Scripture and revelation remain different, only partly congruent entities. Therefore moderate criticism follows the trend of seeking the real meaning of Scripture beyond Scripture. Seventh, it tends in the direction of a theology of experience by separating Scripture and revelation from each other and acknowledging only certain dimensions of the Bible's statements as God's Word.

Our own position shall therefore be worked out cognizant of moderate criticism, yet constructed independently of it.

# CHAPTER FOURTEEN

# Developing a Biblical-Historical Interpretation

The most urgent hermeneutical task facing us in theology today is the development of a biblical-historical interpretation. The final pages of our study will be devoted to this task.

## TERMINOLOGY

First, comment is in order regarding the term *biblical-historical*.

In previous publications I used the term *historical-biblical*.[1] That reflected direct response to the term *historical-critical*. In critical interaction with the historical-critical method and its distinctive history, *historical-biblical* functioned well.

In the course of time, however, some disadvantages to our term surfaced. E.g., occasionally the misunderstanding arose that the "historical-biblical" approach sought to be just a variation of the "historical-critical." Further, the connotation of both "historical-critical" and "historical-biblical" lays the accent on the historical. This feeds the misconception that interpretation of the biblical texts is only a subcategory of historical work. This gives short shrift to the theological dimension of the Bible, i.e., to what makes it unique.

Considerations like these have moved me now to select the term *biblical-historical*. It does more justice, I feel, to the distinctive nature of the Bible, which demands no less than an interpretive approach distinctively suited to it. Yet at the same time it preserves the serious historical interest that cannot be abandoned. But this brings us to a related problem.

## IMPORTANCE OF THE TERM *HISTORICAL*

To put it sharply: the great deficiency of this whole study could in hindsight prove to be that we remain too strongly attached to the "historical."

Our generation still languishes in the grip of the "historical" way of putting questions. The relation of European civilization to the wider world, however, has in the meantime altered drastically. A Bible-Babel dispute today would not begin to create the excitement that it did at the onset of the twentieth century. Today ethical questions have supplanted historical-cognitive ones. E.g., we are divided today by peace issues or man's use of the environment, not specific individual historical problems. The "new religiosity" of our time has far more to do with man's integration into the cosmos and with his personal and collective survival than with "the way things used to be"—including things religious. Not what "used to be" but what is "real" or "right" dominates modern concern.

Indeed, the entirety of previous history is being read with an incriminating eye. The modern man or woman seeks to reinterpret the entire stream of history and give it a quite different sense than it ever had before. For the modern person, the continuation of human history as previously understood would result only in decline and ruin.

Along with the reorientation of post-Roman European civilization, we must note the impulse of the burgeoning church in the two-thirds world. Its cultures feel the Western historical impetus only partially, if at all. To them the mystery of the faith speaks far more compellingly than the deciphering of the historical. Dynamic and ethical understanding of the Bible ranks higher than the cognitive or even analytical.

It would be foolish for us as theologians to shut our eyes to these profound changes and to continue to treat the historical as if it were obviously the most important thing.[2] Today it is rather concern for the historical that requires justification. Are we not already outmoded, then, in suggesting "biblical-historical interpretation"? The answer to this question runs along two lines. First, insofar as the Bible comprises a document of the history of God with man, it must be understood and interpreted historically. Even if all mankind wished to "climb out" of history—people who hallow the Bible could never follow suit. Second, the term *biblical-historical* fairly invites other "biblical" ways of understanding. If, as we propose, "biblical" is made the overarching rubric, then alongside of "biblical-historical" we may readily expect to find "biblical-ethical," "biblical-spiritual" or "typological," and so on.

We remain aware, then, of the limited serviceability of the term *biblical-historical*. But the nonnegotiable historical interest that must inhere in every salvation-historical interpretation and that the Bible itself provokes—to say nothing of the present theological situation, still strongly affected by the historical—gives us the right to propose first of all a biblical-historical interpretive procedure.

## PROCEDURAL OPENNESS AND CONSTRAINTS

Our methodical interpretive procedure must first be an open one. This primarily means that it is constantly subject to refinement. It must orient itself in an ongoing way with a careful eye to its object and to the necessities of its service in the Christian community. It may never claim the status of a dogma or a dogmatic-like position. Such dogmatic ossification is precisely the objection we have to the historical-critical mode of thinking. We may never, then, claim that our method is the "only one possible" or "the scientific one" or "the absolutely legitimate one" or the like. It goes without saying that it can therefore also not serve as the identification card of our faithfulness or even the object of our faith.

Openness of procedure, then, means the constant willingness to be corrected. We wish to keep the thoughts in view that others have contemplated. We desire, by a sort of *ars semper reformanda* (art of always reforming), to hold open the method's process, teachability, and further development, most of all in relation to a constantly improving grasp of biblical statements.

At the same time, "openness of procedure" serves notice that a guarantee of errorless, biblically perfect results can never by any means be provided. The polemical objection is sure to arise that a biblical manner of interpretation such as we are proposing seeks to vouchsafe an error-free exegesis. Such polemic, however, would be quite misplaced.

On the other hand, every interpretation is carried out in the framework of certain restrictions. As we noted earlier, inherent in the character of scientific activity is that it clearly states to itself and to others what these restrictions are. They are, so to speak, positive prejudgments—and therefore obviously prejudgments that admit of correction.

Three such restrictions may be cited in this connection. First, we view ourselves bound by the results that we have worked out in previous chapters. Yet the interpretive event itself is always a fresh occasion for the testing of these results. Second, in principle we maintain binding ties with other modes of interpretation. We attempt to keep before us such matters as wherein a historical interpretation necessarily remains descriptive rather than prescriptive, or where, e.g., a dynamic, ethical, dogmatic, or typological understanding helpfully supplements the historical. Third, our interpretive possibilities remain rooted in the Christian community which interpretation is called to serve. We remind ourselves that scientific, or in particular biblical-historical, interpretation, while possessing a distinct character, does not possess a fundamentally higher quality or value than the Spirit-led and Scripture-based interpretation of other members of the church. Prayer, exchange of ideas, discussion, correction, and praxis bind the scientific Bible interpreter with the overarching reality of the Christian community in which he lives.

But with the above we have already taken the first step into the procedure itself, the exploration of which will now occupy us in the pages ahead.

## THE SETTING OF A BIBLICAL-HISTORICAL INTERPRETATION

At this point we must discuss more fully the embeddedness of the interpreter. What embeddedness? Embeddedness in the faith and in the Christian community. Both have fundamental significance for interpretation.[3] Man seldom tends to speak truth to *himself*. Much more typically he speaks *his* truth—i.e., the truth that has resulted from his own life story to that point and which he practices. To paraphrase a proverbial saying, "Tell me the story of your life and I'll tell you how you interpret."

The way we interpret, then, begins in the history of our life. This life history forms, first, our dynamic and ethical understandings of Scripture. It does this before our cognitive, and then our historical, understandings of Scripture take shape. The priority of dynamic and ethical understanding often results in our talking past each other without realizing the reason why.

An understanding that the Bible suggests to us, in light of our discussion in previous chapters, presupposes personal faith. A biblical-historical interpretation consciously integrates itself, therefore, into a *theologia regenitorum* (theology of regeneration). How can one apply Bengel's leading principle ("Apply yourself totally to the text . . .") otherwise? "Totally" signifies the opposite of reservation, of cool, critical distance. On the other hand, being rooted in faith means that the interpreter is not faced with an isolated text, with some absolutized medium of speech. He rather steadily hears the voice of the living God. The voice that "pierces our heart" (cf. Ac 2:37), the voice that becomes our answer to the question "What shall I do?"—this voice encounters us on the cognitive and historical level. Biblical-historical questions can basically never be separated from faith questions.

Along with embeddedness in faith we must consider embeddedness in the Christian community, the fellowship of faith. True, the Bible speaks to every age and will do so till the end of time. Yet the specific challenges of every age serve to cast sharper light on respective specific features of the biblical message. Such challenges are first and foremost community challenges and not research challenges or challenges for some pedagogical guild. Biblical-historical interpretation, therefore, takes place consciously within the framework of the challenges that impinge on the community. To that extent the effects that an interpretation elicits in a certain situation justly reflect back on the interpreter.

This serves as a reminder to the interpreter of his responsibility for the community. How the community's present mission, e.g., of winning people to Christ, fares is of concern to him, also in his activity as interpreter. He is not free to stipulate his own chosen sphere of responsibility; it is given to him. It is one of the excesses of self-serving, self-exalting reason that it dangles before the interpreter the illusion that he lives in an open zone beyond the concerns of the community, and that he can pursue theology "etsi congregatio sanctorum non daretur" ("as if the holy congregation did not exist").

Earlier we named prayer, exchange of ideas, discussion, correction, and praxis as forms of interfacing with the community. The heading "prayer" is concrete reminder of the supplication that bears up and accompanies the interpreter. Prayer is interpretive aid in a primal sense. The heading "exchange of ideas" reminds us of the various gifts among community members (cf. Ro 12 and 1Co 12). Only seldom will the interpreter possess the gift of the evangelist. He does preliminary work for the evangelist and in a manner of speaking carries on his work through the evangelist's ministry. On the other hand there are cases in which, e.g., the interpreter is dependent on those who pray over him for healing (Jas 5:13ff.). "Discussion" reminds us, e.g., of the necessity of using understandable language. The paucity of discussion between theologians and nontheologians in recent times is closely related to theologians' failure to strive for lucidity—indeed, they sometimes seem to fear that understandable language is tantamount to superficiality. But how can there be correction when there first has to be a linguistic miracle to bring about understanding?

"Correction" brings us to an especially delicate issue. To deflect misunderstanding let it be said at the outset that the ideal here cannot lie in a compromise between "university theology" and "practical Christian piety." Nor is it to be sought through tallying opinions and computing the average. It is not a matter of "getting along well together," of arriving at a "most conservative possible theology," or the like. We speak here rather of a genuine, indeed even equal participation of church members regarding a common understanding of Scripture. This calls on theologians to concede that the Holy Spirit is active in places other than the scholar's study and the history of theology. We may cite two examples here. According to Wilfried Joest, God himself has made it clear to us through the history of theology since the Enlightenment that the Bible is error-prone.[4] He forgets that during the same era the same Holy Spirit made clear to the church that modern theology was heading up a box canyon. Another example involves James Barr. He advocates the thesis that the decisive criterion for interpretation lies neither in the Bible nor in the teaching of the church but rather in "research."[5] This thesis enthrones a papacy of experts and excludes the correction of the church. But what is correction? It cannot replace personal conscience and hard-earned knowledge gained over many years. Yet it constantly reminds the interpreter of his membership in the body of Christ and of his—at best—fragmentary knowledge (cf. 1Co 13:9). Further, correction makes him grateful for the gifts of others. It thus prepares the way for modesty and agreement on a common interpretation of Scripture.

We also spoke of "praxis." Let us try to express what that means concretely. Every church member is expected to take up some task in the fellowship in addition to his or her work outside the church. Analogous to this, every interpreter should take up an additional task in the church along with his work of interpretation. Among the many possibilities we may list visiting the sick, attending Christian meetings and small-group get-togethers, supply preaching, and missionary trips. In general J. T. Beck's counsel applies: practice what you know in order to advance in knowledge.[6] In this way the interpreter is most likely to avert the nemesis that Franz Mussner called "Privatgnosis" ("private specialized knowledge").[7]

We have now sketched the general features of the setting of a biblical-historical interpretation. It has its prehistory in the earlier faith- and life-story of the interpreter. It is embedded in the Christian community. Together with other church members it seeks biblical answers to the challenges of the day. It hears in Scripture the voice of the living God.

Now let us look at a concrete example of how the event of interpretation gets underway.

The interpreter approaches his text in continuity with his ongoing life history. This history is not only background, not just a foil, but a real presupposition for the step that places him before the text. He does not do this in as nonparticipatory a mood as possible or in as distanced a fashion as he can; he rather affirms fundamental trust that previous encounter with the voice of the living God through his Word has infused him. He does this in prayer. The goal of his prayer is to work filled with the same Holy Spirit by which the authors of the Bible labored. He knows that his prayer—here one thinks of Luther's *oratio* (prayer)!— does not preserve him from error. But at the same time he knows that he can, despite his failures, serve the church to which he is called as interpreter. He knows that his prayer is determinative for the connection of his life with God—the God who also in this, perhaps unusual, text speaks with him. And he knows that this life connection is decisive for his interpretation and for any fruit that it might bear.

He also comes to the text realizing that here, quite possibly, a battle awaits. This can be a battle between God and man—him, the interpreter. He is aware of his inherent determination to modulate and alter God's Word according to his own ideas. He knows the limits of his own willingness to see this or that feature of the text. He recognizes the disparity between his praxis and how God has charged him to live. In all of this he lives out the *tentatio* (struggle) of which Luther likewise spoke. He also knows that that battle may hinder as well as further his understanding. What could await, however, is also a battle with the Evil One. *Tentatio* can become an hour when the Tempter does his work. The interpreter's errors can lose their harmlessness and lead to deception. Or he may be tormented by the prospect of succumbing to such danger. In any case he knows that decisions await him. Likewise, just as every thought carries a will within it (Schlatter), an interpreter's every thought is itself already the consequence of certain decisions (Oepke). To that extent every exegesis consists in an act of the will. Here we are obviously far removed from the view of U. Wilckens, according to whom "a scientifically responsible interpretation of the Bible" consists "solely" in an investigation of the texts that comes about "through methodologically consistent application of historical reason."[8] What a bloodless and abstract conception! Such a view is, in the literal sense of the word, "utopian" ("leads nowhere").

The setting of a biblical-historical interpretation is, finally, characterized by an inner exchange between the interpreter and his text. Here we encounter traces of what Luther called *meditatio* (reflection). Our modern word *meditation* utterly fails to grasp the meaning.[9] For the essential focus here is not concentration on oneself and immersion in oneself but rather a hearing of that which is beyond oneself.[10] The interpreter makes his way toward the text. He implores God to open his heart so that his limitations will be overcome. He knows that he is dealing with an *apokalupsis*, a revelation, that defies and eludes all manipulation (cf. Mt 16:17). He waits, we might say, on the text. Or more precisely, he waits on a sort of *parousia* of the text, its "arrival" in his presence. If the text fails to "arrive," if this "arrival" does not come about, then he is forced to go no farther than a philological, literary, or at best isolatedly cognitive "explanation."

To summarize: biblical-historical interpretation begins at that point where an interpreter approaches a text and expects its "arrival" in continuation of his faith- and life-history and his embeddedness in the Christian community. First and most importantly he hears in this text the voice of the living God. He thereby enters into a tension resulting from the fact that every interpretation in the realm of church and personal faith brings about battle and decision, on the one hand, and yet boon to those who remain open to it, on the other. The interpreter's basic posture is one of expectant prayer and humble openness.

## THE BIBLICAL TEXT AS STARTING POINT

The first step of our interpretation is devoted to the text. In this way we are remaining true to the procedure of the church's interpretation of Scripture down through the centuries. Even historical criticism did not break out of this traditional approach. That was a great blessing, since in this way the biblical texts continued to receive a hearing.

Numerous considerations from previous chapters support the decision to take the text as our point of departure. If the Bible facilitates encounter between God and man, this encounter must indeed be opened through his Word. We receive it. From this grace, this gift of encounter, is derived the right of these biblical texts to speak. If we wish to hear what they say, and what they are authorized to say, then we must hear them in their concrete form—just as we find them in the text. In this way our revelatory starting point comes into play as well.

With the church through all the centuries, then, we ask more precisely: what do we find written there? This question leads us to the task of *determining the text*. From the numerous manuscripts, translations, and other documents, we must ascertain the oldest and most original text, insofar as this can be determined.

Relevant specialized studies furnish orientation in the available possibilities and technical procedures. Here we will add only a few remarks.

First, a word about nomenclature and what it implies. Normally one speaks of "textual criticism," whereas our term is *determining the text*.[11] "Criticism" in view of textual transmission is a thoroughly apt word inasmuch as it connotes differentiating and evaluating discrimination. Since, however, historical criticism continually tried to rob this word of innocence and to make "criticism" its chief argument to justify its own existence, a certain caution is advisable in its use. We speak of neither criticism of the text nor of a dogmatic-critical procedure. Ours is rather the comprehensive concern to recover the original text to the extent that this is possible.

A second comment relates to the matter at hand itself. Are we not, one might ask, here granting priority, or at least equality, to critical human reason rather than to revelation? And is this not taking place at the decisive juncture at which revelation as such first encounters us? Is it not then precisely critical reason, as it determines the presumably oldest text, that dictates to us what revelation is? As plausible as a positive answer to this question appears, to say yes here would ultimately be unjustified. For the transmission of the biblical tradition is not characterized by various messages, by *different* texts, that compete with each other in their conflicting demands to be "the" revelation. We are dealing rather with a single message, with variants of *the same* text. We decide from among these *variants* and not from among independent texts. So our decision rests on the pregiven, fundamentally preserved substance of the text as passed along in the course of transmission. Since its substance and parameters are already firmly in place, a decision in individual cases where there are differences is possible. The possibility of seriously mistaken decisions is narrowly circumscribed. To that extent the earlier so-called Textus Receptus is basically not a different text than the more recent textus receptus of Nestle-Aland.[12]

In this connection we should recall that in the work of determining the text we move virtually wholly in the realm of what we may term "receptive reason." Reason is thoroughly capable of such reception, even in the view of Reformation dogmatics. Parallel events would be, e.g., the mastery and use of the biblical languages, observation of archaeological evidences, or the transference of the biblical message into modern speech. Here reason's receptive and ordering capability remains intact (cf. 1Co 14:19) despite the Fall. If we give this insight up, then we could also no longer account for how people ever heard the preaching of Jesus, the apostles, and the prophets, and understood them in at least an outward sense. We would end with an a-rational or radically ecstatic faith hardly to be found in either Scripture or mainstream Christian history.

It would not be theology, nevertheless, if worldview-theological viewpoints did not make their presence felt even at the foundational level of determining the text. Our third remark pertains to this problem. Instructive here is the food for thought that the history of "textual criticism" offers us. According to the introduction to the 1979 edition of the Nestle-Aland Greek text of the New Testament, "the special theories of Westcott/Hort" had a "decisive influence" on the form that the early Nestle text assumed.[13] The 1979 Nestle-Aland consciously freed itself from commitment to these theories. Instead, it opted for a "local-genealogical method,"[14] gave up preference for any particular text group, and made its decisions eclectically "from case to case."[15] In fact, a careful investigation of each individual case seems to be the best means of avoiding illegitimate biases. Similarly, one must maintain sober awareness that already in the rise of textual variants, theological points of view played a role.

## OPENING UP THE TEXT

1. After determining the text, the next step is *philological exegesis* of the text. Such exegesis investigates overarching structural features and more immediate context as well as grammatical and linguistic structure. It illuminates word meanings and literary forms (genre) and flows naturally into a suitable translation.

Once more it should be said that making philological exegesis primary has been common throughout church history. We recall that even medieval exegesis took the *sensus literalis* (literal sense) as its starting point. Historical criticism with its own philological concern took over a tradition many hundreds of years old. As a result, theological science in partnership with the more restricted field of philology has put together outstanding technical tools and a nearly incalculable wealth of illustrative material.

In contrast to the previous area of determining the text, we observe that now in philological exegesis the interpreter has a far larger area of free play for his decisions. The possibilities multiply of making theologically grounded judgments. Temptations and dangers multiply as well. We will shortly see how this area of free play for decisions increases with every exegetical step.

In this connection two items bear special mention. First, biblical-historical interpretation attempts to implement the principle of proximity in its philological focus. That is, it explains the words, the linguistics, and the literary forms of the New Testament first of all with an eye to the Old Testament and to Judaism. It does this not for traditional or arbitrary reasons but because it proceeds from the basis of a historical connection between the new covenant and the old covenant, a connection dealt with sufficiently in earlier chapters of this study. To cite a well-known example: it explains the *logos* of John 1, not as the immanent cosmic nexus to which man has universal access but as the Word God addresses to the creature. Another example: it explains the light of John 8:12 not from gnostic-Hellenistic speculations but based on the God who grants illumination (Ps 36:10), and who does this especially through the medium of his Word (Ps 119:105). It is worth noting that Kittel's *Theological Dictionary of the New Testament* is constructed with this principle of proximity in prominent view.

Second, biblical-historical interpretation at the philological level pays heed to the possibilities and boundaries of form-critical investigation. Biblical genres and forms can give valuable clues to content and purpose of biblical expressions. Thus it is improbable just on the basis of form that Jesus wants to commend negligence in Luke 16:1ff. On the other hand, the form-critical enterprise that found special favor most of all in Germany is now shattered—I speak here of historical criticism's, and specifically form criticism's, quest to describe the rise of the Gospel on the basis of assumptions about forms having their origin in collective consciousness and activity. Today form criticism finds itself in a state of upheaval. In general we may say that the rise and history of a text cannot be explained solely through its form, and that form and history respectively are to be considered on their own terms.

2. From philological exegesis interpretation progresses to historical exegesis. This too was already practiced long ago in the days of a Flacius or a Bengel.

Once again the interpreter's latitude for judgment and decision rachets upward. For here he gains additional interpretive possibilities.

He can, e.g., illuminate his text from ancient history. Contours emerge from this. By such historical comparison e.g., Matthew 22:15ff. appears as a time of decision in view of the Zealots; the distinctiveness of the Lucan prologue (Lk 1:1–4) comes into view; the peculiarities of the trials of Jesus take shape.

Broadened possibilities of understanding result as well from comparative religious illumination. It its light we grasp more clearly Jesus' striking behavior at Jacob's well (Jn 4:5ff.), his critical interaction with Jewish Halacha (oral tradition; cf. Mt 15:1ff.), or his dissatisfaction with the title of Son of David (Mt 22:41ff.). The history behind the rise of the New Testament epistles helps us, not just to write early-church history, but also to understand the queries and responses that abound in them.

In addition there is the expansive area of tradition history. Leading images, motives, and underlying reasons can sometimes be traced through several biblical writings and to an extent over large temporal distances. Placement of themes and entire chains of expression repeat themselves with various modifications. Thus, e.g., one can follow the attitude of the believing community toward the state from the Jewish Diaspora (Daniel, Esther, Ezra, Nehemiah) on down into apostolic times (Ro 13:1ff.; 1Pe 2:13ff.). The process of revelation that tradition history makes accessible unveils to us the rise of resurrection hope as biblical promises found increasing assent. On the other hand, e.g., the evangelists in their individuality as redactors draw from this tradition history, applying oral and written transmissions and making them serviceable for new purposes. Luke 18:1ff., the parable of the unjust judge, offers an interesting example here; Luke builds an appeal against weariness in prayer into his gospel.

Biblical-historical interpretation devotes concentrated attention to all historical dimensions. It places high priority on understanding and interpreting the Bible historically.

At the same time, however, it will pay heed to its special orientation points on that very same plane of history. The following comments serve to demarcate such points.

The biblical-historical interpreter will remember, first, that he does not labor as historian or even as a sort of historical design engineer but as theologian in service to the church. History will therefore not take on independent status for him but rather remain the sphere of God's activity. Precisely in the text's historical characteristics he hears anew the voice of the living God.

For biblical-historical interpretation, then, there can never be a question of working historically "etsi deus non daretur" ("as if God did not exist"). It can never accept an atheistic conception of history. Here lies a weighty difference with historical criticism, whose fundamental and majority-supported starting point is that historical research knows no God, at least not as a factor of history.[16]

In contrast, biblical-historical interpretation reckons at every turn, not only with the historical or self-understanding of the biblical witnesses, but also with God *himself*, who testifies to his presence in history. In the very course of its work biblical-historical interpretation seeks to encounter him.

Basically we have already said above that the goal of biblical-historical interpretation can never lie simply in explaining the genesis of a text. With such explanations the interpreter leaves the one seeking understanding all alone at the decisive point where he most needs help.[17] The genesis of a text can—not must!—be at most a preliminary stage of understanding.

The next point of orientation may be subsumed under the heading "formation of hypotheses." Historical work remains closely related to hypothesis formation. Revelation and faith, however, aim at certainty. Exegesis with its historical work therefore ventures constantly onto a stormy, ever-changing sea. This sea, however, is not boundless but rather has secure banks. But it is not the hypotheses that can form these banks; it is only the canonical text. Hypotheses, then, only furnish lines of assistance. Because of this every interpreter has the task to divulge with full honesty where he is arguing on the basis of hypotheses. It is an important concern of biblical-historical interpretation that the distinction between hypotheses and facts, between value judgments and actual observations, again be carried out with as much clarity as possible. Hypotheses are, e.g., the acceptance of a Gospel-sayings source (Q), the dominant source divisions in the Pentateuch, the acceptance of a Second or Third Isaiah. It is a hypothesis that there was ever an adoptionist Christology in the early Christian church. It is a hypothesis that the New Testament contains pseudepigraphical writings.

What we have said regarding formation of hypotheses in the course of historical exegesis leads naturally to our judgment concerning *literary criticism*. In general we may say that the results of so-called literary criticism must be classified as hypothesis formation. Exceptions may be found especially where literary sources become visible in the biblical reports themselves, as, e.g., the songs of Yahweh's wars (Nu 21:14f.), in the documents mentioned in Ezra (Ezr 4–6), or in the citations from Greek authors (Ac 17:28; Tit 1:12).

In distinction from previously ascendant biblical-critical opinion, a biblical-historical interpretation will therefore in any case base itself on the final form of the canonical text. "In," "with," and "under" the historical emergence of a biblical text God was indeed at work. The historical event of revelation permitted these texts to arise the way they did, conformed them to their final shape, and placed them in their determined position within the canon. The voice of the living God was at best faintly audible in the prestages of this development; but it sounds loud and clear when it comes to the goal of the text he intended to bring into being—and did.

Precisely the difference from historical criticism moves us along now to a further point of orientation regarding the kind of historical exegesis we are proposing. This point can be characterized with the key word *analogy*. As is well known, post-Enlightenment exegesis stood in danger of making a possible analogy into the criterion of the truth of reports. Theologians have succumbed to this danger even more than historians. Troeltsch's triad (criticism-analogy-correlation) with analogy at its heart has not even been repudiated in recent Tübingen theology.[18] Since a biblical-historical interpretation at its very heart emphasizes that encounter with the living God is without analogy, at least as Troeltsch defined it, it can no longer use analogy as a criterion of truth. That also applies for the historical sphere of its interpretation.

This position has wide-ranging consequences. The supernatural, the terror of entire generations of interpreters,[19] returns to its legitimate place—not as a calculable element of religious *ratio* (reason), but also no longer "off-limits," as it is for irreligious *ratio*. It comes to us with the mystery of revelation in order to transform us through communication with this mystery.

Miracle again returns to the scene. We will not through our categories be able to determine what a miracle is or even may be. Precisely here all previous experiences have limited explanatory value. Miracle can be grasped only in the light of revelation. Divisions such as (possible) healing miracles and (impossible) nature miracles are rationalistic, indeed laughable.

Prophecy makes a return, as well. That Jesus could not have known of his resurrection, that Daniel 11 is too exact in what it foretells to be actual prophecy, that the prophecy of Jerusalem's trampling by the Gentiles (Lk 21:24) must be the terminus a quo for the composition of Luke's gospel—those are all critical Enlightenment notions that a biblical-historical interpreter can no longer take as a standard. His thinking is conditioned by the God who created time and who will abolish time (Rev 10:6f.), the God who beyond all temporal barriers revealed his secrets to the prophets (Rev 10:7). In short, with the return of God into historical interpretation, genuine prophecy again becomes a theme of interpretation. History is now a "history that God has with mankind and thereby with his entire creation."[20]

Let us once more take a characteristic example: the report of Jesus' baptism (Mt 3:13ff. par.). Historical-critical interpretation is content to accept the text's statement that Jesus was baptized by John. It holds this text to be accurate on the grounds that the (early) Christian church would not have invented a baptism of Jesus by the Baptist. But historical-critical interpretation regards as superfluous all that goes beyond the actual baptism event; it is suspicious, indeed not acceptable on methodological grounds. "When for example," writes Weder, "it is said that the Spirit of God descended on Jesus like a dove, and that a divine voice spoke from heaven, the historian cannot accord the value of historical truth to these expressions for methodological reasons."[21] Why not? Because in the modern worldview the supernatural and superhistorical do not occur. Bultmann, on whose work Weder builds,[22] declared that the New Testament's view of history is in fact "mythological."[23] He pondered whether the dove of Matthew 3:13ff. might not be derived from other accounts that make use of the ancient Near Eastern kingbird[24] and saw in the divine voice an interpretive device of the church, not an event.

We will leave the question open here whether modern man actually no longer believes in miracles. Contemporary "new religiosity" seems to take a different view, at any rate. We will also leave open whether the modern historian, like a Machiavelli and Guicciardini, is as desirous of keeping "God" so entirely "out of the picture"[25] as histori-cal-critical interpreters claim. The decisive matter here is the concept of history. If one uses the concept of history that revelation provides, if one begins from history as constituted by God, then historical interpretation runs an entirely different course than in classic historical criticism. The tyranny of analogy is broken. The deficient verificational capacity of the world around us, our understanding of which can reflect more what we project onto it than what we observe in it, no longer decides every ques-tion. The voice from heaven and the dove were God-enabled, thoroughly possible events. The occurrence stamps my understanding—and not the opposite. The horizon of previous experience widens. Just because something is unusual, or "supernatural" to use the customary term, that does not mean it must be excluded from having "the value of historical truth." To put it positively, the voice and the descent of the Spirit were intended by the text to be understood as events. The report that these events took place becomes true in "the reality characterized by God's continually new activity."[26] With this, biblical-historical interpretation takes an immense step forward in its possibilities for understanding and explication. It no longer has a fixation with the history of an early church who had to explain Jesus' baptism by using John and thereby also jus-tified its own baptismal practices. It is liberated to affirm knowledge of the actual occurrence, in which Jesus receives the lasting gift of the Spirit for the purpose of his messianic activity. It is likewise liberated to affirm knowledge of the commission which the divine voice imparted for this activity. The acceptance of Old Testament statements (Ge 22:2; Ps 2:7; Isa 42:1) through the divine voice clarifies Jesus' mission of dying for sin. Biblical-historical interpretation hears, therefore, the voice of the living God here, which speaks of his will to bring about redemp-tion and salvation. That means that it encounters real salvation history, not just a narrow slice of the history of the early church.

## SYNTHETIC INTERPRETATION

Opening up the text, treated in previous sections, involved details and differentiations. Synthetic interpretation involves getting at the whole.

It would seem reasonable from the outset to speak of a theological exegesis at this point, having covered philological and historical exegesis in the previous section. We recall that in the basic framework of Reformation interpretation of Scripture, as we encounter it, e.g., in Flacius, *theologica tractatio* (theological preparation) followed *grammatica intellectio* (philological understanding). And at this point, in fact, subsequent to philological and historical exegesis, theological viewpoints push more decisively into the foreground. Nevertheless: the entire process of interpreting the Bible is theological, and theological viewpoints were accordingly not absent from the exegetical steps discussed above. So the heading "Theological Interpretation" for this section could give rise to the misunderstanding that it is first at this point that theology comes into play. Therefore we have chosen the heading "Synthetic Interpretation," which seems better suited. For it indicates that now the process of opening up the text must bear fruit, and that most of all the points of view of a synthetic outlook must have their turn.

The conspicuous mark of a synthetic interpretation is discussion. The text, now already laid open in earlier steps, must be brought into dialogue with the following: #1) other texts of enscripturated revelation; #2) previous interpreters, including dogmaticians; #3) the believing Christian fellowship, the church; and #4) the challenges of the surrounding world. The following remarks are intended to facilitate this dialogue.

In speaking first of discussion with other revelatory texts, we are expressing a real priority. Discussion with other participants is senseless until we have taken the trouble to understand a biblical text within the entirety of biblical revelation. Here is where justice is done to the point of view of *tota scriptura* (the whole of Scripture). The knowledge that the biblical texts, according to their own claim, are inspired, and that all of Holy Scripture arose from the basis of a history of inspiration, requires that we take seriously the canonical placement of a text. This placement is the basis from which inner-biblical discussion ensues. On the other hand, the other texts also possess their respective canonical position and a function in the entirety of the canon derived from that position. The "canonical approach" proposed by B. S. Childs proves once more to be justified.

But it is not only canonical classification that plays a role here. Discussion with other revelatory texts can only succeed if we encounter there the voice of the same living God. That is, this discussion presupposes the unity of Scripture. Whoever gives up the unity of Scripture can at best partially, and perhaps not at all, carry out a biblical classification or an inner-biblical comparison. Clearly, at this point a biblical-historical interpretation differs powerfully from a historical-critical one. For the essence of historical criticism is precisely that it, stamped with the idea of difference, nullifies the unity of the Bible.

Let us take the relation between Romans 3 and James 2 as an example. If one places Romans 3:28 ("For we maintain that a man is justified by faith apart from observing the law" [NIV]) directly next to James 2:24 ("You see that a person is justified by what he does and not by faith alone" [NIV]), the impression arises that only one of the two can be correct. Things change, however, as soon as the context is considered. Romans 1–3 deals with the question, "Where does salvation come from?" James 2, in contrast, speaks from within the experience of salvation. While the epistle to the Romans must deny the expectation that man can achieve his salvation through works, James's epistle must deal with the expectation that we obviously cannot achieve our own salvation because it was long since given to us in Christ. In other words, Romans 3 leads toward the Cross; James 2 speaks from the point of already having arrived there. Romans 3 says: we can be saved only through Jesus. James 2 says: we forsake salvation if our faith is empty and dead. Both passages are rightly accorded their canonical place. Both statements are necessary and correct. In both passages the voice of the living God speaks to us. They contradict each other as little as two different lines in a father's letter to one of his sons, in which he first writes, "Dear Son, I leave you my entire estate," and then at the end writes, "Please share it with your brother."

This example makes clear once more that discussion with various revelatory texts in a biblical-historical interpretation proceeds from the assumption that the same Divine Author stands behind all these texts and that they therefore comprise a unity.

But what is the situation when not just individual texts but complexes of large dimensions are compared with each other? Let us take the example of the history of Israel. Since Wellhausen, critical theology has been dominated by the assumption of various narrative threads in the Pentateuch or Hexateuch, threads which were later redactionally connected and reworked. The narrative unity of the Pentateuch was thereby dissolved. Wellhausen's approach drastically altered the historical picture presented by the text. Now the invasion of Canaan is the result of the infiltration of various groups. These groups first united to form the entirety of "Israel" after they all entered Canaan independently. Each group brought with it respective bodies of tradition that in the course of time were intermingled with each other.

A biblical-historical interpretation proceeds quite differently here. It would first note that Israel's fellowship of faith, as far as we can follow its convictions, never took any other historical shape than the one that lies before us in the Pentateuch or Hexateuch. It would further note that both prophetic and anti-Jewish texts proceed from the same historical picture (cf. e.g., Jos 24:2ff.; 2Ki 14:6; Pss 78; 106; Hos 2:17; 9:10ff.; 11:1; 12:4ff.; Mic 6:4f.; Mal 3:22; also the non-canonical Sirach 44–49). It will ultimately find the same historical picture in the New Testament (cf. Ac 7; Heb 11). Biblical-historical interpretation finds, therefore, that revelation furnishes a unified historical portrait. It will be loathe to contradict this portrait. It will rather find it confirmed by the agreement of the texts, and it will make it its starting point for subsequent deliberations.

Such acceptance of the texts, precisely in the horizon of discussion with as many revelatory texts as possible, is of a piece with the *openness* that a biblical-historical interpretation wants to maintain in its synthetic work. Openness here means readiness to listen and the willingness to let previous experiences and knowledge be corrected by revelation. Also on this level, biblical-historical interpretation—in contrast to historical criticism—will not make its own "worldview" into the grid through which understanding must pass. Biblical-historical interpretation can only champion an open worldview, whereas historical criticism seeks "in that sense" to be "content-critical [*sachkritisch*]" "as it makes its own contemporary understanding of reality into the critical standard of statements found in the sources."[27] Biblical-historical interpretation is open in the sense that it does not rule out the contents of revelation. It is also open in the sense that it permits revelation, as the case may be, to pass along *no* closed worldview to us at all!

In the course of this openness it becomes more and more apparent that an interpretation suited to revelation can only proceed *inductively*. E.g., it may not simply replace an (allegedly?) modern worldview with an (allegedly?) biblical one. It must rather feel its way forward, step by step and issue by issue, under constantly renewed listening. In the course of this openness it becomes further apparent that a biblical-historical interpretation must pay attention to the progressive character of revelation. Since revelation itself is historical and accompanies the people of God along its way, some of its messages emerge very gradually. It therefore makes no sense to seek to trace out a comprehensive messianic doctrine or resurrection message already back in the Pentateuch.

And finally, a result of openness to discussion is that individual statements, passages, and the like may not be loaded with more freight than they can bear. That which is unclear, if it does not admit of clarification from the context, must remain in its obscurity. Where various interpretations are possible, they must be listed and perhaps left open alongside each other. Wide-ranging consequences cannot be pressed on the basis of disputed passages. The danger must be held firmly in view that the interpreter might make bold to become an extrabiblical source of Scripture—violating Deuteronomy 4:2 and Revelation 22:18.

To return to the rubric "discussion," which plays such a large role in synthetic interpretation, until now we have spoken of discussion with other revelatory texts. It has become clear that this is a particular weighty feature of biblical-historical interpretation.

Now, however, we must ponder *discussion with previous interpreters*. Texts, as is well known, have their own history of interpretation and effect. They influence individual interpreters, even generations, indeed even whole Christian communions. Whether this is for the good or for ill we may leave to the side for now. Discussion with other interpreters is especially important if we assume that the Holy Spirit has worked in other church members and in the church of all ages. Such discussion is grounded in the expectation of learning from other thinkers of other times and places.

In this form *analogia fidei* (analogy of faith) and *interpretatio fidei* (interpretation of faith) report back to us from earlier discussion. In light of the history of interpretation in recent generations we must advance here a trio of exclamation points, so to speak. #1) The first relates to the weight accorded various periods of church history. It has become customary to pay heed almost exclusively to post-Enlightenment voices. Only Luther and Calvin receive anything like the same degree of consideration. The result of this emphasis on the most "modern" possible interpretive literature is the neglect of patristics, at least by Protestants. Such neglect is especially regrettable because valuable material for shedding light on biblical statements can be found in the most ancient utterances from church history. Naturally the wheat has to be separated from the chaff here. Yet study of the church fathers remains a rewarding task in any case. #2) A second exclamation point concerns dogmatics. As a rule, dogmatics is an embodiment of stability, continuity, and conservative character. Its disadvantage is its natural attachment to tradition. Yet it can warn exegesis, which is sometimes too interpretively fleet-footed for its own good, of blind alleys and thin ice. #3) The third exclamation point has to do with confessions. Confessions furnish, among other things, a concentrated history of interpretation and effect. Where they hinder observation of the text they are damaging. The time should be past when they worked as filters, or in league with dogmatics even prescribed entire doctrinal systems. No responsible interpreter, however, will facilely knock down the warning signs or step beyond the guideposts that the confessions of the church have erected in the course of time.

In addition to discussion with other interpreters there is also *discussion with the Christian church*. We have already said much about this as we reflected on the embeddedness of the interpreter in the church. We will therefore restrict ourselves here to what is most salient. First, lively discussion with other adherents of our believing community is irreplaceable. No amount of myriads of secondary literature is able to offset the lack that arises from sundering the interpreter from the church. Discussion, witnessing, preaching are the best means of testing the sense or senselessness of an interpretation. That is quite simply the very character of revelation, which wants to mediate, encounter, and establish fellowship. Its goal is not the isolated writing desk. Next, the church embodies the antidote against an interpreter's cognitive one-sidedness. The text that he interprets certainly has more levels than the merely cognitive. It is, however, his occupational hazard and constant danger that he threatens to lose sight of the dynamic and ethical understanding— modes of understanding that in themselves set boundaries for the cognitive element and furnish necessary supplementation. And precisely these modes of understanding are alive in the church, as a rule, with stronger force. Further, the church often preserves nonscientific traditions that may have long since proven themselves and may assume virtual confessional status. It may be that such traditions are unbiblical cultural accommodations. But it may also be the case that behind them lies a concentrated, partially even notable history of interpretation and effect. That would be precisely the point at issue in discussion, and in common prayer and witness.

Finally, above we mentioned *discussion with the challenges of the surrounding world*. German-language literature that researches this point is scanty. This state of affairs conceals a curious contradiction to the blithe confidence with which many theologians appeal to the "spirit" of their time or a "modern understanding of man and world."[28] Our discussion must avoid two extremes. One extreme would be to make, consciously or unconsciously, this much-appealed-to spirit of the age into a second *norma normans* (normative standard) alongside of Scripture. The person who says that we should talk in such a way that "there is no need to feel ashamed before the bar of reason"[29] is at least on the way to setting up such a second authority. The other extreme would consist in alienation from the world or ghetto isolation. An exegete who no longer hears whom or what is affected by recent local and world developments will hardly be in any position to offer helpful answers in service to the church. It is no coincidence that the age of the "apologists" marked an entire epoch in early church history. In this connection we must once more point to the character of revelation, whose goal is encounter and which seeks no less than to make telling contact with our own time and its specific challenges, too.

Now we must touch on the *goal* of all these levels of discussion. They take place in a quite particular framework, namely, as contributions that should facilitate a comprehensive interpretation. It was already pointed out that this comprehensive or synthetic interpretation possesses the character of a theological interpretation. If this interpretation is to be comprehensive, then in certain cases it will proceed from the basis of a multiple sense of Scripture. If the task, e.g., is to interpret a historical text, then the interpreter will utilize typology so as to render the voice of the living God audible in the present. Often the impetus for a typological, prophetic, or when appropriate allegorical interpretation will come from interchange with other interpretations in the history of the church or from discussion with other church members.

The interpreter arrives at a goal, however, only when he is in the position to grasp the purpose of a text. In any case, as encounter revelation is conditioned by its purposeful intent. That is true of even the small units of a text. If the interpreter misses this purpose that revelation itself establishes, then his interpretation runs aground at a decisive point. This insight gives rise once more to rejection of all content criticism (*Sachkritik*) of the Bible. For content criticism transforms the bent of the statements and the specific intent of the text. At this point we once more observe in all its sharpness the difference between a historical-critical and a biblical-historical interpretation. For historical criticism by its very nature reserves the right to subject the text to content criticism.

The purpose of a Bible text has been expressed for centuries as its *scopus* (major point). The *scopus* requires the interpreter to ponder once more the special features of a given text along with the features that it has in common with other texts. He must weigh wherein the particular profile of the text he is dealing with lies.

In this last-mentioned interpretive decision, that of determining *scopus*, it becomes absolutely clear how great the space has grown for the interpreter to exercise his own discretion. This discretion has grown from a small amount in determining the text, to ever-larger proportions at the stages of philological and historical exegesis, and then increased yet again in synthetic interpretation with its plurality of possibilities. What has also grown much larger is the weightiness of the presuppositions from which the interpreter proceeds. Finally, the differences we have seen between historical-critical and biblical-historical exegesis have also grown.

By now it is all the more evident to the interpreter that in the presence of the text he has become "contemporary" together with other interpreters and other church members. By "contemporary" we mean that he takes his place, alongside other hearers who possessed this text and will possess it in the future, in a fundamentally similar situation. The encounter that revelation seeks to mediate through him is fundamentally none other than the encounter that it offers to other persons. All splitting up of the listening audience, whether into "ancient" and "modern" man, whether into pre- or post-Enlightenment man, whether into "primitive" or "civilized" man—all these and any similar divisions are dashed by the voice of the living God, who addresses all persons for their salvation. But the interpreter has not only become "contemporary." He is, at least from now on, a "participant" in this encounter. There is no need to repeat what we wrote above about this involvement, about the decisions and the struggles, the bewilderment in *oratio-tentatio-meditatio* (prayer-struggle-reflection), the gift of possibilities of understanding, the interweaving of one's own life story. But we would underscore simply this: as a participant the interpreter will in any case go forth from this encounter as a transformed person, whether he agrees with or denies the text's claims which have mediated the encounter to him.

## COMMUNICATIVE INTERPRETATION

With this final step we leave the sphere in which historical-critical interpretation, which is often parallel with our biblical-historical approach, labors. For since the Enlightenment the tendency has become established to terminate exegesis with *scopus* (the text's major point). True, still in 1810 the entire second part of K. A. G. Keil's *Lehrbuch der Hermeneutik* (*Hermeneutics Handbook*) was devoted to this theme: "The instruction of others about the rightly understood meaning of the books of the New Testament."[30] But even Keil distinguishes between "popular" interpretation of Scripture and that of "experts" and eventually makes it known that he much prefers the second, which is intended "for the actual theologians."[31] In the course of the history of interpretation, then, popular (which also means practical) Scripture interpretation was left to the side. That had calamitous consequences. A vast quantity of material languished on the far side of the *scopus* barrier, hidden in the journals of historical exegesis, guarded by the disdain of professional exegetes for the "popular." Conversely, "popular" evangelists left scientific resources lie untouched. They laid out their message along traditional lines, almost unaffected by scientific-exegetical discoveries and disputes—and met with considerable success. There were only a few theologians—Karl Heim would be an example—who were also effective in popular evangelism.

With our step into communicative interpretation we draw nearer, however, to the basic principles of precritical, reformational Scripture interpretation. We recall that such interpretation in Flacius' presentation had three major components: *grammatica intellectio—theologica tractatio—cognitio practica* (philological understanding—theological preparation—practical knowledge). The last step led to practical application. Flacius did, to be sure, distinguish between simple application for laypersons and scholarly application for theologians.[32] We also recall the role of application in Francke, who demanded of his students that they "become more spiritual" through their labor on the Bible.[33] Finally we recall Bengel's exegesis which issued in homiletical application. All these examples encourage us to press a biblical-historical interpretation past the point of synthetic interpretation, past the *scopus* (major point).

But what do we mean by the expression "communicative interpretation"? It refers to transforming our interpretation into praxis. What was earlier worked out is now shared with others, communicated. To whom? First to the church, then to the surrounding world. To both we owe the interpreted message at which we have arrived. But in that the interpreter himself is responsible for this transformation, his interpretation gains additional dimensions once more. This is less true for the cognitive sphere, which could end with the *scopus*. It holds much more true for the unified sphere in which the interpreter labors, e.g., the dynamic and ethical levels of understanding. His service in the church takes on concrete form not least here.

Classical forms of this transformation are the sermon outline, the lecture précis, and the evangelistic presentation. By such means, of course, exegesis is also throwing up a bridge to "practical theology."

As an example let us take Luke 4:16–21. Determination of the text has presumably led us to its original form and in the process clarified the extent of the quotation from Isaiah 61:1. Opening up the text showed us the characteristics of synagogue worship of that time, the prevailing messianic expectation, the tradition history of messianic texts and interpretations, the institution of the jubilee year, and more. Synthetic interpretation has made Jesus' messianic claim clear, a claim about which more is learned from interaction with other Gospel texts. We realize, likewise in discussion with other revelatory texts, how Jesus woos Israel, how he loves the synagogue, and how he is willing to enter into battles and disputes, indeed how he is also willing to walk the way of suffering—the way of the cross. It has become clear, further, that all Jesus' ministry was grounded in Israel's Holy Scriptures. We realize that he is a Messiah of the Word who offers redemption from guilt and judgment, not a Messiah of armed struggle seeking to bring down existing structures. In discussion with previous interpreters we have become conscious of the spectrum of interpretations, ranging, e.g., from Luther's Magnificat interpretation to Müntzer's of a revolutionary appeal. In the midst of this spectrum the question continually rings: who was—no, who *is* Jesus? In discussion with the church and the challenges of the surrounding world we next saw that various understandings of Jesus to this very day, on the part of both Christians and Jews, are often malignant, that they create tensions like unto those that arose in our text in Nazareth, so that Jesus' claims impinge on the present in provocative fashion. We recognized the purpose of the section as being Jesus' self-testimony about his messiahship. Our *scopus* (major point) turned out like this: "Jesus is the announced and expected Messiah!" But . . . now what? How does the result of our interpretation make its way into the present, filled as it is with opinions, currents, doubts, and conflicts? Does the *scopus* remain entrusted to silent paper, or will its words be urged on the church in the midst of its ongoing striving for the truth? How does the interpreter bear the claim of his text into the surrounding world which revelation strives to penetrate? There is only one way: that the text becomes message.

The communicative interpretation of which we speak is basically already demanded by the encounter-character of revelation. Revelation does not only take aim at the interpreter. It rather aims through him to others beyond and draws the interpreter into the event of mediation which knows no bounds until the end of the earth (cf. Ac 1:8).

Let us return to our example. The *scopus* (major point), "Jesus is the announced and expected Messiah!" forms the starting point for the subsequent communicative interpretation. This can take various shapes, e.g., as a doctrinal sermon, as a unit of instruction in religious education, or as a component in an evangelistic application.

Here we choose an evangelistic application. It might be sketched out roughly as follows:

1. A world full of expectancy. Nazareth has a sensation: a local resident worked miracles in Capernaum (cf. Lk 4:23 with 4:31ff.). Now he is there. The Sabbath is anxiously awaited. The synagogue will function as the contemporary theater. And he comes! Masterful, how he threads himself into the reading at an appropriate moment. Behind all this lie expectations spanning many generations: prophets are to return, finally even the Messiah. Behind all this lie disappointments spanning many generations: again and again hopes were dashed. Even the Maccabees turned out to be entirely normal overlords. And our world? What are our expectancies? What are our disappointments? Is this Jesus any better . . . ?

2. A word full of power. "Coincidence," that Jesus is handed the Isaiah scroll? He did not ask for it. It is God's leading. God's leading also lets him alight on the passage in Isaiah 61. What an explosive text! It is centuries old. Interpreted again and again, sifted through repeatedly and then some more. But now its actual meaning: "On me," "he anointed me"! Anointed: that means Christ, Messiah. And over the long arc of many centuries this Word is fulfilled: "Today"! God's Word never fails (Ps 33:4).

3. He's the one! Jesus! He himself says so. We don't have to wait for the Messiah any longer. We don't need some other salvation-bearer. And Israel will also not have any other Messiah. Jesus has the liberating, indeed the redemptive, Word: you are free from guilt. You are freed from Satan's clutches. You enter God's kingdom. You receive under-

standing, illumination about the truth. Your life may fall to pieces, sickness may ravage you externally. Charges that you have wasted your life come to nothing—nothing can take the kingdom of God from you, or rather you from it. Jesus remains the Liberator, for he dies for you. He invites you to come to him—"Today"!

Certainly, a communicative interpretation always remains an outline. But this necessity of saying the most important in briefest possible compass is healthy, indeed compulsory. It is the culmination and touchstone of our interpretation. Let us reflect on this once more in what follows.

Communicative interpretation is healthy first just because it demands intelligibility from us. It is, so to speak, medication against the tendency of the theologian to artificial, affected ways of speaking or writing. It does away, then, with language barriers. The interpreter must now himself undertake the job of transforming his results. Here he discovers once again what is nourishing food and what is just gawdy wrapping. In this connection one may perhaps speak of a "second naivete." Simplifications are permissible when they arise through adequate reflection.

Further, we now recognize the justification for that old arrangement in which the "meditation" had to precede the sermon outline. Such a—legitimate—meditation once again penetrates to the Word that bears fruit; it serves as a test of all interpretations derived from this fruitful Word and reveals whether those interpretations are worthy. Such a meditation can satisfy the counsel that J. T. Beck once offered: "Spare no pains to seek more and more the most basic original sense of the biblical words, and let this be the root-sense of everything additional."[34]

To express it plainly: this transformation, this "second naivete," this essential simplifying, also means humiliation for the interpreter. Much that he was proud of is unmasked as empty, glittering wrapping. What's more, he discovers how narrow the wavelength is on which he communicates. He will be surprised again and again at how modest the wavelength appears that carries the fruit of his labor and ability, whether he seeks to communicate as a religious educator, a preacher or Bible teacher, or an evangelist.

But with this humiliation we have already touched on something actually quite positive. Through concern for communicative interpretation the interpreter is reminded anew of the supplementary unity of his person and his work. He takes to heart once more that what is demanded is that he be a Christian and not just a theologian. He once more enters naturally into the modes of understanding which he was in danger of forgetting: the dynamic, the ethical, and so on. In a word, the exegete becomes a witness. Where this is nullified, as is the case in many quarters of historical criticism, the interpreter is robbed of his existential, complete breadth and his original vocation.

In life with the church, in the communicability of his research, he discovers in a salutary manner the gifts that he has. He discovers how his interpretation becomes helpful, how his exegesis bears fruit. It is first the church that teaches him how to deal aright with critical interaction and polemic. For the Christian community is where the bitter fruits of polemic become visible. That lack of restraint which reduces the opponent to the level of a beast is certainly not without precedent in exegetical literature, but it is not to be taken up in interpretation and communication that has the church as its basis and model.

Finally, there is one more point to mention.

Earlier we explained communicative interpretation in the concrete forms of sermon outline, lecture précis, or evangelistic presentation. We gained insight into the fact that exegesis that leads to the final step of communicative interpretation already extends into the area of practical theology. We reminded ourselves of the communication, the lively exchange within the Christian fellowship, exchange which requires the interpreter to be a complete person and which first enables his service to be fruitful. In all this we observe that the interpreter is a member of the Christian community. As such he is, like every other church member, called to be a witness.

Let us explore this calling to bear witness a bit farther. Certainty is a central component to bearing witness in the full sense. If the witness is uncertain about someone or something, he can only testify to his uncertainty about this someone or this something. He cannot testify to those things. In that communicative interpretation, as participation in the church, calls on the interpreter as witness, it obligates him to the clarification of his certainty. If previously, most of all in his historical investigations, he tended to dwell on hypotheses or languish in indecisiveness, then communicative interpretation now fetches him back onto the ground of certainty. The *assertio* which lay so much on Luther's heart becomes indispensable in the conveying of the message.

An example from church history may illustrate this. In his studies entitled *Evangelium als Schicksal* Karlmann Beyschlag pictures for us the role that the biblical word about seeking and finding (Mt 7:7) played in the early stages of Christendom.[35] "The Christians"—thus the apologist Aristides described existence renewed by biblical revelation— "moved about, and searched, and found the truth." Is there any better way to characterize the interpretive enterprise? At its end something is "found." He who has "found," however, has become a witness.

## FINAL COMMENT

We have traversed the way of a biblical-historical interpretation as far as communicative interpretation. In continuity with his previous faith-and life-history, the interpreter has approached his text. His renewed discussion with revelation, the process of interpretation that he pursues, issues again into the totality of his life history. He communicates with others what he has "found." Out of this "finding" emerges his certainty. With this certainty he steps into the world around him. Now he personifies the transformation that is created through encounter with revelation. In passing along the interpretation that has transformed him and made him into a witness, his interpretation itself becomes testimony.

Only in these categories—in discussion, in communication, in testimony, and in encounter—can the event of interpretation be grasped aright. Out of it, by necessity, a "hermeneutic of encounter" must arise. For encounter is the fundamental character of revelation. True, its goal is not in encounter with itself. Its goal is rather . . . Jesus (Jn 21:4; Mt 17:8).

# Appendix

Below is a table showing possible steps for a biblical-historical interpretation.

- I. DETERMINING THE TEXT
    1. Assessing variants
    2. Translation
- II. OPENING UP THE TEXT
    1. Overarching structural features of the text
    2. Context
    3. Grammatical and linguistic structure
    4. Important word meanings; exegesis of concepts where called for
    5. Genre
    6. Reassessment of translation
    7. Integration into historical setting
    8. Comparative religions analysis
    9. Tradition history and where appropriate redaction history
    10. Literary sources (if any)
- III. SYNTHETIC INTERPRETATION
    1. Discussion with other revealed texts (inner-biblical comparison)
    2. Discussion with previous interpreters (church-historical

comparison; history of interpretation and its effects; prior use of text in dogmatics)

3. Discussion with the Christian community
4. Discussion with the challenges of the surrounding world
5. Purpose of the text
6. Summarized theological interpretation
7. Major point (*scopus*)

IV. COMMUNICATIVE INTERPRETATION

# Bibliography

Entries below include abbreviations used in footnotes. Abbreviations follow those given in Siegfried Schwertner, *Internationales Abkürzungsverzeichnis für Theologie und Grenzgebiete*, Berlin/New York, 1974.

An addendum to Schwertner's list is JSOT = *Journal for the Study of the Old Testament.*

Full bibliographic data for titles cited just once is often found in the relevant footnote. These titles normally do not appear below but may be accessed via the author index.

Abraham, W. J. *The Divine Inspiration of Holy Scripture.* Oxford/New York/Toronto/Melbourne, 1981.
  abbreviation: Abraham.
Abrey, L. J. "La vie d' un anabaptiste strasbourgeois au seizième siècle: Michael Meckel." *RHPhR* 57 (1977): 195–207.
  abbreviation: Abrey.
Achtemeier, P. J. *An Introduction to the New Hermeneutic.* Philadelphia, 1969.
  abbreviation: Achtemeier.
Ahn, B.-M. *Draussen vor dem Tor.* Göttingen, 1986.
  abbreviation: Ahn.
Aland, K. "Das Problem des neutestamentlichen Kanons." In Käsemann, 134–58.

abbreviation: Aland, Kanon.

Aland, K. "Der Hallesche Pietismus und die Bibel." In O. Söhngen, ed., *Die bleibende Bedeutung des Pietismus*, 29–69. Witten/Berlin, 1960.
abbreviation: Aland, Hallescher Pietismus.

Amberg, E.-H. *Die Autorität der Heiligen Schrift in der deutschen evangelischen Dogmatik seit der Jahrhundertwende.* Dissertation photocopy. Leipzig, 1956.
abbreviation: Amberg.

Aner, K. *Die Theologie der Lessingzeit.* Halle, 1929.
abbreviation: Aner.

Asmussen, H. *Die Heilige Schrift.* Berlin, 1967.
abbreviation: Asmussen.

Aune, D. "On the Origins of the 'Council of Jamnia' Myth." *JBL* 110/3 (1991): 491–93.
abbreviation: Aune


Barnikol, E. "Der Briefwechsel zwischen Strauss und Baur." *ZKG* 73 (1962): 74–125.
abbreviation: Barnikol, ZKG.

Barnikol, E. *Ferdinand Christian Baur als rationalistisch-kirchlicher Theologe.* Berlin, 1970.
abbreviation: Barnikol.

Barr, J. "Childs' Introduction to the Old Testament as Scripture." *JSOT* 16 (1980): 12–23.
abbreviation: Barr, JSOT.

Barr, J. *Holy Scripture.* Philadelphia, 1983.
abbreviation: Barr.

Barth, H.-M. "Gottes Wort ist dreifaltig." *ThLZ* 113 (1988): col. 241–54.
abbreviation: H. M. Barth.

Barth, K. *Die kirchliche Dogmatik*, I, 2. 4th ed. Zollikon-Zürich, 1948.
abbreviation: Barth, KD I, 2.

Baur, F. C. *An Herrn Dr. Karl Hase.* Tübingen, 1855.
abbreviation: Baur, An Hase.

Bayer, O. "Hamann." *TRE* 14 (1985): 395–403.
abbreviation: Bayer, TRE.

Beale, G. K. "Did Jesus and His Followers Preach the Right Doctrine from the Wrong Texts?" *Themelios* 14/3 (1989): 89–96.
abbreviation: Beale.

Beck, J. T. *Gedanken aus und nach der Schrift.* 2d ed. Tübingen, 1868.
abbreviation: Beck, Gedanken.

Beck, J. T. *Leitfaden dern christlichen Glaubenslehre für Kirche, Schule und Haus.* Pt. 1, 2d ed. Stuttgart, 1869.
abbreviation: Beck, Leitfaden.

Beisser, F. *Claritas scripturae bei Martin Luther.* Forschungen zur Kirchen- und Dogmengeschichte, 18. Göttingen, 1966.
abbreviation: Beisser, Claritas.

Beisser, F. "Irrwege und Wege der historisch-kritischen Wissenschaft." *NZSTh* 15 (1973): 192–214.
abbreviation: Beisser, NZSTh.

Die *Bekenntnisschriften* der evangelisch-lutherischen Kirche. 5th ed. Göttingen, 1963.
abbreviation: BELK.

Bengel, J. A. *Erklärte Offenbarung Johannis oder vielmehr Jesu Christi.* 2d ed. Stuttgart, 1773.
abbreviation: Bengel, Erkl Offb.

Bengel, J. A. *Gnomon Novi Testamenti.* Tubingae, 1742.
abbreviation: Bengel, Gnomon.

Berg, J. van den. "De uitdraging van het historisch–kritisch onderzoek." *GTT* 77 (1977): 239–59.
abbreviation: van den Berg.

Berger, K. *Exegese des Neuen Testaments.* Heidelberg, 1977.
abbreviation: Berger.

Berkhof, L. *Principles of Biblical Interpretation (Sacred Hermeneutics).* Grand Rapids, 1974.

abbreviation: L. Berkhof.

Betti, E. *Die Hermeneuetik als allgemeine Methodik der Geisteswissenschaften.* PhG, 78/79, 2d ed. Tübingen, 1972.

abbreviation: Betti.

Beumer, J. "Die Kanonfrage und ihre katholische Lösung in den Versuchen der Aufklärungszeit und der Theologie der Gegenwart." *Cath(M)* 18 (1964): 268–90.

abbreviation: Beumer, Cath.

Beumer, J. *Die katholische Inspirationslehre zwischen Vatikanum I und II.* SBS, 20, 1966.

abbreviation: Beumer, SBS.

Beyschlag, K. *Evangelium als Schicksal.* München, 1979.

abbreviation: Beyschlag.

Bittner, W. J. *Jesu Zeichen im Johannesevangelium.* WUNT, 2d series, 26. Tübingen, 1987.

abbreviation: Bittner.

Blank, J. "Exegese als theologische Basiswissenschaft." *ThQ* 159 (1979): 2–23.

abbreviation: Blank.

Blau, L. *Studien zum althebräischen Buchwesen und zur biblischen Literaturgeschichte.* Budapest, 1902.

abbreviation: Blau.

Blenkinsopp, J. "A New Kind of Introduction, Professor Childs' *Introduction to the Old Testament as Scripture.*" *JSOT* 16 (1980): 24–27.

abbreviation: Blenkinsopp.

Blomberg, C. L. "The Legitimacy and Limits of Harmonization." In Hermeneutics, 139–74.

abbreviation: Blomberg.

Bockmühl, K., ed. *Die Aktualität der Theologie Adolf Schlatters.* Giessen/Basel, 1988.

abbreviation: Bockmühl.

Boeckh, A. *Encyclopädie und Methodologie der philologischen Wissenschaften.* Leipzig, 1877.
abbreviation: Boeckh.

Bonwetsch, G. N. *Die Theologie des Irenäus.* BFchTh, 2d series, 9. 1925.
abbreviation: Bonwetsch.

Bornkamm, H. *Martin Luther in der Mitte seines Lebens.* Göttingen, 1979.
abbreviation: Bornkamm, Luther.

Bornkamm, H., ed. *Martin Luthers Vorreden zur Bibel.* Hamburg, 1967.
abbreviation: Bornkamm, Vorreden.

Bring, R. *Luthers Anschauung von der Bibel.* Luthertum, 3. 1951.
abbreviation: Bring.

Brunner, E. *Erlebnis, Erkenntnis und Glaube.* 3d ed. Tübingen, 1923.
abbreviation: Brunner, Erlebnis.

Brunner, E. "Geschichte oder Offenbarung." *ZThK* NF, 6 (1925): 266–78.
abbreviation: Brunner, Geschichte.

Büchsel, E. *Biblisches Zeugnis und Sprachgestalt bei J. G. Hamann.* Giessen/Basel, 1988.
abbreviation: E. Büchsel.

Bürgener, K. *Die Auferstehung Jesu Christi von den Toten.* Bremen, 1970.
abbreviation: Bürgener.

Bultmann, R. "Das Problem der Hermeneutik." In *Glauben und Verstehen*, II, 2d ed., pp. 211–35. Tübingen, 1958.
abbreviation: Bultmann, GV II.

Bultmann, R. "Die Bedeutung des Alten Testaments für den christlichen Glauben." In *Glauben und Verstehen*, I, 5th ed., pp. 313–36. Tübingen, 1964.
abbreviation: Bultmann, GV I.

Bultmann, R. "Neues Testament und Mythologie." KuM, 2d ed., pp. 15–48. Hamburg-Volksdorf, 1951.

abbreviation: Bultmann, Mythologie.

Burkhardt, H. *Die Inspiration heiliger Schriften bei Philo von Alexandrien.* Giessen/Basel, 1988.
abbreviation: Burkhardt.

Calvin, J. *Unterricht in der christlichen Religion (Institutio religionis christianae).* Translated from the last edition by Prof. D. E. F. Karl Müller. 2d ed. Neukirchen, 1928.
abbreviation: Calvin, Inst.

Campenhausen, H. Freiherr v. *Die Entstehung der christlichen Bibel.* BHTh, 39. Tübingen, 1968.
abbreviation: Campenhausen.

Carson, D. A. "Hermeneutics: A brief assessment of some recent trends." *Themelios* (1980): 12–20.
abbreviation: Carson, Hermeneutics.

Carson, D. A. "Recent Developments in the Doctrine of Scripture." In Hermeneutics, 5–48.
abbreviation: Carson, Developments.

Catchpole, D. R. "Tradition History." In Marshall, 165–80.
abbreviation: Catchpole.

"Chicago Statement on Biblical Inerrancy, The." In *Journal of the Evangelical Theological Society* 21/4 (1978): 289–96.
abbreviation: Chicago

Childs, B. S. *Biblical Theology in Crisis.* Philadelphia, 1970.
abbreviation: Childs, Theology.

Childs, B. S. *Introduction to the Old Testament as Scripture.* Philadelphia, 1979.
abbreviation: Childs, Introduction.

Chmiel, J. "L'inspiration biblique chez Saint Justin." *Analecta Cracoviensia* 9 (1977): 155–64.
abbreviation: Chmiel.

Choisy, E. "Turrettini." *RE* 20 (1908): 165–71.
abbreviation: Choisy.

Cole, S. G. *The History of Fundamentalism.* Westport, 1931. Reprint 1971.
abbreviation: Cole.

Conzelmann, H., and Lindemann, A. *Arbeitsbuch zum Neuen Testament.* 3d ed. Tübingen, 1977.
abbreviation: Conzelmann-Lindemann.

Courth, F. "Die Evangelienkritik des D. Fr. Straub im Echo seiner Zeitgenossen." In Schwaiger, 60–98.
abbreviation: Courth.

Daube, D. *The New Testament and Rabbinic Judaism.* Jordan Lectures in Comparative Religion, 2. London, 1956.
abbreviation: Daube.

Delitzsch, F. *Jesaja.* 5th ed. Reprint of 3d ed., 1879. Giessen/Basel, 1984.
abbreviation: Delitzsch.

Delling, G. "Johann Jakob Griesbach." *ThZ* 33 (1977): 81–99.
abbreviation: Delling.

"Des Herrn Wort bleibt in Ewigkeit." Beschliessung der Mitgliederversammlung des Gnadauer Verbandes, *Gemeinschaft*, 68, pp. 176–77, 1981.
abbreviation: Des Herrn Wort.

Dibelius, M. *Geschichtliche und übergeschichtliche Religion im Christentum.* Göttingen, 1925.
abbreviation: Dibelius.

Diem, H. *Grundfragen der biblischen Hermeneutik.* TEH, new series, 24. München, 1950.
abbreviation: Diem.

Dilschneider, O. *Ich glaube an den Heiligen Geist.* Wuppertal, 1969.
abbreviation: Dilschneider.

Dilthey, W. "Das Problem der Religion." *Gessamelte Schriften*, VI, pp. 288–305. Leipzig/Berlin, 1924.
abbreviation: Dilthey, Schriften VI.

Dilthey, W. "Die Entstehung der Hermeneutik." *Gessamelte Schriften*, V, pp. 317–38. Leipzig/Berlin, 1924.
abbreviation: Dilthey, Schriften V.

Dinkler, E. "Bibelautorität und Bibelkritik." SgV, 193. Tübingen, 1950.
abbreviation: Dinkler.

Dobschütz, E. von. *Vom Auslegen des Neuen Testaments*. 2d ed. Göttingen, 1927.
abbreviation: Dobschütz.

Doeve, J. W. *Jewish Hermeneutics in the Synoptic Gospels and Acts.* Assen, 1954.
abbreviation: Doeve.

Drewermann, E. *Tiefenpsychologie und Exegese*, II. 2d ed. Olten/Freiburg, 1986.
abbreviation: Drewermann.

Droysen, J. G. *Grundriss der Historik.* 1858. Reprint. Halle, 1925.
abbreviation: Droysen.

Duhm, B. *Das Buch Jesaja*. Göttinger Handkommentar zum Alten Testament. Vol. 1, pt. 3, 3d ed. Göttingen, 1914.
abbreviation: Duhm.

Du Plessis, I. "Once More: The Purpose of Luke's Prologue (Lk 1, 1–4)." *Nov Testamentum* 16 (1975): 259–71.
abbreviation: Du Plessis.

Eakins, J. K. "Moses." *RExp* 74 (1974): 461–71.
abbreviation: Eakins.

Ebeling, G. "Hermeneutik." RGG, 3, 3d ed., col. 242–62, 1959.
abbreviation: Ebeling, RGG.

Ebeling, G. "Die Bedeutung der historisch–kritischen Methode für die protestantische Theologie und Kirche." *ZThK* 47 (1950): 1–46.
abbreviation: Ebeling, ZThK.

Egg, G. *Adolf Schlatters kritische Position, gezeigt an seiner Matthäusinterpretation.* AzTh, 2d series, 14. 1968.
abbreviation: Egg.

Egger, W. *Methodenlehre zum Neuen Testament.* Leipzig, 1989 (Lizenzausgabe).
abbreviation: Egger.

Elert, W. *Der christliche Glaube.* 3d ed. Hamburg, 1956.
abbreviation: Elert, Glaube.

Elert, W. *Morphologie des Luthertums.* I. München, 1931.
abbreviation: Elert, Morphologie.

Ellis, E. E. *Prophecy and Hermeneutic in Early Christianity.* 2d ed. Grand Rapids,1980.
abbreviation: Ellis.

Esking, E. *Glaube und Geschichte in der theologischen Exegese Ernst Lohmeyers.* ASNU, 18. Kopenhagen/Lund, 1951.
abbreviation: Esking.

Evertz, A. "Die Theologie im Zwielicht, Erneuerung und Abwehr." *Ev. Notgemeinschaft in Deutschland.* 19 (1984): 4–7.
abbreviation: Evertz.

Eybers, I. H. "Some Remarks About the Canon of the Old Testament." *Theologia Evangelica* (University of South Africa) 8 (1975): 88–117.
abbreviation: Eybers, Remarks.


Falckenberg, R. *Geschichte der neueren Philosophie.* 8th ed. Berlin/Leipzig, 1921.
abbreviation: Falckenberg.

Fascher, E. *Vom Verstehen des Neuen Testaments.* Giessen, 1930.
abbreviation: Fascher.

Fee, G. D. *New Testament Exegesis.* Philadelphia, 1983.
abbreviation: Fee.

Finlayson, R. A. "Contemporary Ideas of Inspiration." In *Revelation and the Bible*, pp. 219–34. London, 1959.
abbreviation: Finlayson.

Fitzmyer, J. A. *Die Wahrheit der Evangelien.* SBS, 1. 1965.
abbreviation: Fitzmyer.

Foerster, W. *Von Valentin zu Herakleon.* Giessen, 1928.
   abbreviation: Foerster.
Frankemölle, H. "Evangelist und Gemeinde. Eine methodische Besinnung." *Biblica* 60 (1979): 153–90.
   abbreviation: Frankemölle.
Frei, H. W. *The Eclipse of Biblical Narrative.* New Haven/London, 1974.
   abbreviation: Frei.
Frey, H. *Die Krise der Theologie.* Wuppertal, 1971.
   abbreviation: Frey, Krise.
Frey, H. "Um den Ansatz theologischer Arbeit." In *Abraham unser Vater* (Festschrift für Otto Michel zum 60. Geburtstag), pp. 153–80. Leiden/Köln, 1963.
   abbreviation: Frey, Ansatz.
Frick, H. *Wissenschaftliches und pneumatisches Verständnis der Bibel.* SgV, 124. Tübingen, 1927.
   abbreviation: Frick.
Fuchs, E. *Zum hermeneutischen Problem in der Theologie.* 2d ed. Tübingen, 1965.
   abbreviation: Fuchs.
Funk, R. W. "The Watershed of the American Biblical Tradition: The Chicago School, First Phase, 1892–1920." *JBL* 95 (1976): 4–22.
   abbreviation: Funk.

Gadamer, H.-G. *Wahrheit und Methode.* 3d ed. Tübingen, 1972.
   abbreviation: Gadamer.
Gallas, H. *Marxistische Literaturtheorie.* Neuwied/Berlin, 1971.
   abbreviation: Gallas.
Gass, W. *Geschichte der Protestantischen Dogmatik in ihrem Zusammenhange mit der Theologie überhaupt.* Vol. I. Berlin, 1854. Vol. IV, 1867.
   abbreviation: Gass I, etc.

Geiger, W. *Spekulation und Kritik.* FGLP, 10th series, vol. 28. München, 1964.
abbreviation: Geiger.

Geisler, N. L., ed. *Biblical Errancy.* Grand Rapids, 1981.
abbreviation: Geisler, Errancy.

Geisler, N. L. *Decide for Yourself. How History Views the Bible.* Grand Rapids, 1982.
abbreviation: Geisler, Decide.

Gemmer, A., and Messer, A. *Søren Kierkegaard und Karl Barth.* Stuttgart, 1925.
abbreviation: Gemmer/Messer.

Gennrich, P. *Der Kampf um die Schrift in der deutsch-evangelischen Kirche des neunzehnten Jahrhunderts.* Berlin, 1898.
abbreviation: Gennrich.

Gese, H. "Hermeneutische Grundsätze der Exegese biblischer Texte." In *Standort und Bedeutung der Hermeneutik in der gegenwärtigen Theologie,* edited by A. H. J. Gunneweg und H. Schröer, pp. 43–62. Bonn, 1986.
abbreviation: Gese, Grundsätze.

Gese, H. *Zur biblischen Theologie.* München, 1977.
abbreviation: Gese, Theol.

Gigon, O. *Erwägungen eines Altphilologen zum Neuen Testament.* Basel, 1972.
abbreviation: Gigon.

Girgensohn, K. *Der Schriftbeweis in der evangelischen Dogmatik einst und jetzt.* Leipzig, 1914.
abbreviation: Girgensohn, Schriftbeweis.

Girgensohn, K. "Die Grenzgebiete der systematischen Theologie." In *Greifswalder Reformgedanken zum theologischen Studium,* pp. 73–96. München, 1922.
abbreviation: Girgensohn, Reformgedanken.

Girgensohn, K. *Die Inspiration der Heiligen Schrift.* 2d ed. Dresden, 1926.

abbreviation: Girgensohn, Insp.

Girgensohn, K. *Grundriss der Dogmatik.* Leipzig/Erlangen, 1924.
abbreviation: Girgensohn, Grundriss.

Gnilka, J. "Methodik und Hermeneutik." In *Neues Testament und Kirche*, Festschrift für Rudolf Schnackenburg, pp. 458–75. Freiburg/Basel, Wien, 1974.
abbreviation: Gnilka.

Gollwitzer, H. *Kann man der Bibel glauben?* Düsseldorf, 1967.
abbreviation: Gollwitzer.

Goppelt, L. *Typos.* BFchTh, 2d series, Vol. 43, 1939. Reprint. Darmstadt, 1969.
abbreviation: Goppelt, Typos.

Grant, R. M. *A Short History of the Interpretation of the Bible.* 2d ed. New York, 1963.
abbreviation: Grant.

Grässer, E. "Antwort auf P. Stuhlmacher." *Evangelische Kommentare* (1977): 272–74.
abbreviation: Grässer, Ev Komm.

Grässer, E. "Offene Fragen im Umkreis einer Biblischen Theologie." *ZThK* 77 (1980): 200–21.
abbreviation: Grässer, ZThK.

Grillmeier, A. "Die Wahrheit der Heiligen Schrift und ihre Erschliessung." *Theologie und Philosophie* 41 (1966): 161–87.
abbreviation: Grillmeier

Gross, H., and Mussner, F. "Die Autorität der Bibel heute." *Bibel und Kirche* 26 (1971): 74-77.
abbreviation: Gross-Mussner.

Güttgemanns, E. *Offene Fragen zur Formgeschichte des Evangeliums.* BEvTh, 54. München, 1970.
abbreviation: Güttgemanns.

Gunkel, H. *Zum religionsgeschichtlichen Verständnis des Neuen Testaments.* Göttingen, 1903.
abbreviation: Gunkel.

Gunneweg, A. H. "Sola scriptura." *WPKG* 65 (1976): 2–16.
abbreviation: Gunneweg, WPKG.

Gunneweg, A. H. *Vom Verstehen des Alten Testaments.* ATD,
Ergänzungsreihe, 5, 2d ed. Göttingen, 1988.
abbreviation: Gunneweg, Verstehen.

Haacker, K., et al. *Biblische Theologie heute.* Neukirchen-Vluyn, 1977.
abbreviation: Haacker.

Harnack, A. *Die Aufgabe der theologischen Facult ä ten und die allgemeine Religionsgeschichte.* Giessen, 1901.
abbreviation: Harnack.

Hartlich, C. "Historisch-kritische Methode in ihrer Anwendung auf
Geschehnisaussagen der Hl. Schrift." *ZThK* 75 (1978): 467–84.
abbreviation: Hartlich.

Hasel, G. F. *New Testament Theology.* Grand Rapids, 1978.
abbreviation: Hasel.

Hauff, J., et al. *Methodendiskussion.* Arbeitsbuch zur Literaturwissenschaft, II. Frankfurt a.Main, 1971.
abbreviation: Hauff.

Heim, K. *Ich gedenke der vorigen Zeiten.* Hamburg, 1957.
abbreviation: Heim, Ich gedenke.

Heinisch, P. *Der Einfluss Philos auf die älteste christliche Exegese.*
Alttestamentliche Abhandlungen, I, 1/2. Münster, 1908.
abbreviation: Heinisch.

Heinrici, G. "Hermeneutik, biblische." *RE* 7 (1899):718–50.
abbreviation: Heinrici.

Hempelmann, H. *Gott—ein Schriftsteller.* Wuppertal, 1988.
abbreviation: Hempelmann.

Hengel, M. "Die Bergpredigt im Widerstreit." *ThB* 14 (1983): 53–67.
abbreviation: Hengel, ThB.

Hengel, M. *Zur urchristlichen Geschichtsschreibung.* Stuttgart, 1979.
abbreviation: Hengel, Gesch.

Henkel, H. *Goethe und die Bibel.* Leipzig, 1890.
abbreviation: Henkel.

Hennig, G. *Zurück zur Sache.* Stuttgart, 1973.
abbreviation: Hennig.

Henry, C. F. H. *God, Revelation and Authority.* Vol. II. Waco, 1976. Vol. IV. Waco, 1979.
abbreviation: Henry II or IV.

*Hermeneutics, Authority and Canon.* Edited by D. A. Carson and J. D. Woodbridge. Grand Rapids, 1986.
abbreviation: Hermeneutics.

Herodot. *Historien.* 4th ed. Stuttgart, 1971.
abbreviation: Herodot, Hist.

Hesse, F. *Das Alte Testament als Buch der Kirche.* Gütersloh, 1966.
abbreviation: Hesse, AT.

Hesse, F. "Zur Frage der Wertung und der Geltung alttestamentlicher Texte." In Probleme, 266–94.
abbreviation: Hesse.

Hirsch, E. *Geschichte der neueren evangelischen Theologie.* 5 vols. 5th ed. Gütersloh, 1975.
abbreviation: Hirsch I, II, etc.

Hirsch, E. *Hilfsbuch zum Studium der Dogmatik.* 4th ed. Berlin, 1964.
abbreviation: Hirsch, Hilfsbuch.

Hoffmann, P., et al., eds. *Orientierung an Jesus.* Josef Schmid zum 80. Geburtstag. Freiburg/Basel/Wien, 1973.
abbreviation: Hoffmann.

Hofmann, J. C. K. v. *Biblische Hermeneutik.* Edited by W. Volck. Nördlingen, 1880.
abbreviation: Hofmann.

Holl, K. "Luthers Bedeutung für den Fortschritt der Auslegungskunst." *Gesammelte Aufsätze zur Kirchengeschichte,* I, pp. 544–82. Tübingen, 1948.
abbreviation: Holl.

Holmes, M. W. "The 'majority text debate': new form of an old issue." *Themelios* 8/2 (1983): 13–19.
abbreviation: Holmes.

Holtz, G. *Die Pastoralbriefe*. ThHK, 13. 2d ed. 1972.
abbreviation: Holtz.

Hornig, G. "Die Anfänge der historisch-kritischen Theologie." FSThR, vol. 8. 1961.
abbreviation: Hornig.

Iwand, H. J. "Wider den Missbrauch des pro me als methodisches Prinzip in der Theologie." *ThLZ* 79 (1954): col. 453–58.
abbreviation: Iwand.

Jaschke, H.-J. "Das Johannesevangelium und die Gnosis im Zeugnis des Irenäus von Lyon." *MThZ* 29 (1978): 337–76.
abbreviation: Jaschke.

Jenson, R. W. "On the Problem(s) of Scriptural Authority." *Interpretation* 31 (1977): 237–50.
abbreviation: Jenson.

Jepsen, A. "Wissenschaft vom Alten Testament." In Probleme, 227–65.
abbreviation: Jepsen.

Jeremias, J. *Die Pastoralbriefe*. NTD, 3. 1st (= 2d) ed., pp. 1–56. 1935.
abbreviation: Jeremias.

Joest, W. "Die Frage des Kanons in der heutigen evangelischen Theologie." In Joest, 173–210.
abbreviation: Joest, Kanon.

Joest, W. "Fundamentalismus." *TRE* 11 (1983): 732–38.
abbreviation: Joest, TRE.

Joest, W. et al. *Was heisst Auslegung der Heiligen Schrift?* Regensburg, 1966.
abbreviation: Joest.

Josephus, F. *De Bello Judaico*. Vol. I. Edited by O. Michel und O. Bauernfeind. Darmstadt, 1959.

abbreviation: Josephus BJ.

Jung, C. G. *Briefe*, III, 1956–61. Olten/Freiburg, 1973.
abbreviation: Jung.

Jüngel, E. *Gott als Geheimnis der Welt.* 3d ed. Tübingen, 1978.
abbreviation: Jüngel.

Kähler, M. *Die Heilsgewissheit.* Biblische Zeit- und Stretfragen, VII, 9/10. Berlin-Lichterfelde, 1912.
abbreviation: Kähler, Heilsgewissheit.

Kähler, M. *Die Wissenschaft der christlichen Lehre von dem evangelischen Grundartikel aus im Abrisse dargestellt.* 3d ed. Leipzig, 1905.
abbreviation: Kähler, Wissenschaft.

Kalin, E. R. "How Did the Canon Come to Us?, A Response to the Leiman Hypothesis." In *Currents* 4 (1977): 47–51.
abbreviation: Kalin.

Käsemann, E., ed. *Das neue Testament als Kanon.* Göttingen, 1970.
abbreviation: Käsemann.

Keil, K. A. G. *Lehrbuch der Hermeneutik des Neuen Testamentes nach Grundsätzen der grammatisch-historischen Interpretation.* Leipzig, 1810.
abbreviation: Keil.

Keller, R. *Der Schlüssel zur Schrift, Die Lehre vom Wort Gottes bei Matthias Flacius Illyricus.* Arbeiten zur Geschichte und Theologie des Luthertums, NF., 5. Hannover, 1984.
abbreviation: Keller.

Kihn, H. *Theodor von Mopsuestia und Junilius Africanus als Exegeten.* Freiburg/Bresigau, 1880.
abbreviation: Kihn.

Kittel, B. "Brevard Childs' Development of the Canonical Approach." *JSOT* 16 (1980): 2–11.
abbreviation: B. Kittel.

Klassen, W. "Anabaptist Hermeneutics, The Letter and the Spirit." *MQR* 40 (1966): 83–111.
abbreviation: Klassen.

Klatt, W. *Hermann Gunkel.* FRLANT, 100. 1969.
abbreviation: Klatt.

Klauck. "Adolf Jülicher—Leben, Werk, Wirkung." In Schwaiger, 99–150.
abbreviation: Klauck.

Knopf, R. "Bibel." RGG, vol. 1, col. 1086–1131. 1909.
abbreviation: Knopf.

Köberle, A. *Gottes Offenbarung in Niedrigkeit.* Sonderdruck aus *Lutherische Kirche in der Welt.* Jahrbuch des Martin-Luther-Bundes, series 34/1987. Erlangen, 1987.
abbreviation: Köberle.

Koole, J. L. "Die Gestaltung des alttestamentlichen Kanons." *GTT* 77 (1977): 224–38.
abbreviation: Koole.

Kramer, D. G. *August Hermann Francke.* 2 pts. Halle, 1880/1882.
abbreviation: Kramer I or II.

Kraus, H.-J. *Calvins exegetische Prinzipien.* ZKG, 79, pp. 329–41. 1968.
abbreviation: Kraus, ZKG.

Kraus, H.-J. *Die Biblische Theologie.* 2d ed. Berlin (East), 1974.
abbreviation: Kraus, Bibl Theol.

Kropatscheck, F. *Das Schriftprinzip der lutherischen Kirche*, I. Leipzig, 1904.
abbreviation: Kropatscheck.

Krüger, G. *Das Dogma vom Neuen Testament.* Giessen, 1896.
abbreviation: Krüger.

Kühne, H.-J. *Schriftautorität und Kirche.* Berlin (East), 1979.
abbreviation: Kühne.

Kümmel, W. G. *Das Neue Testament, Geschichte der Erforschung seiner Probleme.* 2d ed. Freiburg/München, 1970.

abbreviation: Kümmel.

Kürzinger, J. "Lk 1: 3." *BZ*, NF, 18 (1974): 249–55.

abbreviation: Kürzinger.

Kuppler, A. "10 Punkte zur Selbstkontrolle christlichen Redens über Juden." In *Friede über Israel* 64 (1981): 115–17.

abbreviation: Kuppler.

Ladd, G. E. *A Theology of the New Testament.* Guildford/London, 1975.

abbreviation: Ladd.

Latacz, J. *Perspektiven der Gräzistik.* Freiburg I.Br./Würzburg, 1984.

abbreviation: Latacz.

Lau, F. "Orthodoxie." RGG, 4, 3d ed., col. 1719–30. 1960.

abbreviation: Lau.

Le Brun, J. "Das Entstehen der historischen Kritik im Bereich der religiösen Wissenschaften im 17. Jahrhundert." *TThZ* 89 (1980): 100–117.

abbreviation: Le Brun.

Lehmann, K. "Der hermeneutische Horizont der historisch–kritischen Exegese." In *Einführung in die Methoden der biblischen Exegese,* edited by J. Schreiner, pp. 40–80. Würzburg, 1971.

abbreviation: Lehmann.

Leiman, S. Z. *The Canonization of Hebrew Scripture.* Hamden, 1976.

abbreviation: Leiman.

Lerle, E. *Voraussetzungen der neutestamentlichen Exegese.* Frankfurt am Main, 1951.

abbreviation: Lerle.

Lessing, G. E. "Axiomata, wenn es deren in dergleichen Dingen gibt." In *Die Erziehung des Menschengeschlechts und andere Schriften.* Reclam Nr. 89685, pp. 44–79, Stuttgart.

abbreviation: Lessing, Axiomata.

Lessing, G. E. "Die Erziehung des Menschengeschlechts." In *Die*

*Erziehung des Menschengeschlechts und andere Schriften.*
Reclam Nr. 8968, pp. 7–31. Stuttgart, 1965.
abbreviation: Lessing, Erziehung.

Lessing, G. E. "Über den Beweis des Geistes und der Kraft." In *Die Erziehung des Menschengeschlechts und andere Schriften.*
Reclam, Nr. 8968, pp. 31–38. Stuttgart, 1965.
abbreviation: Lessing, Beweis.

Lewis, J. P. "What Do We Mean By Jabneh?" *JBR* 32 (1964): 125–32.
abbreviation: Lewis.

Liebing, H. "Historisch-kritische Theologie." *ZNW* 57 (1960): 302–17.
abbreviation: Liebing.

Lindemann, W. *Karl Barth und die kritische Schriftauslegung.* ThF, 54.
Hamburg-Bergstedt, 1973.
abbreviation: Lindemann.

Lindner, H. *J. G. Hamann.* Theologie und Dienst, 54. Giessen/Basel,
1988.
abbreviation: Lindner.

Lönning, I. *Kanon im Kanon.* Oslo/München, 1972 (= FGLP, 10 series,
vol. 43. Reihe, Bd. 43).
abbreviation: Lönning.

Löser, W. "Was gilt in der Kirche? Katholische Fragen an die
Evangelische Kirche." In *Evangelisch und Ökumenisch.* Jahrbuch
des Evangelischen Bundes, XXX, pp. 49–67. Göttingen, 1987.
abbreviation: Löser.

Lohfink, N. "Über die Irrtumslosigkeit und die Einheit." *Stimmen der
Zeit* 89 (1963/64): 161–81.
abbreviation: Lohfink.

Longenecker, R. N. *Biblical Exegesis in the Apostolic Period.* Grand
Rapids, 1975.
abbreviation: Longenecker.

Lotz, D. W. "Sola Scriptura: Luther on Biblical Authority."
*Interpretation* 35 (1981): 258–73.
abbreviation: Lotz.

Ludwig, E. *Schriftverständnis und Schriftauslegung bei Johann Albrecht Bengel.* Stuttgart, 1952 (= BWKG. series 9).
abbreviation: Ludwig.

Lücke, F. *Grundriss der neutestamentlichen Hermeneutik und ihrer Geschichte.* Göttingen, 1817.
abbreviation: Lücke.

Lutz, J. L. S. *Biblische Hermeneutik.* Pforzheim, 1849 (posthum).
abbreviation: Lutz.

Luz, U. *Das Evangelium nach Matthäus (Mt 1–7).* EKK 1/1, 1985.

Machen, J. G. *Christianity and Liberalism.* Reprint. Grand Rapids, 1985.
abbreviation: Machen.

McGinley, L. J. *Form-Criticism of the Synoptic Healing Narratives.* Woodstock, 1944.
abbreviation: McGinley.

Mac Lean, J. "Jean Buenderlin, Theoricien du christianisme non-institutionnel." *RHPhR* 57 (1977): 153–66.
abbreviation: Mac Lean.

Maier, G. *Die Johannesoffenbarung und die Kirche.* WUNT, 25. Tübingen, 1981.
abbreviation: Maier, Joh-Offb.

Maier, G. *Mensch und freier Wille.* WUNT, 12. Tübingen, 1971.
abbreviation: Maier, Mensch und freier Wille.

Maier, G. "Zur neutestamentlichen Wunderexegese im 19. und 20. Jahrhundert." In *Gospel Perspectives*, vol. 6, edited by D. Wenham und C. Blomberg, pp. 49–87. Sheffield, 1986.
abbreviation: Maier, Wunderexegese.

Marshall, I. H. *Biblical Inspiration.* London/Sydney/Auckland/Toronto, 1982.
abbreviation: Marshall, Insp.

Marshall, I. H. "Historical Criticism." In Marshall, 126–38.
abbreviation: Marshall, Criticism.

Marshall, I. H., ed. *New Testament Interpretation.* Exeter, 1979.
abbreviation: Marshall.

Martin, R. P. "Approaches to New Testament Exegesis." In Marshall, 220–51.
abbreviation: Martin.

Melzer, F. *Innerung.* Kassel, 1968.
abbreviation: Melzer.

Merk, O. "Anfänge neutestamentlicher Wissenschaft im 18. Jahrhundert." In Schwaiger, 37–59.
abbreviation: Merk, Anfänge.

Merk, O. "Bibelwissenschaft II, Neues Testament." *TRE* 6 (1980): 375–409.
abbreviation: Merk, TRE.

Meyer, G. W. *Geschichte der Schrifterklärung für die Wiederherstellung der Wissenschaften.* 5 vols. Göttingen, 1802–9.
abbreviation: Meyer I, II, etc.

Meyer, R. *Bemerkungen zum literargeschichtlichen Hintergrund der Kanontheorie des Josephus.* Josephus-Studien, pp. 285–99. Göttingen, 1974.
abbreviation: R. Meyer.

Michel, K.-H. *Anfänge der Bibelkritik.* Wuppertal, 1985.
abbreviation: Michel, Anfänge.

Michel, K.-H. *Sehen und glauben.* Theologie und Dienst, 31. Wuppertal, 1982.
abbreviation: Michel, Sehen.

Mickelsen, A. B. *Interpreting the Bible.* Grand Rapids, 1963.
abbreviation: Mickelsen.

Moldaenke, G. *Schriftverständnis und Schriftdeutung im Zeitalter der Reformation.* Part I of *Matthias Flacius Illyricus,* FKGG, 9. Stuttgart, 1936.
abbreviation: Moldaenke.

Moltmann, J. "Er ist wahrhaftig auferstanden." *Evangelische Kommentare* 22/3 (1989): 13–17.

abbreviation: Moltmann, Ev Komm.

Mussner, F. "Aufgaben und Ziele der biblischen Hermeneutik." In Joest, 7–28.
abbreviation: Mussner, Aufgaben.

Mussner, F. *Geschichte der Hermeneutik von Schleiermacher bis zur Gegenwart.* Handbuch der Dogmengeschichte, I, fascicle 3c (2. Teil). Freiburg/Basel/Wien, 1970.
abbreviation: Mussner.

Mussner, F. "Kathexes im Lukasprolog." In *Jesus und Paulus*, Festschrift für Werner Georg Kümmel zum 70. Geburtstag, pp. 253–55. Göttingen, 1975.
abbreviation: Mussner, FS.

Nadler, J., ed. *J. G. Hamann, Sämtliche Werke.* 6 vols. Wien, 1949–57.
abbreviation: N I, etc.

Neill, S. *The Interpretation of the New Testament.* London/New York/Toronto, 1964.
abbreviation: Neill.

Neuer, W. *Adolf Schlatter.* Wuppertal, 1988.
abbreviation: Neuer, Schlatter.

Neuer, W. *Der Zusammenhang von Dogmatik und Ethik bei Adolf Schlatter.* Giessen/Basel, 1986.
abbreviation: Neuer, Zusammenhang.

Nitzsch, F. A. B. *Lehrbuch der evangelischen Dogmatik.* Edited by Horst Stephan. 3d ed. Tübingen, 1912.
abbreviation: Nitzsch-Stephan.

Noll, M. A., ed. *The Princeton Theology 1812–1921.* Grand Rapids, 1983.
abbreviation: Noll.

Oberman, H. A. *Spätscholastik und Reformation.* Vol. 1. Zürich, 1965.
abbreviation: Oberman.

Oehler, W. *Geschichte der deutschen evangelischen Mission*, II. Baden-Baden, 1951.
abbreviation: Oehler.

Oepke, A. "Bibloi apokryphoi im Christentum." *ThWNT* 3 (1938): 987–99.
abbreviation: Oepke, ThWNT.

Oepke, A. *Geschichtliche und übergeschichtliche Schriftauslegung*. 2d ed. Gütersloh, 1947.
abbreviation: Oepke.

Ohlig, K.-H. *Die theologische Begründung des neutestamentlichen Kanons in der alten Kirche*. Düsseldorf, 1972.
abbreviation: Ohlig.

Olson, O. K. "Flacius Illyricus." *TRE* 11 (1983): 206–14.
abbreviation: Olson.

Osborne, G. R. "Evangelical Theological Society: 1982, Annual Meeting." *TSF Bulletin* (March-April 1983): 15.
abbreviation: Osborne.

Ott, H., (ed.). *Die Antwort des Glaubens*. Stuttgart/Bertlin, 1972.
abbreviation: Ott.

Otto, W. F. "Einleitung" to Herodot, *Historien*. 4th. ed. Stuttgart, 1971.
abbreviation: Otto.


Packer, J. I. *Beyond the Battle for the Bible*. Westchester, 1980.
abbreviation: Packer, Battle.

Packer, J. I. *Fundamentalism and the Word of God*. London, 1958.
abbreviation: Packer, Fundamentalism.

Palmer, I. S. "The Authority and Doctrine of Scripture in the Thought of John Calvin." *EvQ* 49 (1977): 30–39.
abbreviation: Palmer.

Pannenberg, W. *Grundfragen systematischer Theologie*. Gessamelte Aufsätze, 2d ed. Göttingen, 1971.
abbreviation: Pannenberg.

Pannenberg, W. *Heilsgeschehen und Geschichte*. In Probleme, 295–318.
abbreviation: Pannenberg, HG.

Pedersen, S. "Die Kanonfrage als historisches und theologisches Problem." *StTh* 31 (1977): 83–136.
abbreviation: Pedersen.

Petzke, G. *Die Traditionen über Apollonius von Tyana und das Neue Testament*. Leiden, 1970.
abbreviation: Petzke.

Peukert, H. *Wissenschaftstheorie-Handlungstheorie-Fundamentale Theologie*. Düsseldorf, 1976.
abbreviation: Peukert.

PGB (= Pfarrergebetsbruderschaft [pastors' prayer brotherhood]), personal correspondence, series 92, January 1984.
abbreviation: PGB.

Philippi, F. A. *Kirchliche Glaubenslehre*. 6 vols. Stuttgart, 1854–79.
abbreviation: Philippi I, II, etc.

Picht, G., ed. *Theologie, was ist das?* Stuttgart/Berlin, 1977.
abbreviation: Picht.

Pieper, F. *Christliche Dogmatik*. Revised by D. Dr. J. T. Mueller. St. Louis, 1946.
abbreviation: Pieper.

Pinnock, C. H. *The Scripture Principle*. San Francisco, 1984.
abbreviation: Pinnock.

Pius XII (Pope). *Rundschreiben über die zeitgemässe Förderung der biblischen Studien*. Freiburg/Breisgau, 1947.
abbreviation: Pius XII.

Popkin, R. H. *The History of Scepticism from Erasmus to Descartes*. Assen, 1960.
abbreviation: Popkin.

Preus, R. *The Inspiration of Scripture*. 2d ed. Edinburgh/London, 1957.
abbreviation: Preus.

Procksch, O. *Theologie des Alten Testaments.* Gütersloh, 1949.
abbreviation: Procksch, AT.
Procksch, O. "Über pneumatische Exegese." *CuW* 1 (1925): 145–58.
abbreviation: Procksch, CuW.

Rad, G. von. "Das Alte Testament ist ein Geschichtsbuch." In *Probleme,*
11–17.
abbreviation: v. Rad.
Ramm, B. *Protestant Biblical Interpretation.* 2d ed. Boston, 1956.
abbreviation: Ramm, Interpr.
Ramm, B. *Special Revelation and the Word of God.* Grand Rapids,
1961.
abbreviation: Ramm, Rev.
Ratschow, C. H. *Lutherische Dogmatik zwischen Reformation und
Aufklärung.* 2 vols. Gütersloh, 1964/66.
abbreviation: Ratschow I or II.
Redlich, E. B. *Form Criticism.* 2d ed. London, 1948.
abbreviation: Redlich, Form Criticism.
Redlich, E. B. *The Early Traditions of Genesis.* London, 1956.
abbreviation: Redlich, Traditions.
Reinhard, J. *Die Prinzipienlehre der lutherischen Dogmatik von 1700
bis 1750 (Hollatz, Buddeus, Mosheim).* Leipzig, 1906.
abbreviation: Reinhard.
Rendtorff, R. "The 'Yahwist' as Theologian? The Dilemma of
Pentateuchal Criticism." *JSOT* (1977): 2–10.
abbreviation: Rendtorff.
Reventlow, H. "Graf, Richard Simon und seine Bedeutung für die kritische Erforschung der Bibel." In Schwaiger, 11–36.
abbreviation: Reventlow.
Richter, W. *Exegese als Literaturwissenschaft.* Göttingen, 1971.
abbreviation: Richter.
Ricoeur, P. "The Hermeneutics of Testimony." *AThR* 61 (1979): 435–61.
abbreviation: Ricoeur, AThR.

Ricoeur, P. "Toward a Hermeneutic of the Idea of Revelation." *HThR* 70 (1977): 1–37.
abbreviation: Ricoeur, HThR.

Ridderbos, H. *Begründung des Glaubens.* Wuppertal, 1963.
abbreviation: Ridderbos.

Riesenfeld, H. *The Gospel Tradition and Its Beginnings.* London, 1957.
abbreviation: Riesenfeld.

Riesner, R. *Jesus als Lehrer.* WUNT, 2d series, no. 7, 3d ed. 1988.
abbreviation: Riesner.

Robinson, J. A. T. "The New Look on the Fourth Gospel." *Studia Evangelica,* edited by K. Aland, F. L. Cross, J. Daniélou, H. Riesenfeld and W. C. van Unnik (= TU 73), pp. 338–50. Berlin, 1959.
abbreviation: Robinson, New Look.

Robinson, J. M., and Cobb, J. B. Jr., *Neuland in der Theologie.* Vol. II, *Die neue Hermeneutik.* Zürich/Stuttgart, 1965.
abbreviation: Robinson-Cobb.


Sanders, J. A. "Biblical Criticism and the Bible as Canon." *USQR* 32/3 and 4 (1977): 157–65.
abbreviation: Sanders.

Sasse, H. "Heilige Kirche oder Heilige Schrift?" In *In statu confessionis,* II, edited by F. W. Hopf, pp. 290–314. Berlin, 1976.
abbreviation: Sasse.

Sauer, G. *Jesus Sirach.* JSHRZ, III/5. 1981.
abbreviation: Sauer.

Schadewaldt, W. "Die Zuverlässigkeit der synoptischen Tradition." *ThB* 13 (1982): 201–23.
abbreviation: Schadewaldt.

Schäfer, P. "Die sog. Synode von Jamnia." *Jud.* 31 (1975): 54–64; 116–24.
abbreviation: Schäfer.

Scheel, O. *Luthers Stellung zur heiligen Schrift.* SgV, 29. Tübingen/Leipzig, 1902.
abbreviation: Scheel.

Schlatter, A. *Das christliche Dogma.* 2d ed. Stuttgart, 1923.
abbreviation: Schlatter, Dogma.

Schlatter, A. *Die Geschichte des Christus.* Stuttgart, 1923.
abbreviation: Schlatter, Christus.

Schlatter, A. *Erläuterungen zum Neuen Testament.* Vol. 2. Calw/Stuttgart, 1909.
abbreviation: Schlatter, Erläuterungen.

Schlatter A. *Rückblick auf meine Lebensarbeit.* 2d ed. Stuttgart, 1977.
abbreviation: Schlatter, Rückblick.

Schleiermacher, F. "Hermeneutik und Kritik mit besonderer Beziehung auf das Neue Testament." Edited by Friedrich Lücke. In *Friedrich Schleiermacher, sämtliche Werke*, 1. Abteilung, *Zur Theologie*, vol. 7. (= *Friedrich Schleiermacher's literarischer Nachlass, Zur Theologie*, vol. 2). Berlin, 1838.
abbreviation: Schleiermacher.

Schlingensiepen, H. *Die Wunder des Neuen Testaments.* Gütersloh, 1933.
abbreviation: Schlingensiepen.

Schloemann, M. *Siegmund Jacob Baumgarten.* Göttingen, 1974.
abbreviation: Schloemann.

Schmid, H. *Die Dogmatik der evangelisch = lutherischen Kirche.* 3d ed. Frankfurt/M. and Erlangen, 1853.
abbreviation: Schmid.

Schmidt, W. *Bibel im Kreuzverhör.* Gütersloh, 1968.
abbreviation: Schmidt, Kreuzverhör.

Schmidt, W. *Zur Inspirationsfrage.* Gotha, 1869.
abbreviation: W. Schmidt, 1869.

Schnabel, E. *Inspiration und Offenbarung.* Wuppertal, 1986.
abbreviation: Schnabel.

Schneider, E. E. "Die Wahrheit als Zentralbegriff der Theologie." *ThZ* 23 (1967): 257–66.
abbreviation: Schneider.

Schöffler, H. *Deutscher Geist im 18. Jahrhundert.* Göttingen, 1956.
abbreviation: Schöffler.

Scholder, K. "Ferdinand Christian Baur als Historiker." *Ev Th* 21 (1961): 435–58.
abbreviation: Scholder, Ev Th.

Scholder, K. *Ursprünge und Probleme der Bibelkritik im 17. Jahrhundert.* FGLP, series 10, vol. 33. München, 1966.
abbreviation: Scholder.

Schottroff, L. "How My Mind Has Changed." *Ev Th* 48 (1988): 247–61.
abbreviation: Schottroff.

Schrenk, G. *Der heutige Geiteskampf in der Frage um die heilige Schrift.* Zürich, 1952.
abbreviation: Schrenk.

Schürmann, H. *Traditionsgeschichtliche Untersuchungen zu den synoptischen Evangelien.* Düsseldorf, 1968.
abbreviation: Schürmann, Untersuchungen.

Schürmann, H. "Wie hat Jesus seinen Tod bestanden und verstanden?" In Hoffmann, 325–63.
abbreviation: Schürmann, Jesu Tod.

Schulz, W. *Der Gott der neuzeitlichen Metaphysik.* Pfullingen, 1957.
abbreviation: Schulz.

Schwaiger, G., ed. *Historische Kritik in der Theologie.* Studien zur Theologie und Geistesgeschichte des Neunzehnten Jahrhunderts, 32. Göttingen, 1980.
abbreviation: Schwaiger.

Schweizer, E. "Kanon?" *Ev Theol* 31 (1971): 339–57.
abbreviation: Schweizer, Ev Th.

Schweizer, E. "Plädoyer der Verteidigung in Sachen: Moderne Theologie versus Lukas." *ThLZ* 105 (1980): col. 241–52.
abbreviation: Schweizer, ThLZ.

Scott, J. J., Jr. "Some Problems in Hermeneutics for Contemporary Evangelicals." *JETS* 22 (1979): 67–77.
abbreviation: Scott.

Seeberg, R. "Zur Frage nach dem Sinn und Recht einer pneumatischen Schriftauslegung." *ZSTh* 4 (1927): 3–59.
abbreviation: Seeberg.

Séguenny, A. "A l'origine de la philosophie et de la théologie spirituelles en Allemagne au XVI siècle: Christian Entfelder." *RHPhR* 57 (1977): 167–81.
abbreviation: Séguenny.

Seils, M., ed. *Johann Georg Hamann, Eine Auswahl aus seinen Schriften, "Entkleidung und Verklärung."* 2d ed. Wuppertal, 1987.
abbreviation: Seils.

Semler, J. S. *Abhandlung von freier Untersuchung des Canon; nebst Antwort auf die tübingische Vertheidigung der Apocalypsis.* Halle, 1771–75.
abbreviation: Semler I, etc.

Semmelroth, O., and Zerwick, M. *Vaticanum II über das Wort Gottes.* SBS, 16. 1966.
abbreviation: Semmelroth-Zerwick.

Sierszyn, A. *Die Bibel im Griff?* Wuppertal, 1978.
abbreviation: Sierszyn.

Smalley, S. S. "Redaction Criticism." In Marshall, 181–95.
abbreviation: Smalley.

Smend, R. "Nachkritische Schriftauslegung." In *Parrhesia*, Karl Barth zum achtzigsten Geburtstag, pp. 215–37. Zürich, 1966.
abbreviation: Smend.

Smend, R. "Questions About the Importance of the Canon in an Old Testament Introduction." *JSOT* 16 (1980): 45–51.
abbreviation: Smend, JSOT.

Sneen, D. J. "An Exegesis of Luke 1:1–4 with Special Regard to Luke's Purpose as a Historian." *ET* 83 (1971/72): 40–43.
abbreviation: Sneen.

Spranger, E. *Der Sinn der Voraussetzungslosigkeit in den Geisteswissenschaften.* 3d ed. Heidelberg, 1964.
abbreviation: Spranger.

Spurgeon, C. H. *Es steht geschrieben.* Wuppertal und Kassel, 1980.
abbreviation: Spurgeon.

Stadelmann, H. *Grundlinien eines bibeltreuen Schriftverständnisses.* Wuppertal, 1985.
abbreviation: Stadelmann.

Stanton, G. N. "Presuppositions in New Testament Critiicism." In Marshall, 60–71.
abbreviation: Stanton.

Steubing, H., ed. *Bekenntnisse der Kirche.* Vol. 1. Taschenbuchauflage. Wuppertal, 1985.
abbreviation: Steubing.

Stibbs, A. M. "The Witness of the Scripture to Its Inspiration." In *Revelation and the Bible*, pp. 105–18. London, 1959.
abbreviation: Stibbs.

Stolzenburg, A. F. *Die Theologie des Jo. Franc. Buddeus und des Chr. Matth. Pfaff.* Berlin, 1926.
abbreviation: Stolzenburg.

Strasburger, H. "Die Entdeckung der politischen Geschichte durch Thukydides." In *Thukydides*, edited by H. Herter, Wege der Forschung, 98, pp. 412–76. Darmstadt, 1968.
abbreviation: Strasburger.

Strauss, L. *Die Religionskritik Spinozas als Grundlage seiner Bibelwissenschaft.* Darmstadt, 1981 (Nachdruck der Ausgabe von 1930).
abbreviation: Strauss.

Strecker, G., ed. *Das Problem der Theologie des Neuen Testaments.* Wege der Forschung, 367. Darmstadt, 1975.
abbreviation: Strecker.

Stroth, F. A. *Freymüthige Untersuchungen die Offenbarung Johannis betreffend usf.* Halle, 1771.
abbreviation: Stroth.

Stuhlmacher, P. "Der Geist der Wahrheit wird euch in alle Wahrheit leiten (Joh 16,13)." In *150 Jahre Calwer Verlag 1836–1986*, pp. 13–36. Stuttgart, 1986.
abbreviation: Stuhlmacher, Geist.

Stuhlmacher, P. *Jesus von Nazareth—Christus des Glaubens.* Stuttgart, 1988.
abbreviation: Stuhlmacher, Jesus.

Stuhlmacher, P. *Vom Verstehen des Neuen Testaments.* NTD, Ergänzungsreihe, 6, 2d ed. Göttingen, 1986.
abbreviation: Stuhlmacher, Verstehen.

Stuhlmacher, P. "Zur hermeneutischen Bedeutung von 1 Kor 2,6–16." *ThB* 18 (1987): 133–58.
abbreviation: Stuhlmacher, ThB.

Stupperich, R., (ed.). "Briefe Karl Holls an Adolf Schlatter." *ZThK* 64 (1967): 169–240.
abbreviation: Stupperich.

Sundberg, A. C. "The Bible Canon and the Christian Doctrine of Inspiration." *Interpretation* 29 (1975): 352–71.
abbreviation: Sundberg.


Tappeiner, D. A. "Hermeneutics, The Analogy of Faith and New Testament Sacramental Realism." *EvQ* 49 (1977): 40–52.
abbreviation: Tappeiner.

*125 Jahre Theologisches Seminar der Evangelisch-methodistischen Kirche 1858–1983* (Festschrift). Edited by W. Klaiber und M. Weyer. Reutlingen, 1983.
abbreviation: Theol. Seminar EmK.

Thiselton, A. C. "The New Hermeneutic." In Marshall, 308–33.
abbreviation: Thiselton.

Thurneysen, E. "Schrift und Offenbarung." *ZZ* 6 (1924): 3–30.
abbreviation: Thurneysen.

Titi Livi. *Ab urbe condita.* I. Libri I–V, edited by Robertus Maxwell Ogilvie. Oxonii, 1979.

abbreviation: T. Livius.

Torm, F. *Hermeneutik des Neuen Testaments*. Göttingen, 1930.
abbreviation: Torm.

Traub, F. "Wort Gottes und pneumatische Schriftauslegung." *ZThK*, NF, 8 (1927): 83–111.
abbreviation: F. Traub.

Travis, S. H. "Form Criticism." In Marshall, 153–64.
abbreviation: Travis.

Trillhaas, W. *Dogmatik*. Berlin, 1962.
abbreviation: Trillhaas.

Troeltsch, E. "Ueber historische und dogmatische Methode in der Theologie." *Gesammelte Schriften*, vol. 2, pp. 729–53. Aalen, 1962 (Neudruck der 2d ed. 1922).
abbreviation: Troeltsch.


Utzschneider, H. "Das hermeneutische Problem der Uneindeutigkeit biblischer Texte—dargestellt an Text und Rezeption der Erzählung von Jakob am Jabbok (Gen 32,23–33)." *Ev Th* 48 (1988): 182–98.
abbreviation: Utzschneider.


Vermes, G. "The Qumran Interpretation of Scripture in Its Historical Setting." *ALUOS* 6 (1966/8): 85–97.
abbreviation: Vermes.

Vielhauer, P. "Einleitung in das Neue Testament (Fortsetzung)." *ThR* 42 (1977): 175–210.
abbreviation: Vielhauer.

Vögtle, A. "Die Schriftwerdung der apostolischen Paradosis nach 2. Petr 1,12–15." In *Neues Testament und Geschichte* (Oscar Cullmann zum 70. Geburtstag), pp. 297–305. Zürich/Tübingen, 1972.
abbreviation: Vögtle, Schriftwerdung.

Vögtle, A. "Was heisst 'Auslegung der Schrift'?" In Joest, 29–83.
abbreviation: Vögtle, Auslegung.

Vogels, H. J. "St. Augustins Schrift *De consensu evangelistarum.*"
Biblische Studien, 13, 5. Freiburg, 1908.
abbreviation: Vogels.

Völkel, M. "Exegetische Erwägungen zum Verständnis des Begriffs
kathexes im lukanischen Prolog." *NTS* 20 (1974): 289–99.
abbreviation: Völkel.

Vorländer, K. *Philosophie der Neuzeit. Die Aufklärung.* Geschichte der
Philosophie, V. München, 1967.
abbreviation: Vorländer.


Wach, J. *Das Verstehen.* 3 vols. Tübingen, 1926–33.
abbreviation: Wach, Verstehen I or II or III.

Wach, J. "Verstehen." RGG, 5, 2d ed., col. 1570–73. 1931.
abbreviation: Wach, RGG.

Wächter, O. *Johann Albrecht Bengel.* Stuttgart, 1865.
abbreviation: Wächter.

Wagner, S. "'Biblische Theologien' und 'Biblische Theologie.'" *ThLZ*
103 (1978): col. 785–98.
abbreviation: Wagner.

Warfield, B. B. "Inspiration." In Noll, 280–88.
abbreviation: Warfield, Insp.

Warfield, B. B. "The Divine and Human in the Bible." In Noll, 275–79.
abbreviation: Warfield, Divine.

Warfield, B. B. "The Inerrancy of the Original Autographs." In Noll,
268–74.
abbreviation: Warfield, Inerrancy.

Warfield, B. B. *The Inspiration and Authority of the Bible.* London,
1951.
abbreviation: Warfield, Inspiration and Authority.

Weber, H. E. *"Eschatologie" und "Mystik" im Neuen Testament.*
BFchTh, 2d series, no. 20. Gütersloh, 1930.
abbreviation: Weber, Esch.

Weber, H. E. *Historisch = kritische Schriftforschung und Bibelglaube.* 2d ed. Gütersloh, 1914.
abbreviation: Weber, Schriftforschung.

Weber, O. *Grundlagen der Dogmatik,* I. Neukirchen-Moers, 1959.
abbreviation: O. Weber.

Weder, H. *Neutestamentliche Hermeneutik.* Zürich, 1986.
abbreviation: Weder.

Weidlich, W. "Fragen der Naturwissenschaft an den christlichen Glauben." *ZThK* 64 (1967): 241–57.
abbreviation: Weidlich.

Weinel, H. *Die Wirkungen des Geistes und der Geister im nachapostolischen Zeitalter bis auf Irenäus.* Freiburg/Leipzig/Tübingen, 1899.
abbreviation: Weinel.

Wellhausen, J. *Israelitische und jüdische Geschichte.* 6th ed. Berlin, 1907.
abbreviation: Wellhausen.

Wenham, D. "Source Criticism." In Marshall, 139–52.
abbreviation: David Wenham.

Wenham, G. J. "The place of biblical criticism in theological study." *Themelios* 14/3 (1989): 84–89.
abbreviation: Wenham.

Westermann, C., ed. *Probleme alttestamentlicher Hermeneutik.* Munich, 1960.
abbreviation: Probleme.

Westermann, C. "Zur Auslegung des Alten Testaments." In Probleme, 18–27.
abbreviation: Westermann.

Wilckens, U. "Über die Bedeutung historischer Kritik in der modernen Bibelexegese." In Joest, 85–133.
abbreviation: Wilckens.

Wille, G. "Zu Stil und Methode des Thukydides." In *Thukydides,* edited

by H. Herter. Wege der Forschung, 98, pp. 683–716. Darmstadt, 1968.
abbreviation: Wille.

Windisch, H. "Der Apokalyptiker Johannes als Begründer des neutestamentlichen Kanons." *ZNW* 10 (1909): 148–74.
abbreviation: Windisch.

Wingren, G. *Die Methodenfrage in der Theologie.* Göttingen, 1957 (= Theologie der Oekumene, 5).
abbreviation: Wingren.

Wink, W. *Bibelauslegung als Interaktion.* Stuttgart, 1976.
abbreviation: Wink.

Wolff, H. W. "Zur Hermeneutik des Alten Testaments." In *Probleme,* 140–80.
abbreviation: Wolff.

Wolter, M. "Die anonymen Schriften des Neuen Testaments." *ZNW* 79 (1988): 1–16.
abbreviation: Wolter.

Wrede, W. *Über Aufgabe und Methode der sogenannten Neutestamentlichen Theologie.* Göttingen, 1897.
abbreviation: Wrede.


Yri, N. *Quest for Authority.* Kisumu/Nairobi, 1978.
abbreviation: Yri.


Zahn, T. *Grundriss der Geschichte des Neutestamentlichen Kanons.* 2d ed. Leipzig, 1904.
abbreviation: Zahn, Grundriss.

Zöckler, O. *Der Prophet Daniel.* THBW, 17. Bielefeld/Leipzig, 1870.
abbreviation: Zöckler.

Zuntz, G. "Ein Heide las das Markusevangelium." In *Markus–Philologie,* edited by H. Cancik. WUNT, 33. 1984.
abbreviation: Zuntz.

# Endnotes

CHAPTER ONE: *Defining the Hermeneutical Task*
1. Cf. Heinrici, p. 719.
2. Cf. recently Carson, Hermeneutics, pp. 12ff.
3. Lücke, p. 18.
4. Heinrici, p. 719.
5. Dilthey, Schriften V, pp. 320, 332. Cf. Bultmann, GV II, p. 211.
6. Mussner, Aufgaben, p. 7.
7. Dilthey, Schriften V, p. 331, refers to Schleiermacher's views as "foundational."
8. Schleiermacher, p. 3.
9. J. S. Semler, "Lebensbeschreibung von ihm selbst abgefasst." Vol. 1. (Halle, 1981): 208. Cf. Heinrici, p. 737.
10. Bultmann, GV II, pp. 211, 215.
11. Ibid., p. 213. Cf. Fuchs, p. 116 ("theory of scientific understanding").
12. Harnack, p. 8.
13. Bultmann, GV II, p. 216; Lehmann, p. 61; Wach, RGG, col. 1572; Spranger, p. 21.
14. Heinrici, p. 719; cf. Torm, p. 1.
15. Lücke, p. 18; cf. p. 5.
16. Ibid., p. 4.
17. Schleiermacher, p. 32.
18. Dilthey, Schriften V, p. 331.
19. Ibid.; cf. Betti, p. 13: "inversion . . . of the creative process."
20. Torm, p. 1f.
21. According to Torm (ibid., p. 1), this "theory of interpretation" goes back to J. C. Dannhauer (1654).
22. Ricoeur, HThR, p. 23.
23. Ibid. Ricoeur's ultimate aim is then the self-understanding of the person "in front of the text" (p. 29).
24. Barth, KD I, 2, p. 512.
25. Ricoeur, HThR, p. 29.
26. Dilthey, Schriften V, pp. 331, 334.

27. Betti, pp. 43, 35.
28. Ibid., pp. 42, 30.
29. Ibid., pp. 20, 13.
30. Ibid., pp. 55, 42.
31. Cf. ibid., p. 12 and Spranger, pp. 16, 23. Already Dilthey, Schriften V, p. 319.
32. Spranger, pp. 16, 20, 23.
33. Ibid., p. 28.
34. Ibid.
35. Ibid., p. 11.
36. Dilthey, Schriften V, p. 319.
37. Oepke, p. 54.
38. So F. Traub, p. 100.
39. Cf. Wach, RGG, col. 1570; Torm, p. 3.
40. That is not even the case in Islam, which in modified form recognizes Old Testament and New Testament among the "possessors of Scripture."
41. Ricoeur, HThR, p. 26
42. With this definition we also take into account the element of the "continually fixed life utterances." This element was important to Dilthey (Schriften V, p. 319).

CHAPTER TWO: A Special Biblical Hermeneutic?

1. Cf. Liebing, pp. 307ff.; Harnack, p. 8; Hofmann, p. 1; Lutz, p. 172; Schleiermacher, p. 22.
2. The Koran does not do this but rather presupposes Old Testament and New Testament.
3. So Harnack, p. 8.
4. Girgensohn, Insp, p. 40.
5. Droysen, p. 8.
6. Fascher, p. 28.
7. Torm, p. 5. Cf. Childs, Introduction, p. 71.
8. Dilthey, Schriften V, p. 334.
9. Spranger, pp. 28, 31.
10. Schmid, p. 11, in summarization of orthodox dogmatics.
11. Cf. the essays from Bring and Holl. Cf. Gadamer, p. 262: the Enlightenment wanted "all authority to be under subjection to reason."
12. Fascher, p. 98.
13. As Fascher (ibid.) rightly states.
14. Fascher, p. 95.
15. Gadamer, p. 255.
16. E. g. in Ricoeur, HThR, pp. 27ff.
17. An example would be Conzelmann-Lindemann, p. 37.
18. Girgensohn, Schriftbeweis, pp. 37ff.
19. Ibid. p. 43; cf. Girgensohn, Insp, p. 34.
20. Cf. again Ricoeur, HThR, pp. 27ff.
21. So also Beisser, NZSTh, p. 212.
22. Lücke, pp. xi, xvii, 7. Cf. Heinrici, p. 723; Keil, p. v.

23. Procksch, CuW, pp. 150f.
24. Ibid., p. 150.
25. Oepke, p. 17. Otherwise Ricoeur, HThR, p. 37: the Bible directs itself not "to our obedience," but rather "to our imagination"; this still amounts to an appeal." Cf. Beisser, NZSTh, p. 212.
26. Ricoeur, HThR, p. 35.
27. Wingren, p. 7.
28. Weber, Schriftforschung, p. 185.
29. Jung, p. 49.
30. Bultmann, GV II, p. 232. Baur, among others, anticipates Bultmann at this point (cf. Liebing, pp. 307f.).
31. Schmid, p. 11.
32. Cf. Frei, p. 52.
33. Lessing, Beweis, p. 34. Cf. Dilthey, Schriften V, p. 317.
34. Thus Dibelius, p. 97, characterizes Christianity.
35. Harnack, p. 8.
36. Cf. on this point Michel, Sehen, pp. 39ff.
37. Cf. Moldaenke, pp. 14, 126; Gadamer, p. 163; Heinrici, pp. 723, 737; Hofmann, p. 1; Keil, p. v; Lücke, p. 6; Mussner, Aufgaben, p. 7; Oepke, p. 9.
38. Dobschütz, pp. 5, 2.

*CHAPTER THREE: The Starting Point of Hermeneutics*

1. Scholder, p. 132.
2. Cf. ibid., p. 133.
3. Ibid.
4. Schulz, pp. 34ff., 64.
5. Cf. Scholder, pp. 73f.
6. Ibid., p. 90.
7. Ibid., p. 108.
8. Ibid., p. 107.
9. Grant, p. 142. Lücke, p. 41, wants to return to this position!
10. Scholder, p. 106. Strangely, this same interest crops up today in the case of some who reject a *hermeneutica sacra* on biblical grounds.
11. Ibid., p. 105. Cf. p. 147.
12. Schulz, p. 72: *Deus est natura* (God is nature).
13. Ibid., p. 67.
14. Scholder, p. 147.
15. So a title by John Locke; cf. Frei, p. 327.
16. Taken up e.g., by D. Hume and Th. Woolston; cf. Frei, p. 328.
17. Aner cites, among others, Cherbury, Whiston, Shaftesbury, Lyttleton, Warburton, Tindal, Locke, Doddridge, Baxter, Peirce, Benson, Sykes (pp. 27f., 166, 208).
18. Aner, p. 3.
19. "combiner la raison et la révélation, sans qu'elles se contredisent l'une l'autre"; according to Aner, p. 145.
20. According to Aner, p. 200.

21. Frei, p. 55.
22. According to Schulz, p. 74.
23. Ibid., p. 76.
24. Aner, p. 4.
25. Ibid., p. 162; cf. p. 158.
26. Scholder, p. 90.
27. Droysen, p. 11.
28. Spranger, p. 28.
29. Droysen, p. 9.
30. Bultmann, GV II, p. 232; cf. p. 222.
31. Fuchs, pp. 119, 134.
32. Bultmann, GV II, p. 228.
33. Ibid., pp. 215ff.
34. Ibid., p. 235.
35. See Carson, Hermeneutics, p. 14.
36. Gadamer, p. 162.
37. Ibid., p. 168.
38. Carson, Hermeneutics, pp. 14ff. In contrast Stuhlmacher wishes to develop a "hermeneutic of consent"—a late fruit of Gadamer and Fuchs.
39. Ricoeur, HThR, pp. 27, 20.
40. Ibid., pp. 31, 34, 37.
41. Ibid., p. 37.
42. Ibid., p. 30.
43. Ibid., pp. 15, 31. He also speaks, however, of a "hermeneutic of testimony"; cf. HThR, p. 31; Ricoeur, AThR, p. 438.
44. "scriptura sacra sui ipsius interpres" (Luther WA VII, pp. 97 ff.); cf. Holl, p. 559.
45. Moldaenke, p. 12, cites Dilthey, who calls Flacius the "creator of the science of a Protestant hermeneutic."
46. Cf. Moldaenke, pp. 144f.
47. According to Schmid, p. 50.
48. Cf. Kramer II, p. 383, on Francke. It is superfluous here to cite specific passages from Bengel, who likewise held this view.
49. Philippi I, p. 86.
50. Cf. Troeltsch, pp. 729ff.
51. Stuhlmacher attempts this by adding the "principle of hearing" as a fourth standard next to Troeltsch's three (Verstehen, pp. 243ff.).
52. BELK, p. 777.
53. Cf. Schmid, p. 11.
54. Cf. here Merk, Anfänge, p. 44; Frei, p. 51.
55. Courth, pp. 63, 66.
56. Barnikol, p. 24; cf. Liebing, pp. 307f., 310; Lücke, p. 36.
57. Cf. Esking, p. 104; Egg, p. 63.
58. Bultmann, GV II, pp. 226f., 232.
59. Schulz, p. 46.
60. Even Ricoeur falls prey to this danger; HThR, p. 26.

61. Harnack, pp. 8, 12.
62. Wellhausen, p. 386.
63. Dilthey, Schriften VI, p. 288.
64. So Gunkel, p. 95; cf. p. 35 and p. 1.
65. Gunkel (ibid., p. vi) speaks of "seizure by the Spirit" and the necessary "separation from the letter."
66. Kähler, Wissenschaft, p. 390; cf. pp. 53f.
67. Packer, Battle, p. 52.
68. Packer, Fundamentalism, p. 72; cf. Packer, Battle, pp. 42, 95, 117.
69. Henry IV, p. 168.
70. Ibid., p. 191.
71. Succumbing to this danger is e.g., Jenson, p. 237. Cf. also Abraham, pp. 16ff.
72. Philippi I, p. 92.
73. E.g., Ramm, Interpr, p. 119. Cf. however also Packer, Fundamentalism, pp. 75, 96.
74. Cf. Schulz, p. 64.
75. Cf. Abraham, p. 8.
76. Lücke, p. 19. Cf. on p. 10 the lament about "the tyrannical force and sole sovereignty of historical knowledge."
77. Fascher, p. 1.
78. Cf. my essay in Gospel Persp 6, p. 75f.
79. Kähler, Heilsgewissheit, pp. 53f. Cf. again Fascher, pp. 6, 16ff. Otherwise e.g., Lücke, p. 144: we may proceed only "according to the laws of historical possibility."

CHAPTER FOUR: *Theological Hermeneutics as Science*
1. Cf. Peuckert, p. 69.
2. Cf. Grant, p. 142.
3. Girgensohn, Insp, p. 14.
4. Cf. ibid., p. 34.
5. Cf. Girgensohn, Schriftbeweis, p. 36.
6. So however Fascher, p. 6; cf. p. 18.
7. Cf. Harnack, p. 6.
8. Krüger, p. 4; cf. Weinel, p. vi.
9. Harnack, p. 16; cf. p. 8, where he—in contrast to Troeltsch—recognizes the "entirely singular" in history.
10. Ibid., p. 22.
11. Cf. Oepke, p. 41. Of interest here is the comparison with the Catholic "Instructio de historica Evangeliorum veritate" of April 21, 1964 (Fitzmyer, p. 39).
12. Spranger, p. 19.
13. Blank, pp. 3, 5.
14. Bultmann, GV II, p. 235. Cf. Klauck, p. 99.
15. Cf. here Blank, p. 3; Richter, p. 9.
16. Contemporary Protestant theology wields "criticism" so dogmatically that it hinders this necessary self-criticism.

17. Spranger, p. 21.
18. Blank, p. 6.
19. Ricoeur, HThR, p. 37
20. Dibelius, p. 96. Cf. Harnack, pp. 19ff.
21. Wrede, p. 10.
22. Cf. Richter, pp. 12, 11.
23. Harnack, pp. 8, 19ff.
24. Ibid., p. 18.
25. Blank, pp. 4f. Cf. Mickelsen, p. 44; Lehmann, p. 61.
26. Cf. Scholder, pp. 48ff.
27. Aner, p. 4.
28. Wach, RGG, col. 1571.
29. Spranger, p. 6. Cf. pp. 9f., 17.
30. Ibid., p. 17.
31. Gadamer, p. xxii.
32. Ibid., p. xxi.
33. Dinkler, p. 7. Cf. Hesse, AT, p. 20; Jepsen, p. 232. More reservedly Stanton, pp. 66, 69.
34. So also Stuhlmacher, Verstehen, pp. 253ff.
35. Oepke, p. 41. Cf. p. 12.
36. Girgensohn, Insp, p. 15.
37. Cf. A. Schlatter's interaction with P. Jäger.
38. Cf. Schulz, pp. 92, 86.
39. Droysen, pp. 21f.
40. Ibid.
41. Erasmus. Cf. Grant, p. 142.

*CHAPTER FIVE: The Interpreter*

1. Cf. Merk, Anfänge, pp. 42f.
2. Cf. Heinrici, p. 737 as well as Merk, Anfänge, p. 43; Seeberg, p. 47.
3. Barr, p. 114.
4. Ibid., p. 111.
5. Weber, Schriftforschung, p. 185; likewise Bultmann, GV II, p. 216; F. Traub, p. 97. For the same view much earlier see Hofmann, p. 23.
6. Weber, Schriftforschung, p. 185.
7. "préjugés légitimes"; cf. Gadamer, p. 255.
8. Dilthey, Schriften V, p. 319.
9. Spranger, p. 16.
10. Procksch, CuW, p. 150, for whom however this is not enough. Cf. Dibelius, p. 97.
11. F. Traub, p. 100.
12. Among others Betti, p. 53; Dilthey, Schriften V, p. 332; Dobschütz, pp. 50, 28; Droysen, p. 9; Heinrici, p. 720; Keil, p. x; Torm, p. 13; Wach, RGG, col. 1573.
13. So Dilthey, Schriften V, p. 318.
14. So Weinel, p. v.
15. So Droysen, p. 10.

16. So F. Traub, p. 100; cf. Keil, p. x.
17. So Heinrici, p. 720.
18. So Dobschütz, p. 51.
19. So Wach, RGG, col. 1573; Torm, p. 13.
20. So Bultman, GV II, p. 217. Cf. a certain parallel in Ricoeur, HThR, p. 30.
21. Dobschütz, p. 28.
22. Cf. Dilthey, Schriften V, p. 330, and Torm, p. 2.
23. Dilthey, Schriften V, p. 330.
24. Ibid., p. 332.
25. Cf. the role that "intellectual breadth" (capacity) plays in Spranger (p. 16)!
26. Cited in Heinrici, p. 720.
27. Droysen, p. 22.
28. Treitschke, cited in Heinrici, p. 720.
29. Philippi I, p. 214; cf. p. 215.
30. Ibid., p. 199; cf. p. 111.
31. Here see Stuhlmacher, Verstehen, pp. 135ff., 238ff. He decisively rejects such a theology.
32. Grant, p. 36.
33. De princ I, praef 3, according to Campenhausen, p. 359.
34. On Calvin cf. Palmer, p. 35; Grant, p. 134.
35. Holl, p. 547, n. 4, from WA 4, p. 305. Cf. Holl, pp. 547ff.; Bring, p. 16; Torm, p. 16; Procksch, AT, p. 36; Grant, p. 132; Scheel, p. 36.
36. Cf. Reinhard, p. 17. On Flacius cf. Moldaenke, pp. 486ff.
37. Reinhard, pp. 52f.
38. Ibid., p. 85.
39. Francke's own statement from 1692 according to Kramer I, p. 5.
40. Francke according to Kramer II, p. 388.
41. Ibid.
42. Ibid., pp. 389, 392.
43. Cf. Heinrici, p. 736; Kramer II, p. 394.
44. Cf. Frei, p. 38; Heinrici, pp. 736f.
45. Lücke, pp. vff.
46. Ibid., pp. vii, ix.
47. Ibid., p. 46.
48. Ibid.
49. Cf. Lutz, p. 84; Philippi I, pp. 86, 214f., 226f.
50. Kähler, Wissenschaft, p. 35; cf. Esking, p. 37.
51. Weber, Schriftforschung, p. 186.
52. Seeberg, p. 44; Beisser, NZSTh, p. 213.
53. Examples: Packer, Fundamentalism, p. 111; Ramm, Interpr, pp. 12f.
54. Cf. Girgensohn, Insp, pp. 6f.; Procksch, CuW, pp. 145, 150f.; Frey, Ansatz, pp. 161, 167ff.
55. Cf. Fitzmyer, p. 37.
56. So Stuhlmacher, Verstehen, pp. 135ff., 221, 238ff.
57. Cf. Holl, p. 559.

58. Cf. my essay *Heiliger Geist und Schriftauslegung* (*Holy Spirit and Biblical Interpretation*) (Wuppertal, 1983), p. 22; also Bring, pp. 14ff.
59. Calvin, Inst. I, 3, 2.
60. Ibid. I, 3, 3; 4, 4.
61. Ibid. I, 5, 11, 13.
62. Cf. Heinrici, p. 734.
63. Cf. Reinhard, pp. 17, 20.
64. Cf. ibid., p. 16.
65. Lutz, p. 93; similarly Fascher, p. 23.
66. Cf. Philippi I, p. 227; Hofmann, p. 30; Fascher, p. 23.
67. Cf. Bring, pp. 15f. Cf. also Procksch, CuW, p. 151; Torm, p. 14; F. Traub, p. 100; Seeberg, pp. 43f.; Vögtle, Auslegung, p. 29.
68. Spranger, pp. 17, 21.
69. Barnikol, p. 10.
70. Jepsen, pp. 227f.
71. Dibelius, p. 97.
72. Dobschütz, p. 64; cf. pp. 28, 62.
73. Girgensohn, Schriftbeweis, p. 65.
74. Ibid. p. 69.
75. Inst I, 7, 5. Cf. the entire context of Inst I, 2–8.
76. Reinhard, p. 52.
77. Ibid.
78. Cf. Hofmann, p. 101. Cf. on the same point Hollaz in Reinhard, p. 17; also Luther according to Holl, p. 555.
79. Hoffmann, p. 101.
80. Kähler, Wissenschaft, p. 390.
81. Girgensohn, Schriftbeweis, p. 63.
82. Ibid., p. 72.
83. Torm, p. 22.
84. Cf. e.g., regarding Bengel my Joh-Offb, pp. 422f.; also Lutz, pp. 84f.
85. Stuhlmacher, Verstehen, p. 136. Similarly Fascher, p. 26.
86. E.g., Fuchs falls prey to this misunderstanding: "Theological interpretation is existential to the extent it is scientific, i.e., proceeds methodically" (p. 134).
87. Frick, p. 22.
88. Ricoeur, HThR, p. 30.
89. Ibid.
90. Likewise e.g., Stadelmann emphasizes the "encounter" factor; on p. 121 he even speaks of a "hermeneutic of encounter." Cf. already Schrenk, p. 7.
91. But Hafenreffer in his Loci already called the Holy Scriptures "epistolae de patria aeterna nobis transmissae" (Elert, Morphologie, pp. 157, 2).
92. Cf. my Joh-Offb, pp. 345, 414f.
93. Oepke, p. 17.
94. Cf. Oepke's view in contrast to that of F. Traub, p. 27.
95. Stanton, p. 65.
96. Stadelmann, p. 121.

97. Contra Conzelmann-Lindemann, p. 37, and already Reimarus (Wilckens, p. 98).
98. Ricoeur, HThR, p. 37.
99. Ibid.
100. Girgensohn, Insp, p. 18.
101. Girgensohn, Schriftbeweis, p. 63 (citing Bengel). Representing a similar view have been Frey, Ansatz (p. 170); Packer, Battle (pp. 11, 13f.); and Ramm, Interpr (p. 87); as well as Vögtle, Auslegung (p. 50).
102. Elert, Glaube, p. 194.
103. Statements like "we cannot revert to the time before the Enlightenment" are foolish. For factually everyone who takes the Bible seriously reverts "to the time before the Enlightenment"—and this was as true at the time of the Enlightenment as it is today!
104. Barmen Declaration of 1934, first thesis, according to Steubing, p. 300.
105. Cf. my Joh-Offb, p. 418; Reinhard, pp. 61ff., 65.
106. Philosophically parallel is the plea of e.g., Gadamer for a new, favorable assessment of "tradition" (pp. 265f.).
107. Marshall, Criticism, p. 134; similarly Girgensohn, Insp, p. 28.
108. Luther puts it more strongly: "Scripturas sacras sciat se nemo gustasse satis, nisi centum annis cum Prophetis Ecclesias gubernarit" ("Let no one suppose he has fed enough on Scripture who has not led the church for a century using the prophets"); on this point cf. Torm, p. 24. In any case our position is not the same as that of the so-called Erlangen theology, in which Christian experience played a more dominant role (see e.g., Hofmann, p. 100, among many passages that could be cited).
109. Fascher (pp. 108, 132) also uses the term transsubjective.
110. Hofmann, p. 30.
111. Ibid., p. 100.
112. On the "principle of effect in history" (*Wirkungsgeschichte*) cf. Gadamer, pp. 284ff. Cf. also Seeberg, p. 9.
113. Mussner, p. 21.
114. Ibid.
115. Fitzmyer, p. 37.
116. Ibid., pp. 39, 37, 51. Cf. p. 47 and Gnilka, p. 460.
117. Vögtle, Auslegung, p. 60.
118. Diem, p. 43.
119. Ibid.
120. Cf. Kramer II, p. 396.
121. Dobschütz, p. 64. Cf. Frey, Ansatz, pp. 177f.; Ramm, Interpr, pp. 88f.
122. E. g. in Wrede, pp. 15, 47. Cf. also Jepsen, p. 227 (regarding Wellhausen); Krüger, p. 8.
123. Lücke, p. 41.
124. Cf. on this point Stadelmann, pp. 78ff.
125. Cf. my Joh-Offb, p. 423.

*CHAPTER SIX: Ways of Understanding Revelation*

1. Gunkel, pp. 10f.; Wilckens, p. 133.
2. Torm, p. 37. Cf. the long list of predecessors that Karl August Gottlieb Keil looked back on in 1810.
3. Cf. Ricoeur, HThR, p. 30.
4. Keil, pp. 7f.
5. Cf. Schleiermacher, p. 21.
6. Keil, p. 8.
7. Dilthey, Schriften V, p. 322.
8. Cf. Heinrici, p. 738.
9. Cf. Torm, p. 29.
10. Wilckens, p. 133.
11. Theodosius Harnack according to Gennrich, p. 87.
12. Cf. Gennrich, p. 60; Oepke, pp. 53f. A similar view was expressed in Protestant Scholasticism; cf. Preus, pp. 164ff.
13. Philippi I, p. 224, cf. pp. 222ff.; similarly Lutz, p. 83: "Every now and then it happens that farmers and young girls know how to interpret the Scripture better than all the scholarly commentaries."
14. Cf. Kramer I, p. 56.
15. Spranger, p. 16.
16. Cf. Barr, p. 84.
17. Barr, p. 108.
18. Mussner, Aufgaben, p. 25.
19. Bring, p. 40.
20. Oepke, p. 27.
21. Westermann, p. 20.
22. Torm, p. 22.
23. Egger, pp. 20ff.; Lehmann, p. 67. Cf. Frankemölle, p. 155; Mussner, p. 27; Vögtle, Auslegung, p. 36.
24. Cf. Pius XII, p. 35.
25. Longenecker, p. 28.
26. Ibid., pp. 29ff. Cf. Grant, p. 40.
27. Cf. Longenecker, pp. 67ff.; Doeve, pp. 91ff,. 206; Grant, pp. 24ff.
28. Longenecker, p. 39, according to W. H. Brownlee.
29. Cf. Grant, pp. 31, 54f.; Longenecker, p. 126.
30. Grant, p. 65. Cf. Campenhausen, p. 109.
31. Cf. Grant, p. 62.
32. Ibid., pp. 70ff.; Jaschke, p. 346. Tertullian was also careful (Campenhausen, pp. 328ff.).
33. Grant, pp. 79f., 81ff.
34. Cf. Dinkler, p. 12; Grant, pp. 84f.; Campenhausen, p. 361; Heinrici, p. 730.
35. Cf. my Joh-Offb, pp. 87ff. and Grant, p. 89.
36. Grant, p. 93.
37. Ibid., p. 97.
38. Ibid., p. 98.
39. Cf. my Joh-Offb, pp. 112ff.

40. Cf. Vogels, p. 79.
41. According to Vogels, p. 80, this conception of Augustine's contrasts to that of other church fathers. Cf. further Grant, pp. 109ff.
42. Cf. Heinrici, p. 734; Grant, p. 119; Dinkler, p. 13; Hofmann, pp. 15f.
43. Cf. the example involving Jerusalem (see Dinkler and Grant in previous note). Jerusalem is #1) the capital of Palestine (historical), #2) the church (dogmatic), #3) an ordered political commonwealth (ethical), and #4) eternal life (eschatological).
44. Cf. Grant, pp. 116ff. E.g., Thomas Aquinas emphasized the literal sense (p. 122).
45. Bring, pp. 9f. Cf. Kropatscheck, pp. 446ff.
46. According to Heinrici, p. 734.
47. Scheel, p. 38. Cf. Grant, p. 132.
48. According to Torm, p. 24. Cf. Grant, p. 132.
49. Cf. here Holl, p. 551 and WA 10, p. 169.
50. Scheel, p. 38.
51. Holl, p. 548.
52. Ibid., p. 553. Cf. Grant, pp. 129ff.
53. Cf. on this point Grant, p. 128.
54. Cf. Abrey, p. 199 on Michael Meckel.
55. Cf. Mac Lean, pp. 158ff. and my Joh-Offb, pp. 216f.
56. Cf. Séguenny, pp. 167ff. and my Joh-Offb, p. 217.
57. Heinrici, p. 735.
58. Moldaenke, p. 248.
59. Ibid., pp. 241f., 215, 9.
60. On these concepts cf. Frei, p. 1.
61. Schmid, pp. 45ff.
62. Cf. Frei, p. 38.
63. Cf. my Joh-Offb, p. 325.
64. Ibid., p. 424.
65. Ibid., pp. 460ff.
66. Frei, pp. 6f.
67. Grant, pp. 146ff.
68. Ibid., p. 154.
69. Nevertheless Schleiermacher defended allegorical interpretation (Schleiermacher, p. 21). Interestingly, Hofmann rejected it (pp. 11ff.).
70. Lutz, pp. 156ff.
71. Girgensohn, Insp, p. 9.
72. Ibid.
73. Cf. the concept of a "graduated approach" (*Stufengang*) in Girgensohn, Insp, p. 23.
74. Cf. here Girgensohn, Insp, pp. 6, 8, 22f., 27; Girgensohn, Schriftbeweis, pp. 63, 73; Oepke, pp. 17, 36; Procksch, AT, p. 36; Schrenk, p. 7; Frey, Ansatz, p. 169. Cf. also Weber, Schriftforschung, p. 48.
75. Girgensohn, Insp, pp. 46ff.
76. Cf. also Oepke, p. 43.

77. Pius XII, p. 35.
78. Vögtle, Auslegung, p. 49, with Schlier. Cf. the first hermeneutical canon in Betti, p. 14.
79. Cf. here G. Schrenk, *Studien zu Paulus*, AThANT, 28, 1955, pp. 107ff.
80. Ibid., p. 125.
81. Long ago Flacius endorsed a primal knowledge possessed by man which can detect divine revelation (cf. Moldaenke, p. 190). We differ from Flacius, however, in placing the accent on the use God makes of man's knowledge rather than on that which lies within human competence.
82. Betti, p. 19.
83. Torm, pp. 208ff.
84. Martin, pp. 220ff. Sanders' (pp. 159ff.) suggestions suffer from lack of systematic clarity.
85. According to Le Brun, p. 106.
86. Spranger, p. 18.
87. Cf. Gennrich, pp. 35f.
88. Lutz, pp. 72ff.
89. Weber, Schriftforschung, p. 35; similarly Diem, p. 38.
90. Beisser, NZSTh, p. 192. A reconciliation of the two disciplines will not come about as easily as Stuhlmacher, who calls for discussion between them, appears to expect (Verstehen, p. 252). Cf. already the lament by Lücke, pp. 45f.
91. Examples include e.g., Clévenot, Gallas, Hauff (pp. 83ff.).
92. Cf. already Philippi I, pp. 87ff.
93. Cf. Ro 5:14; Ps 95:7ff.; Heb 3:7ff.; 1Pe 2:21. See also Grant, pp. 43, 54f.
94. Cf. once more Longenecker's investigation as well as the commentaries at the verses cited and Goppelt, Typos, passim.
95. Cf. Wolff, p. 162.
96. Aner, pp. 155, 152.
97. Cf. my Joh-Offb, p. 450.
98. Cf. J. Jeremias, *Die Gleichnisse Jesu*, 6th ed. (Göttingen, 1962), pp. 87f.
99. Cf. especially Longenecker, pp. 37, 28.
100. Cf. D. Flusser, *Die rabbinischen Gleichnisse und der Gleichniserzähler Jesus*, pt. 1 (Bern/Frankfurt/Las Vegas, 1981), pp. 119ff.
101. So also Girgensohn, Insp., p. 46.
102. E.g., Da 2:36ff.; 4:3ff.; 7:16ff.; 8:15ff.; Zec 1:9ff.; 2:4; 4:11ff.
103. Cf. Longenecker, p. 39.
104. Cf. my investigation of Revelation, esp. p. 372 (Petersen), p. 422 (Bengel), p. 492 (Delitzsch), pp. 494ff. (Auberlen).
105. Cf. my Joh-Offb, p. 431.
106. Cf. L. Goppelt, "Heilsoffenbarung und Geschichte nach der Offenbarung des Johannes," ThLZ 77 (1952): 513ff.
107. Cf. my Joh-Offb, p. 206.
108. Cf. Frankemölle, p. 155. Here we part company with the strict separation that e.g., Wrede (p. 8) demanded between New Testament exegesis and dogmatics.

*CHAPTER SEVEN: The Inspiration of Scripture*

1. Girgensohn, Insp, p. 3.
2. Gennrich, pp. 88f. Cf. Gunkel, p. 5; Girgensohn, Insp, p. 4.
3. Merk, Anfänge, p. 41.
4. Ibid., p. 44.
5. Ibid., p. 49.
6. Aner, p. 175.
7. Schleiermacher, pp. 22ff.; Gennrich, pp. 29ff.
8. Aner, p. 222; cf. pp. 220ff.
9. Cf. Gennrich, p. 23.
10. Gennrich, pp. 44ff., 50ff.
11. Ibid., pp. 44ff.
12. Ibid., pp. 50ff.
13. Ibid., pp. 75ff.
14. Similarly Schleiermacher; cf. Gennrich, pp. 30f.
15. Gennrich, p. 87.
16. According to Gennrich, p. 105.
17. Ibid., p. 111.
18. Ibid., pp. 117f.
19. Ibid., p. 113.
20. Wrede, p. 8.
21. Ibid., p. 9.
22. Ibid., p. 8.
23. Funk, pp. 9ff.
24. E. g. B. Lang, *Ein Buch wie kein anderes* (Kevelaer/Stuttgart, 1980), pp. 213ff.
25. Frick, p. 5.
26. Elert, Glaube, pp. 169, 171.
27. Joest, Kanon, p. 184.
28. Dinkler, p. 16.
29. So Schmidt, Kreuzverhör, p. 50.
30. Finlayson, p. 221.
31. E. g. Gennrich, p. 80.
32. The "Gnadauer Verband" is the major pietistic body within the German state church.
33. Des Herrn Wort, p. 177.
34. Cf. Philippi I, pp. 183ff. On Gaussen cf. Gennrich, pp. 41ff.
35. E. g. W. Schmidt (1869): the Protestant Scholastic doctrine was present among the Reformers "only in an incomplete, raw form" (p. 5).
36. Pius XII, p. 7.
37. Ibid., pp. 33, 43, 45.
38. Fitzmyer, p. 45: "mentes quoque sanctorum . . . gubernans et regens" ("governing and leading also the understanding of the saints").
39. Ibid., p. 47.
40. E. g. Stuhlmacher, Verstehen, pp. 47ff.; Childs, Theology, p. 103.
41. This is all the more true in light of recent declarations from evangelicals in the

German-speaking sphere. See e.g., Stadelmann, pp. 14ff.; Schnabel, pp. 103ff.; Sierszyn, pp. 39f.

42. Cf. here Seeberg, pp. 16f.

43. This is the locus classicus of the doctrine of inspiration. From here, and from the Latin translation "inspirata," comes the concept of "inspired" Scripture.

44. Stuhlmacher, Verstehen: "Every Scripture [passage] is filled with God's Spirit" (p. 54); Jeremias: "Every Scripture passage originates in God's Spirit" (p. 44); Holtz: "Every Bible passage is given [to the human writer] by God's Spirit" (p. 183). Tholuck and Wilhelm Schmidt (1869) are advocates of a restrictive translation: "If this or that Scripture or Scripture passage is breathed out from God, then it is also useful . . ." (Schmidt, p. 39). Similarly Schrenk, 1869, pp. 28f.

45. Cf. Schmid, p. 26; Preus, pp. 36f.

46. Justin would emphasize this some years later (Chmiel, p. 161).

47. For W. Schmidt (1869) is Jn 10:35 merely a view of Jesus' opponents (p. 40); according to Abraham, p. 98, Jesus speaks only ad hominem. Both these views evade the obvious.

48. Cf. Leiman, pp. 19ff.

49. Cf. Ramm, Rev, pp. 164ff.

50. See here ibid., Rev, pp. 166, 176.

51. Cf. once more ibid., Rev, p. 165.

52. A list of passages is impossible due to their large number. Examples are 1Sa 10:10ff.; Jer 1:4ff.; Eze 2:2; Da 4:6.

53. Longenecker, pp. 19, 48.

54. Likewise Pedersen, p. 96.

55. It is not insignificant that 1Co 2:10 was a key text for the doctrine of inspiration among dogmaticians of past eras; cf. Schmid, p. 26.

56. Cf. Sneen, p. 40.

57. Likewise Pedersen, pp. 94ff.

58. Cf. the discussion in Du Plessis, p. 269; Kürzinger, p. 254; Mussner, FS, pp. 254f.; Sneen, p. 41.

59. Cf. Du Plessis, pp. 270f.; Schadewalt, p. 223; Sneen, p. 42.

60. Du Plessis, pp. 270f. Similarly Sneen, p. 40.

61. Cf. Du Plessis, pp. 262f., 268; Sneen, pp. 40f.; Kürzinger, p. 254.

62. Cf. my investigation along these lines in D. Wenham, ed., *Gospel Perspectives*, vol. 6 (Sheffield, 1985), pp. 85–128.

63. Regarding eyewitness status see 1Pe 5:1; 2Pe 1:16ff. James and Jude qualify by virture of being the Lord's brothers (cf. Jude 1).

64. Stibbs, p. 116.

65. Sundberg, p. 352.

66. W. Schmidt, 1869, p. 48.

67. According to Gennrich, p. 53.

68. Stuhlmacher, Verstehen, p. 57.

69. Cf. Schleiermacher, pp. 23f.; Gennrich, pp. 30f.; Mussner, p. 7.

70. Schleiermacher, p. 24.

71. Gennrich, p. 31.

72. According to Gennrich, p. 54.
73. Cf. Weber, Schriftforschung, p. 3 with p. 7; Girgensohn, Insp, p. 57 with p. 64; Abraham, pp. 32ff.; Stuhlmacher, Verstehen, pp. 47ff.; Schrenk, p. 33.
74. Abraham, p. 63.
75. See "The Answer of Revelation" above, pp. 101-108.
76. Cf. Schmid, p. 24.
77. Chmiel, p. 160.
78. According to Campenhausen, p. 364.
79. Moldaenke, pp. 300, 314. On Protestant Scholasticism cf. Preus, p. 33.
80. Beck, Leitfaden, p. 7.
81. Fitzmyer, p. 45.
82. Gennrich, p. 19.
83. Cf. Funk, p. 14.
84. Ricoeur, AThR, p. 454.
85. Ricoeur, HThR, p. 17.
86. Ibid., p. 18.
87. Gennrich, p. 19.
88. Cf. Preus, p. 36.
89. Ibid. p. 35. Cf. p. 47 regarding Jesuits.
90. Ibid., p. 45.
91. Aner, p. 220.
92. E. Bloch, *Werkausgabe*, vol. 5, 1st ed., 1985, p. 1113.
93. Cf. Gennrich, pp. 50ff. and pp. 28ff. Girgensohn, Insp, p. 56, heads in the same direction.
94. Gennrich, p. 34.
95. Ibid., pp. 44ff.
96. Lutz, p. 94.
97. According to Gennrich, pp. 95ff. Similarly W. Schmidt, 1869 ("the didactic and historical" are not inspired); Weber, Schriftforschung, pp. 7ff.; Girgensohn, Insp, p. 64 (only the "pneumatic" is inspired).
98. Cf. Vogels, p. 66. For Protestant Scholasticism see Schmid, p. 24.
99. The earlier view is still detectable in Mosheim (Reinhard, pp. 86ff.).
100. Here 2Ti 3:16 was translated restrictively (Tholuck, W. Schmidt, Schrenk): "Every Scripture that is inspired . . .", not "All Scripture is inspired."
101. Gennrich raises this question on pp. 94f.
102. Cf. Philippi's criticism, I, p. 182.
103. In view of Mt 5:17f. Grant speaks of "a rigorous doctrine of scripture." The toning down of this passage to which e.g., W. Schmidt, 1869, pp. 40f., resorts in order to justify his rejection of verbal inspiration does not sound very convincing. Schmidt suggests that Mt 5:18 applies only to the law and that Jn 10:35 is only a principle held by Jesus' opponents.
104. Campenhausen, p. 35; cf. pp. 33ff.
105. Ibid., p. 81.
106. Cf. the investigation by Chmiel.
107. Campenhausen, pp. 121ff., 320ff. (Tertullian shows "acceptance of a formal inspiration," p. 324.) Cf. Grant, pp. 70ff.

108. Campenhausen, p. 354. Cf. Grant, pp. 81ff. Origen worked this out most of all in De principiis, IV.
109. Campenhausen, pp. 355, 362, 364, 367, 370.
110. Vogels, p. 72.
111. The quote is from Epist 82, 3, 24. Cf. Vogels, pp. 72ff., 53f.
112. Vogels, pp. 65f.
113. Ibid., pp. 69f.
114. Tract in Joann 30, 1; Serm 85, 1,1. Cf. Vogels, p. 69.
115. Kropatscheck, p. 425.
116. Ibid.
117. Ibid., pp. 439f. Cf. however the very much more differentiated presentation by Oberman, pp. 335ff. Regarding Biel's stress on the authority of Scripture see Oberman, p. 365. Cf. however also Grant, pp. 122ff.
118. Bring, p. 23. Likewise Grant, p. 135.
119. Scheel, p. 69. Lotz makes a similar judgment (p. 267).
120. Cf. Scheel, pp. 76f.
121. Cf. Palmer, pp. 31ff.; Childs, Introduction, p. 44.
122. Moldaenke, p. 300. Cf. also Augustine, DCD XX, 1; XVIII, 43; En in ps 144; Serm 85,1,1. When Moldaenke, pp. 300, 303, opines that according to Flacius it is not the Scriptures but only their authors that are inspired, he is refuted by Flacius himself.
123. Cf. Schmid, pp. 20ff.
124. So Hollaz (Schmid, p. 25); cf. Quenstedt, according to Preus, p. 35.
125. Cf. Schmid, p. 25; Preus, p. 40; Philippi I, p. 183.
126. Schmid, p. 20. Cf. Preus, p. 53 (Schröder); Reinhard, p. 7.
127. Preus, p. 27 (Quenstedt); cf. Reinhard, p. 7 (Hollaz).
128. Cf. Schrenk, p. 9; Girgensohn, Insp, p. 3.
129. Cf. recently Stadelmann, pp. 14ff.; Schnabel, pp. 160ff. Cf. also Schrenk, p. 26; Stuhlmacher, Verstehen, pp. 30ff. On Catholic doctrine cf. the dogmatic constitution on divine revelation produced during Vatican II (excerpts in Ott, pp. 42f.).
130. Ott, p. 46.
131. Ibid.
132. Cf. here Gennrich, p. 46 (regarding Beck, Lange, Stier) as well as Girgensohn, Insp, p. 25 (regarding Hamann) and Frey, Ansatz, p. 157.
133. So Hofmann, p. 19.
134. Thus e.g., Schrenk, pp. 33ff.; Abraham, p. 56; Gollwitzer, pp. 16f.; W. Schmidt, 1869, pp. 35ff.
135. Hofmann, pp. 23, 30, 75ff. Similarly Beck (Gennrich, p. 56).
136. Girgensohn, Insp, p. 3.
137. Seeberg, p. 22.
138. Girgensohn, Grundriss, pp. 61ff. Cf. Schrenk, p. 36.
139. Moldaenke, pp. 377f.
140. Cf. Preus, pp. 35f. Schrenk (p. 35) therefore flails at empty space.
141. Cf. Preus, pp. 60ff.; Schmid, p. 26.
142. Cf. my Joh Offb, pp. 416f. Philippi takes the same tack (I, pp. 167ff.).

143. So however Schrenk, pp. 30f.
144. Schrenk, pp. 30f., makes this claim.
145. Abraham, pp. 27f.
146. Gollwitzer, p. 15. Likewise Abraham, p. 40.
147. Gollwitzer, p. 15. Cf. Abraham, p. 56; Schrenk, pp. 5ff.; Gennrich, p. 18; Weber, Schriftforschung, p. 3; Lutz, p. 85.
148. Cf. Gennrich, pp. 30f.
149. According to Gennrich, p. 31. Gennrich called this "the word of solution," a "knowledge of the truth given to us by God" (pp. 28f.). Arguing similarly are e.g., Abraham (p. 32) and Schrenk (p. 35).
150. Thus e.g., Zöckler, according to Gennrich, p. 105; also Stuhlmacher, Verstehen, pp. 238ff.; Gollwitzer, pp. 11ff.; the Chicago school (Harper, Mathews, and others) according to Funk, pp. 11ff. Cf. also Frick, pp. 4f.
151. Cf. the idea of "in step with the times" in Stuhlmacher, Verstehen, p. 222.
152. Abraham, p. 91.
153. So e.g., Gollwitzer, pp. 16f.; Schrenk, pp. 34f.; W. Schmidt, 1869, pp. 35f.; Stuhlmacher, Verstehen, p. 240; Keil, p. 108.
154. Cf. Seeberg, p. 15; W. Schmidt, 1869, p. 72; Keil, p. 134. Cf. much earlier Erasmus, according to Holl, p. 552.
155. Agreeing on this point are Lutz, p. 88; Philippi I, p. 183; Girgensohn, Grundriss, p. 65; Hofmann, p. 24; Ramm, Interpr, p. 85; Packer, Fundamentalism, pp. 78, 113f.; Henry IV, pp. 129ff.; Geisler, Decide, pp. 69ff.; Ladd, p. 32; Stibbs, pp. 107ff.; Mickelsen, pp. 91ff.; Beck, Leitfaden, pp. 7ff.; Stadelmann, pp. 62ff.; Pius XII, p. 59; Finlayson, p. 234. Much earlier advocates of the same view include Protestant Scholasticism and Pietism, notably Bengel (cf. my Joh-Offb, pp. 414ff.).
156. E.g., Jeremias, p. 44; Stuhlmacher, Verstehen, p. 54; Schrenk, ThWNT I, p. 753 (English edition: TDNT, p. 754).
157. E.g., Holtz, p. 183.
158. The New Jerusalem Bible's translation is interesting: while it translates restrictively in the text ("Every Scripture given by God"), in the apparatus it states, "Literally: Every Scripture is given by God."
159. Schlatter, Erläuterungen, on 2Ti 3:16.
160. Cf. Origen, de princ IV, 2,2 and Campenhausen, pp. 354ff.
161. Among others: Geisler, Decide, p. 71; Henry IV, p. 160; Ramm, Interpr, p. 86; Warfield, Inspiration and Authority, p. 113.
162. E.g., Gaussen (cf. Gennrich, pp. 41ff.).
163. Preus, p. 33.
164. So e.g., Hofmann, p. 34.
165. Cf. my Joh-Offb, p. 420f.
166. Des Herrn Wort, p. 177.
167. Cf. Grant, p. 145.
168. Semler I, p. 75.
169. Keil, p. 134.
170. Kähler, Wissenschaft, p. 390.
171. Ibid.

172. Ibid.
173. Ibid.
174. Weber, Schriftforschung, pp. 8f.; prior to Kähler there were similar thoughts in Lutz, p. 94.
175. F. Traub, p. 110.
176. Ibid.
177. Ibid., p. 102; similarly once more Lutz, p. 94.
178. Further examples in Gennrich, p. 129; Joest, Kanon, p. 181; Fascher, pp. 29f.; Seeberg, p. 15; W. Schmidt, 1869, p. 72; Procksch, AT, p. 17; Gunkel, p. 15; Diem, p. 38; Mussner, Aufgaben, p. 27; Dinkler, p. 31. Cf. Geisler, Decide, pp. 57ff.; Geisler, Errancy, p. 233.
179. Cf. Scheel, pp. 20f., 69f.; Lutz, pp. 263ff.
180. Cf. Preus, p. 16.
181. Cf. my Joh-Offb, pp. 414ff.
182. Thus e.g., Hofmann, p. 82; but also orthodox Lutheranism, e.g., Philippi I, p. 93.
183. Barth, KD I, 2, p. 512.
184. Ibid.
185. Ibid., pp. 512f.
186. Barth, *Das Wort Gottes und die Theologie,* 1922, p. 20. Cf. on this Esking, p. 67.
187. E.g., Diem, p. 4.
188. Cf. Fascher, p. 42; Dinkler, p. 32.
189. Cf. Joest, Kanon, p. 183.
190. E.g., Stuhlmacher, Verstehen, pp. 49, 175ff.
191. Harnack, p. 15.
192. Cf. Barth's foreword to his *Römerbrief:* we must peer through into the "Spirit" of the Bible.
193. Schmidt, 1869, p. 50. Cf. also pp. 60, 71.
194. According to Grant, p. 145.
195. Girgensohn, Grundriss, p. 65; Insp, p. 56.
196. Schrenk, p. 37.
197. Esking, p. 72; F. Traub, p. 49. Cf. my Joh-Offb, pp. 553f., as well as Fascher, p. 34; Geisler, Decide, p. 89; Geisler, Errancy, p. 232; Ridderbos, pp. 5ff.; Finlayson, pp. 225, 230.
198. F. Traub, p. 102.
199. Cf. on Luther, Lotz, p. 263. On Flacius cf. Moldaenke, pp. 55, 286. On Protestant orthodoxy (Gerhard) cf. Preus, p. 14.
200. Cf. Schrenk, pp. 30f.
201. Thus rightly Finlayson, p. 223.
202. Acute awareness of the difficulties is present e.g., in Bengel (cf. my Joh-Offb, pp. 413ff.), as well as in Philippi (I, p. 198), who wished to teach "inspiration of word" ("Wortinspiration") rather than "inspiration of words" ("Wörterinspiration").
203. Cf. Bengel to Jeremias Friedrich Reuss, as Bengel compared Bible word to bread: "don't bother yourself whether you find a grain of sand mixed in here

and there with the fine meal" (cf. my Joh-Offb, p. 414). Cf. Hofmann, p. 34; Ramm, Rev, p. 177.

204. Bengel, Gnomon, Praef, §14.
205. Cf. Chmiel, pp. 158f.
206. Cf. Campenhausen, p. 323.
207. Origen, De princ IV,2,2.
208. Contra Adimant c. 11: "Spiritus Sanctus . . . his etiam verbis uti voluit" ("The Holy Spirit also wanted to use *these* words") (according to Vogels, p. 72).
209. Cf. Grant, p. 122.
210. Cf. Scheel, pp. 68ff.
211. According to Moldaenke, p. 293; cf. p. 230. On Protestant Scholasticism see Preus, p. 53.
212. Cf. my Joh-Offb, p. 416.
213. E.g., Spener and Bengel (Joh-Offb, pp. 345, 414).
214. Cf. Beck, Leitfaden, p. 9; Procksch, AT, p. 17; Henry IV, pp. 129, 159.
215. Sasse, p. 305.
216. Barr, p. 27 ("a product of the church"); cf. pp. 2ff.
217. Sundberg, p. 364. Stadelmann (pp. 17ff.) lists German representatives of this outlook.
218. Likewise Stadelmann (pp. 17ff.); Girgensohn, Grundriss, p. 65.
219. Ramm states it this way: "Inspiration is infallible, but not illumination" (Interpr, p. 14).
220. Cf. Preus, pp. 27f. Philippi I, p. 151, speaks similarly of a "specific dignity"; cf. Preus, pp. 99f.
221. Thus e.g., Stuhlmacher, Verstehen, pp. 55ff.
222. Chmiel, pp. 159, 16.
223. Ibid., p. 160.
224. Campenhausen, p. 366.
225. Cf. Vogels, pp. 72ff.
226. Kropatscheck, p. 427.
227. According to Preus, pp. 57ff.
228. Cf. Burkhardt, pp. 221ff.
229. Cf. his remarks in Contra Ap I, 37–43. German translations in Koole, pp. 226f.; R. Meyer, pp. 285f.
230. Otherwise Stuhlmacher, Verstehen, pp. 55f.
231. Cf. Scheel, p. 68; Kropatscheck, p. 428.
232. Pius XII, p. 39. Warfield, Inspiration and Authority, p. 119: "media." Regarding Protestant Scholasticism see Preus, p. 54. On Bengel see my Joh-Offb, pp. 416ff.
233. Clearly visible in the dogmatics of Gottlieb Christian Storr (1793), which attempts to grant "complete latitude to the individual intellectual activity of the writers of sacred scripture" (according to Gennrich, pp. 20f.).
234. Le Brun, p. 114.
235. Childs, Introduction, p. 80.
236. This thought is present in Flacius (Moldaencke, p. 484), also later e.g., in W. Schmidt, 1869, p. 56.

237. Philippi I, p. 205. Cf. Pius XII, p. 39; Preus, pp. 69ff.
238. Cf. Vogels, pp. 73ff. On Calvin cf. Palmer, p. 35.
239. Protestant Scholastics saw this (Preus, p. 66ff.; Reinhard, p. 55).
240. Again already realized by Augustine (Vogels, p. 76).
241. Cf. my Joh-Offb, pp. 416f. This is denied by Henry IV, p. 160.
242. Cf. my Joh-Offb, pp. 416f.
243. Augustine is clearer on this point than Bengel.
244. On Augustine cf. Vogels, pp. 69f., 76; on Bengel cf. my Joh-Offb, pp. 417f.
245. Flacius made the same observation (Moldaenke, p. 298).
246. Protestant Scholasticism devoted attention to the problematic of this; cf. Preus, pp. 29ff.
247. Beck, Leitfaden, p. 8.
248. It is likely that Protestant Scholasticism sensed this as well; cf. Preus, p. 54.
249. Girgensohn, Grundriss, p. 63.
250. Ibid., pp. 63, 65; Girgensohn, Insp, p. 64.
251. Girgensohn, Grundriss, p. 63.
252. Cf. Marshall, Insp, pp. 40ff. with Packer, Fundamentalism, passim.
253. Marshall, Insp, p. 42.
254. Both citations from Vogels, p. 79.
255. Moldaenke, pp. 270, 484.
256. Similarly e.g., Frey, Ansatz, p. 157; Philippi I, pp. 166, 173, 215; Stibbs, p. 111 (calling attention to Jn 11:50); Asmussen, p. 25.
257. Cf. Gennrich, p. 18; Esking, p. 81; Wrede, p. 9.
258. Jung, p. 186.
259. Statements in this direction also in Flacius (Moldaenke, p. 323).
260. Cf. Augustine, DCD XVIII, 41, 43; XX, 1.
261. Cf. Preus, pp. 39ff.; Reinhard, pp. 86ff.
262. On Calvin cf. Palmer, p. 35; on Flacius cf. Moldaenke, pp. 9, 283, 303; on Protestant Scholasticism cf. Preus, pp. 57, 66ff., 195ff.; on Philippi cf. I, p. 185.
263. Cf. Moldaenke, p. 303.
264. E.g., Packer, Fundamentalism, passim.
265. Thus Elert, Glaube, p. 171.
266. Cf. my Kommentar zu Daniel in WStB.
267. So rightly Stadelmann, pp. 19, 25.
268. Cf. Preus, pp. 195ff.
269. Cf. Philippi I, pp. 194ff.
270. Cf. Preus, pp. 34f., 47.
271. Preus, pp. 35f.; Philippi (see n. 269); Schmid, p. 25.
272. Wrede, p. 35.
273. Ibid., p. 42.
274. Cf. Fitzmyer, pp. 39ff. Cf. however also the criticism of Dobschütz, pp. 33ff.; Frankemölle, pp. 163ff.; McGinley, p. 154; Ridderbos, p. 31; and Schlatter (Egg, p. 133).
275. Gnilka, p. 466.
276. Travis, p. 153.
277. So Ridderbos, p. 31.

278. Cf. Travis (n. 276 above).
279. Cf. Ellis, pp. 240f.; Riesner, passim.
280. Cf. here J. A. T. Robinson, *Redating the New Testament* (Philadelphia, 1976), and C. P. Thiede, *Die älteste Evangelien-Handschrift* (Wuppertal, 1986).
281. Cf. Ellis, pp. 242ff.; Travis, p. 159; Riesner, pp. 350, 422, 491ff.
282. Ellis, pp. 243ff.; Riesner, p. 502.
283. Cf. W. Marxsen, *Einleitung in das Neue Testament*, 2d ed. (1964), pp. 143ff.
284. Wrede, p. 35.
285. "et ideo, licet varia singulis evangeliorum bibris principia doceantur, nihil tamen differt credentium fidei. . . ." Translation above follows B. F. Westcott, *A General Survey of the History of the Canon of the New Testament* (Grand Rapids: Baker, 1980 [1889, 6th ed.]), p. 215.
286. Cf. Grant, p. 68; Campenhausen, p. 335.
287. Cf. the Daniel commentary in the Wuppertaler Studienbibel (p. 27).
288. Cf. Campenhausen, p. 81.
289. Chmiel, pp. 162f.; Campenhausen, pp. 111ff.
290. Dial 65,2 according to the translation in Campenhausen, p. 111.
291. Adv. haer. II, 28, 2. Cf. IV, 33, 8; IV, 32, 1; also Grant, p. 73.
292. Campenhausen, pp. 323, 355, 374.
293. Cf. Vogels, pp. 71, 53.
294. Luther's "open criticism of the Bible" is occasionally exaggerated, e.g., in Nitzsch-Stephan, pp. 268f.
295. Cf. Scheel, pp. 53, 70.
296. Moldaenke, pp. 295f.
297. Ibid., p. 268.
298. Lau, col. 1724.
299. Cf. Reinhard, pp. 10ff.; Preus, pp. 72ff.
300. According to Preus, p. 77.
301. Ibid., pp. 77f.
302. Ibid., p. 79.
303. Ibid., pp. 80ff.: "Si enim in uno alterove errare potuerunt Scripturae S. quis certos reddet nos, quod in aliis non erraverunt?" ("For if Holy Scripture could err in one or two things, who gives us the certainty that it has not also erred in other matters?"). Cf. H. Schmidt, pp. 20, 28.
304. Cf. my Joh-Offb, p. 418.
305. Ibid.
306. Le Brun, p. 100.
307. Reventlow, p. 14.
308. Ibid., p. 25; cf. Le Brun, p. 105; Kümmel, pp. 41ff.
309. According to Kümmel, p. 42.
310. Reventlow, pp. 33f.
311. Ibid., pp. 35f.; cf. Grant, p. 153.
312. Cf. Aner, p. 238.
313. Grant, p. 151.
314. Hofmann, p. 82.
315. Ibid., pp. 123, 75f., 79ff.

316. According to Gennrich, p. 77. Similarly Lutz, p. 94.
317. Thus W. Schmidt, 1869, pp. 35f.; cf. p. 60.
318. Schrenk, p. 31.
319. Ibid., pp. 34f.; cf. pp. 33, 36.
320. Childs, Theology, p. 104.
321. Jenson, p. 244.
322. Herrnhuter Losungen [daily devotional readings], 1986, for the 10th of September: "Mein Erbarmer selbst verspricht's; sollt ich ihm sein Wort verdrehen? Nein, er lässt mich ewig nicht; das ist meine Zuversicht."
323. Günter Balders in foreword to Spurgeon, p. 3. Cf. Philippi I, p. 117.
324. Spurgeon, p. 31.
325. Ibid., pp. 31, 33.
326. Pius XII, p. 51 (cf. p. 43); papal Bible commission, 1964 (in Fitzmyer, p. 47). Cf. Grant, pp. 166ff., who however refers to a turn in Pius XII's views (pp. 172f.); also Kühne, pp. 36ff.
327. Cf. Geisler, Decide, pp. 49, 75f.; idem, Errancy, pp. 11ff.; Henry IV, pp. 167ff.; Packer, Battle, pp. 17ff.; Ramm, Interpr, pp. 183ff.
328. Campenhausen, p. 35.
329. Ibid., pp. 33f.
330. Cf. R. Meyer's translation, pp. 285f. as well as Koole, pp. 226f. (with divergences at individual points).
331. Longenecker, p. 19.
332. To cite only a few examples: Hofmann, p. 82; Henry IV, p. 103; Packer, Fundamentalism, p. 96; Stibbs, p. 117; article 2 of the Lausanne Covenant; Schlatter, Dogma, p. 375.
333. Cf. my essay *Wie legen wir die Schrift aus?* (*How Do We Interpret Scripture?*), 2d ed. (Giessen/Basel, 1982), pp. 39f.
334. Even Schlatter does this: Dogma, pp. 375ff.
335. Schlatter writes: "The infallibility of the Bible consists in this: it calls us to the God" (Dogma, p. 376). We would say: "consists also in this . . ." Schlatter's understanding is too narrowly circumscribed and is not marked off clearly enough from that of A. von Harnack, F. Traub, and others.
336. In his foreword to the first volume of his German writings of 1539 (see H. H. Borcherdt and G. Merz, eds., *Martin Luther, Ausgewählte Worte*, vol. 1, 3d ed. [Munich, 1951], p. 15).

*CHAPTER EIGHT: The Canon*

1. Zahn defined the canon as "the list of books accepted as holy writings by the church" (Grundriss, p. 9). Cf. H. W. Beyer in *ThWNT* 3 (1938): 600–606.
2. Leiman, p. 29. Otherwise e.g., Kalin, p. 51. Eybers, Remarks, p. 111: ca. 200 B.C.; likewise Schäfer, p. 116.
3. E.g., Campenhausen, p. 6; Oepke, ThWNT, p. 986; Koole, p. 230; R. Meyer, p. 299; Trillhaas, p. 72.
4. Lewis, pp. 125 (referring to H. H. Rowley), 128, 132; Kalin, p. 48; Leiman, p. 125; Sanders, p. 161; Eybers, Remarks, pp. 96ff. See also Aune, "On the Origins of the 'Council of Jamnia' Myth."

5. Contra Apionem I, 38ff. as translated by R. Meyer, p. 285.
6. Thus Koole, p. 229.
7. Thus R. Meyer, p. 290.
8. Thus also Leiman, pp. 32f.; Lewis, p. 128; Eybers, Remarks, p. 99.
9. Cf. R. Meyer, p. 286; Leiman, pp. 32f.; Koole, pp. 228ff.
10. Oepke, ThWNT, p. 988; Eybers, Remarks, p. 102.
11. Qumran is disputed; cf. Koole, p. 228 with Lewis, p. 128; Eybers, Remarks, pp. 108ff.
12. Cf. Lewis, p. 128; Eybers, Remarks, pp. 106ff.
13. Likewise Eybers, Remarks, pp. 100f.; Schäfer, p. 116.
14. Cf. Sauer, p. 505; Lewis, p. 128.
15. Cf. my essay on man and free will, pp. 24f.; Sauer, p. 490, places the date somewhat earlier, "ca. 190 B.C."
16. Leiman, p. 30. Likewise Eybers, Remarks, p. 113. For other views see e.g., Aland, Kanon, p. 136; Sanders, p. 161; Gese, Theol, p. 13.
17. Cf. Zahn, Grundriss, pp. 59ff., 65ff.; Aland, Kanon, pp. 141f.; Ohlig, p. 21.
18. Windisch, pp. 158f.
19. Pedersen, pp. 99f.; cf. Aland, Kanon, p. 140; Zahn, Grundriss, pp. 35ff.
20. Pedersen, pp. 100ff.; Aland, Kanon, p. 140.
21. Zahn, Grundriss, p. 26; cf. p. 15.
22. Cf. Eusebius, H. E. III, 25.
23. Thus likewise Campenhausen, p. 80
24. Aland, Kanon, p. 147; cf. Barth, KD I, 2, pp. 524ff.
25. Oepke, ThWNT, p. 988; Aland, Kanon, pp. 136ff.
26. Scheel, p. 10. Cf. on the early church Eybers, Remarks, pp. 114ff.
27. According to Bornkamm, Vorreden, p. 175.
28. Ibid., p. 177.
29. Cf. Nitzsch-Stephan, p. 288; Preus, p. xiv.
30. Nitzsch-Stephan, p. 288. Cf. already Flacius (Moldaenke, p. 259).
31. Philippi I, pp. 123f.
32. According to Hennig, p. 38.
33. Cf. Palmer, pp. 38f.
34. Cf. Ridderbos, pp. 6, 1f.
35. Cf. Kümmel, pp. 32ff.
36. Cf. Dinkler, p. 16; Ridderbos, p. 10.
37. Schleiermacher, p. 254.
38. Thus Krüger, p. 15.
39. So e.g., Nitzsch-Stephan, p. 292; Aland, Kanon, pp. 151ff.; O. Weber, pp. 290ff.; Trillhaas, p. 73; Barth, KD I, 2, pp. 530f.
40. Cf. Blank, p. 7: The canon forms "the factual, pre-given foundation of biblical science. Pragmatically speaking its work centers there." Cf. also the comments on the canon's historical-pragmatic importance in Stuhlmacher, Verstehen, pp. 35ff.
41. Cf. Ridderbos, p. 6; Sasse, pp. 310f.
42. Calvin, Inst I, 8, 6.

43. This is clearly seen in e.g., Ohlig, p. 313. Cf. also the critique of Ridderbos, p. 57.
44. Cf. Preus, p. xiv.
45. Sundberg (p. 369) maintains that for the early church inspiration was not a criterion for distinguishing canonical from noncanonical writings.
46. According to Bornkamm, Vorreden, p. 178. To the contrary: Flacius (Moldaenke, p. 217). For a recent critique see Ridderbos, pp. 12f.
47. Cf. O. Weber, pp. 285f.; Ohlig, p. 313.
48. So e.g., the Confessio Virtembergica, art. 30.
49. Ridderbos (pp. 11, 49ff.), e.g., rejects the attempt to use apostolicity as a basis because of such historical uncertainty.
50. Ridderbos, pp. 22, 58.
51. O. Weber, p. 284.
52. They could not, of course, be multiplied by words of inspired persons, contrary to R. Bultmann's claims in *Geschichte der synoptischen Tradition*, 6th ed. (1964), p. 135.
53. Cf. Riesenfeld, pp. 21ff.
54. Aland, Kanon, p. 147; cf. pp. 151f. To the contrary however Barr, pp. 72f.
55. O. Weber, p. 280; cf. pp. 275, 277f.
56. The canon is made to appear a product of the church even where e.g., Trillhaas, p. 72, wants to explain it as arising "from the need for religious security."
57. Cf. Moldaenke, p. 266.
58. Thus rightly Aland, Kanon, p. 152; also Philippi I, p. 115; Kähler, Wissenschaft, p. 387.
59. Gese, Theol, p. 13.
60. Sundberg, pp. 356ff. Critical of Gese is Schäfer, pp. 117ff.
61. Cf. Barth, KD I, 2, pp. 524ff.
62. Lönning, p. 45.
63. Thus e.g., Lotz, p. 272.
64. Lönning, pp. 72ff.
65. Cf. Moldaenke, pp. 281ff.
66. Ibid., p. 284.
67. Barr, p. 72, totally overlooks this.
68. Hofmann, p. 89.
69. Cf. ibid., pp. 82ff.
70. Pedersen, p. 90.
71. Thus Blank, p. 15.
72. Ibid., p. 9.
73. Thus Joest, Kanon, p. 198. Such subjectivism is taken to an even greater extreme in Barr, p. 73.
74. In Käsemann, pp. 175ff. and 205ff.
75. Lönning, pp. 271f.
76. Hesse, AT, p. 34. Cf. p. 106.
77. Ibid., AT, p. 35.
78. Cf. my *Das Ende der historisch-kritischen Methode*, 5th ed. (Wuppertal, 1984).
79. Gese, Theol, p. 29.

80. Cf. Martin, p. 225.
81. Cf. Beisser, NZSTh, p. 209; Hasel, pp. 165ff.; Childs, Introduction, p. 44; Childs, Theology, p. 102; Küng in Käsemann, pp. 191ff.
82. Cf. Hasel, pp. 165ff.; Küng in Käsemann, p. 192; Ridderbos, pp. 16f., 45ff.
83. Cf. Ohlig, pp. 12f.
84. Cf. Girgensohn, Insp, p. 64.
85. Examples of such (willful!) dissolution are found in Wrede (pp. 10ff.) and Gunkel (Klatt, p. 265).
86. This is another point at which we find ourselves in agreement with Barth (KD I, 2, pp. 545ff.).
87. Apart from Childs cf. James A. Sanders; J. Kenneth Eakins along with the discussion in Barr, JSOT; Blenkinsopp; B. Kittel and R. Smend, JSOT. While in the last-named writer's judgment "Childs' book is to me the most important new publication of recent years in our discipline" (p. 45), Barr rejects Childs' Old Testament introduction as "a simple intellectual error" (JSOT, p. 16).
88. Cf. Childs, Theology, p. 99, along with the fuller statement on pp. 91ff.; idem, Introduction, p. 45.
89. Among other problems: he has in mind at the same time "to make full and consistent use of the historical critical tools" (Introduction, p. 45). Still more radical at this point is Sanders, pp. 162ff.

*CHAPTER NINE: The Authority of Scripture*
1. Schadewaldt, p. 216.
2. Spurgeon, p. 73.
3. Scholder, pp. 132f.
4. Jung, p. 344.
5. Trillhaas, p. 80. Cf. Barnikol, p. 38, especially on F. C. Baur. Cf. also Sasse, p. 306.
6. So Berger, pp. 243f.
7. Semmelroth-Zerwick, p. 80. Cf. Grillmeier, pp. 161ff.
8. Cf. here Amberg, pp. 25f.
9. Strauss, p. 2.
10. Ibid., p. 126.
11. Ibid., p. 255.
12. Ebeling, RGG, col. 254.
13. Cf. Amberg, p. 9; Klatt, pp. 268, 28.
14. Cf. Girgensohn, Reformgedanken, p. 88.
15. So Wrede, p. 8.
16. Funk, p. 11. Cf. regarding the Continent Girgensohn, Schriftbeweis, pp. 62f.
17. Funk, p. 5.
18. Stuhlmacher, Verstehen, pp. 222ff.; earlier e.g., Ebeling, ZThK, pp. 25ff. Cf. also Grässer, Ev Komm, p. 273.
19. Wilckens, p. 133.
20. Ibid., p. 133. Stuhlmacher, Verstehen, pp. 222ff., essentially follows this same line.
21. Funk, p. 14.

22. Bultmann, GV II, p. 235. Cf. Ebeling, ZThK, p. 43. Interestingly, the commemoration of Bultmann's 100th birthday (Dt Pf Bl, August 1984) appeared under the title "Veracity."
23. Weber, Schriftforschung, p. 3. Cf. Girgensohn, Schriftbeweis, p. 76.
24. Kropatscheck, p. 454. Cf. Luther's views in Hirsch, Hilfsbuch, pp. 94ff., 84.
25. Hirsch, Hilfsbuch, p. 85, citing the Assertio omnium articulorum of 1520 (WA VII, pp. 96ff.). Cf. Scheel, pp. 33, 62f.
26. Scheel, p. 71. Cf. my Joh-Offb, p. 419.
27. Cf. Kramer II, p. 399; also my Joh-Offb, pp. 414ff.
28. Des Herrn Wort, p. 176.
29. Weber, Schriftforschung, pp. 122ff.
30. Amberg, p. 51.
31. Thus e.g., Ebeling, ZThK, p. 2.
32. Amberg, p. 61.
33. Contra Ap I, 38ff. Cf. Koole, p. 226; R. Meyer, pp. 285f.
34. Cf. Elert, Morphologie, p. 173.
35. Moldaenke, pp. 583ff.
36. Cf. Preus, pp. 106ff. On Buddeus cf. Reinhard, p. 48.
37. Thus e.g., Philippi I, p. 93. Similar thoughts are found in Girgensohn, Grundriss, p. 65.
38. Cf. Lutz, p. 81 with p. 72.
39. Seeberg, p. 9.
40. Cf. Semmelroth-Zerwick, pp. 79f.
41. Barr, pp. 28 and 2ff.
42. Cf. Courth, p. 67.
43. Girgensohn, Grundriss, pp. 56ff.
44. Trillhaas, p. 84.
45. Ebeling, ZThK, p. 28, clearly expressed this state of affairs.
46. Cf. Amberg, p. 100.
47. E.g., Lotz, p. 273.
48. Cf. the interesting discussion in Reinhard, p. 104, as well as in Ebeling, ZThK, pp. 27ff.
49. Cf. Reinhard, pp. 97ff. Similarly Joh. Franz Buddeus (Reinhard, pp. 39ff.).
50. Inst I, 7, 4. Cf. Kraus, ZKG, p. 330.
51. Cf. Campenhausen, p. 323.
52. Cf. Ridderbos, p. 20.
53. Preus, pp. 12f.
54. Ibid., p. 13.
55. Cf. my Joh-Offb, pp. 345, 414.
56. Schmid, pp. 29ff.
57. E.g., in Pius XII (pp. 9, 47).
58. Kraus, ZKG, pp. 330ff., points out rightly that there are, however, certain differentiations and emphases that need to be noted.
59. Preus, p. 89. Cf. Palmer, pp. 35f. on Calvin; Preus, p. 38 on Quenstedt; Pius XII, p. 43; Pieper, p. 143.
60. Cf. Kraus, ZKG, p. 330.

61. Cf. again ibid.; Ridderbos, p. 20.
62. Interestingly Philippi (I, pp. 93ff.) here follows largely in Calvin's train. Cf. however also Preus, pp. 108f.; Pieper, p. 143.
63. Thus Gross-Mussner, p. 74.
64. Philippi I, p. 97; cf. p. 92.
65. WA VII, pp. 96ff., according to Hirsch, Hilfsbuch, p. 85. Cf. Frei, p. 19.
66. Cf. Henry IV, p. 50.
67. Abraham, pp. 100ff., 106.
68. Barr, pp. 14ff., 22 (appealing to Abraham).
69. Stuhlmacher, Verstehen, pp. 64f. (The judgment above is based on the second edition, 1986).
70. Ibid., p. 65.
71. Cf. Campenhausen, pp. 13f.; Stadelmann, pp. 23ff.
72. This false impression should be abandoned.
73. Cf. among others Packer, Fundamentalism, pp. 56ff.
74. Abraham, p. 98.
75. Cf. Henry IV, p. 50.
76. Cf. Vögtle's essay on enscripturation.
77. Theses for debate of 11 Sept. 1535, in Hirsch, Hilfsbuch, p. 94.
78. Cf. Stadelmann, p. 25.
79. On dominical tradition in 1 Peter cf. my essay in *Gospel Perspectives*, vol. 5 (1985), pp. 85ff.
80. Cf. Vögtle, Schriftwerdung, pp. 297ff.
81. Cf. Stuhlmacher, Verstehen, pp. 54f.
82. Cf. Preus, p. 207.
83. Wellhausen, p. 135.
84. BELK, p. 767; cf. O. Weber, pp. 298f.
85. O. Weber, p. 298.
86. Ibid., p. 299. Cf. Schmid, pp. 30f.; Pieper, pp. 83ff.
87. Reinhard, p. 43. On Baumgarten cf. Schloemann, pp. 72ff.
88. Cf. Girgensohn, Insp, p. 9. For an example see Grässer, ZThK, p. 201.
89. Ebeling, ZThK, pp. 25, 27, 30.
90. Redlich, Traditions, p. 12; cf. p. 11.
91. Ricoeur, HThR, p. 37.
92. Cf. Preus, pp. 88ff. For a more recent example see Pieper, p. 143.
93. Inst I, 12, 1.
94. Inst I, 7, 5.
95. Cf. my Joh-Offb, p. 419.
96. Cf. ibid., pp. 399, 418.
97. Cf. Beisser, Claritas, passim.
98. Cf. the quotation from De servo arbitrio in Hirsch, Hilfsbuch, p. 87.
99. Holl, p. 551.
100. According to Hirsch, Hilfsbuch, p. 86.
101. Cf. Preus, pp. 156ff. On Flacius cf. Moldaenke, p. 306.
102. Cf. still Pieper, p. 158.
103. Schmid, pp. 44ff.

104. Luther also pondered this matter (WA 8, 236).
105. Cf. O. Weber, p. 310; Schmid, pp. 44ff.; recently Pieper, p. 156.
106. De doctr christ II, 9.
107. Schmid, p. 45; O. Weber, p. 310; Pieper, p. 156.
108. Luther, Assertio omnium articulorum, 1520 (WA 7, 96ff.; cf. Hirsch, Hilfsbuch, p. 85); Flacius in Moldaenke, p. 351.
109. O. Weber, p. 310.
110. Moldaenke, p. 306.
111. Cf. Riesner, pp. 408ff.
112. Diem, p. 12; Grässer, ZThK, passim.
113. Cf. O. Weber, pp. 303f.
114. Cf. again ibid., pp. 306f.
115. Prax 18, 2. Cf. Campenhausen, p. 329.
116. Cf. Moldaenke, p. 356; Schmid, pp. 40ff.; Preus, pp. 76, 147ff.
117. Inst III, 21, 3 as translated in Hirsch, Hilfsbuch, p. 109. Cf. Preus, pp. 147ff.
118. Cf. Preus, pp. 134ff. On Bengel's more carefully grounded judgment see my Joh-Offb, pp. 413ff.
119. Cf. K. Junack, Bibelreport, 1, 1976.
120. O. Weber, pp. 308f.
121. Ibid. p. 309.
122. Girgensohn, Insp, p. 24.
123. Ibid., pp. 25f., following Hamann. Cf. Amberg's criticism, p. 49.
124. Grässer, ZThK, pp. 201, 209.
125. Geiger, p. 227.

CHAPTER TEN: *The Unity of Scripture*

1. Hesse, AT, p. 35. Cf. p. 294; Wrede, pp. 79f.; Dibelius, p. 93; Jenson, p. 243; Gunkel, p. 35; Fuchs, p. 22.
2. Redlich, Traditions, p. 11.
3. Dibelius, p. 93. Cf. Girgensohn, Grundriss, p. 63.
4. Thus Barr, p. 3.
5. Examples: Elert, Glaube, p. 190; Joest, Kanon, p. 196; Weber, Schriftforschung, p. 36; Schrenk, p. 33; Stuhlmacher, Verstehen, p. 240. To my chagrin also my own teacher Köberle, pp. 16ff.
6. Grant, p. 68.
7. Frei, p. 8.
8. Contra Ap I, 38. Cf. R. Meyer, p. 285.
9. Cf. Heinisch, pp. 47, 52ff.; Burkhardt, p. 75.
10. Heinisch, pp. 47ff.
11. Campenhausen, p. 111; Chmiel, p. 162.
12. Campenhausen, p. 335; cf. p. 362; Grant, pp. 70ff.; Bonwetsch, p. 39.
13. Cf. Vogels, pp. 2, 13, 53, 88. On Theodore of Mopsuestia cf. Kihn, p. 121.
14. Cf. Scheel, p. 18, along with Bring, pp. 10, 21; Popkin, p. 7; Beisser, Claritas, p. 129.
15. Kraus, ZKG, p. 341.
16. Cf. Moldaenke, pp. 10, 604; Preus, pp. 17ff.; also Gadamer, pp. 163f.

17. Moldaenke, p. 604: Scripture is not a "chaotic confusion."
18. Cf. my Joh-Offb, p. 421.
19. Strauss, pp. 120, 254.
20. Frei, p. 8. Cf. Hornig, pp. 84ff.; Meyer II, p. 169.
21. Merk, Anfänge, p. 45.
22. Keil, p. 108.
23. Lücke, p. 60.
24. Cf. Hofmann, pp. 30ff., 34, 100.
25. Lutz, p. 14.
26. Thus Philippi I, p. 199.
27. Ibid., p. 206.
28. Wrede, pp. 27, 3.
29. Examples: Beisser, NZSTh, pp. 205, 214; Pieper, pp. 110ff.; Lerle, pp. 49ff.
30. Example: Heim, Ich gedenke, p. 208.
31. Here Schlatter comes to mind (Dogma, pp. 369ff.), although Schlatter balked at every attempt to pigeonhole his views.
32. Examples: Ladd, p. 32; Henry IV, pp. 450ff.; Packer, Fundamentalism, pp. 84, 109f., 113f. and Battle, pp. 23, 41; Mickelsen, pp. 86ff.; L. Berkhof, p. 53.
33. So e.g., Packer, Fundamentalism, pp. 84, 110, 113f. and Battle, pp. 23, 41; L. Berkhof, p. 53.
34. Packer, Fundamentalism, p. 109; cf. p. 114. In Battle, p. 53, Packer speaks of a "method of harmonizing."
35. Girgensohn, Insp, p. 41. Cf. Procksch, AT, p. 33; Frey, Ansatz, p. 175.
36. Girgensohn, Insp, p. 44.
37. Ibid., pp. 42ff.; Procksch, AT, pp. 42ff.
38. Examples: Wolff, p. 145; Jepsen, pp. 258ff.; Gese, Theol, passim; Kraus, Bibl Theol, passim.
39. Cf. Vögtle, Schriftwerdung, passim.
40. Already in Philo; cf. Heinisch, pp. 47ff.
41. Cf. Semmelroth-Zerwick, p. 79; Grillmeier, p. 186; Lohfink, p. 162; Procksch, AT, p. 33; Berkhof, p. 53; Packer, Fundamentalism, p. 84; Packer, Battle, p. 23. Concerning Bengel cf. my Joh-Offb, pp. 415f.
42. Schlatter, Dogma, p. 369.
43. Cf. my Joh-Offb, p. 416.
44. Incidentally, Schlatter relates what he says here to Ötinger! Cf. Schlatter, Dogma, p. 590 n. 215.
45. Cf. Bengel in my Joh-Offb, p. 416; Schlatter, Dogma, p. 370.
46. Käsemann, p. 371.
47. Cf. Schlatter, Dogma, p. 369.
48. Ibid.
49. Modern examples: Berkhof, p. 53; Ladd, p. 32; Packer, Battle, pp. 22f.; Ramm, Interpr, pp. 111ff.; Vögtle, Auslegung, p. 43.
50. Cf. Packer's concept of "complex unity" (Battle, p. 23).
51. Weber, Schriftforschung, p. 36.
52. This is the point from which to understand Wrede's fierce aversion to a

"method of doctrinal concepts" (Wrede, pp. 17ff.). Cf. Hofmann, p. 14: Scripture is "the record of a history" and not a "revelation of doctrine."

53. Goppelt, Typos, pp. 239, 248f.
54. Ibid., pp. 240ff.
55. Campenhausen, p. 46.
56. Cf. ibid., pp. 109, 116, 121, 320; Grant, pp. 70ff.; O. Weber, p. 336.
57. Cf. my Joh-Offb, pp. 113ff.
58. Cf. ibid., pp. 174ff.
59. Klassen, pp. 96ff.
60. Cf. Moldaenke, pp. 60, 577.
61. Cf. my Joh-Offb, pp. 325ff.
62. Cf. ibid., pp. 353ff., 415ff.
63. Cf. Hofmann, p. 9.
64. Weber, Schriftforschung, p. 20.
65. Cf. Procksch, AT, pp. 44f.; Frey, Ansatz, p. 163.
66. E.g., Packer, Battle, p. 41; Yri, p. 17.
67. E.g., Wolff, p. 161.
68. Schadewaldt, passim.
69. Schlatter, Dogma, p. 369, thus objects to the "reformation use of Scripture."
70. Goppelt, Typos, pp. 70ff., 239.
71. Aner, p. 4.
72. Cf. ibid., pp. 52, 156, and 49ff.
73. Ibid., p. 206.
74. Semler takes this view.
75. Bultmann, Mythologie, pp. 23, 26, 16, 48.
76. Bultmann, GV I, pp. 333ff.
77. Bultmann, ThLZ 64 (1939): col. 254.
78. Ricoeur, HThR, p. 35.
79. Schlatter, Dogma, p. 369: "[The Bible] leaves gaps in our sequence of thought and is quite aware that it possesses such gaps, yet sees no deficiency in this."
80. The phrase is from Schadewaldt, p. 216.
81. One of the most recent attempts is that of Bürgener.
82. We honor Luther by following his desire that "no one bind himself to my thinking or judgment" (Bornkamm, Vorreden, p. 179).
83. Käsemann, pp. 368, 405.
84. Küng in ibid., pp. 175ff.; Löser, pp. 53ff.
85. Bengel, Erkl Offb, p. 964.
86. Lotz, p. 270.
87. It even crops up in Erasmus (Scheel, p. 10)! On the contemporary situation cf. Beisser, Claritas, pp. 210ff.
88. Scheel, p. 18.
89. Cf. here Pieper, pp. 133f.
90. Cf. Grant, p. 131.
91. Coming to the same result is Schlatter, Dogma, p. 370. Otherwise e.g., Weber, Schriftforschung, p. 13; Joest, Kanon, p. 198; Lönning, pp. 72ff.
92. Löser, p. 53.

93. Ibid., p. 54.
94. Ibid.
95. Käsemann, pp. 175ff.
96. Amberg, p. 65, appealing to Barth's *Christliche Dogmatik im Entwurf*, I (Munich, 1927).
97. Schlatter, Dogma, p. 370.
98. All quotes in this paragraph from Schlatter, Dogma, p. 370.
99. O. Weber, p. 264.
100. Ibid., p. 334.
101. Cf. the standpoint of the Old Testament specialist Procksch, AT, p. 2.
102. Cf. once more O. Weber, pp. 334ff., who draws on Jn 8:58 and other passages.
103. Ibid., p. 336, according to Inst II, 11, 4.
104. Against Blank, p. 16; also Beisser, Claritas, p. 214.
105. Cf. Schlatter, Dogma, p. 370.
106. Le Brun, pp. 104f.
107. Keil, p. 108. Cf. also Lücke, p. 60.
108. Wrede, pp. 27, 3.
109. Philippi I, p. 206.
110. Ibid., p. 199.
111. Packer, Battle, p. 53. Cf. Packer, Fundamentalism, pp. 113f.
112. Cf. especially Blomberg, pp. 166ff.
113. Ibid., p. 161.
114. This must be said, regrettably, also against Köberle, p. 21.
115. Thus also Lutz, p. 14.
116. To this extent Köberle, p. 16, is correct.
117. Cf. Henry II, p. 311.

*CHAPTER ELEVEN: The Historical Nature (Historicality) of Scripture*
1. Heinisch, p. 43. But see now the opposing views of Burkhardt, passim.
2. Cf. Heinisch, pp. 42f.
3. Köberle, p. 24.
4. V. Rad, p. 11.
5. Henry II, p. 312.
6. Ibid., p. 247.
7. Ibid., p. 311. Cf. Packer, Battle, p. 22.
8. Pannenberg, p. 299. Cf. Hofmann, pp. 118ff.
9. Pannenberg, p. 295.
10. Ibid., pp. 296, 295. Cf. here Semmelroth-Zerwick for the Catholic position (p. 85).
11. Cf. also Procksch, AT, p. 17.
12. Weber, Schriftforschung, pp. 6, 20; cf. Oepke, p. 30; Procksch, AT, pp. 17, 13.
13. Procksch, AT, p. 15.
14. Marshall, Criticism, p. 126.
15. Henry II, p. 321. Already Baumgarten (Schloemann, pp. 165f.).
16. Cf. again Henry II, p. 321.
17. Cf. Marshall, Criticism, p. 127; Weber, Schriftforschung, p. 4.

18. That remains true despite Henry's remarks (II, p. 314, on Kähler).
19. Schloemann, pp. 189f.; cf. pp. 186ff.
20. Ibid., p. 188.
21. On Bengel cf. Ludwig, p. 28.
22. Bornkamm, Luther, p. 207.
23. Ibid.
24. Aner, p. 4. Cf. Henry II, p. 312.
25. Hornig, p. 90.
26. Meyer II, pp. 352ff.
27. Weber, Schriftforschung, p. 48.
28. Nicely presented in ibid., pp. 47f.
29. Cf. Henry's critique (II, p. 314).
30. Girgensohn, Schriftbeweis, pp. 73, 1. On Bousset cf. Kümmel, p. 331.
31. Girgensohn, Schriftbeweis, p. 76.
32. Ibid.
33. Ibid., pp. 73, 1. Note the similarity to Brunner.
34. Schrenk, pp. 4f. Cf. also Weber, Schriftforschung, p. 35.
35. Brunner, Geschichte, p. 270.
36. Brunner, Erlebnis, pp. 106f. Like Bultmann, Brunner appeals here to 2Co 5:16.
37. Ibid., p. 127.
38. Ibid., pp. 107, 112.
39. Cf. Lindemann, p. 26; my Joh-Offb, pp. 550ff.; Oepke himself, p. 30.
40. Oepke, p. 30.
41. Ibid.
42. Ibid., pp. 36f.
43. Wellhausen, pp. 385f.
44. But not only them! Cf. Pannenberg.
45. Cf., to name just two examples, the papal Bible commission in Fitzmyer, p. 41 (obviously directed against Bultmann, Ebeling, and similar theologians), and Henry II, pp. 247ff.
46. The term is from W. J. Bittner, *Jesu Zeichen im Johannesevangelium*, WUNT, 2d series, 26 (Tübingen, 1987), p. 76.
47. Thurneysen, p. 25. Cf. Diem, p. 38.
48. Geiger, p. 242.
49. Kümmel, p. 162. Cf. Liebing, p. 311.
50. Quoted from Geiger, p. 225. Cf. Liebing, p. 315.
51. Cf. Klatt, p. 264.
52. Cf. Kümmel, pp. 325ff., on this point.
53. According to Klatt, p. 261.
54. Ibid., p. 268.
55. Cf. on this point Ahn, passim, and most of all pp. 79ff.
56. Bultmann, GV II, p. 229.
57. Gemmer/Messer, p. 18.
58. Droysen, p. 12.
59. Ibid.
60. Ibid., p. 24.

61. Ibid., p. 5.
62. Ibid., p. xii.
63. Frei, p. 57, speaks of the "meaning-and-fact issue."
64. Schneider, pp. 257f.
65. Fuchs, p. 116.
66. Dinkler, p. 22.
67. Diem, pp. 40ff., saw the impossibility of this position and wishes to uphold the "happened-ness" of the events attested in Scripture, even if these amount to "tales" and "legends"—a solution having little plausibility.
68. Schloemann, p. 166.
69. On this contradiction cf. from the early twentieth century Weber, Schriftforschung, p. 33; Fascher, pp. 94, 99; more recently Frey, Ansatz, p. 173. On the Catholic situation see Fitzmyer, p. 41.
70. That comes to light e.g. in Diem, pp. 16ff.
71. Betti, pp. 20, 27ff., 34f., 46. Cf. Schadewaldt, passim.
72. Ricoeur (AThR, p. 446) refers to Strathmann, *ThWNT* 4.
73. Ibid.
74. Ibid.
75. Ibid.
76. Ibid., p. 445.
77. Ricoeur, HThR, p. 33. Cf. Frey, Ansatz, p. 173.
78. Ricoeur, HThR, p. 35.
79. Otto, p. xviii.
80. Ibid., p. xxi.
81. Ibid.
82. Ibid.
83. Ibid., p. xxii.
84. Ibid., p. xxi.
85. Josephus BJ, I, 2f.
86. Ibid., I, 9, 16.
87. Ibid., I, 1, 2, 9, 12, 16.
88. Schadewaldt, p. 222.
89. Cf. the introduction by Michel-Bauernfeind in Josephus BJ, pp. xxiiiff.
90. Cf. n. 87 above.
91. Livius, Praefatio, 6.
92. Ibid., 10.
93. Sneen, p. 40. Cf. on Josephus Michel-Bauernfeind in Josephus BJ, p. xxiv.
94. Cf. Kürzinger, p. 254.
95. Sneen, pp. 40, 41.
96. This was known already by Flacius (Moldaenke, p. 324). Cf. Mickelsen, p. 45; Westermann, p. 26.
97. In Ricoeur, HThR, p. 33.
98. Cf. Mishna, Pesachim, X, 1ff.
99. G. von Rad, *Das fünfte Buch Mose. Deuteronomium*, ATD, 8, 2d ed. (Göttingen, 1968), pp. 113f.
100. Dibelius, p. 32.

101. Weber, Schriftforschung, p. 53.
102. Schlingensiepen, pp. 47, 76f.; Petzke, p. 7.
103. Cf. Elert, Morphologie, p. 173; Moldaenke, pp. 583ff.
104. Reinhard, p. 48.
105. Strauss, p. 117.
106. Schulz, p. 64.
107. Cf. Grant, pp. 146ff.; Strauss, pp. 106ff.; my article on miracle exegesis in *Gospel Perspectives*, vol. 6, pp. 50ff.
108. Grant, p. 151.
109. Frei, p. 328.
110. Ibid., p. 53.
111. Ibid.
112. Allusions to this in Aner, pp. 166, 208; Schöffler, pp. 39f.
113. Cf. Reinhard, p. 48; Stolzenburg, p. 112.
114. Stolzenburg, p. 108.
115. Cf. e.g., Aner, p. 216, on Christoph August Heumann.
116. Aner, pp. 306f.
117. Cf. my article on miracle exegesis, pp. 52f.
118. Cf. Lücke, p. 134.
119. Cf. Girgensohn, Schriftbeweis, pp. 20f.; my article on miracle exegesis, pp. 53ff.
120. Baur, An Hase, p. 20.
121. Barnikol, ZKG, p. 89.
122. Cf. e.g., Weber, Schriftforschung, p. 177; Henry II, pp. 324ff.; Frey, Ansatz, p. 171. The opposite view in e.g., Dinkler, p. 21; my article on miracle exegesis, pp. 72ff.
123. Fitzmyer, pp. 41f.
124. Against Trillhaas, pp. 168ff.
125. Cf. Maier, Wunderexegese, pp. 71f.
126. E.g., in the Talmud b Sota 47a; b Sanhedrin 106a/106b; 43a.
127. Schlatter, Dogma, p. 58.
128. Ibid.
129. Still held by Buddeus (Reinhard, p. 48).
130. On Flacius see Moldaenke, pp. 583ff.; on Buddeus see Reinhard, p. 48.
131. Cf. my Joh-Offb, pp. 112f.
132. Cf. the numerous pesherim and florilegia.
133. Fitzmyer, p. 41.
134. E.g., Ramm, Interpr, p. 68.
135. Frei, p. 53.
136. Lessing, Erziehung, §85.
137. According to Frei, pp. 327, 7; cf. p. 83.
138. Reinhard, p. 88.
139. Stroth, p. 262.
140. Cf. my Joh-Offb, p. 462.
141. Ibid., pp. 463f.
142. Wellhausen, p. 128.

143. Ibid., p. 155.
144. Ibid., p. 382.
145. Zöckler, p. v.
146. Delitzsch, p. xxxii.
147. Hesse, AT, p. 82.
148. Ibid., p. 84.
149. Ibid., p. 86.
150. An example is Trillhaas, pp. 471ff.
151. Hesse, AT, p. 101.
152. Ibid., p. 86.
153. Thus Duhm, p. xvi.
154. Ricoeur, HThR, p. 3.
155. Thus Duhm, p. xvii.
156. This line of analysis was surely employed in the trial of Jesus.
157. Rejection of requests for signs also takes place but would require a separate discussion.
158. Likewise the Talmud (b Sota 47a; b Sanh 43a, 106a/b).
159. b Sanh 43a in R. Mayer's translation.
160. Schlatter, Dogma, p. 327.
161. What Matthew writes here is enigmatic.
162. Schlatter, Dogma, p. 328.
163. Cf. the fulfillment citations in Matthew and the messianic disputations in John; also Ro 1:2f.; Heb 7–10.
164. According to Kümmel, p. 83 (related first to the apostolic epistles).
165. Ricoeur, HThR, p. 18.
166. Cf. Schlatter, Dogma, pp. 536, 538.
167. Hesse, AT, p. 86, says that the future announced in the Old Testament will "never become fact."
168. Daube, p. 408.
169. Ibid.
170. Ibid., p. 412.
171. Sneen, p. 41.
172. German-language versions like the revised Elberfelder Bible and the New Jerusalem Bible retain this translation.
173. Cf. Kürzinger, p. 253, who translates it as "in what follows," "as follows," as well as Pedersen, p. 93.
174. Sneen, p. 41.
175. Blomberg, p. 157.
176. Ibid.
177. Vogels, p. 120.
178. Cf. Euseb H.E. III, 39, 15.
179. Quite similarly Blomberg, p. 156.
180. Blomberg, passim.
181. Wächter, p. 108.
182. Such a flight to a safe haven is taken by both the advocates of a theology of

"paradox" and the advocates of an existential theology, as well as by Platonist theologians and speculative lay believers in churches.
183. On *sensus plenior* cf. recently Douglas J. Moo in Hermeneutics, pp. 175ff.

*CHAPTER TWELVE: Revelation and Criticism*
 1. Latacz, pp. 13f. All citations in this paragraph are from this source.
 2. Cf. Schadewaldt, pp. 201ff.
 3. Cf. Ramm, Interpr, p. 9; Stanton, p. 68.
 4. Marshall, Criticism, p. 131.
 5. Mickelsen, p. 45. Cf. Osborne, p. 15.
 6. Pinnock, pp. 85ff., 136ff., 222ff.
 7. Ibid., pp. 136ff.
 8. E.g., Ramm, Interpr, pp. 9, 101.
 9. According to Amberg, p. 86.
 10. The spectrum extends from Ebeling (ZThK, p. 7) to Schrenk (p. 5), from Amberg (p. 118) to the Theol. Seminar EmK (pp. 82ff.) and to Evertz (pp. 4ff.).
 11. Ritcher, p. 18.
 12. Cf. on the Protestant side e.g., Barr, p. 121; Dobschütz, p. 24 ("the interpreter ... has ... the obligation ... to come to the text critically"); on the Catholic side e.g., Blank, p. 9.
 13. Grässer, ZThK, p. 220.
 14. Schrenk, p. 6; cf. Amberg, p. 121.
 15. Ebeling, ZThK, p. 43; Hirsch in Amberg, p. 86.
 16. Courth, p. 74.
 17. Klauck, p. 99.
 18. Ibid., p. 99.
 19. Weber, Esch, p. 222.
 20. In Barnikol, p. 88 (letter of 19 August 1836 to F. C. Baur).
 21. Ibid. (in the same letter).
 22. Dobschütz, p. 56.
 23. Ebeling, ZThK, p. 5.
 24. Ibid., p. 30.
 25. Grässer, ZThK, p. 220. In Lerle, p. 60, there is a further example of an insult that pretty well pushes the limits from ZThK, p. 358 (by H. Schuster).
 26. Ebeling, ZThK, p. 6.
 27. Yet reference may be made here to the other chapters of this book, which for the most part *ad locum* contain historical discussions.
 28. Scholder, p. 7.
 29. Ibid., p. 14.
 30. Ebeling, RGG, col. 253.
 31. Cf. Scholder, p. 73.
 32. Le Brun, p. 109. Cf. Hasel, p. 18.
 33. Not counting the first chapter which deals with prehistory.
 34. Kümmel, p. 42. Cf. Le Brun, pp. 110ff.
 35. Kümmel, p. 42.
 36. Ibid.

37. Ibid., p. 43.
38. Cf. Le Brun, pp. 106ff.
39. Hornig, p. 184; Merk, Anfänge, p. 53.
40. E.g., Dinkler, p. 15; Kümmel, pp. 41ff.; Meyer I, pp. 24f.; III, p. 315.
41. Cf. Le Brun, pp. 109f. (who nevertheless remarks that the Socinians have "still not yet been thoroughly researched"); Scholder, pp. 48ff.
42. Scholder, p. 132.
43. Picht, p. 19.
44. Cf. Scholder, p. 133.
45. Picht, p. 19.
46. Le Brun, p. 110.
47. Scholder, p. 147.
48. Balthasar Bekker, according to Scholder, p. 147. Cf. Reinhard, p. 46.
49. Picht, p. 15.
50. Cf. Hasel, p. 18; Gass IV, p. 11; Aner, pp. 22 (on Lessing), 27f., 68ff.; Schöffler, pp. 39f.; Schloemann, pp. 160ff. (on Baumgarten); Kümmel, pp. 55ff.; Dilthey, Schriften V, p. 325.
51. Meyer V, pp. 7f.
52. This is effectively worked out by Schloemann, pp. 96ff., 166ff.
53. Cf. Aner, p. 3.
54. Cf. Meyer III, p. 328.
55. Meyer I, p. 6.
56. Ibid., p. 15.
57. E.g., Meyer II, pp. 335ff.; Aner, p. 37.
58. Stolzenburg, p. 435.
59. Meyer II, pp. 352ff., 378.
60. Schöffler, p. 51.
61. Ibid., p. 55.
62. Ibid., pp. 26ff.
63. Ibid., pp. 54, 29.
64. Aner, p. 12.
65. Choisy, p. 166.
66. According to Gass IV, p. 28. Similarly still A. Jülicher (Klauck, p. 100).
67. Cf. Aner, passim; Barr, p. 122; Hornig, passim; Pinnock, p. 131; Sanders, p. 157; Wilckens, p. 95.
68. Cf. Meyer I, pp. 5ff., 18.
69. Gadamer, p. 170; Stolzenburg, p. 446.
70. Aner, p. 4.
71. Lessing, Erziehung, §74. Cf. Aner, p. 158.
72. Aner, pp. 49ff.
73. Ibid., p. 80. Cf. Stolzenburg, p. 440.
74. Stolzenburg, p. 105.
75. Thus Pfaff (Stolzenburg, pp. 95f.); Meyer V, p. 13.
76. The latter expression e.g., in Meyer III, p. 315.
77. Schloemann, p. 233.
78. Stolzenburg, p. 94.

79. Schloemann, pp. 227ff.
80. Ebeling, ZThK, p. 32.
81. Ibid. Cf. Stolzenburg, p. 438.
82. In Gennrich, p. 99.
83. Van den Berg, p. 251.
84. Cf. Courth, p. 97.
85. Girgensohn, Insp, p. 4; cf. F. Traub, p. 83; Seeberg, p. 7.
86. The author: Hermann Risch (Pfarrergebetsbruderschaft, Persönliche Mitteilungen, Folge 92, January 1984).
87. Cf. Esking, pp. 78f.
88. Childs, Theology, p. 140.
89. Cf. ibid., p. 141; idem, Introduction, pp. 40f.
90. Seeberg, p. 5. Similarly Stuhlmacher, Verstehen, p. 31.
91. Güttgemanns, p. 253.
92. Fascher, p. 20.
93. Güttgemanns, pp. 253f.
94. Dibelius, p. 94.
95. Ibid. Cf. Beisser, NZSTh, pp. 197, 206.
96. Dibelius, pp. 46ff.
97. Beisser, NZSTh, p. 206.
98. Gadamer, p. 262.
99. Ibid., p. 263.
100. Ricoeur, HThR, pp. 30ff., 36.
101. Ibid., p. 31.
102. Cf. Picht, pp. 20ff.
103. Ibid., p. 11.
104. Ibid.
105. Ibid., p. 21.
106. Ibid., p. 12.
107. Girgensohn, Schriftbeweis, p. 2.
108. Girgensohn, Insp, pp. 12, 16f.
109. Ibid., pp. 13f. Similarly Ramm, Rev, p. 174.
110. Girgensohn, Insp, p. 14.
111. Procksch, AT, pp. 1f.
112. Sanders, p. 157. Cf. Lücke's prophetic statement on p. 153: for lack of humility historical criticism must "annihilate itself."
113. Childs, Theology, pp. 139ff.; idem, Introduction, pp. 15ff.
114. Cf. Schlatter, Dogma, p. 115.
115. Cf. Bengel in my Joh-Offb, pp. 398f.
116. Thus e.g., Cappel or Bengel.
117. Cf. Schrenk, pp. 38f.; Abraham, pp. 97ff.; Dinkler, p. 9; Grant, p. 25.
118. Thus Schrenk, pp. 38f.
119. Thus e.g., also Packer, Fundamentalism, pp. 56ff.
120. E.g., in Abraham, p. 101; Grant, p. 25; Schrenk, pp. 38ff.
121. Abraham, p. 101; Schrenk, p. 39.
122. E.g., in Abraham, p. 101, and Schrenk, pp. 38f.; Grant, p. 24.

123. Schrenk, p. 101.
124. Cf. Grant, p. 61.
125. Hornig, pp. 165ff.
126. Moldaenke, pp. 6f.
127. Frick, p. 5.
128. Dinkler, p. 8.
129. Ebeling, ZThK, pp. 21, 41. Cf. Kümmel, pp. 16f.
130. Ebeling, ZThK, pp. 39f., 42.
131. Cf. Hirsch, Hilfsbuch, p. 94; Ebeling, RGG, col. 252.
132. Cf. Hirsch, Hilfsbuch, p. 94.
133. Ebeling, RGG, col. 252; cf. Bornkamm, Luther, p. 207.
134. Philippi I, p. 105.
135. Scheel, p. 74.
136. Beisser, Claritas, p. 51.
137. Lönning, pp. 72ff.
138. Bring, pp. 39, 32.
139. Scheel, p. 60; Beisser, Claritas, pp. 125, 180.
140. Scholder, p. 15. Cf. further Beisser, NZSTh, pp. 206, 1; Girgensohn, Insp, p. 41; Popkin, pp. 6f.
141. Cf. Bornkamm, Vorreden, most of all on the antilegomena of the New Testament.
142. Ebeling, RGG, col. 253.
143. Baur, An Hase, p. 8. Cf. already Meyer I, p. 29.
144. According to Grant, p. 155, Baur was "the most important New Testament critic of the nineteenth century."
145. Liebing, p. 310.
146. Ibid., pp. 310, 315.
147. Courth, pp. 63, 66.
148. Ibid., p. 65.
149. Ibid., p. 63.
150. Cf. Kümmel, p. 149; Courth, p. 64.
151. Von Meyer, "a Cartesian friend of Spinoza" (Grant, p. 151).
152. Ibid.
153. Lessing, Beweis, p. 34.
154. Kümmel, p. 76.
155. Cf. ibid., p. 74.
156. Aner, p. 4.
157. Wellhausen, p. 383.
158. Ibid., p. 375.
159. Ibid., p. 385.
160. Dibelius, p. 87.
161. Ibid., p. 46.
162. Ibid., pp. 46, 94.
163. Ibid., p. 82.
164. Cf. also Kümmel, pp. 490ff.
165. Joest, Kanon, p. 192.

166. Ibid.
167. Frei, p. 56.
168. McGinley, p. 22.
169. Ibid., p. 154.
170. Ibid., p. 22.
171. Cf. still Vielhauer, p. 183, who in 1977 placed "patristic testimonies" and "historical criteria" in opposition to one another, and gave preference to the latter!
172. Cf. Barr, p. 34; Meyer I, p. 6; Westermann, p. 18. Cf. Ebeling, ZThK, pp. 27, 31; Pinnock, p. 131. It is one of the enigmas of the history of theology that Ebeling, ZThK, p. 2, can characterize the historical-critical method "as one of the decisive essential features of so-called Neo-Pietism."
173. Reventlow, p. 34; Ebeling (previous note); Lehmann, p. 40.
174. Cf. Aner, passim; Baur, An Hase, p. 22; Liebing, p. 315.
175. Picht, p. 19. Cf. Ebeling, ZThK, p. 30.
176. Picht, p. 15.
177. Cf. Ebeling, ZThK, p. 27.
178. Grant, p. 154. Likewise Mickelsen, p. 44. In the case of Baur cf. again Liebing, pp. 310ff. Cf. still Ebeling, ZThK, p. 2.
179. Schwaiger, p. 7.
180. Westermann, p. 18.
181. Ebeling, ZThK, p. 27.
182. Frei, p. 55. Cf. Gnilka, pp. 473f.
183. Ebeling, ZThK, p. 30. Cf. Dilschneider, pp. 13ff.; Hirsch V, p. 492.
184. Ebeling, ZThK, p. 30.
185. Ibid., p. 42. Cf. Barr, p. 34.
186. Ebeling, ZThK, p. 45. Similarly also Bultmann.
187. Ebeling, ZThK, p. 36.
188. Ibid.
189. Trillhaas, p. 476.
190. Schadewaldt, p. 203.
191. Ibid., pp. 202f. Cf. Latacz at the beginning of this chapter.
192. Cf. Gigon, passim.
193. The Allgemeiner Evangelisch-Protestantischer Missionsverein (1884), since 1929 called Ostasienmission; cf. Oehler, pp. 37ff.
194. Semler I, p. 55; cf. Aner, pp. 270ff.
195. Kümmel, p. 476.
196. Lessing, Axiomata, p. 63.
197. Ibid., p. 73. Cf. the following pages.
198. Ibid., p. 77.
199. Aner, p. 151. Cf. Picht, p. 19; Gadamer, pp. 174, 186.
200. Aner, p. 151.
201. Wellhausen, p. 386.
202. In Courth, p. 67. Cf. Kümmel, p. 149.
203. Gemmer/Messer, p. 18.
204. Trillhaas, p. 1.

205. Ibid., p. 463.
206. Ibid., pp. 475ff.
207. Ibid., pp. 471, 492.
208. Ibid., p. 500.
209. Cf. Meyer I, p. 6; Aner, pp. 163f.
210. Here Barr is correct: "Its basic perceptions seem to derive from the Renaissance."
211. Cf. here Vorländer, p. 246.
212. Lessing, Menuschengeschlect,§4.
213. Semler, according to Kümmel, p. 76.
214. Lessing, Axiomata, p. 69.
215. Cf. ibid., pp. 47ff.
216. Aner, p. 51.
217. Merk, Anfänge, p. 59.
218. Cited by Kümmel, pp. 124f. (Translation follows that by S. L. Gilmour and H. C. Kee of Kümmel, *The New Testament: The History of the Investigation of Its Problems* [Nashville/New York, 1972], p. 105.)
219. Cf. Kümmel, pp. 250ff.
220. Cf. Girgensohn, Schriftbeweis, pp. 37ff. Regarding F. C. Baur, Geiger stated that for him "the autonomy of the subject" is a central concept (p. 227). Cf. also Lerle, p. 27; Ebeling, ZThK, p. 30.
221. Cf. Hirsch V, p. 3: "Faith in reason" had "by 1790 . . . become a major power."
222. Reventlow, pp. 33f.
223. Conzelmann-Lindemann, p. 37.
224. E.g., in Barr, p. 3 (1983).
225. Scholder, p. 133. Cf. Gadamer, p. 255.
226. Lehmann, p. 46.
227. Neill, p. 4. Cf. Still Wilckens, p. 98.
228. Gadamer, p. 255.
229. Lessing, Beweis, p. 34.
230. According to Kümmel, p. 121.
231. Ibid.
232. Cf. Amberg, p. 86.
233. Barr, p. 93.
234. Lehmann, p. 46.
235. Also long before now: see Lücke, p. 153.
236. Hengel, Gesch, p. 9.
237. Ibid., p. 54.
238. Ibid., p. 55.
239. Seeberg, p. 5.
240. Reventlow, p. 34.
241. Bürgener, p. 56, in his otherwise valuable work which even attempts a harmony of the Easter narratives.
242. Hengel, ThB, p. 60.
243. Kuppler, p. 116.
244. Luz, e.g., pp. 141, 171.

245. Scholder, p. 7.
246. According to Strauss, p. 126; cf. p. 260.
247. Lessing, Axiomata, p. 67.
248. Ibid.
249. Hirsch V, p. 6.
250. Lessing, Erziehung, p. 8.
251. On Luther cf. e.g., Bornkamm, Luther, p. 207.
252. Schmidt, Kreuzverhör, p. 51.
253. Ibid.
254. Cf. Amberg, p. 16.
255. Ibid., p. 86.
256. Dinkler, pp. 7f.
257. Moves in this direction have been made e.g., by Stuhlmacher.
258. Strauss, p. 260.
259. Ibid.
260. According to Merk, Anfänge, p. 43; cf. Kümmel, p. 65.
261. Merk, Anfänge, p. 43.; Kümmel, p. 66.
262. According to Kümmel, p. 67.
263. Keil, p. 1.
264. Cf. Frei, pp. 17f.; Mickelsen, p. 44; Packer, Fundamentalism, pp. 111f.; Pinnock, p. 131.
265. Cf. Bultmann, GV II, p. 231.
266. Ebeling, ZThK, p. 32.
267. Ibid.
268. Ibid.
269. Girgensohn, Schriftbeweis, p. 65.
270. Kümmel, p. 98.
271. Ibid., p. 99.
272. Example: Dibelius, p. 13.
273. Girgensohn, Schriftbeweis, p. 3.
274. Dinkler, p. 7.
275. Bultmann, GV II, pp. 231f.
276. Ibid., p. 232. The quote is from Augustine's Confessions, I, 1: "Tu nos fecisti ad Te."
277. Stuhlmacher, Verstehen, p. 253.
278. Cf. the Stuhlmacher-Grässer feud.
279. Kümmel, pp. 69f.
280. Cf. Hornig, p. 68; Kümmel, pp. 82ff.
281. Kümmel, p. 83.
282. Ibid., pp. 116f.
283. Gass IV, p. 22.
284. Kümmel, p. 389.
285. Ibid., p. 393.
286. Thus e.g., Hirsch I, p. 323.
287. According to Kümmel, p. 60.
288. Ibid., p. 62.

289. Dinkler, p. 16.
290. Amberg, p. 52.
291. Cf. Kümmel, pp. 466ff.
292. Stuhlmacher, Verstehen, p. 57, and then pp. 52ff.
293. Thus Weber, Schriftforschung, p. 31.
294. An example would be his "Beweis des Geistes und der Kraft."
295. Weber, Schriftforschung, p. 126.
296. Lessing, Beweis, p. 32. Cf. E. Hirsch's judgments, which Amberg, p. 86, cites.
297. Thus Geiger, p. 225, on F. C. Baur.
298. Schloemann, p. 229.
299. Hornig, p. 73.
300. Kümmel, pp. 132f.
301. Redlich, Traditions, p. 12.
302. Ibid., p. 10.
303. Cf. Le Brun, pp. 107ff.
304. E.g., Weber, Schriftforschung, p. 36.
305. Dinkler, p. 16.
306. Schweizer, Ev Th, p. 344.
307. Cf. Joest, Kanon, pp. 177, 184, 190.
308. Ibid., pp. 177, 190, 196.
309. Cf. Barr, pp. 106f.; Redlich, Traditions, p. 10.
310. Cf. again Kümmel, pp. 62ff.
311. An example is once more Weber, Schriftforschung, p. 36.
312. Dinkler, p. 16.
313. Cf. Grässer, ZThK, pp. 211ff.; Trillhaas, p. 74.
314. Thus Hesse, p. 294, in view of Ps 109. Similarly Hesse, AT, p. 107, in view of Ex 32:27.
315. Thus Stuhlmacher, Verstehen, p. 240.
316. Cf. Dilschneider, pp. 13, 61; Schulz, p. 83.
317. Schulz, p. 43.
318. E.g., Semler, cf. Aner, p. 237.
319. Aner, pp. 173f., 300.
320. Ibid., p. 241.
321. Ibid., pp. 285ff.
322. Ibid., pp. 291ff.
323. Ibid., pp. 174f.
324. Ibid., pp. 270ff.
325. Cf. Aner, p. 200.
326. Beisser, NZSTh, p. 197.
327. Oepke, p. 29. Similarly Funk, p. 236.
328. Geiger, p. 227.
329. Ebeling, ZThK, p. 30.
330. F. Traub, p. 111.
331. On the sources in Spinoza cf. again Strauss, pp. 106ff., 260f.
332. Funk, p. 236.
333. Cf. Aner, p. 4.

334. Baur, An Hase, p. 11.
335. E. g. Strauss (Courth, p. 66; Barnikol, ZKG, 73, p. 118).
336. According to Klatt, p. 261. Cf. Gunkel himself in Vorwort, p. v (1903).
337. Esking, p. 6.
338. Cf. Stuhlmacher, Verstehen, pp. 240ff.
339. According to Aner, p. 24.
340. Lessing, Erziehung, § 81–82.
341. Ibid., § 80.
342. Ibid., § 85–86.
343. Aner, p. 49.
344. Jerusalem, according to Aner, p. 162.
345. Aner, pp. 49f.
346. Ibid., p. 164.
347. Barnikol, p. 32.
348. According to Courth, p. 67.
349. Cf. Ahn, pp. 66ff.
350. Lehmann, p. 52.
351. Cf. Stanton, pp. 60f.; Mickelsen, p. 44.
352. Ebeling, RGG, col. 256.
353. According to Stanton, p. 66.
354. Cf. Bultmann, GV II, pp. 226f.
355. Liebing, p. 310.
356. Klatt, p. 261.
357. Klauck, p. 100.
358. Smend, p. 232.
359. Ibid. Cf. Frick, pp. 13f.; Barnikol, p. 27 (on Baur).
360. Meyer IV, pp. 428ff.
361. In Klauck, p. 108.
362. Two examples (which could easily be multiplied): Duhm's interpretation of Isa 29:17ff., and Käsemann's "criterion of underivability."
363. Stuhlmacher, Verstehen, p. 253.
364. Rightly Bring, p. 38.
365. Bultmann, GV II, pp. 231f.
366. Ebeling, ZThK, p. 32.
367. Ibid.
368. Bultmann, GV II, p. 232.
369. Barr, p. 84.
370. Ibid., p. 46.
371. Ibid., p. 47.
372. Thus already Lücke, p. 144.
373. Cf. Strauss, pp. 2, 106ff., 126, 247, 261.
374. Cf. Hirsch V, p. 6.
375. Trillhaas, p. 78.
376. Cited in Kümmel, p. 74. Cf. Hornig, pp. 84ff.
377. Cf. again Hornig, p. 84.
378. Ibid., pp. 112ff.

379. Beisser, Claritas, p. 180; Cf. Luther, WA V, p. 184.
380. Cf. Preus, p. 9.
381. Axiomata I (p. 3).
382. Axiomata, p. 48.
383. Ibid.
384. Ibid., pp. 48f.
385. Ibid., p. 63.
386. Courth, p. 64.
387. Amberg, p. 7.
388. Dibelius, pp. 14, 46. Cf. Esking, pp. 49ff.
389. Dobschütz, p. 61.
390. Jüngel, p. 210.
391. Meyer I, p. 5.
392. Cf. on Baur and his school Frankemölle, p. 175; Geiger, p. 183. On Reimarus see Merk, Anfänge, p. 55.
393. According to Esking, p. 8.
394. Weber, Schriftforschung, p. 9 (following Semler?).
395. Ebeling, ZThK, p. 13. Cf. Thurneysen, pp. 15, 21.
396. Esking, p. 69.
397. Hesse, AT, p. 14.
398. Girgensohn, Grundriss, p. 61.
399. Thurneysen, p. 13. Cf. Preus, p. vi.
400. Esking, p. 9.
401. Stuhlmacher, Verstehen, p. 247. His essay in ThB, p. 158, says nothing different.
402. Stuhlmacher, Geist, p. 27.
403. Ibid.
404. Ibid. Cf. Stuhlmacher, ThB, pp. 157f.
405. Blank, p. 9.
406. Cf. also Beisser, NZSTh, p. 195.
407. Cf. Falckenberg, p. 283.
408. Wellhausen, p. 206.
409. Stuhlmacher, Geist, pp. 27f.
410. Cf. Robinson-Cobb, p. 50.
411. Ibid., p. 94.
412. Ebeling, ZThK, p. 27. Cf. Barr, p. 121; Blank, p. 9; also the statements by Stuhlmacher above.
413. Grässer, ZThK, p. 209.
414. Funk in Robinson-Cobb, p. 298.
415. Thus Jüngel, p. 266.
416. Cf. Fascher, p. 18.
417. Thus however Thurneysen, who with this statement represents the Barth school.
418. Cf. Falckenberg, p. 285.
419. Cf. Jüngel, pp. 211ff.; Thurneysen, pp. 30, 25.

420. Making use of Lessing's term in Axiomata, p. 63, but in sense opposite from Lessing's.
421. Fascher, p. 18.
422. Fuchs in Robinson-Cobb, p. 182.
423. Lücke, p. 153.
424. Ebeling, ZThK, p. 6. Cf. Weber, Schriftforschung, p. 1.
425. Weber, Schriftforschung, pp. vii, 2.
426. Thus e.g., Thurneysen(!), p. 19; Ebeling, ZThK, pp. 31ff.; Girgensohn, Schriftbeweis, p. 22; Dinkler, p. 17 ("never"!).
427. Thus e.g., Stuhlmacher, Verstehen, pp. 223, 243.
428. Ibid., pp. 222ff.; Stuhlmacher, ThB, pp. 157f.
429. Cf. Rendtorff, p. 10.
430. See e.g., Evangelische Mission, 1985, pp. 83ff.
431. Cf. Drewermann, pp. 18ff.; Wink, p. 7.
432. Cf. Beisser, NZSTh, p. 195.

*CHAPTER THIRTEEN: Revelation and Method*

1. Cf. Longenecker, pp. 67ff.
2. Cf. Wellhausen, p. 135.
3. Cf. here Papias in Eusebius, H. E. III, 39, and in Irenaeus, Adv. Haer., V, 33. See also the Hypotyposes of Clement of Alexandria, also entire documents such as the Didache.
4. Cited according to the *Jahrbuch der Theologischen Schule Bethel,* 6, 1935, p. 128.
5. Diem, p. 45.
6. Girgensohn, Insp, p. 24.
7. Ibid.
8. Girgensohn, Schriftbeweis, pp. 2f.
9. Cf. *Theologie und Dienst,* vol. 43, 1985, in which the essays of Schlatter and Jäger are newly reprinted with an afterword by Heinzpeter Hempelmann.
10. Wrede, pp. 79f.
11. Cf. Kümmel, p. 282.
12. Ibid., p. 466.
13. Cf. Heinrici, p. 739; Dobschütz, pp. 19, 50.
14. Beck, Leitfaden, p. 10.
15. Ibid., p. 9. Cf. Wach, Verstehen II, p. 209.
16. Beck, Leitfaden, p. 9.
17. Ibid.
18. Cf. Wach, Verstehen II, pp. 206ff.
19. Cf. Lutz, p. 172; Heinrici, p. 739; Wach, Verstehen II, pp. 318ff.
20. Girgensohn, Reformgedanken, pp. 92f.
21. Girgensohn, Insp, pp. 25f.
22. Ibid., pp. 42f.
23. Girgensohn, Schriftbeweis, p. 60.
24. Ibid., p. 3.
25. Ibid., p. 2.

26. Ibid., pp. 37–43.
27. Ibid., p. 65.
28. Ibid., p. 52.
29. Ibid.
30. Ibid., p. 63.
31. Ibid., pp. 63f.
32. Ibid., p. 63.
33. Ibid., pp. 73, 76.
34. Ibid., pp. 73, 1.
35. Ibid., p. 76; cf. p. 72.
36. Girgensohn, Reformgedanken, p. 92.
37. Girgensohn, Schriftbeweis, p. 73.
38. Ibid., pp. 66–69.
39. Theol Bl, 1928, 3, col. 64, 10.
40. Torm, p. 17.
41. Seeberg, p. 46.
42. Seeberg, pp. 41ff.; cf. Torm, p. 24.
43. Fascher, p. 28. Dobschütz also mentioned that Girgensohn came to his pneumatic exegesis through Elias Schrenk (p. 49). Schrenk, born 1831 in Hausen ob Verena, Württemberg, was one of the fathers of the awakening and cofounder of tent evangelism. On Girgensohn's own appeal to Schrenk cf. Insp, p. 43.
44. Girgensohn, Insp, p. 16. The parallel to K. Barth's formulation in the foreword of his Romans commentary is striking.
45. Cf. Dobschütz, p. 19.
46. Girgensohn, Insp, p. 21.
47. Ibid., p. 40.
48. Stressed in Girgensohn's Reformgedanken, p. 90.
49. Girgensohn, Insp, p. 45.
50. Cf. Stuhlmacher, Verstehen, pp. 253f.
51. Girgensohn, Insp, pp. 21ff.
52. From the second edition, 1921, p. 42, cited by Torm, pp. 29, 1.
53. Girgensohn, Insp, pp. 61ff.
54. Cf. Amberg, pp. 47ff.; Fascher, p. 27; Lerle, p. 26; Seeberg, p. 39.
55. Girgensohn, Insp, p. 27.
56. Cf. ibid., p. 64, and idem, Reformgedanken, p. 90. See also Lerle, p. 26.
57. Girgensohn, Insp, p. 28; idem, Schriftbeweis, p. 73.
58. Girgensohn, Insp, p. 27; cf. p. 18.
59. Cf. Dobschütz, pp. 51, 63, appealing to J. Behm; also Fascher, p. 28; Oepke, pp. 24, 9.
60. Fascher, p. 27.
61. Procksch, CuW, p. 145.
62. Ibid., p. 150.
63. Ibid.
64. Ibid.
65. Ibid., p. 156.

66. Procksch, AT, pp. 13, 15.
67. Ibid., p. 17.
68. Ibid., p. 36.
69. Oepke, p. 26.
70. Ibid., pp. 17ff.
71. Ibid., p. 36.
72. Ibid., p. 18.
73. Ibid., p. 19.
74. Ibid., p. 36.
75. Ibid., pp. 37, 43.
76. Cf. Frey, Ansatz, pp. 156, 1.
77. Ibid., p. 178.
78. Ibid., p. 180.
79. Ibid., p. 155.
80. Ibid., p. 156.
81. Ibid., p. 171.
82. Ibid., p. 170.
83. Ibid., p. 154; Frey, Krise, pp. 86ff.
84. Frey, Ansatz, pp. 170, 167.
85. Ibid., pp. 168f.
86. Ibid., p. 169.
87. Ibid., pp. 161, 166.
88. Ibid., pp. 163ff.
89. Ibid., pp. 175, 173.
90. Ibid., pp. 177f.
91. Ibid., p. 157.
92. Ibid.
93. Ibid., p. 158 (appealing to Luther and Barth!).
94. Ibid.
95. Cf. e.g., ibid., pp. 154, 158.
96. Ibid., p. 158.
97. Ibid., p. 154.
98. Ibid., p. 169.
99. Cf. Frey, Krise, p. 81.
100. Cf. ibid., pp. 80ff.
101. Richter, p. 18.
102. Ibid., p. 9.
103. Ibid.
104. Wolff, p. 140.
105. Merk, TRE, p. 395.
106. Gunneweg, WPKG, p. 16. Cf. Stuhlmacher, Verstehen, p. 223. Hartlich, p. 476, is still more radical: The historical-critical method is "the only [one] possible"!
107. Richter, p. 19.
108. Philippi I, p. 110.
109. Ramm, Interpr, pp. 60ff.

110. Henkel, p. 2.
111. Ibid., p. 6.
112. Cf. ibid., pp. 14f.
113. Dobschütz, pp. 28f.
114. Oepke, p. 20.
115. Dibelius, p. 97.
116. Ibid., p. 46.
117. Ibid., p. 97.
118. Esking, pp. 121, 81. Esking himself turned decisively against a "dualistic conception of the Word of God," or against a dualism of methods (p. 80).
119. Boeckh, p. 80.
120. Ibid., p. 81.
121. Wolff, p. 143.
122. Stuhlmacher, ThB, p. 156.
123. Ibid. Cf. p. 153.
124. Ibid., pp. 157f.
125. On the different situation in the Anglo-Saxon realm cf. Travis, p. 155; Ellis, p. 238.
126. Dobschütz, pp. 33ff.
127. Ibid.
128. Riesenfeld, pp. 7ff. For the continuance of the impetus his work provided cf. R. Riesner, *Jesus als Lehrer.*
129. Riesenfeld, pp. 23f.; cf. pp. 15ff., 28.
130. Ibid., pp. 14f., 19f.
131. Ibid., pp. 21, 26.
132. Schürmann, Untersuchungen, p. 46.
133. Ibid., pp. 45f.
134. Ibid., p. 47. Cf. the dissertation by that name authored by R. Riesner (cf. n. 128 above).
135. Ibid., p. 56.
136. Ibid., p. 45.
137. Subtitle in Schürmann's Tod Jesu, p. 325.
138. Schürmann, Jesu Tod, p. 359.
139. Güttgemanns, p. 36.
140. Ibid., pp. 253f.
141. Subtitle of "Evangelist und Gemeinde."
142. Frankemölle, p. 180. Cf. the axioms in Travis, pp. 153f.
143. Richter, pp. 17f.
144. Yri, pp. 17f. ("a proper historical-theological methodology").
145. Cf. Childs, Theology, pp. 91ff.; idem, Introduction, passim.
146. Wink, p. 7.
147. Not even Frey, who wants to proceed methodically when it comes to individual passages!
148. Vermes, p. 95: "a fundamental unity of exegetical tradition."
149. Cf. Longenecker, p. 28, with Goppelt, Typos, p. 67.
150. Cf. again Longenecker, pp. 29, 19, along with Heinisch, pp. 47, 52ff.

151. Daube, passim; Grant, p. 24; Longenecker, pp. 67ff. Travis, p. 159, in disagreement with J. Jeremias, calls attention to the fact that even allegory is used by Jesus.
152. Longenecker, p. 67.
153. Ibid., pp. 68f.
154. Cf. D. A. Carson, *Matthew*, The Expositor's Bible Commentary, 8 (1984), p. 114.
155. Cf. Riesenfeld, p. 24; Schürmann, Untersuchungen, pp. 47ff.
156. Cf. Daube, passim; Travis, p. 159 (referring to H. Riesenfeld and B. Gerhardsson).
157. Goppelt, Typos, pp. 70ff., 239; Grant, pp. 54f.
158. Cf. Grant, pp. 33, 40.
159. Ibid., pp. 31, 33; cf. Goppelt, Typos, p. 152.
160. Longenecker, p. 126; Heinisch, p. 35; Grant, p. 31.
161. Cf. Chmiel, pp. 155ff.; Heinisch, pp. 36ff.
162. Bonwetsch, passim, most of all pp. 42ff.
163. Cf. Kramer II, p. 380.
164. Boeckh, p. 80.
165. Cf. Nestle-Aland, *Novum Testamentum Graece,* 26th ed., p. 775, where New Testament references to Greek authors are catalogued.
166. One is reminded of what value Beck placed on this unity of doctrine and praxis!
167. Childs, Theology, pp. 139ff.
168. Strecker, p. 19.
169. E.g., ibid., p. 2.
170. Lehmann, pp. 75ff.
171. Baur, An Hase, p. 8. Cf. on Rückert, 1831, Heinrici, p. 738.
172. Wrede, p. 9.
173. Cf. Esking, p. 6; Troeltsch, passim.
174. Cf. Robinson, New Look, pp. 338ff.
175. So Diem, p. 16. Much more crassly Hartlich, pp. 467ff.
176. Gunneweg, WPKG, pp. 13, 16.
177. Strecker, pp. 2f.
178. Schloemann, p. 231.
179. Funk, p. 19.
180. Hasel, p. 19.
181. Frei, p. 1.
182. Cf. Kihn, p. 122.
183. Cf. Heinrici, p. 737.
184. Cf. Dobschütz, pp. 33, 49.
185. Keil, pp. viiif., 9. The complete title runs *Lehrbuch der Hermeneutik des Neuen Testaments nach Grundsätzen der grammatisch-historischen Interpretation* (*Handbook of Hermeneutics According to the Basic Principles of Grammatical-Historical Interpretation*). Hasel's claim (pp. 28f.) that Gottlob Philipp Christian Kaiser was in 1813 the first to propose the "grammatico-historical method" needs to be revised.

186. Frei, p. 2.
187. Dilthey, Schriften V, p. 324.
188. Moldaenke, p. 121.
189. See Moldaenke, p. 300: "Spiritus s. et Pater ipse per os Prophetarum et Apostolorum locutus est conscripsitque sacram Scripturam" ("The Holy Spirit and the Father himself have spoken through the mouth of the prophets and the Apostles and have written the sacred Scripture"). Cf. Keller, pp. 44f., 139.
190. Moldaenke, pp. 351f. Cf. Keller, pp. 168, 109.
191. Moldaenke, p. 67. Cf. Keller, pp. 121f.
192. Moldaenke, pp. 573, 484.
193. Ibid., p. 59.
194. Cf. ibid., p. 190.
195. Ibid., pp. 476ff., 306ff.
196. Ibid., pp. 484ff.
197. Ibid., p. 497. Cf. Keller, p. 122.
198. Moldaenke, p. 495.
199. Ibid., pp. 519ff.
200. Ibid., p. 492.
201. Ibid., p. 518.
202. Ibid., pp. 195ff.
203. Ibid., pp. 127, 617f.
204. Ibid., pp. 617f., 144f. Cf. Keller, p. 134.
205. Moldaenke, pp. 197ff., 206f.
206. Ibid., p. 203.
207. Ibid., p. 207.
208. Ibid., p. 572. Moldaenke lists the following as individual central components: Gospel, Decalogue, confessions, catechism, salvation history with creation, fall, and redemption (pp. 562ff.; cf. p. 356).
209. Hasel, p. 20 (with Dentan). Cf. Merk, Anfänge, pp. 49ff.
210. Cf. the themes in Preus, p. xvii, as well as Preus, passim; Ratschow I, pp. 101ff. Cf. Colovius, *Systema Locorum Theologicorum*, 1655–77; König, *Theologia Positiva Acroamatica*, 1665; Hollaz, *Examen Theologiae Acroamaticae*, ed. by Teller, 1750; Quenstedt, *Theologia Didacticopolemica*, 1685.
211. Frei, p. 19.
212. It remains a mystery how Frei (p. 4) can make Coccejus and Bengel into forerunners of historical criticism.
213. Kramer II, p. 396.
214. Frei, p. 38.
215. Cf. Kramer I, p. 5.
216. Ibid., p. 60; cf. Kramer II, p. 388.
217. Kramer II, p. 388.
218. Kramer I, p. 5.
219. Kramer I, p. 152.
220. He is senselessly therefore always being styled as one of the fathers of historical criticism. Thus unfortunately even Frei, pp. 39f.; Stuhlmacher, Verstehen, pp. 139f.

221. Cf. Kihn, p. 77.
222. Cf. my Joh-Offb, pp. 416f.
223. Frei, p. 40.
224. Cf. Jüngel, pp. 171ff.
225. Cf. H. Burkhardt, *Wiederkehr der Religiosität?*, 1990.
226. Büchsel, p. iii.
227. Stuhlmacher, Verstehen, p. 142. Cf. regarding the newly wakened interest in Hamann the treatises by E. Büchsel, 1988; H. Hempelmann, 1988; K. H. Michel, Anfänge, 1985; H. Lindner, 1988; M. Seils, 1987; along with the bibliography in Bayer, TRE, p. 403 and Lindner, pp. 47–49. Cf. further Hempelmann, p. 18.
228. "Entkleidung und Verklärung," according to Seils, p. 495.
229. Thus C. M. Wieland, cited in Seils, pp. 390, 1.
230. "Entkleidung und Verklärung," in Seils, pp. 498, 500. Cf. Bayer, TRE, p. 399; E. Büchsel, p. v.
231. Lindner, pp. 27f.
232. "Über die Auslegung der Heiligen Schrift" (N I, pp. 5f.).
233. N I, p. 91.
234. "Gedanken über meinen Lebenslauf," in Seils, p. 62.
235. N I, p. 5.
236. In Seils, pp. 63, 184 (in "Gedanken über meinen Lebenslauf" or "Die Magi aus Morgenlande").
237. Cf. note 234.
238. Cf. again note 234. Cf. Jer 38:13.
239. From the first letter in "Kleeblatt Hellenistischer Briefe," in Seils, p. 263; cf. p. 262.
240. Ibid., in Seils, p. 265.
241. Nicely worked out in Lindner, pp. 26f.
242. In Seils, p. 235.
243. Ibid.
244. Ibid.
245. In "Biblischen Betrachtungen eines Christen," in Seils, p. 13. Cf. Michel, Anfänge, pp. 114f.
246. In "Gedanken über meinen Lebenslauf," in Seils, p. 62.
247. In the first of the Hellenistische Briefe in Seils, p. 263.
248. Lindner, p. 28; Hempelmann, p. 10; Michel, Anfänge, p. 115. Cf. Büchsel, p. 33.
249. Cf. note 248 along with Lindner, pp. 16, 18; Hempelmann, p. 29; Michel, Anfänge, p. 120.
250. In "Golgatha und Scheblimini," in Seils, p. 238.
251. "Biblischen Betrachtungen eines Christen" (N I, p. 5).
252. In "Gedanken über meinen Lebenslauf," in Seils, p. 62.
253. Ibid., p. 61.
254. In "Biblischen Betrachtungen eines Christen," in Seils, p. 24.
255. In the first of the Hellenistische Briefe in Seils, p. 264.
256. Cf. E. Büchsel, p. 43.

257. In "Komnxompax," in Seils, pp. 217f.; cf. Seils, p. 235.
258. In "Die Magi aus Morgenlande," in Seils, pp. 182f.
259. In "Biblischen Betrachtungen eines Christen" (N I, pp. 5f.).
260. Cf. Lindner, p. 18.
261. "Am Himmelfahrts-Tage, 4 May 1758." In Seils, p. 20.
262. In "Gedanken über meinen Lebenslauf," in Seils, p. 60. Cf. E. Büchsel, p. 48.
263. E. Büchsel, p. 59.
264. Cf. N III, pp. 277ff.; Bayer, TRE, p. 401.
265. E. Büchsel, p. 99.
266. Ibid., p. 41.
267. It is better to avoid the expression "philological-historical work" (Stuhlmacher, Verstehen, p. 141) in view of its weighty associations from the history of theology. It does not fit what Hamann has in mind.
268. Cf. Lindner, pp. 18, 22, along with Hempelmann, p. 61, and Michel, Anfänge, p. 113.
269. Bayer, TRE, p. 397.
270. Hempelmann, p. 17.
271. Cf. Lindner, pp. 26f. with Hempelmann, pp. 14ff.
272. Cf. Hempelmann, pp. 11ff.; Lindner, p. 25; Michel, Anfänge, p. 114.
273. Cited and discussed in Lindner, pp. 28f.
274. Ibid., p. 29.
275. N II, p. 43. Cf. Hempelmann, p. 11.
276. Other critical questions in E. Büchsel, pp. 96, 99.
277. Cf. the opinion of Wach, Verstehen II, p. 318.
278. Lutz, p. 172.
279. Beck, Gedanken, pp. 84, 98f., 179.
280. Cf. Lutz, p. 172; Wach, Verstehen II, p. 332; also Wach, Verstehen II, pp. 206ff. on Beck.
281. Wach, Verstehen II, p. 332.
282. Ibid.
283. Heinrici, pp. 738f.; Wach, Verstehen II, p. 206.
284. Wach, Verstehen II, p. 206.
285. Ibid., pp. 209, 327f.
286. Schöffler, p. 67. Schöffler names the following as examples (among others): Bodmer, Goggsched, Klopstock, Lessing, Schlözer, Lichtenberg, Hölty, Bürger, Lenz.
287. Schlatter, Dogma, p. 367.
288. Hasel, p. 43.
289. Dobschütz, p. 56. Cf. Riesner and Bittner, in Bockmühl, pp. 36ff. and p. 116.
290. On Schlatter cf. Egg, pp. 108, 135, 239. Cf. Neuer, Schlatter, pp. 50ff.
291. Schlatter, Dogma, p. 369. Cf. Egg, p. 134.
292. On Schlatter cf. his Dogma, pp. 364ff.
293. Cf. ibid., pp. 372ff.
294. Ibid., p. 93.
295. Ibid., p. 109.
296. Ibid., p. 199.

297. Egg, p. 242.
298. Schlatter, Dogma, p. 5.
299. Ibid., p. 12.
300. Ibid.
301. Cf. Egg, p. 82.
302. Schlatter, Dogma, p. 89.
303. Ibid., pp. 12, 18, 19, 41, 94.
304. Ibid., pp. 25ff.
305. Ibid., pp. 15, 38ff.
306. Ibid., p. 27.
307. Ibid., p. 121.
308. Ibid., p. 18.
309. Ibid., p. 19.
310. Ibid., p. 98. Cf. Egg, p. 82; also Neuer, Zusammenhang, pp. 43ff., 139ff.
311. Cf. Beck, Gedanken, pp. 98f., 118.
312. Schlatter, Dogma, pp. 20ff.
313. Ibid., p. 14.
314. Thus ibid., p. 370.
315. Ibid., p. 367. Cf. Neuer, Schlatter, pp. 55f.
316. Cf. Schlatter, Dogma, pp. 364ff.
317. Ibid., pp. 591, 217.
318. Cf. Schlatter, Christus, pp. 226ff.
319. Cf. Egg, p. 135.
320. Schlatter, Dogma, p. 14.
321. Ibid., p. 11.
322. Ibid., p. 525.
323. Cf. Hasel, pp. 36ff.
324. Cf. ibid.; Wach, Verstehen II, p. 359.
325. Wach, Verstehen II, p. 360.
326. Cf. Beyschlag, p. 9. The quote is from Hofmann, *Der Schriftbeweis*, I, 2d ed. (1857), p. 10.
327. Wach, Verstehen II, p. 367.
328. Ibid., p. 372.
329. Ibid., p. 369.
330. Ibid., pp. 370ff.
331. Ibid., pp. 366f. Cf. Hofmann, p. 5.
332. Hofmann, p. 9 (*Biblische Hermeneutik*).
333. Wach, Verstehen II, p. 364. Cf. the similar judgment of Beyschlag (p. 9).
334. Joest, TRE, p. 732.
335. Ibid.
336. Ibid.
337. Wenham, pp. 84f.
338. Lönning, pp. 13, 10.
339. Gratefully we can report that P. Stuhlmacher in the 2d ed. of his Verstehen (cf. pp. 199, 238ff.) toned down his antifundamentalist polemic. How deeply the ruts run can still be seen in Joest's "critical assessment" in TRE, pp. 736ff.

340. Cf. Cole, pp. 52ff.; Packer, Fundamentalism, p. 28.
341. Packer, Fundamentalism, p. 29.
342. Joest, TRE, p. 732.
343. Ibid., p. 734.
344. Cf. here Machen, pp. 75, 78; Warfield, Inspiration and Authority, pp. 110ff.; Warfield, Insp, pp. 280ff.; Chicago, Art. 16; Geisler, Decide, p. 32.
345. Cf. Packer, Fundamentalism, p. 25.
346. Machen, p. 73.
347. Thus e.g., ibid., pp. 73f.; Ramm, Interpr, p. 86; Henry IV, p. 160; Geisler, Decide, p. 71.
348. Thus Ramm, Interpr, p. 86; Chicago, Art. 6.
349. Thus Chicago Short Statement, number 4.
350. Thus Geisler, Decide, p. 71.
351. Machen, pp. 73, 1. Cf. Warfield, Divine, pp. 275ff.; Henry IV, p. 202; Chicago, Art. 8 and the exposition; Geisler, Decide, p. 75.
352. Machen, p. 73. Cf. Warfield, Divine, p. 276.
353. Warfield, Divine, p. 278.
354. Cf. Marshall, Insp, pp. 40ff.; also Carson, Developments, p. 45.
355. Machen, p. 75; cf. p. 74.
356. Geisler, Decide, p. 22.
357. Thus e.g., Ramm, Interpr, pp. 183ff.; Geisler, Decide, pp. 75, 102ff.; Packer, Battle, pp. 44ff.; Henry IV, pp. 167ff.; Pinnock, pp. 222ff.; Chicago, Art. 12ff.
358. Cf. Chicago, Art. 17 ("in its entirety") and 19 ("full inerrancy of Scripture").
359. Geisler, Decide, p. 76, according to John R. Rice, *Our God-Breathed Book— The Bible* (1969).
360. Kropatscheck, p. 425; cf. p. 434.
361. According to Preus, p. 77.
362. Cf. Preus, p. 77; Ratschow I, p. 71.
363. Cf. Keller, p. 132.
364. Cf. Warfield, Inerrancy, pp. 270ff.
365. Carson, Developments, pp. 24f.; Ramm, Interpr, p. 119.
366. Packer, Fundamentalism, pp. 115ff.
367. Marshall, Insp, p. 72; cf. also pp. 70f.
368. Cf. again ibid., pp. 70ff.
369. Cf. Machen, pp. 77ff.; Chicago, Art. 3.
370. Cf. Chicago, Art. 14; Berkhof, p. 53; Mickelsen, pp. 86ff.; Packer, Battle, p. 41; Ramm, Interpr, p. 186.
371. Thus Packer, Battle, p. 41, and Berkhof, p. 53.
372. Cf. Chicago, Art. 5; Berkhof, p. 53; Pinnock, pp. 175ff.; Ramm, Interpr, pp. 111ff.
373. Machen, p. 70: "centre and core."
374. Ibid., p. 74.
375. Ibid., p. 70.
376. Chicago, Art. 8, 18.
377. Henry IV, p. 168. Cf. IV, p. 68, and Packer, Battle, p. 52.
378. On the term *moderate criticism* cf. Merk, TRE, p. 388.

379. See the essay by R. Smend.
380. Thus Stuhlmacher, Verstehen, pp. 183ff., appeals expressly to "post-critical Scripture interpretation" and the essay by Smend (previous note).
381. Smend, pp. 233, 236.
382. Those engaged in this line of thinking include e.g., Hahn, Hengel, Merk, Stuhlmacher.
383. Both citations from Merk, TRE, p. 395 (1980).
384. H. M. Barth, col. 241ff.
385. Ibid., col. 241f.
386. Stuhlmacher, ThB, p. 155; cf. Stuhlmacher, Jesus, p. 39.
387. Stuhlmacher, ThB, pp. 133ff.
388. Cf. Stuhlmacher, Verstehen, pp. 34, 47ff.
389. Stuhlmacher, ThB, p. 138.
390. Ibid., p. 153.
391. Stuhlmacher, Verstehen, pp. 253ff.
392. Here we may cite B. S. Childs as an example from outside Continental theological circles. He places weight most of all on the final form of the text in a so-called canonical approach.
393. Examples are Barr, Grässer, Hartlich, Strecker, and recently Utzschneider, pp. 182ff.
394. Thus Hartlich, p. 483; Smend, pp. 226f.
395. Thus Strecker, pp. 19f.; Joest, Kanon, p. 184.
396. Hirsch V, p. 492.
397. Ibid.
398. Ibid., p. 6.
399. Merk, Anfänge, p. 52.
400. H. M. Barth, col. 242, 252.
401. Strecker, p. 31.
402. Stuhlmacher, Jesus, p. 17.
403. Stuhlmacher, ThB, p. 158.
404. Hartlich, p. 473.
405. Ibid., p. 478.
406. Cf. here Stuhlmacher, Verstehen, p. 56f.
407. Stuhlmacher, ThB, p. 158, and idem, Jesus, pp. 16f.
408. Blank, pp. 7f.
409. Schottroff, p. 253.
410. Thus Stuhlmacher, ThB, pp. 157f., especially n. 85 on p. 158.
411. Reinhard, p. 102.
412. Cf. Hartlich, pp. 474f.; Strecker, p. 21.
413. Strecker, p. 22.
414. Stuhlmacher, Verstehen, pp. 91, 222.
415. Schottroff, p. 255.
416. R. Simon traced everything back to one authority: the teaching office of the church. On Enlightenment theology cf. Aner, passim.
417. Cf. Wach, Verstehen II, p. 294.
418. Rothe, according to Wach, Verstehen II, p. 296.

419. Beck, Gedanken, p. 179.
420. Stuhlmacher, Jesus, pp. 16f.
421. Stuhlmacher, Verstehen, pp. 240, 249f.
422. Cf. Für Arbeit und Besinnung, Zeitschrift für die Evang. Landeskirche in Württemberg, 41, 1987, p. 90.
423. Ibid., p. 95.
424. Schottroff, p. 251.

CHAPTER FOURTEEN: *Developing a Biblical-Historical Interpretation*
1. Most of all in my *Das Ende der historisch-kritischen Methode* (*The End of the Historical-Critical Method*).
2. In this connection cf. also Moltmann, Ev Komm, passim.
3. Therefore the church's interest in the calling of theological teacher-scholars should be acute and vital, not hesitant and bashful.
4. Cf. Joest, Kanon, pp. 184ff.
5. Barr, p. 108.
6. Beck, Leitfaden, pp. 9f.
7. Mussner, p. 25.
8. Wilckens, p. 98.
9. Melzer, p. 14: "The foreign word 'meditation' is unclear." Melzer proposes rather the designation "internalization" (p. 16).
10. Ibid., pp. 11ff., speaks of "meditation as a way inside," "meditation as self-absorbtion," "meditation as internalization." Cf. ibid., pp. 77ff.
11. The phrase "locating the text" from my book *Das Ende der historisch-kritischen Methode* is to be abandoned in favor of the more precise phrase "determining the text."
12. Cf. Nestle-Aland, *Novum Testamentum Graece*, 26th ed. (1979), p. 2, along with Holmes, passim.
13. Nestle-Aland, p. 3.
14. Ibid., p. 5.
15. Ibid.
16. Very clearly expressed again by Weder, pp. 27, 68, 74: "Methodologically it is essential to exclude God as historical factor" (p. 74).
17. Cf. Thurneysen, p. 20.
18. Thus Stuhlmacher only adds one more to the established Troeltschian principles; he replaces none of them.
19. Also in Weder, pp. 48ff., 73ff.
20. Pannenberg, p. 22. Pannenberg, however, does not orient himself by revelation but on a concept of universal history that incorporates revelation.
21. Weder, p. 74.
22. Ibid., pp. 48ff.
23. Cf. Bultmann, Mythologie, passim.
24. Bultmann, *Die Geschichte der synoptischen Tradition*, 6th ed. (Tübingen, 1964), pp. 263ff.
25. Cf. Strasburger, p. 475.
26. Pannenberg, p. 25.

27. Weder, pp. 69f.
28. Thus e.g., ibid., pp. 48, 73.
29. Ibid., p. 96.
30. Keil, pp. 123ff.
31. Ibid., p. 124.
32. Cf. Moldaenke, p. 597.
33. Cf. Kramer I, p. 60.
34. Beck, Gedanken, p. 159.
35. Beyschlag, pp. 27ff., especially p. 31.

# Scripture Index

# Author Index

# Subject Index